"Dr. Sun sheds light on the problem ~~and absent, is social and transcend~~... ~~and reveals himself and hides himself.~~ She states the problem sympathetically and analyzes it with evident ecclesial concerns. I commend her for the artistry she exhibits in her analysis of the Song of Songs and Esther. I greatly value her contribution because I have raised more and more the questions entailed in God's hiddenness over the years."

Willem A. VanGemeren, professor emeritus of Old Testament and Semitic languages, Trinity Evangelical Divinity School

"This fascinating book focuses on two of the more neglected books of the Bible. At first glance, Esther and Song of Songs are a mismatched pair. Their differences appear to outnumber their similarities. But through a meticulous cross-examination, Chloe Sun finds many fruitful connections, not the least of which is the apparent absence of God. Dr. Sun explores the links between these books, and interbiblical connections with other books in the Old Testament. Along the way, the motifs of time and space are visited, as well as feasting—all in relation to God's perceived absence. We find out how Esther and Song of Songs present an alternative voice to that of most of the Old Testament. Dr. Sun also outlines the implications of God's seeming absence for us today and how we might still find him. Highly recommended for all who wrestle with the mystery of this aspect of God's character."

Peter H. W. Lau, researcher and writer, OMF International, and Old Testament book review editor for *Themelios*

"We seek God's presence, but sometimes we experience God's absence. Chloe Sun moves the theme of the absence of God found in the book of Esther and the Song of Songs from the margins to the center to remind us that 'experiencing divine absence is part of the faith journey.' She masterfully employs a sensitive understanding of genre, intertextuality, close reading, and the canon to disrupt our stereotypical understanding of God to lead us to a more profound faith. I enthusiastically recommend this book to all who want a better understanding of the Bible and, indeed, of God."

Tremper Longman III, distinguished scholar and professor emeritus of biblical studies, Westmont College

"With *Conspicuous in His Absence*, Sun offers an inviting and reaffirming treatment of key theological questions. Building on the conceptual pillars of divine presence and absence, she guides readers from a broad picture of Old Testament theology, through a series of carefully selected topics that elucidate the theological issues in question. She arrives at the conclusion that the Song of Songs and Esther complement and challenge the normative biblical theology based on the Torah and the Prophets, which foregrounds God's presence. Henceforth, these two books—through Sun's compassionate exposition—provide a much-needed companion for contemporary believers, so that they may acquire a more felicitous framework to think of God's nature during the perceived divine absence and act accordingly with human responsibility."

Sarah Zhang, associate professor of biblical studies at GETS Theological Seminary, California, and author of *I, You and the Word "God": Finding Meaning in the Song of Songs*

"Dr. Sun provides a thorough analysis of the scholarly works and differing views on the difficult topic of the hiddenness of God in Song of Songs and Esther. She demonstrates how these books, which begin and conclude the Megilloth, respond to the conundrum of divine absence in faith and canon. Her writing is both theologically astute and pastorally sensitive. Dr. Sun's book is an important contribution to the theology of absence in times of suffering and uncertainty (which both love and potential genocide can engender). God's absence intensifies the longing for his presence. In a canonical reading, these books point to a God who expects his people to pursue love and do justice even when he is silent."

Ingrid Faro, visiting professor of Old Testament at Northern Seminary

"What is the significance of books in the Bible that don't mention God? Chloe Sun has been thinking around this question and reading around what other scholars have written about it, and she here offers a book full of insights on whether God is there when you can't see him and what this God is like. In *Conspicuous in His Absence* you get the fruit of wide reading in the scholarly literature and discerning reflection in light of this reading. It's easy to stay with the mainstream of scriptural teaching and ignore its more exotic byways, and Professor Sun invites readers to profit from the margins without losing the mainstream."

John Goldingay, David Allan Hubbard Professor of Old Testament emeritus, Fuller Theological Seminary, Pasadena, California

"In her latest book, Chloe T. Sun moves seamlessly between Old Testament theology and practical theology discussions centered around 'a theology of absence.' In so doing, the dynamism of her methodology mirrors the life of faith, which seeks divine presence in the face of apparent absence. The curated conversations—on theology, time, temple, feast, and canon—illustrate well the riches that can be gleaned when one reads often-neglected texts in the canon, especially alongside one another. This work is to be commended for the insightfulness and honesty it offers to those who desire to know God more fully."

Brittany N. Melton, assistant professor of biblical and theological studies at Palm Beach Atlantic University and chair of the Old Testament study group of Tyndale Fellowship

"Chloe T. Sun reminds us that God's presence does not always conform to human expectations. As Sun brings together the Song of Songs and the book of Esther as conversation partners, she retrieves the theological theme of divine absence from the margins of scholarly discourse and brings it front and center. In this timely, thought-provoking work, Sun draws us in to consider how the absence of God in the Song and Esther attests to part of the real-life, multidimensional human experience with God."

Denise C. Flanders, assistant professor of biblical studies at Taylor University

CONSPICUOUS

IN

HIS

ABSENCE

STUDIES IN THE
SONG *of* SONGS *and* ESTHER

CHLOE T. SUN

An imprint of InterVarsity Press
Downers Grove, Illinois

InterVarsity Press
P.O. Box 1400, Downers Grove, IL 60515-1426
ivpress.com
email@ivpress.com

InterVarsity Press® is the book-publishing division of InterVarsity Christian Fellowship/USA®, a movement of students and faculty active on campus at hundreds of universities, colleges, and schools of nursing in the United States of America, and a member movement of the International Fellowship of Evangelical Students. For information about local and regional activities, visit intervarsity.org.

All Scripture quotations, unless otherwise indicated, are taken from the New American Standard Bible®, copyright 1960, 1962, 1963, 1968, 1971, 1972, 1973, 1975, 1977, 1995 by The Lockman Foundation. Used by permission.

While any stories in this book are true, some names and identifying information may have been changed to protect the privacy of individuals.

Cover design and image composite: David Fassett
Interior design: Jeanna Wiggins
Images: gold frame © Tomekbudujedomek / Moment Collection / Getty Images
   biblical engraving © bauhaus1000 / DigitalVision Vectors / Getty Images
   smoke © James Harris / EyeEm / Getty Images

ISBN 978-0-8308-5488-2 (print)
ISBN 978-0-8308-5489-9 (digital)

Printed in the United States of America ♾

InterVarsity Press is committed to ecological stewardship and to the conservation of natural resources in all our operations. This book was printed using sustainably sourced paper.

Library of Congress Cataloging-in-Publication Data
A catalog record for this book is available from the Library of Congress.

P	25	24	23	22	21	20	19	18	17	16	15	14	13	12	11	10	9	8	7	6	5	4	3	2	1
Y		36		35		34		33		32		31		30		29		28		27		26		25		24		23		22		21

CONTENTS

ACKNOWLEDGMENTS

THROUGHOUT MY JOURNEY AS A CHRISTIAN, the teachings about the presence of God have dominated many spiritual formation courses and Sunday sermons, while the theme of the absence of God is seldom mentioned or acknowledged. Yet, the experience of the absence of God is a grim reality to be reckoned with and a necessary question to be raised. When God seems absent, does it mean he is no longer there? Does it mean he does not care? Or worse yet, does it mean I have sinned somehow and offended him? Infinite questions abound as one tries to align mind and soul, theology with reality, and knowledge with experience.

The idea to write a book on the absence of God sparked as I taught the Megilloth and poetic books at Logos Evangelical Seminary. In one of the classes, a student suggested to me: Why not write about Song of Songs and Esther? Since then, I have embarked on this journey of exploring, contemplating, and reflecting on the subject of divine absence in these two books. I would like to thank Jeanne Roach, my spiritual director, for her encouragement and prayers throughout the process of writing this book. Her insightful questions and affirmations of both divine presence and absence have been a valuable guide in my quest. To Dennis Ngien, I am indebted for his support of the book from the very outset, to Sarah Zhang and Barbara Leung Lai, I am grateful for their reading portions of earlier drafts of this book and offering helpful suggestions, as well as to the anonymous reviewers whose candid comments prevented me from many mistakes. Thanks are due to my dissertation adviser, John Goldingay, for instilling the love of the First Testament and its theology during my graduate studies. I am thankful for my husband, Eddie, and son,

Jedidiah, for their loving support and offering me the space to pursue what I love.

Last but not least, my gratitude goes out to Anna Gissing, associate editor at InterVarsity Press, who kindly took on this project and saw it to fruition, and for all the InterVarsity Press staff who have helped in making this book possible.

ABBREVIATIONS

AB	Anchor Bible
BBR	*Bulletin for Biblical Research*
BDB	*The Brown-Driver-Briggs Hebrew and English Lexicon*
CBQ	*Catholic Biblical Quarterly*
DOTWPW	*Dictionary of the Old Testament: Wisdom, Poetry and Writings.* Edited by Tremper Longman III and Peter Enns. Downers Grove, IL: InterVarsity Press, 2010
ESV	English Standard Version
FCB	Feminist Companions to the Bible
GCT	Gender, Culture, Theory
HBM	Hebrew Bible Monographs
JBL	*Journal of Biblical Literature*
JSJ	*Journal for the Study of Judaism in the Persian, Hellenistic, and Roman Periods*
JSOT	*Journal for the Study of the Old Testament*
JSOTSup	Journal for the Study of the Old Testament Supplementary Series
LHBOTS	Library of Hebrew Bible/Old Testament Studies
MT	Masoretic Text
NASB	New American Standard Bible
NIV	New International Version
NKJV	New King James Version
NLT	New Living Translation
NRSV	New Revised Standard Version
NSBT	New Studies in Biblical Theology
OTL	Old Testament Library
ResQ	*Restoration Quarterly*
RPT	Religion in Philosophy and Theology

RSV	Revised Standard Version
SJT	*Scottish Journal of Theology*
VT	*Vetus Testamentum*
WBC	Word Biblical Commentary

INTRODUCTION

"MY GOD, MY GOD, why have you forsaken me"? (Ps 22:1). The cry of the psalmist reverberates deep into the heart of the human soul. In the journey of believers, divine forsakenness is a real experience. This religious experience presumes that God is there but he refuses to act. Throughout human history, events such as war, natural disaster, genocide, pandemic, violence, and injustices of various kinds testify to the persistence of divine absence in human experiences. When suffering abounds, questions of divine absence arise.

How do we talk about God when his name is not even there in the text? In the entire biblical canon, which centers on the story of God and his people from Genesis to Revelation, there are only two books that lack any explicit reference to the name of God—Song of Songs and the book of Esther. Although there are traces and hints of divine presence in these books, they are not overt. God's peculiar absence in these two books creates unsettling resonance both in theological discourses and in the lived experience of believers. Why would these two books conceal the name of God when the references are found throughout the rest of Scripture? Moreover, why would the Jewish people recite these two books at two of their festivals associated with deliverance of God's people when these books forgo any direct mention of God? What does the absence of God's name say about the nature of God and his activities in the world? How do we think of God when he is absent? What do we do when God is silent or hidden? This book attempts to address these questions by attending precisely to Song of Songs and Esther.

Normally, readers associate Song of Songs with love and sexuality. Whether it is a divine love song or a human love song, Song of Songs is a book about erotic love. In two thousand years of its interpretative history, the Song presents itself as a multifaceted and mysterious piece of literature whose influence on biblical interpretation, theology of love, Hebrew poetry, and feminist and gender studies continues to blossom. A close reading of the Song reflects that love is not always rosy and intoxicating. There are times when love makes one sick. There are also times when the pursued lover is absent, and the soul of the other lover tries to search for him, but he is nowhere to be found. It is this theology of strange absence that captures my attention. This absence of the lover not only echoes the absence of God sometimes in believers' experiences but also parallels the literary absence of God in Esther.

In Esther, though human characters occupy center stage to avert a villain's scheme to annihilate the whole Jewish race, the name of God is conspicuously absent. Esther is not merely a tale either of an orphan girl undergoing a transformation to becoming the savior of her people, or of a devout Jew, Mordecai, becoming a hero in a Persian court and riding on a royal horse with royal robe. It is not just a farce ridiculing the king of Persia as a spineless monarch or Haman as the embodiment of evil. Rather, theologically, it is about a story of unsettling divine absence in the most treacherous time in Jewish history. Where was God when his people needed him the most?

Out of the entire Hebrew and Christian canon, Song of Songs and Esther set themselves apart by leaving the name of God out of the texts. This conspicuous absence of God's name becomes the incentive for writing this book. The goal for this book, then, is to examine, meditate, and reflect theologically on the Song of Songs and Esther in relation to the theology of absence and inquire how these two books function in Old Testament theology. It attempts to address three main questions: (1) What is the nature of God as revealed in texts without his name? (2) How do we think of God when he is perceived to be absent? and (3) What should we do when God is silent or hidden?[1]

---

[1]While absence implies nonpresence, silence and hiddenness connote a silent presence and a hidden presence. Divine absence and divine silence/hiddenness are not the same conceptually, but they both reflect the negativity of the divine.

METHOD

I will adopt theological interpretation as the primary method of this book. By theological interpretation, I borrow the analogy of digging from Kevin Vanhoozer. I attempt to dig into the texts of Song of Songs and Esther in order to find gold in them. This interpretation is characterized by a governing interest in God, the word and works of God. Its principal thrust is to direct readers' attention to God, to the acts of God in history, to the extent that it helps readers grow in the knowledge of God.[2] I will also adopt William Brown's proposal of theological interpretation by asking two questions: (1) What is the text's theo-logic, that is, what can be ascertained from the text about God's character and relationship to the world? (2) What is the text's cosmo-logic, that is, what can be ascertained from the text about the world in its relationship to God and humanity's place in it?[3] The intriguing challenge of this study is to consider how we think of God when his name is not mentioned explicitly in the texts. How can we do theological interpretation when God does not reveal himself in plain sight? As we will observe, the absence of God's name in the text does not preclude the knowledge of him, since his literary absence is precisely an aspect of Scripture that needs to be addressed and that readers need to wrestle with, both theologically and in their own lived experience.

Under the umbrella of theological interpretation, I also include other complementary methods to probe the question of absence in Song of Songs and Esther, such as literary analysis of the text concerning time (chap. 3), innerbiblical allusions to Edenic garden and Israel's sacred space as a way to detect divine presence (chap. 4), the early history of interpretation of Passover and Purim in connection to divine deliverance (chap. 5), and canonical connections of the two books within the Hebrew Scripture (chap. 6).

Why Song of Songs and Esther? These two books are part of the Megilloth, a collection of five scrolls in the Hebrew canon that are associated

---

[2]Kevin J. Vanhoozer, ed., *Theological Interpretation of the Old Testament: A Book-by-Book Survey* (Grand Rapids, MI: Baker Academic, 2008), 16, 21, 26.

[3]William P. Brown, "Theological Interpretation: A Proposal," in *Method Matters: Essays on the Interpretation of the Hebrew Bible in Honor of David L. Petersen*, ed. Joel M. LeMon and Kent Harold Richards (Atlanta: Society of Biblical Literature, 2009), 390.

with five Jewish festivals. These five scrolls include Song of Songs, Ruth, Ecclesiastes, Lamentations, and Esther. By placing these five books in a collection, the compiler must have perceived their commonality and interconnectivity within the Hebrew canon. In the Jewish liturgical calendar, Song of Songs heads the Megilloth, and Esther concludes the Megilloth. While Song of Songs is recited during Passover, the first festival in the Jewish calendar, Esther is recited during Purim, the last festival in that calendar, suggesting that these two books open and close the entire liturgical year.

Most scholars consider Ruth and Esther together, but rarely do they consider the Song of Songs and Esther this way, except for Brittany Melton's recent monograph.[4] Perhaps due to their difference in themes and literary forms, the similarities and theological connections of Song of Songs and Esther have been overlooked in past and present scholarship. However, it is their theological connection, namely, the absence of God's name, that binds the two books closely together. Because of this theological proclivity, Song of Songs and Esther belong to the same group of inquiry that centers on the theology of absence, and together they call for theological reflection.

RELEVANCE AND PURPOSE

The study of theology always involves its subject—God. How do we do theology, and how do we know God, when God's name is absent in the text?

---

[4]Brittany N. Melton, *Where Is God in the Megilloth? A Dialogue on the Ambiguity of Divine Presence and Absence* (Leiden: Brill, 2018), especially 59-83. There is an article written on the Song of Songs and Esther. The contents deal with the name of God and its various forms rather than the themes and theology of these two books. See David R. Blumenthal, "Where God Is Not: The Book of Esther and the Song of Songs," *Judaism* 44, no. 1 (1995): 81-92. A book treats Ruth and the Song of Songs together: Peter S. Hawkins and Lesleigh Cushing Stahlberg, *Scrolls of Love: Ruth and the Song of Songs* (New York: Fordham University Press, 2006). For a treatment of Ruth and Esther together, see, e.g., Athalya Brenner, *A Feminist Companion to Ruth and Esther*, FCB (Sheffield: Sheffield Academic Press, 1999). Several commentaries put Ruth and Esther together as a pair, including Frederic William Bush, *Ruth, Esther*, WBC 9 (Dallas: Word Books, 1996). In the Berit Olam series, the commentary on Ruth is written by Tod Linafelt, and Esther by Timothy K. Beal (Collegeville, MN: Liturgical Press, 1999). Another such commentary is by Iain M. Duguid, *Esther and Ruth*, Reformed Expository Commentary (Phillipsburg, NJ: P&R, 2005). Wetter's recent publication takes Ruth, Esther, and Judith together. See Anne-Mareike Wetter, *"On Her Account": Reconfiguring Israel in Ruth, Esther, and Judith*, LHBOTS 623 (London: T&T Clark, 2015). The most recent work on Ruth and Esther appears in three chapters in Brad Embry, *Megilloth Studies: The Shape of Contemporary Scholarship* (Sheffield: Sheffield Phoenix, 2016), 7-19, 20-29, 43-71.

This book addresses that fundamental question. Readers will discover that theological discourse does not necessarily require the name of God to be present. It is precisely the absence of God's name in the text that arouses curiosity, which motivates us to reflect and respond.

Second, the experience of the absence of God reflects a human condition. When God is absent or seems absent, what we think about him and what we should do are two main concerns that deserve reflection and action. Readers will benefit from this book, knowing that God reveals himself in different ways. Sometimes he manifests himself through nature or love. Other times he reveals himself through the miraculous merging of times, the ascension of his people at a foreign court during a time of crisis and the act of executing justice to confront evil. This book will help readers appreciate not only the similarities shared by the Song of Songs and Esther, but also their respective distinctiveness. The juxtaposition of the two books does not obscure each book's uniqueness. On the contrary, it highlights their differences.

Third, readers will gain a profound understanding of the place and purpose of Song of Songs and Esther in the Hebrew Scripture, especially in regard to the theology of absence. For Christians, this book will open another window to comprehend the mystery of God, the reality of love and human responsibility as well as the possibility for faith in the midst of divine absence.

DATING AND AUTHORSHIP

Since the method of inquiry of divine absence is through the lens of theological interpretation and the final form of the texts, issues on authorship and dating are less relevant, but I include a discussion here for interested readers.

Song of Songs. The dating of the Song of Songs is tied up with the issue of authorship and language. As in many other biblical books, proposals for dating the book range from early to late dates. The beginning title, "The Song of Songs, which is Solomon's" (לִשְׁלֹמֹה, Song 1:1), does not necessarily suggest Solomonic authorship, since the preposition לְ has several meanings, including "to Solomon," "for Solomon," "by Solomon," "belonging to

Solomon," or "concerning Solomon."[5] Based on the internal evidence, the presence of Tirzah in Song of Songs 6:4 suggests an early date during the time of King Omri of Israel. Tirzah was a center of the northern kingdom for a brief time in history. First Kings 15:33 says, "In the third year of Asa king of Judah, Baasha son of Ahijah became king of all Israel at Tirzah, *and reigned* twenty-four years."[6] Later, Omri reigned in Tirzah and made it his capital for six years (1 Kings 16:23), while Jerusalem remained the capital city of the southern kingdom. The parallel juxtaposition of Jerusalem and Tirzah—"You are as beautiful as Tirzah, my darling, as lovely as Jerusalem" (Song 6:4)—suggests that at the time of composition of Song of Songs, Tirzah was at the height of its reputation. This would put the drafting of the Song around the ninth century.

The reference to sixty queens and eighty concubines in Song of Songs 6:8 suggests a date during the early phase of Solomon's reign. If indeed the Song was composed by Solomon, as implied by the reference to Solomon in 1 Kings—"He also spoke 3,000 proverbs, and his songs were 1,005. He spoke of trees, from the cedar that is in Lebanon even to the hyssop that grows on the wall; he spoke also of animals and birds and creeping things and fish" (1 Kings 4:32-33)—then an early, tenth-century date during the reign of Solomon is supported by this innerbiblical evidence.[7] However, there are arguments against this view based on the character Solomon in the Song. In the Song, Solomon appears to be a minor character, and the last chapter of the Song portrays him as someone who used money to purchase love (Song 8:11-12). If Solomon was indeed the author, it would be odd for him to cast himself in such negative light. If Solomon was the author, then Rashi's comment that Solomon wrote the Song later in his life as an act of repentance may explain his motivation for writing the Song, but this remains a conjecture.[8]

---

[5]For the various uses of ל in the biblical texts, see Bruce K. Waltke and M. O'Connor, *An Introduction to Biblical Hebrew Syntax* (Winona Lake, IN: Eisenbrauns, 1990), 205-12.

[6]Unless otherwise indicated, translations of the Song of Songs and Esther are my own. Scriptural translations of other biblical books follow the NASB.

[7]There are seven references to Lebanon in the Song (Song 3:9; 4:8 [2×], 11, 15; 5:15; 7:4), cedar (Song 1:17; 5:15; 8:9), trees (Song 1:17; 2:3; 6:11; 7:7-8), and the mentioning of animals such as dove (Song 4:1; 5:12), turtledove (Song 2:12), and gazelle (Song 2:9; 3:5; 4:5; 7:3; 8:14).

[8]Douglas Sean O'Donnell, *The Song of Solomon: An Invitation to Intimacy* (Wheaton, IL: Crossway, 2012), 21.

Geographically, almost all physical locations mentioned in the Song are found in the northern kingdom, Israel, such as Sharon (Song 2:1), Gilead (Song 4:1; 6:5), Hermon (Song 4:8), Damascus (Song 7:4), and Mount Carmel (Song 7:5).[9] This suggests that at the time of composition, the northern kingdom had not been destroyed. If so, this would place the dating of the book before the eighth century BCE. However, Jerusalem also appears eight times in the Song, suggesting its significance and that the mere mention of the cities and sites in the northern kingdom does not necessarily support an early date (Song 1:5; 2:7; 3:5, 10; 5:8, 16; 6:4; 8:4).[10]

In terms of language, the presence of *še* as well as Aramaisms in the Song indicates a late date, during the exilic period or even after the exile.[11] There is also a Persian loanword, *pardes* (פַּרְדֵּס, Song 4:13), present in the Song, but given Solomon's well-established networks of international trade, it is possible for his writing to have a Persian loanword, and his writing style might have been influenced by Aramaisms. Since the Song emerged in ancient Israel over a long period of time, some also argue that Song of Songs is a collection of love songs, an anthology like Proverbs, and that therefore it contains both early and late materials, as reflected by its language of composition.[12] Taking all this evidence into consideration, it is logical to think that Song of Songs was first composed in the ninth century at the height of Tirzah. Whether it went through layers of editorial refinement and when exactly it reached its final form remains unknown.

Esther. The dating of Esther is inconclusive. Carey Moore suggests that the book was composed in either the late Persian (539–332 BCE) or early

---

[9]Othmar Keel, *The Song of Songs*, Continental Commentary (Minneapolis: Fortress, 1994), 5. See the map on 36. Keel proposed the date of composition as being between the eighth and sixth centuries BCE. Scholars who support Solomonic authorship belong to a minority voice. These scholars include Archer, Carr, Snaith, and O'Donnell. See Gleason Archer, *Introduction to the Old Testament* (Chicago: Moody, 1964), 537-40; G. Lloyd Carr, *The Song of Solomon*, Tyndale Old Testament Commentaries 19 (Downers Grove, IL: InterVarsity Press, 1984), 19; John G. Snaith, *Song of Songs*, New Century Bible Commentary (Grand Rapids, MI: Eerdmans, 1993), 5; O'Donnell, *Song of Solomon*, 23.

[10]En Gedi is also located in the Southern Kingdom (Song 1:14).

[11]For details of dating, authorship, and language, see Marvin H. Pope, *Song of Songs*, AB 7C (Garden City, NY: Doubleday, 1977), 22-37.

[12]See, for example, Tremper Longman III, *Song of Songs*, New International Commentary on the Old Testament (Grand Rapids, MI: Eerdmans, 2001), 19; Michael Fishbane, *Song of Songs: The Traditional Hebrew Text with the New JPS Translation* (Philadelphia: Jewish Publication Society, 2015), xxi.

Hellenistic period (331–168 BCE), given its sympathetic attitude toward a "Gentile" king.[13] Jon Levenson places the date of composition after Xerxes but before the watershed of the mid-second century BCE.[14] Michael Fox argues that Esther's language is a mixture of early and late Biblical Hebrew. He suggests a third-century date for the book.[15] Based on the internal historical evidence of Song of Songs and Esther, the former is usually associated with Solomonic tradition (eighth century BCE) and the latter with the postexilic period during the reign of Ahasuerus (Xerxes I, 486–465 BCE).

In the Hebrew canon, Esther was placed among the Writings, at the end of the Megilloth, followed by Daniel, Ezra-Nehemiah, and then the Chronicles. Esther's canonical position and association with Daniel are apparent given their similar genre and themes, especially with regard to Daniel 1–6. Esther's canonical affinity with Ezra-Nehemiah may suggest their similarity in the same historical period and their emphasis on Jewish identity. The place of Chronicles at the end of the canon seems to make it a conclusion to the Writings. The dating of Chronicles ranges from an early date to a late date, that is, from 527–500 BCE to 166 BCE.[16] The intermediary date, around 400 BCE, for Chronicles has the most supporters.

From the perspective of festivals, Song of Songs came to be associated with the Passover, Esther with Purim. The connection between Esther and Purim was established in the first century AD, while the association of Song of Songs and Passover came later, in the second or third century AD. The allegorical reading of Song of Song as God's salvation history of Israel during the Second Temple period has contributed to this association. The earliest textual witness that places the Megilloth as a group is the Leningrad Codex, dating from the early eleventh century AD. Before that, only the book of Esther was known as the Megillah. It was not until the fifteenth century AD that the Megilloth appeared with Song of Songs heading the

---

[13]See Carey A. Moore, *Esther*, AB (Garden City, NY: Doubleday, 1971), lix.

[14]Jon D. Levenson, *Esther: A Commentary* (Louisville, KY: Westminster John Knox, 1997), 26.

[15]Michael V. Fox, *Character and Ideology in the Book of Esther*, 2nd ed. (Grand Rapids, MI: Eerdmans, 2001), 139-40.

[16]Kalimi proposes three possible dates—an early, a late, and an intermediary one. See Julius Steinberg and Timothy J. Stone with the assistance of Rachel Marie Stone, *The Shape of the Writings*, Siphrut 16 (Winona Lake, IN: Eisenbrauns, 2015), 215-18.

group and Esther concluding the group.[17] That said, the Megilloth's association with the festivals does not reflect the respective dating of the books within this collection.

Although a definitive solution regarding the dating and authorship of Song of Songs and Esther is not conclusive, based on the above evidence it is logical to assume that Song of Songs was composed earlier than Esther and that the author of Esther was aware of or even familiar with the text of Song of Songs. Did the author of Esther intentionally use similar vocabulary to the Song, or did the authors of both texts draw their wealth of vocabulary and motifs from the same literary stock of their times? Both options are possible, but we have no way to be certain.

THE STRUCTURE OF THIS BOOK

I have arranged this book in six chapters. The first two chapters place divine absence in a larger context of Old Testament theology. The next four chapters address the issue of divine absence through four themes: time, temple, feast, and canon.

Chapter one focuses on mapping the theological landscape of divine presence and absence in the Hebrew Bible. It first provides an overview of the subject matter in past scholarship and assesses the place of Song of Songs and Esther in the enterprise of Old Testament theology. As the only two books where the name of God is absent, Song of Songs and Esther speak volumes in regard to the theology of absence.

Chapter two regards Song of Songs and Esther as belonging to the broader worldview of wisdom. Divine presence is expressed through nature, erotic love, and human responsibility. I argue that both books serve as countertexts to the nature of God and his work with the rest of the Hebrew Scripture, and therefore they contribute to a fuller picture of who God is.

Chapter three is a meditation and literary reflection on the aspect of time in Song of Songs and Esther. Time is a human concern. Time in the Song of Songs is not static or fixed but fluid and dynamic, whereas time in Esther moves not only in linear fashion but also in retrospective and anticipatory manners. In the Song, the woman yearns for her beloved in his absence,

---

[17]B. C. Gregory, "Megillot and Festivals," *DOTWPW* 457, 459, 463.

while in Esther, many readers search for divine activities in the absence of God's name. Therefore, the two scrolls form two parallel responses to the theology of absence. When the lover is absent, the woman's heart grows even fonder of him. In times of divine absence, God is present in the mind of those who seek him. Absence intensifies the desire for presence.

Chapter four takes a spatial perspective, specifically that of the temple. It uses innerbiblical allusion to probe the theology of absence through the temple theme. The major setting of the Song is a garden, which alludes to the Garden of Eden as the temple of God. The setting of the Esther scroll is the Persian palace, where a Gentile ruler reigns. Both the garden and the palace have close affinity with Israel's tabernacle/temple imagery. In times of divine absence, the love in the garden reflects divine love, whereas the palace-temple connection overlaps with the image of Israel's sacred space. The ascension of Mordecai, along with his royal and priestly clothing, resembles Israel's priestly garment, on the one hand, suggesting that the possibility of divine presence may have shifted from the physical temple to his people. On the other hand, the temple-palace connection bears theological ambiguity in that God is absent entirely in the story, and the survival of his people is all due to the wisdom and just actions of Esther and Mordecai.

Chapter five focuses on the two feasts associated with Song of Songs and Esther after the canon was closed. It cites early reception history regarding the relationship of the two books and the two feasts. In the Jewish liturgical calendar, the Song of Songs is sung during Passover, whereas Esther is recited during the Purim festival. The two festivals are back to back in this calendar, and both commemorate the divine redemption of Israel from its enemies. While the name of God is absent from both books, the two feasts form two varied responses to the exodus event; thus, in the absence of God, the people of God can look back to his faithfulness in the past and have hope for his future deliverance. Although God is absent in these two books, by associating them with two Jewish feasts, the Jewish faith community receives these two books as religious and as contributing to the knowledge of God and divine-human relationship.

Chapter six is written from the angle of the Hebrew canon, particularly how the motifs of these two scrolls relate to the rest of the Hebrew Scripture.

As it will demonstrate, Song of Songs and Esther are both echoes and counterechoes in relation to the rest of the Hebrew Scripture. As echoes, the
motifs of both books resonate with other biblical texts; as counterechoes,
they not only form a dialectical relationship with the rest of the biblical
canon but also challenge, critique, and evaluate the normative motifs reflected in the rest of the canon. Therefore, these two books form a conversation with the canon, serve as a corrective to the dominant motifs in the
canon, and call for readers' reflection on the nature of God and his presence
and absence in human history.

The concluding chapter summarizes the previous six chapters, reflecting
on the questions, What is the nature of God and his work as revealed in
texts without his name? How do we think of God when he is perceived to
be absent? and, What do we do when God is silent or hidden? Based on my
findings, I observe that Song of Songs and Esther contribute to Old Testament theology and biblical theology in that God's absence and silence is
an integral part of his divine nature that counters and creates tension with
his presence and active participation in human history. God's presence and
absence are not mutually exclusive. The way in which God works in the
Writings and Megilloth differs from that in the Torah and the Prophets.
Since Song of Songs and Esther are rooted in creation theology, where
divine presence is not overt but covert, these two books complement and
supplement what the rest of the biblical canon lacks. Consequently they
offer insight into the larger question of the nature of God and how believers
should respond in times of his absence. I invite you to join me in this
journey of exploring the mystery of the theology of absence in Song of
Songs and Esther.

1

THEOLOGY

DIVINE PRESENCE *and* ABSENCE

My God, my God, why have You forsaken me?

PSALM 22:1

IF GOD IS EXPLICITLY PRESENT in every single book of the Bible, how can we make sense of the reality that people do sense divine absence in their lives? Past scholarship has devoted much attention to the absence of God in the book of Esther, and to a lesser extent the theology of absence in Song of Songs, but rarely does this scholarship place these two books together to investigate how this unique literary feature of the absence of God's name contributes to the theology of Hebrew Scripture.

Therefore, this chapter paints in broad strokes a picture of theological inquiries on the theology of divine presence and absence in the Hebrew Scripture.

As a part of the Writings in general and as an essential component of the Megilloth in particular, together having a close affinity with wisdom, Song of Songs and Esther demonstrate a unique yet often overlooked fact—that the way in which God works in this portion of Scripture differs from that in the Torah and the Prophets. Divine absence forms incomprehensibility, which is intrinsic to the ethos of God. Together with divine presence, divine absence presents a fuller picture of who God is. As a result, these two scrolls supplement and complement what the rest of the biblical books lack. This chapter concludes with the thesis that the absence of God in these two biblical books is a theological necessity if one attempts to articulate an Old Testament theology. The dominant mode of divine presence in other biblical books is not the whole picture of God if it does not include and integrate this theme of divine absence. The theme of absence also helps to align theology with real life, especially for those who experience suffering, trauma, loss, crisis, uncertainty, or evil in this world. In light of the global pandemic in 2020 and its aftermath, the inquiry of the absence of God cannot be more pertinent.

DIVINE PRESENCE AND ABSENCE IN SCHOLARSHIP

In *Where Is God? Divine Absence in the Hebrew Bible*, Joel Burnett observes, "The theme of divine absence in the Hebrew Bible involves a crisis of relationship." In the same book, he states, "The theme of divine absence goes hand in hand with the problem of theodicy."[1] In the minds of the believers, God should be present at all times, especially during the times when they need him the most. Yet the lived experience of many believers speaks otherwise. Relationship, by nature, is mutual and dialogical. When one party remains absent, silent, or uninvolved, it creates a relational crisis. I would like to suggest further that divine absence not only creates a crisis of relationship, but also a crisis of intellect and a crisis of faith. By *intellect* I am referring to human reasoning and comprehension. If God is omnipresent, how and why would he be absent or choose to be absent? If we appeal to the compassion of God and to his special relationship with his chosen people, where is God when his people call on him but he is not there, as many lament psalms indicate? By *faith*, I mean the kind of conviction that God is present even though he cannot be felt, and the kind of belief that God is there even though he remains silent and hidden. Divine absence reflects a serious theological

---

[1] The literary review in this chapter is not comprehensive or exhaustive but representative. See Joel S. Burnett, *Where Is God? Divine Absence in the Hebrew Bible* (Minneapolis: Fortress, 2010), 43, 86. In another article, Burnett traces the theme of divine absence in selected ancient Near Eastern texts and the Hebrew Bible and concludes that the perception of divine absence was not a concern limited to ancient Israel alone. Rather, divine absence is a basic religious concern in ancient Israel's broader West Semitic context. See Joel S. Burnett, "The Question of Divine Absence in Israelite and West Semitic Religion," *CBQ* 67 (2005): 215-35.

crisis, which is worth reckoning and grappling with. Yet scholarship on Old Testament theology has relegated this theological theme to the margins.[2] Only in recent years has the subject of divine absence started to appear in individual monographs and gained gradual momentum in the study of the theology of Megilloth.[3]

Past scholarship on the theology of divine presence and absence can be segmented into three major but also overlapping approaches.[4]

1. Diachronic: This approach advocates the position that divine presence gradually decreases and is replaced by divine absence. At the same time, human characters gradually take center stage, with the book of Esther as the ultimate example of this, in which the name of God is entirely absent, but human responsibility comes to the fore.

2. Dialectic: Divine presence and absence is perceived as a dialectical relationship in which divine absence cannot be conceived apart from divine presence. In this view, there is divine presence in absence and

---

[2]For instance, Bruggemann's *Old Testament Theology* does not include Song of Songs and Esther. See Walter Brueggemann, *Old Testament Theology: An Introduction* (Nashville: Abingdon, 2008). His earlier work, *Theology of the Old Testament*, sees laments and complaints as Israel's counter-testimony. Yet Song of Songs is mentioned only once (342), and the book of Esther is not mentioned at all. See Walter Brueggemann, *Theology of the Old Testament: Testimony, Dispute, Advocacy* (Minneapolis: Fortress, 1997), index of scriptural references. House's *Old Testament Theology* is a book-by-book treatment of the Old Testament's theology. For the book of Esther, he titles it "The God Who Protects the Exiles," which may sound too positive and downplays the issue of divine absence. For Song of Songs, House titles it "The God Who Oversees Male-Female Sexuality," which again, interprets a book without God's name as if he were in fact present. See Paul R. House, *Old Testament Theology* (Downers Grove, IL: InterVarsity Press, 1998), 463, 490. Waltke's *Old Testament Theology* places the book of Esther under the umbrella of divine providence, whereas he sees Song of Songs as a type of God and his people. He neglects the motif of divine absence. See Bruce K. Waltke, *An Old Testament Theology: An Exegetical, Canonical, and Thematic Approach* (Grand Rapids, MI: Zondervan, 2007), 163-64. The book of Esther is not mentioned in Moberly's *Old Testament Theology*, and Song of Songs is mentioned only in passing and mostly appears in the footnotes. See R. W. L. Moberly, *Old Testament Theology: Reading the Hebrew Bible as Christian Scripture* (Grand Rapids, MI: Baker Academic, 2013). The latest book by Duvall and Hays relegates both Song of Songs and Esther to less than one page each. See J. Scott Duvall and J. Daniel Hays, *God's Relational Presence: The Cohesive Center of Biblical Theology* (Grand Rapids, MI: Baker Academic, 2019), 90, 109-10.

[3]For example, Brad Embry, ed., *Megilloth Studies: The Shape of Contemporary Scholarship*, HBM 78 (Sheffield: Sheffield Phoenix, 2016). Brittany N. Melton, *Where Is God in the Megilloth? A Dialogue on the Ambiguity of Divine Presence and Absence* (Leiden: Brill, 2018).

[4]Melton's book also groups past scholarship on divine presence and absence similarly for the first two camps. She names them (1) decreasing trajectory from divine presence to divine absence and (2) recurrent divine hiddenness/absence. See Melton, *Where Is God*, 14, 18.

divine absence in presence. The genre in question is concentrated primarily on the lament psalms and the exilic prophets.

3. Canonical: Recent scholarship is starting to pay attention to the theology of the Writings, particularly the presence and absence of God in Wisdom books as well as the theology of Megilloth. Interest in the latter is gaining increasing momentum.

Throughout all three major approaches, the book of Esther has captured the imagination of scholars, whereas Song of Songs continues noticeably to be overlooked. The following synopsis of scholars and their works serves as representative of different approaches and is not meant to be exhaustive by any means.

Diachronic: From divine presence to divine absence. The proponents of this approach use a linear, narrative approach to portray the character of God. Many of them perceive a development or evolvement of the character of God and his activities throughout the course of the Old Testament narratives.

God as a dramatic persona. In the early 1980s, Dale Patrick wrote a biography of God. He claims that God appears as a *dramatis persona* in the Bible. He argues that the rendering of God in the Bible conforms to the principles that govern the mimetic arts. Patrick uses characterization and dramatic action as ways to present God as a consistent character who speaks and acts. This rendering of God proves his identity. For Patrick, there is a consistency of characterization in the biblical descriptions of God as God moves in bodily form among his creatures without harmful effect. The call of Moses provides God with a biographical identity because God identifies himself as "the God of the fathers." The call of Moses also portrays God as one with emotions as he identifies with the suffering of his people. In addition, God also displays consistent virtue, including his power and intelligence, to rule history and to save his people.

For those character traits that are inconsistent, Patrick considers them "out of character." He cites an example from Exodus 4:24-26, where God assumes the guise of a demon, attacking Moses at night, which is inconsistent with his character elsewhere. When the literary approach to the study of the Bible was at its peak in the eighties, Patrick's work advanced this conversation, which opens a trajectory to interpret the character of God as a literary figure. In so doing, God has become susceptible to the reader's analysis rather than being perceived as a transcendent deity to be revered and received incontestably. Patrick acknowledges the difficulty in establishing criteria for assessing God's character. However, he contributes by painting a portrait of God that involves a development of character as well as drawing attention to God's speech, action, and emotion, thus presenting God like a "real" character before readers' eyes.[5]

God gradually disappears. In the 1990s, the prime supporter for this position was Richard Elliot Friedman. In his groundbreaking work, *The Disappearance of God*, Friedman observes the plot of the Bible. He notes that the presence of God first appears to be visible, active, talking to people face to face, and performing miracles, but then progressively becomes hidden, silent, and eventually disappears in the book of Esther. Language that conveys divine presence includes "the spirit of God," "God appeared," and "God said," but these terms gradually disappear as the story line of the Bible unfolds. The presence of God that is apparent, that is a matter of public knowledge at the beginning of the biblical narrative, has turned into a hidden presence, a matter of belief or of hope. Friedman cites examples of God's presence as a flame of fire to Moses (Ex 3:2), as the column of cloud and column of fire, and as the "glory of Yahweh" that is visible to human eyes (Ex 16:7; Lev 9:6; Num 14:10). When God appears on Mount Sinai, fire and thunder accompany his presence and inspire a sense of awe and terror (Ex 19:19). God even issues the Ten Commandments with his divine voice (Ex 20:1-17).[6] Aside from God's public and visible presence to his people, he also appears to individuals such as Moses, speaking directly to him, even mouth to mouth (Num 12:6-8). Friedman traces God's direct interactions with the patriarchs, Joshua, Aaron, Samuel, David, and Solomon to further his argument of divine presence in the Torah and most of the historical books. At the end, he comes to the book of Esther.

---

[5]Dale Patrick, *The Rendering of God in the Old Testament* (Philadelphia: Fortress, 1981), 1-2; Amelia Devin Freedman, *God as an Absent Character in Biblical Hebrew Narrative: A Literary-Theoretical Study* (New York: Peter Lang, 2005), 48-52, 160-62, 167.

[6]Richard Elliot Friedman, *The Disappearance of God: A Divine Mystery* (Boston: Little, Brown, 1995). The revised edition is titled *The Hidden Face of God* (New York: HarperSanFrancisco, 1997), 15, 28.

Friedman cites Mordecai's words to Esther in Esther 4:14 and highlights two phrases: "Who knows?" and "from another place."[7] These two phrases present a striking contrast to the earlier biblical narratives, where the visibility and activity of God are apparent in the public domain. Friedman sees Esther's ascent to the Persian palace as by worldly means and not by divine involvement, as in the case of Joseph's rise. He states, "The narrator does not suggest that this is a divine plan, and Mordecai's words convey that Mordecai is depicted as truly not knowing for sure." In Esther, the presence of God is no longer publicly visible and has turned into a hidden presence, falling into the realm of personal belief. Friedman further remarks that this is only half of the story.[8]

The other half of the story reveals the other side of the same coin, namely, that the weight of human responsibility gradually increases as the storyline of the Bible progresses. In other words, there is a transition from divine visibility to human responsibility. To demonstrate this fact, Friedman uses a parent-children analogy. In the Bible, God acts like a parent, and the people he created are like his children. When Adam and Eve take the forbidden fruit and eat it, they act like naughty children. As the Bible's story line moves forward, Abraham questions God (Gen 18), and Jacob fights God (Gen 32). Human beings are confronting their Creator, and they are gaining participation and power in the divine-human relationship.[9] In his own words, "In the Bible, God creates humans, becomes known to them, interacts with them, and then leaves." For Friedman, this divine exit from the Bible is exemplified in its extreme by the book of Esther. He sees a shift in the divine-human balance, with Eve symbolizing humans' initial estrangement from God and Esther being credited with ensuring humans' salvation.[10]

Friedman's work is both convincing and troubling. For him, God does seem to disappear gradually as the story line of the Bible progresses. God's presence and activities do seem to give way to his absence and silence as

---

[7]Esther 4:14: "If you keep silent at this time, relief and deliverance will arise for the Jews from another place, and you and your father's house will perish; and who knows whether you have attained royalty for just such a time as this?"

[8]Friedman, *Disappearance of God*, 28-29.

[9]See chap. 2, "The Divine-Human Balance," in Friedman, *Disappearance of God*, 30-59.

[10]Friedman, *Disappearance of God*, 58, 76.

the story advances. At the same time, human characters do seem to take matters into their own hands. The book of Esther does leave out the name of God entirely, and this is replaced by the actions and autonomy of the human hero and heroine. These are undeniable facts. Yet there is something we do need to consider further.

First is the question of canon. To which canon does Friedman refer? Friedman's argument presupposes only a portion of the Bible, namely, the Pentateuch and the historical books, which is not the whole story line of the Hebrew Scripture, let alone the storyline of the whole Bible. The story line of this portion of the Bible indeed begins with Genesis and ends with Esther. However, the book of Esther is not the last book in the Christian canon. In the Christian canon, Malachi is the last book, and God does speak in the book of Malachi.[11] In the Hebrew canon (here I am referring to the Masoretic Text), the last book is Chronicles, where God's activity is conveyed through his stirring up the spirit of Cyrus, king of Persia, to issue an edict, allowing God's people to go up to Jerusalem (2 Chron 36:22-23). To pick and choose a portion or a corpus of the Bible and then attempt to determine its plot only tells a partial story, not the whole story. The order of the biblical books varies with different canonical traditions of the Scripture, and this suggests that different communities of faith present different versions of the portrayal of God in different time periods. For example, the Greek version of the book of Esther does include the name of God more than once.[12] Seen

---

[11]Malachi begins with God's chastisement of Israel, recounting their sins (Mal 1), and ends with God's promise to send Elijah the prophet before the coming of the great and terrible day of the Lord (Mal 4:5). God's presence, words, and activities are quietly visible and apparent.

[12]To discuss the different versions of Esther is a complicated task. Basically, there are two versions of the Esther scroll in two divergent biblical canons: the MT as the Hebrew Bible we know, and the Greek version known as the Septuagint (LXX). There are six passages in the LXX that the MT does not have or may have lost. See Jon D. Levenson, *Esther: A Commentary*, OTL (Louisville, KY: Westminster John Knox, 1997). The name of God is absent in the MT but present in the LXX. De Troyer claims that the problem of the absence or presence of God in the book of Esther should not be seen as a problem only within the book of Esther itself but also within the *books* of Esther, meaning the different versions of Esther. Apart from the LXX, there is also another Greek version of Esther, known as the Alpha Text, which mentions God even more than the LXX does. De Troyer does raise a good point in her research on the Greek texts of Esther, namely, that the problem is no longer the presence and absence of God but what kind of God has been created in the books of Esther. See Kristin De Troyer and Leah Rediger Schulte, "Is God Absent or Present in the Book of Esther? An Old Problem Revisited," in *The Presence and Absence of God: Claremont Studies in the Philosophy of Religion, Conference 2008*, ed. Ingolf U. Dalferth, RPT 42 (Tübingen: Mohr Siebeck, 2009), 35-40, esp. 37, 40. Since the scope of this

through the trajectory of biblical canon, Friedman's argument of the "disappearance of God" collapses accordingly.

Second, although Friedman retells the biblical story from only a portion of the Christian canon, which yields an incomplete story, it does provoke troubling thoughts, because God's name does disappear from the book of Esther. This undeniably forms a significant contrast to the presence of God as portrayed in Exodus. This fact alone calls for inquiry. What Friedman may have missed is that God may not work the same way in the Torah as he does in the Writings. The "disappearance of God" or the "hidden face of God" does not necessarily mean that the character of God has changed or evolved through time. The difference in genre and in the historical time period of Esther versus Exodus should be taken into consideration when one attempts to reconcile or make sense of the dynamics between divine presence and absence. I will return to this point later in the next chapter when we discuss the wisdom element in Song of Songs and Esther.

God is like a human character. Following Friedman's arguments, Jack Miles, in his national bestseller, *God: A Biography*, continues a similar thesis, tracing the "biography" of God from a creator in Genesis to a liberator in Exodus, and then ending with the book of Esther as "Absence" and Chronicles as "Perpetual Round." He compares the book of Esther with the exodus story and suggests that regardless of the intent or purpose of the book of Esther, the absence of the divine name is precisely its effect, the point of the story. He states that the story lines between Exodus and Esther are quite similar, since both involve an averted genocide, but the story of Exodus epitomizes divine presence and activity, whereas in the story of Esther, Esther and Mordecai become the incarnation of God's redemptive action. Miles specifically clarifies that Esther and Mordecai are not "God incarnate," because if one calls them that, then the word *God* would have to appear, which is not the case in the book of Esther.[13] Unlike Friedman, who ends his retelling of the biblical story with Esther, Miles ends it with Chronicles,

---

book is limited to the MT, we will focus on this version with the absence of God's name. For more on the three versions of Esther, see Tricia Miller, *Three Versions of Esther: Their Relationship to Anti-Semitic and Feminist Critique of the Story*, Contributions to Biblical Exegesis & Theology 74 (Leuven: Peeters, 2014).

[13]Jack Miles, *God: A Biography* (New Work: Vintage Books, 1995), 361.

particularly with the prayer of David in 1 Chronicles 29:10-19, where Miles construes the prayer as "God's farewell speech." He takes the last few words in 2 Chronicles, "Let him go up," as part of a musical round that harks back to the first few lines of Ezra 1.[14]

As for Song of Songs, Miles uses "Sleeper" as the chapter title, based on the Song's recurrent adjuration formula: "Do not wake or rouse love" (Song 2:7; 3:5; 8:4). Juxtaposing Isaiah and Hosea with Song of Songs, Miles sees a "grievously estranged older couple finding their way back to the love of their youth." Thus, he thinks that Song of Songs cannot be read apart from the tales of God and Israel. The images presented in the Song, with a secret garden, luxury, and safety, do not ring true to the Jewish community in Jerusalem, which was characterized by want, bitterness, and anxiety. Miles focuses our attention on the silence of God in Song of Songs and asks, "Where is he? What has happened?" In addition, Miles places the book of Job alongside Song of Songs and reads God in the book of Job as an over-powering character whose dealings with Job renders his innocence questionable. God's appearance at the end of Job should serve as a moment of truth, yet it also becomes the moment of death because the pervasive mood of the book "is one not of redemption but reprieve." Miles further remarks that the development of the character of God almost breaks down in the book of Job. It is the Song of Songs that breaks this mood by changing the subject, thus saving God's life.[15]

Miles treats God as a literary character, much like a "real human being" with personality, emotions and shortcomings. Miles's God appears to be a

---

[14]The last few verses of 2 Chronicles and the first few verses of Ezra 1 are identical. "Now in the first year of Cyrus king of Persia—in order to fulfill the word of the LORD by the mouth of Jeremiah—the Lord stirred up the spirit of Cyrus king of Persia, so that he sent a proclamation throughout his kingdom, and also *put it* in writing, saying, 'Thus says Cyrus king of Persia, "The LORD, the God of heaven, has given me all the kingdoms of the earth, and He has appointed me to build Him a house in Jerusalem, which is in Judah. Whoever there is among you of all His people, may the LORD his God be with him, and let him go up!"'" (2 Chron 36:23).

"Now in the first year of Cyrus king of Persia, in order to fulfill the word of the LORD by the mouth of Jeremiah, the LORD stirred up the spirit of Cyrus king of Persia, so that he sent a proclamation throughout all his kingdom, and also *put it* in writing, saying: 'Thus says Cyrus king of Persia, "The LORD, the God of heaven, has given me all the kingdoms of the earth and He has appointed me to build Him a house in Jerusalem, which is in Judah. Whoever there is among you of all His people, may his God be with him! Let him go up"'" (Ezra 1:1-3).

[15]Miles, *God, A Biography*, 328, 335, 338, 405.

complex character who is subject to human beings' scrutiny. If one reads the Bible honestly and follows Miles's presentation of God, a lot of what he says would ring true. For instance, God does appear to be capricious, sometimes without reason, and at other times his presence is nowhere to be seen. At times when he is supposed to speak, he remains silent. Borrowing Friedman's parent-children analogy, when we read about God in the Bible, we are reading him from the perspective of young children looking at our parents. From a child's mind and observation, God could appear as distant, difficult to understand, and unpredictable, and may disappear or leave without saying why. A nicer term for this kind of behavior for God is *mysterious*. Children never understand their parents as long as they remain children. Children are incapable of seeing from their parents' perspective. Even when the children grow up and become adults, and even when the children themselves become parents one day, their parents are still not fully comprehensible from the children's vantage point.

From the perspective of relationship, if a person has a personal relationship with God, then divine absence would pose a serious challenge to that relationship, as Burnett asserts. However, if a person does not have that kind of relationship with God and simply reads the text as it is, then the issue is no longer a crisis in relationship but one of human intellectual inquiry. The outcome of reading God as a character, then, would be very different from one who reads the same subject out of a personal relationship with God. For example, Qoheleth's portrayal of God seems distant and incomprehensible (Eccles 3:11; 5:2).[16] There is no suggestion in Ecclesiastes that the author has any personal interaction with the divine. There is no single dialogue recorded in the book that hints at that. Qoheleth seems to take us on an intellectual journey to probe the question of meaningful living under the sun. Yet in Job, it is apparent that regardless of Job's complaint or protest of divine injustice, he has a personal relationship with God, and because of that the presence of innocent suffering poses a crisis in his relationship with God. Although God in Job appears to be transcendent and incomprehensible, which is very much similar to the portrayal of God in

---

[16]Here I use Qoheleth to refer to the author of Eccles 1:12–12:8 and Ecclesiastes to indicate the whole book.

Ecclesiastes, the outcomes of Ecclesiastes and Job are quite different.[17] The former thrives with contradictions and doubts, whereas the latter is satisfied after the unjust experience of innocent suffering, and at the end he dies happy.

God is an absent character. Along the same vein as Friedman and Miles, in *God as an Absent Character in Biblical Hebrew Narrative*, Amelia Freedman perceives the presence of God gradually withdrawing as the biblical narratives progress. Sometimes, God uses stand-ins to represent his presence, such as the angel in Genesis 18, the judges, King David, and the prophets. Other times, the narrator speaks about God in his absence, as in 1 Kings 19:11-12, or the human characters talk about God, as in the story of the servant meeting Rebekah in Genesis 24:34-49. Overall, Freedman perceives a contradiction emerging in the biblical narrative that God is apparently a major character, but he appears in most of these narratives only indirectly. In light of God's absence, Freedman uses four methods, namely, narrative criticism, reader-response criticism, intertextuality, and feminist literary criticism to examine God as an absent character in the Hebrew Bible. Rather than adopting a block of narratives for the investigation, Freedman uses individual narratives first to reach a more nuanced reading of God as a character. Therefore, she rejects Miles's approach, because she thinks that he fails to read individual narratives on their own terms and tends to overgeneralize the character of God based on larger blocks of narratives. Miles also fails to distinguish the poetry and the narrative portions of the book of Job and construes God as one who is "manipulative and controlled." Freedman selects four methods to examine four individual narratives in turn. They are the Joseph narrative, the succession narrative, the book of Esther, and the book of Ruth. For each method, she first presents several scholarly works that advocate for the approach. Then she analyzes the strengths and weaknesses of the approach. Afterward, she examines how each particular approach contributes (or does not contribute) to the understanding of God as an absent character. For example, through narrative criticism, the text acknowledges that God's presence is behind the

---

[17]See Chloe Sun, "Ecclesiastes Among the Megilloth: Death as an Interthematic Link," *Bulletin for Biblical Research* 27, no. 2 (2017): 185-206, esp. 205-6.

scenes of human actions and interactions, as revealed in the Joseph narrative. Through intertextuality, Freedman juxtaposes the ancient Greek novel *Chaereas and Callirhoe* as an intertext with Esther. She describes the similarities shared between these two texts as well as their points of departure. Reading Esther through the lens of Chaer, Freedman argues that God is neither present nor active in the book. In addition, the character's level of assertiveness has direct bearing on the amount of divine presence and activities. Since Esther does not need God's assistance in saving her people, Freedman concludes that God in Esther is indeed absent.[18]

At the end of her research, she affirms that each method has its merit. The choice of method has a lot to do with the reader's interpretive goal, the type of questions the reader is asking of the biblical narrative, and the degree of information that a particular biblical narrative provides about the character of God. Since each chosen method has its own strengths and weaknesses, the outcome of the inquiry does not yield a complete picture. And since Freedman's work is limited to biblical narratives, lyric poetry such as Song of Songs and prophetic texts are not chosen as texts to be examined. This further creates an incomplete portrayal of God as an absent character. The four texts chosen are from different portions of the Old Testament, but although the activities and involvement of God in the Joseph narrative, the succession narrative, Ruth, and Esther do have some common ground, they do not represent the whole corpus of Scripture.

Moving the end to the center. In *Portraits of a Mature God,* Mark McEntire took a diachronic approach by tracing the development of the character of God from Genesis to "the end of the story," that is, Ezra-Nehemiah. Like Friedman and Miles, McEntire attempts to paint a portrait of God that has undergone character evolvement. Yet, McEntire differs from Friedman and Miles in that he proposes to move the end of the story toward the center, that is, to allow the latter books in the Hebrew Bible that depict God as in the shadow to speak for themselves rather than allowing these books to recede to the background and remain overshadowed by the earlier books in the Bible. Patrick, Friedman, and Miles start from the beginning and then trace the character of God from there to the end of the Bible. The

---

[18]Freedman, *God as an Absent Character,* 2-5, 105-17.

problem of this angle, according to McEntire, is a result that focuses more on the present, the visible and active side of God in the earlier biblical books. The selection of this order determines the subsequent trajectory of how one constructs Old Testament theology. Additionally, tracing a development of divine character in the order of the biblical canon is hindered by the uncertainty of the historical timeline of these books. McEntire says that following the character of God through narrative time will arrive at an articulation that is not complete because the voice at the beginning portions of the Bible is too loud and the voice at the end of the story is too timid.[19] I will return to this latter point at the end of the chapter.

A balanced, thorough theology without a predetermined trajectory or theological agenda can only be achieved through rethinking one's entry point. Should we start from the earlier story, or the end of the story, or somewhere in the middle? Different entry points would yield different outcomes of the character of God. In McEntire's analysis of the end of the story, Ezra-Nehemiah receives the most attention. Daniel also receives considerable space, but Esther is mentioned in less than a page, and Song of Songs is not included at all.[20] The present work will attempt to complete what McEntire's book lacks.

Summary. The diachronic description of the character of God along the timeline of the historical narratives presents a logical but also problematic portrayal of God from an active deity to a passive deity, then eventually a retreating or withdrawing deity. Throughout the course of biblical narratives, the character of God and his level of activities appear to evolve and develop over time. All the aforementioned treatments of this aspect of God render him as a literary character, very much like a real human being. While these treatments attempt to provide an "objective" view of who God is as reflected in the Scripture, they are not without problems. The first problem is the issue of canon, which I mentioned earlier. Which biblical canon are we following? When the order of the books is arranged differently, which

---

[19]Mark McEntire, *Portraits of a Mature God: Choices in Old Testament Theology* (Minneapolis: Fortress, 2013), 7, 21. In chap. 1, McEntire provides a literature review of representative scholars and their works in the portrayal of divine character, with very keen and helpful remarks.

[20]Proverbs, Ruth, and Job are also included, but the space devoted to these books is far less than that devoted to Ezra-Nehemiah and Daniel. See McEntire, *Portraits of a Mature God*, chap. 6, esp. 199.

portrayal of God are we talking about? The choice of canon determines its outcome. Another problem, as McEntire points out, is, Where should we begin painting the character of God, from the beginning of the biblical canon or from the end? The two approaches would yield completely different results. If we were to start painting the picture from the middle, what result would it yield? Last but not least, the absence of God in Esther has been acknowledged widely in this approach, but Song of Songs is still marginal in contributing to the discussions concerning the presence and absence of God.

Dialectic: Divine presence in absence and absence in presence. This position places divine presence and absence as a dialectical and sometimes paradoxical relationship rather than a dichotomy. It acknowledges the prevalence of this theme and its complexity through the Hebrew Scripture. Roland de Vaux thinks that the presence and the absence of God alternate. God conceals himself as much as he shows himself. As the psalmists demonstrate, God hides himself so that his people will return to him and seek him. De Vaux also thinks that the salvation history (German *Heilsgeschichte*) of Israel is retrospective. That is, the plan of God is only made clear after the promises have been fulfilled in Jesus.[21] In de Vaux's point of view, to do a biblical theology or an Old Testament theology has to take the whole Scripture into consideration and not just certain books. Below are some of the major representatives of this approach.

The elusive presence of God. In the late twentieth century, Samuel Terrien was one of the first scholars to construe divine presence and absence not as a bipolar relationship or a mutually exclusive phenomenon but an intricate, interwoven, "two sides of the same coin" kind of relationship. He describes this nature of God as "the elusive presence." When speaking of God's hiddenness, Terrien cites the prophet Isaiah's words that God hides his face and hides himself during the exile (Is 8:17; 45:15). The confession

---

[21]Roland de Vaux, "The Presence and Absence of God in History According to the Old Testament," in *The Presence of God*, ed. Pierre Benoit, Roland Murphy, and Bastiaan van Iersel (New York: Paulist, 1969), 7-20, esp. 17-18, 20. From de Vaux's point of view, a biblical theology or an Old Testament theology has to take the whole Scripture into consideration and not just certain books. One of my purposes for this chapter is to see the place and the contribution of two biblical books in light of the Old Testament, rather than seeing them apart from the rest of the Old Testament.

of this lament itself suggests a confession of faith. For Terrien, to be aware of divine hiddenness is to remember God's presence and to yearn for the return of that presence. Therefore, he asserts that "the presence of an absence denies its negativity." He quotes Blaise Pascal, "A religion which does not affirm that God is hidden is not true. And a religion which does not offer the reason [of this hiddenness] is not illuminating." On the Latin version of the verse in Isaiah 45:15, *Deus Absconditus*, Terrien prefers the meaning of its Hebrew original—a self-concealing God. The Latin translation renders the phrase with a passive participle, whereas the Hebrew original uses a reflexive sense, and thus it stresses divine freedom and sovereignty.[22] Divine hiddenness is a result of God's own choice. By stressing the problem of the elusive presence as a result of God's freedom, Terrien attempts to divert the problem to the divine realm, but this does not solve the issue on the human level. What are human beings supposed to do during the times of God's elusive presence? Are we supposed to accept it passively and silently, or are we supposed to protest and question God and make it his problem?

Terrien observes in some psalms that the psalmists are constantly begging for the presence of God, whereas others try desperately to flee from his presence. As a result, Terrien describes this God as a "haunting God." He cites Psalm 139 as an example to illustrate this conflicted nature of yearning and dread for the divine presence.[23] In other words, divine presence may not be perceived as all positive, and divine absence is not all negative. In times of divine absence, the desire for his presence grows even more intently, and this creates the theological notion of "the presence in absence." This is precisely what appears in Song of Songs. In the absence of the male lover, the female lover's heart for him grows even fonder, to the point of feeling physically sick (Song 5:8). Likewise, in Esther, the absence of the explicit reference to God's name makes many readers attempt to read God into the text. The search for the divine presence intensifies precisely when his name is absent.

---

[22]Samuel Terrien, *The Elusive Presence: The Heart of Biblical Theology* (Cambridge: Harper & Row, 1978), 1, 321, 474.

[23]Terrien, *Elusive Presence*, 326-31.

In the theology of Terrien, the paradox between divine presence and absence can be understood in terms of wisdom, Torah, and Jesus.[24] In all three respects, God's presence is displayed and sensed through his absence. Hence, the term "presence in absence" is conceptualized as well as materialized in biblical theology. Terrien captures the paradox of divine presence and absence with a keen observation and acute insight. Freedman, though, criticizes Terrien's approach as synthetic; that is, he deconstructs biblical narratives for the information they yield and fails to take individual narratives or the difference in genre and voices into account.[25] Although Terrien's approach is confessional for the most part, his understanding of the subject has influenced subsequent literature.

Lament psalms as an expression of divine hiddenness. Many scholars have noticed the theology of divine absence appearing recurrently in the Psalms and the prophetic books.[26] For example, Samuel Balentine studies the hiding of the face of God in the Old Testament. The expression "hiding of face" occurs twenty-nine times in the Hebrew Scripture, twenty-three of which occur in the Psalms and the prophetic books. Sometimes the hiding of God's face is due to the sins or transgressions of the psalmists. At other times, the cause for the hiding of God's face is unclear, since the psalmists protest due to their innocence and cannot comprehend the reason for divine hiddenness. However, the consequence of divine hiddenness is stated unmistakably: that the psalmist or his community is separated from God. This separation is manifest in three major ways: (1) that God refuses to see, hear, or answer their prayers (Ps 10:11; 13:4; 69:18; 102:3); (2) that God

---

[24]Terrien, *Elusive Presence*, 473, 476.

[25]Freedman, *God as an Absent Character*, 3-4.

[26]For example, Anderson quotes lament psalms as an expression of the failure of covenant theology. See Bernhard W. Anderson, *Contours of Old Testament Theology* (Minneapolis: Fortress, 1999), 244-46. Doyle devotes a chapter to the theme of divine presence and absence and argues that this theme is a biding element in the composition of the Psalms. The genre of petition to God in distress appears mostly in Ps 52–64. The metaphor of divine absence has to be read between the lines, and in most cases, the psalmists' confidence in divine presence transcends that of divine absence. See Brian Doyle, "Where Is God When You Need Him Most?," in *The Composition of the Book of Psalms*, ed. Erich Zenger (Leuven: Peeters, 2010), 377-79. Dunn's studies on the imageries of the sanctuary in the Psalms explore the theme of divine presence and concealment. One of his conclusions regarding divine concealment in the Psalms is that God's absence is mysteriously mediated through creation. See Steven Dunn, *The Sanctuary in the Psalms: Exploring the Paradox of God's Transcendence and Immanence* (Lanham, MD: Lexington Books, 2016), 80-81.

is absent from the place of cultic worship (Ps 27:9); and (3) that the psalmist faces death or confinement to Sheol (Ps 22:16; 102:4; 143:7). The phrase "hiding the face" appears predominantly in the lament psalms and is accompanied by expressions of protest. The hiding of God's face indeed contributes to a crisis in the divine-human relationship.[27]

Outside the Psalms, the expression "hiding of face" occurs frequently in the prophetic books, mostly in the context of human sin and principally with regard to Israel's collective unfaithfulness toward God. The prophetic books involved are mainly from the eighth to the fifth century BCE, at the time of the exile.[28] The consequence of the divine hiding of face in the prophetic books shares striking similarities with that of the lament psalms. It involves different ways and degrees of people's separation from God. Balentine summarizes the cause for God's hiding of face in the Psalms as ambiguous but less ambiguous in the prophetic books. In the latter case, the hiding of the face is a manifestation of divine judgment on Israel's apostasy.

Overall, the expression "hiding of face" appears in contexts of lament and judgment. Lament is a form of human expression of distress to God, while judgment in the prophetic texts comes from God and is addressed to human beings. Since lament directed to God serves as a way to cope with God's hiddenness, Balentine understands the experience of divine hiddenness as an integral part of Israel's faith. For him, God is both hidden and present, far and near. This realization makes room for doubt and despair in the faith experience. For Balentine, the hiddenness of God does not seem to emerge as a problem. Rather, it is a natural manifestation of who God is. Balentine does not attempt to explain away divine hiddenness. What he tries to show is that divine hiddenness is necessary for God and for Israel. For God, both divine hiddenness and divine presence are part of being God. For Israel, divine hiddenness is not merely a punishment for its disobedience or the inability to perceive his presence; rather, both the experience of divine presence and of absence reflect the nature of Israel's faith journey

---

[27]Samuel E. Balentine, *The Hidden God: The Hiding of the Face of God in the Old Testament*, Oxford Theological Monographs (Oxford University Press, 1983), 45, 50-65. Balentine indicates one positive use of the phrase "hiding of face" in Ps 51:11, where David entreats God, "Do not cast me away from Thy presence." See *Hidden God*, 58.

[28]Balentine, *Hidden God*, 159, 163. Balentine also acknowledges that the hiddenness of God does not just appear during the literature of this period but also prior to this period and after (160).

with God. When one takes all these instances into consideration in one's theological discourse, then one may understand the idea of the absence of a present God.[29]

In his *Theology of the Old Testament*, Walter Brueggemann expounds eloquently on divine hiddenness, ambiguity, and negativity. His argument on divine hiddenness revolves around the lament psalms, in which Israelites cry out, "How long, O LORD?" (Ps 6:3; 13:1-2; 35:17; 62:3) "Why do You stand afar off?" (Ps 10:1; 22:1; 43:2; 44:23-24) and, "Where is your God?"[30] These interrogatives both reflect the real experience of the psalmists and pose a threat to theodicy. These questions originate from a restless persistence that amount to a "reprimand of Yahweh, who has not done for Israel what Israel has legitimately expected."[31] The other genre in which Israel questions divine injustice and hiddenness is the genre of complaint, which appears in Lamentations, in psalms about exile, and in the prophetic texts regarding the exile.[32] The experience of the exile raises a question about God's sovereign power. If God is all-powerful, why did he not prevent exile from happening? The sense of abandonment incurred by the exilic experience reverberates throughout Lamentations and the book of Isaiah: "Why do You forget us forever?" (Lam 5:20); "But Zion said, 'The LORD has forsaken me'" (Is 49:14).[33] In another article, Brueggemann recounts the consequences of the loss of lament. One is the loss of a genuine interaction between God and human beings. The other is the stifling of the question of theodicy.[34]

Employing a courtroom metaphor, Brueggemann identifies these expressions of divine hiddenness, ambiguity, and negativity as the counter-testimony that functions to cross-examine Israel's core testimony where

[29]Balentine, *Hidden God*, 65-72, 77, 157, 172-73, 175-76.
[30]Ps 79:10; 115:2, or "Where is your steadfast love?" in Ps 89:49.
[31]Brueggemann, *Theology of the Old Testament*, 319.
[32]These psalms include the experience of the exile and the destruction of the temple. See Ps 74:1, 10-11; 79:5, 10; 89:46.
[33]Brueggemann identifies four texts (Ps 22; Lam 5:20; Is 49:14; 54:7-8) as "texts that linger, not yet overcome." All four texts have divine inattentiveness in common. See Walter Brueggemann, "Texts That Linger, Not Yet Overcome," in *Shall Not the Judge of All the Earth Do What Is Right? Studies on the Nature of God in Tribute to James L. Crenshaw*, ed. David Penchansky and Paul L. Redditt (Winona Lake, IN: Eisenbrauns, 2000), 21-41.
[34]Walter Brueggemann, "The Costly Loss of Lament," *JSOT* 36 (1986): 57-71, esp. 60-61.

God is present, active, powerful, and faithful to his promises. The countertestimony, he argues, is not an act of Israel's unfaithfulness, but a "characteristic way in which faith is practiced."[35] The latter statement echoes Balentine's notion of perceiving divine hiddenness as an integral part of Israel's faith. McEntire criticizes Brueggemann's presupposition of naming the present and active God as "the core testimony" and his hiddenness as the countertestimony. While acknowledging the validity of Brueggemann's portrait of God as a tension-filled character, McEntire argues instead that "the weight of the 'core testimony' seems to anchor the divine character to a position that restricts the potential for dynamic character development."[36] For McEntire, the dialectic between Israel's core and countertestimony obscures the diachronic aspect of God's character. What if Israel's countertestimony is framed as its core testimony, and its core testimony is framed as its countertestimony? How would that affect the subsequent trajectory? How would that affect one's perception of God and the understanding of Old Testament theology? I believe the outcome would be quite different.

In light of the pervasive and serious nature of the problem of divine hiddenness, Brueggemann rejects the traditional approaches to tackle the issue, including (1) disregarding such texts; (2) justifying divine hiddenness through human sin; (3) seeing divine judgment as a case of human misperception—that God only "seems" to be abandoning us; (4) philosophical subtlety, that even though God is "experienced" as one who abandons, that experience contains within it an assumption of cosmic aspect of presence, that is, the dialectic notion of "presence in absence" or "absence in presence"; and (5) the "evolution" of God, that God has developed from an unsettling character into one with fidelity and justice.[37] The fourth approach is the one Terrien accepts. Brueggemann acknowledges its attractiveness but rejects it based on two indications: (1) The reasoning of "presence in absence" or

---

[35]Brueggemann, *Theology of the Old Testament*, 318.

[36]McEntire, *Portrait of a Mature God*, 4.

[37]Brueggemann, "Texts That Linger," 27-30. The position that God "evolves" is similar to the notion proposed by Friedman and Miles. Yet in their views, God evolves from presence to absence, whereas in the aforementioned position God evolves from absence to presence. Brueggemann cites the incident of Job as an example of the second traditional approach. See Brueggemann, "Texts That Linger," 28.

"absence in presence" is subtle in ways that Israel would not have enter-
tained, and (2) the reasoning requires a judgment that is against the clear,
uncomplicated statement of the text. It would not solve the problem of what
to do with these texts.[38]

For Brueggemann, the bottom line of all these approaches is that its proponents intend to protect the character of Yahweh, but Yahweh has to run
the risk that belongs to him alone in the memory of Israel.[39] Rather than
defending Yahweh's character, Brueggemann calls for Yahweh to defend
himself. Brueggemann's courtroom metaphor presents a vivid contest between divine negativity and Israel's testimony. The result is tension between
Israel's core testimony and countertestimony. What is absent from Brueggemann's picture of Old Testament theology is reference to Song of Songs and
Esther. How do these two books fit in with his courtroom metaphor? How
can one testify for or against God when God's name is not even mentioned
in the book or when the imagined courtroom is not there?[40]

John Goldingay distinguishes laments from protests and thinks that *protests* is a better description than laments, since *lament* implies an acceptance
of victim status, whereas protests do not. Laments may lack a specific audience, but protests are addressed to someone with power. Based on the
texts of protests from the Psalms, Goldingay develops one trajectory of Old
Testament theology under the rubric of "how one lives with God." Its
context involves prayers of "confronting, calling out, summoning, crying
out, asking questions, asking for grace and attention and encounter, challenging and claiming." Although divine hiddenness and divine absence are
not at the forefront of Goldingay's theology of prayer, he articulates the
issue through psalmists' expressions, such as "asking to be heard and seen
and thought about," "asking for encounter with Yahweh," and "holding
Yahweh to account."[41]

---

[38]Brueggemann, "Texts That Linger," 30.

[39]Brueggemann, "Texts That Linger," 31.

[40]Brueggemann's other books on Old Testament theology also dismiss Song of Songs and Esther altogether. See Walter Brueggemann, *Old Testament Theology: Essays on Structure, Theme, and Text*, ed. Patrick D. Miller (Minneapolis: Fortress, 1992); *Old Testament Theology: An Introduction; An Unsettling God: The Heart of the Hebrew Bible* (Minneapolis: Fortress, 2009).

[41]John Goldingay, *Old Testament Theology*, vol. 3, *Israel's Life* (Downers Grove, IL: IVP Academic, 2009), 209, 219, 221, 224.

Patrick Miller, in his study of the relationship between prayer and divine action, comes up with several insightful observations: (1) the active involvement of God in the human situation is invoked by cries to God, by prayers for help; (2) petitionary prayer is fundamentally an act of persuasion, seeking to lure or coax God into responding to the cry for help; (3) intercession is primarily made by the leaders seeking to evoke a change of heart in the intent of God to judge a sinful people. Such intercession is expected by God and incorporated into the divine activity; (4) the prayers of Scripture consistently expect and receive a response from God in a word that has a particular character to it; (5) trust in God is a dimension of the context of prayer and also part of the transforming act; (6) God's providential activity is understood under the rubric of blessing. His providential activity is also to preserve and enhance life as demonstrated by the absence of prayer in the story of Joseph; (7) God's inscrutable work is asserted indirectly in the dialogues of the book of Job where God meets Job from the divine side rather than with words or deeds of deliverance; (8) the cry to God for help in one's suffering and distress implies that there is a moral ground to the universe; and (9) the imagery of God who hears in heaven the cries for help reflects the world in all its particularity with God who rules and acts for the world and in the world.[42]

Although Miller draws scriptural references from both the Torah and the Prophets, the prayers in the Psalms provide the primary basis for his theology of prayer. Prayers, particularly petitionary prayers in the form of cries for help, imply the reality of divine absence in the experience of their petitioners. Yet, when we come to Song of Songs and Esther, there are no such prayers directed to God. Even in the most daunting crisis of the Jewish diaspora in Persia, there was no prayer offered to God. Questions remain as to why that is the case. Those texts prompt us to ask, How do we comprehend divine presence and activity apart from prayers being offered to God?

The book of Ezekiel as an expression of divine presence in absence. Divine hiddenness in the psalms of distress persists as an issue with which the

---

[42]Patrick D. Miller, "Prayer and Divine Action," in *God in the Fray: A Tribute to Walter Brueggemann*, ed. Tod Linafelt and Timothy K. Beal (Minneapolis: Fortress, 1998), 211-32.

psalmists grapple. Yet, it does not encompass all the questions regarding divine absence in the human experience. The presence of the lament psalms in relation to divine absence has indeed generated profound interest in scholarly endeavor. The other frequently observed genre regarding divine absence appears in the prophetic books, particularly texts addressed to the exilic community of Israel. Among these texts, the book of Ezekiel typically receives the most attention.[43] For Ezekiel, the theological issue at stake is not just about divine absence but also divine presence. The two are in a dialectical relationship, so the reader cannot speak of one without the other.

John Kutsko's study addresses the complexity of the paradox of divine presence and absence in Ezekiel. He structures Ezekiel according to this overriding theme. Ezekiel 1–11 focuses on the shift from divine presence to divine absence, while Ezekiel 40-48 revolves around the shift from divine absence to divine presence. The middle of the book, Ezekiel 12–39, concerns preparation for destruction, oracles against the nations, and preparation for restoration. Kutsko asks a fundamental question being raised in the exile: How can God be present when the temple has been destroyed and the Israelites have been relocated to a foreign place? Additionally, in an aniconic tradition, when the gods are represented by graven images in Babylon and Yahweh is not, how can people perceive Yahweh's presence and worship him there? Therefore, Kutsko sees the theme of God's absence and presence as the cord that holds the composition of the book of Ezekiel together.[44]

Kutsko presents an intricate relationship between divine presence and absence in Ezekiel that centers on the exile. According to Kutsko, the exile underlines three fundamental issues: (1) theodicy: Why is Israel in exile? (2) theophany: Where is God in exile? and (3) theonomy: What power does God have in exile? The exilic experience forces Ezekiel to confront Israel's defeat and deportation and to face the loss of national and cultic identity.[45] For Ezekiel, exile is understood as "the wilderness revisited." Ezekiel

---

[43]The book of Daniel also receives some attention. See Hans van Deventer, "Daniel, Prophet of Divine Presence and Absence," in *The Lion Had Roared: Theological Themes in the Prophetic Literature of the Old Testament*, ed. H. G. L. Peels and S. D. Snyman (Eugene, OR: Pickwick, 2012), 221-34.

[44]John F. Kutsko, *Between Heaven and Earth: Divine Presence and Absence in the Book of Ezekiel* (Winona Lake, IN: Eisenbrauns, 2000), 1, 4, 150. The title aptly captures the contents of the book.

[45]Kutsko, *Between Heaven and Earth*, 4.

employs the mobile glory of Yahweh (*kəbôd-YHWH*) to portray the complementary nature of God's presence and absence. In the exile, God's absence is implied by the absence of his temple, but since the glory of Yahweh is mobile, as in the journey of wilderness wandering, God's presence transcends a physical locale. This mobility of the glory of Yahweh serves as a means to convey divine judgment. At the same time, it emphasizes divine presence in exile.

For Kutsko, the temple serves as a structuring device in the book, where Ezekiel adapts the Priestly tradition of a wilderness sanctuary to emphasize divine judgment and divine guidance. The temple is a stage that links divine presence and absence. The two both exist as polar opposites and complement each other. The absence of the temple does not equate with the absence of God. In the exile, God himself becomes Israel's sanctuary (Ezek 11:16).[46] Therefore, Kutsko argues that for Ezekiel's theology, "exile is both a means of punishment and an opportunity for divine presence."[47] He concludes that Yahweh's presence will not fail in front of the Babylonian idols, the loss of the temple, or the victorious enemy of the nations. Yahweh is apparently absent, but is present in exile.[48] Kutsko's articulation of divine presence and absence in exile contributes to Ezekiel's understanding of this paradox and demonstrates Terrien's notion of divine presence in absence. In this sense, divine presence and absence coexist as a dialectical relationship throughout Israel's history, particularly in lament psalms and in the exilic texts.

Ezekiel scholar Daniel Block recognizes five specific dimensions of Yahweh's abandonment in the Old Testament: (1) Yahweh's absence from an individual; (2) Yahweh's absence from his people, Israel; (3) Yahweh's absence from the land of Israel; (4) Yahweh's absence from Jerusalem; and (5) Yahweh's absence from his sanctuary.[49] Block identifies the motif of divine abandonment in the ancient Near Eastern texts and concludes that

---

[46]Kutsko, *Between Heaven and Earth*, 99-100.

[47]Kutsko, *Between Heaven and Earth*, 152. For details regarding the glory of God in the wilderness tradition, see chap. 3.

[48]Kutsko, *Between Heaven and Earth*, 4, 154.

[49]Daniel I. Block, "Divine Abandonment: Ezekiel's Adaptation of an Ancient Near Eastern Motif," in *The Book of Ezekiel: Theological and Anthropological Perspectives*, ed. Margaret S. Odell and John T. Strong (Atlanta: Society of Biblical Literature, 2000), 16-17.

this same motif appears in Ezekiel but with adaptation. Based on Ezekiel 8:12; 9:9, the people of Judah perceive divine abandonment not in terms of their sin or apostasy, as one would expect, but as a betrayal of Yahweh's earlier commitment to them. They reverse the logic that divine abandonment of the land is due to the sin of the people of Israel. Instead, they sin because they perceive Yahweh as abandoning the land. Through this reversal of cause and effect, Ezekiel intends to demonstrate the extent of Judah's perversion. Ezekiel offers several rationales for Yahweh's abandonment, including people's action as well as his own volition. The latter reveals the freedom of Yahweh, who cannot and will not be forced to leave his temple by the sin of his people or the Babylonian king. Yahweh remains sovereign "not only over the fate of his people, but over his own destiny as well."[50] Ezekiel's vision of the future restoration of the temple, people, and land reflects Yahweh's commitment to his people even if he chooses to leave the temple. Block's conception of the absence of God once again brings out the dialectic between God's response of his people's sin, on the one hand, and God's own free choice, on the other.

When rethinking divine presence and absence, Steven Tuell argues for treating the written text as a replacement of the temple in conveying the concept of divine presence. Tuell proposes that the divine glory links the three major sections of the book: thus, the first vision of divine presence in Ezekiel 1–3 as the glory revealed to the exiles beside the River Chebar, the absence of God in Ezekiel 8–11 as God abandons the temple and the city, and divine presence as reinhabiting the future temple in Ezekiel 40–48 in the prophet's eschatological vision. Tuell notes from Priestly tradition that divine presence is always conveyed through a fixed sacred space, a cultic image, or a king, but this is not the case in Ezekiel. In Ezekiel, the divine glory does not appear in the boundaries of a fixed sacred space; rather, it comes to the prophet in exile, in a foreign land. The divine glory does not take place on a sacred mountain, as in the Sinai theophany. Instead, it appears in the valley of the River Chebar, among the exiles.

Building on the research of several scholars, Tuell is convinced that the words of Ezekiel should be taken as a written composition. The prophecy

---

[50]Block, "Divine Abandonment," 36, 42.

comes to him in the form of a scroll, which is covered with words front and back. Ezekiel is then asked to eat it (Ezek 2:8–3:3). The consistency of style and theme of the scroll further supports it as a written composition. For Ezekiel, his prophecies become the bridge connecting Yahweh and the exilic community. In this way, the text of Ezekiel itself has become a medium for the divine presence in exile. When the people of Israel in exile read this scroll, they would have been aware of God's presence with them.[51] The exile profoundly transforms the understanding of divine presence. It is no longer a fixed external symbol but a mobile icon. Ellen Davis has long noticed that Ezekiel was a written text, which was both the locus and medium of the prophetic enterprise.[52] Tuell ties this understanding of the text to the theme of divine presence and absence.

Two other studies also focus on the divine presence and absence in Ezekiel. William Tooman's study centers on divine presence in relation to covenant and the structure of the book of Ezekiel. He sees the covenant and divine presence going hand in hand. The breaking of the covenant results in divine absence. Likewise, the new gift of divine presence accompanies the unbreakable covenant with an incorruptible people. Tooman demonstrates this interconnectedness of covenant and presence through the vision accounts and oracles of deliverance in Ezekiel.[53] Moreover, John Strong stresses that the *kābôd* of Yahweh is his hypostasis.[54] Ezekiel attempts to maintain Zion theology to affirm Yahweh's presence in the earth and on the divine throne. The aspects of Zion theology include Yahweh enthroned as the divine king during the exile. One day, he will return and again be accessible through his temple on Zion.[55]

---

[51]Steven S. Tuell, "Divine Presence and Absence in Ezekiel's Prophecy," in Odell and Strong, *Book of Ezekiel*, 97-116.

[52]Ellen F. Davis, *Swallowing the Scroll: Textuality and the Dynamics of Discourse in Ezekiel's Prophesy*, JSOTSup 78 (Sheffield: Sheffield Academic Press, 1989), 133.

[53]See William A. Tooman, "Covenant and Presence in the Composition and Theology of Ezekiel," in *Divine Presence and Absence in Exilic and Post-exilic Judaism*, ed. Nathan McDonald and Izaak J. De Hulster (Tübingen: Mohr Siebeck, 2013), 151-82.

[54]Strong borrows from S. Dean McBride's definition of *hypostasis*. It is "a quality, epithet, attribute, manifestation or the like of a deity which through a process of personification and differentiation has become a distinct divine being in its own right." See John T. Strong, "God's *Kābôd*: The Presence of Yahweh in the Book of Ezekiel," in Odell and Strong, *Book of Ezekiel*, 72.

[55]Strong, "God's *Kābôd*," 69-95.

Jill Middlemas argues for "multiple imaging" to understand the theology of divine presence in absence, which summarizes the multiple understandings of the presence of God in his absence. She defines multiple imaging as a literary technique of using many images (metaphors) of Yahweh. These metaphors not only serve as literary devices that replace an idea but also "exert cognitive force by which their use generates new meanings, promotes associations, and results in the interaction and response of an audience." The focus of such is on idolatry and the meaning and implication of aniconism in Yahwistic tradition. Middlemas concludes that the result of using multiple imaging is resistance to forming God in a single, concrete, and stable form. For her, divine presence is near and at the same time far. God emerges as both transcendent and imminent, and this dual nature realizes the theology of divine presence in absence.[56]

Summary. So far, we have seen that the theology of divine presence in the exile can be conceived through the *kābôd* theology and the written text. Divine presence in absence indeed presents itself in multifaceted manners. Studies on the theology of divine presence and absence culminate in the genre of lament psalms and prophetic texts, especially those texts that originate in the context of the exile. Both genres are rooted in Israel's experience of its God. While some studies are confessional in nature, defending God's character, other studies raise candid questions regarding the injustice of divine hiddenness. Stephen Davis thinks that when contemplating the two opposing qualities of God, such as

> God is absent and God is present.
> God is transcendent and God is immanent.
> God is unlike us and God is like us.
> God is hidden and God is revealed.
> God is silent and God speaks.

the danger of focusing too much on the left side of God is that God will become too distant and therefore irrelevant to human life and concerns. On the other hand, the danger of going too far to the right side is either anthropomorphism or idolatry. A sensible Christian thinking of God, he proposes,

---

[56]Jill Middlemas, "Divine Presence in Absence: Aniconism and Multiple Imaging in the Prophets," in McDonald and Hulster, *Divine Presence and Absence*, 183-211, esp. 206-7.

is one that must be done in tension between the opposite poles of transcendence and imminence. Both sides of the claims are true, and neglect of either side leads to false theology.[57] This is precisely the paradoxical tension between divine presence and absence.

In Old Testament theology, the second approach—that is, conceiving a dialectical relationship between divine presence and absence—seems to overpower the first approach, that of seeing a decreasing trajectory from divine presence to divine absence in the chronological arrangement of the Christian and the Hebrew canons. In the examples of lament psalms and the exilic prophetic texts such as Ezekiel, the boundary between the disappearance of God and a God who is present in absence blurs. Nevertheless, in the second approach, although the texts of protest appears in the forefront as a way to comprehend the paradox of divine presence and absence, it presupposes the existence of God. Both the psalmists and Israel address God as a specific dialogic partner to express their protests: "My God, my God, why have You forsaken me?" (Ps 22:1). "The LORD does not see us; the LORD has forsaken the land" (Ezek 8:12). Although experienced by the psalmists as an absent God, he is without doubt present in the minds and souls of the psalmists. By contrast, when we come to the literary absence of God in Song of Songs and Esther, how do we articulate the theology of divine presence and absence? The second approach, though it contains provocative thoughts and profound insights, fails to address this grave theological concern. This leads us to the third approach.

Divine absence in the Writings. In recent scholarship, there has been a growing interest in the theology of the Writings. Among the books in the Writings, the image of God and his action in Wisdom texts has received particular attention. The Megilloth also gains increasing significance as a distinct corpus in both Jewish and Old Testament theology. As previously observed by Friedman, Miles, and McEntire, the visibility and activity of God gradually diminishes as the biblical books progress to the end. If we take the canon of the Hebrew Bible, with its tripartite division—the Torah, the Prophets, and the Writings—into consideration, the trajectory of a

---

[57]Stephen T. Davis, "God as Present and God as Absent," in Dalferth, *Presence and Absence of God*, 147-60, esp. 149-50.

disappearing God emerges. This trajectory at the same time presents a dialectic relationship between divine visibility and divine invisibility, particularly in the Psalms and in the exilic and postexilic books, such as Ezekiel
and Ezra-Nehemiah.[58] Therefore, the first two approaches are not mutually
exclusive but overlapping.

In the third approach, divine activity in the Writings appears drastically
different from that in the Torah and the Prophets. So it is helpful first to
locate the place of Wisdom in the Writings.[59] Since the twentieth century,
scholars have sought to do so. The so-called center approach, such as Walter
Eichrodt's statement that covenant is the center (*mitte*) of Old Testament
theology, fails to do justice to the entire realm of the Old Testament, because the concept of covenant is not a dominant theme in Israel's Wisdom
tradition.[60] Likewise, Gerhard von Rad's salvation history (*Heilsgeschichte*),
which runs through the historical narratives of Israel, does not receive the
same significance in wisdom books.[61] In order to confront this phenomenon,
von Rad later wrote *Wisdom in Israel* as a way to counterbalance what the
tradition-historical approach fails to resolve.[62]

The place of Wisdom in Old Testament theology. By nature, Wisdom theology is not concerned with national interests such as covenant, Israel's
history, Jerusalem, temple worship, idolatry, or restoration from the exile.
Rather, its theological basis lies in creation, and its concern is universal. Von
Rad perceives that Israel was aware of the power of God in all spheres of life,
and so Israel speaks of the world in all its inexplicableness. Therefore, there
are limits to human wisdom, in light of the unsearchable nature of the
world and divine presence, as in the story of Job.[63] Although Israel, its

[58]The motif of divine presence and absence in postexilic Judaism can be conceived through the
perspectives of the spirit of Yahweh, the temple vessels, the rebuilding of the temple, and the
written law code. See the various articles in McDonald and Hulster, *Divine Presence and Absence*.

[59]For the purpose of the present study, we will only consider primarily the books of Proverbs, Job,
and Ecclesiastes as wisdom texts in the Christian canon. Though what constitutes "wisdom
texts" is contested, it is one way of grouping the aforementioned three books. Due to the scope
of the study, the text of Ben Sira and other ancient Near Eastern wisdom texts are not included.

[60]Walter Eichrodt, *Theology of the Old Testament*, 2 vols., trans. J. A. Baker (Philadelphia: Westminster, 1961, 1967).

[61]Gerhard von Rad, *Old Testament Theology*, 2 vols., trans. D. M. G. Stalker (Edinburgh: Oliver &
Boyd, 1962, 1965).

[62]Gerhard von Rad, *Wisdom in Israel* (Harrisburg, PA: Trinity Press International, 1972).

[63]Von Rad, *Wisdom in Israel*, 106-8.

history, religion, and culture are not at the center of its theology, wisdom theology nevertheless is a vital part of Scripture and needs to be reckoned with. Wisdom scholar Leo Perdue responds to the "collapse" of the use of the history of the Israelite religion as the trajectory for doing Old Testament theology. Instead, he proposes a more inclusive approach, in which one acknowledges the diversity of interpretations in the canon, the multiplicity of theologies under the dynamic matrix of creation and history, the recognition of how biblical texts and their theologies have been construed within the history of interpretation, and critical reflection between theologies of the Old Testament and past interpretations with the horizons of meaning that derive from contemporary discourse.[64] In his earlier work, *Wisdom and Creation*, Perdue attempts to locate the place of wisdom in Old Testament theology by evaluating several approaches, such as the relationship between history and creation, wisdom from the canonical theology, and wisdom from feminist theology. Each of these approaches offers significant understandings of the place of wisdom in Israelite faith. He concludes that wisdom theology is theologically grounded in cosmology and anthropology. It affirms a universal orientation to faith and ethics. The role of Woman Wisdom also challenges the predominant image of male metaphors for God.[65] Therefore, Perdue asserts that wisdom and creation are integrated concepts within Old Testament theology.

In previous decades, the place of wisdom in Old Testament theology was typically dismissed or excluded by those who wrote Old Testament theology.[66] In recent decades, however, those who undertake the task of doing Old Testament theology often include wisdom in their endeavors, though they differ in their methods. For instance, Goldingay places "wisdom"

---

[64]Leo G. Perdue, *Reconstructing Old Testament Theology: After the Collapse of History* (Minneapolis: Fortress, 2005), 347-49.

[65]Leo G. Perdue, *Wisdom and Creation: The Theology of Wisdom Literature* (Nashville: Abingdon, 1994), 34-48.

[66]Such as Eichrodt, von Rad, and Brueggemann. There are a few exceptions. For example, Zimmerli places "wisdom" under "life before God." See Walther Zimmerli, *Old Testament Theology in Outline*, trans. David E. Green (Edinburgh: T&T Clark, 1978). Kaiser places Wisdom literature in Israel's historical timeline under "Sapiential Era." See Walter C. Kaiser Jr., *Toward an Old Testament Theology* (Grand Rapids, MI: Zondervan, 1978), 165-81. Though Anderson identifies covenant as a major contour of Old Testament theology, he nevertheless incorporates wisdom in his part 3, "Trials of Faith and Horizons of Hope." See Anderson, *Contours of Old Testament Theology*, 237.

under "humanity," alongside God, Israel, the world, and the nations in his *Old Testament Theology.*[67] John Kessler situates wisdom theology as one of the theologies of the Old Testament alongside creation theology, Sinai covenant theology, promise theology, Priestly theology, and others. He frames wisdom theology as "the relationship of faith seeking understanding."[68] R. W. L. Moberly titles his last chapter "Where Is Wisdom?" in his *Old Testament Theology*. He argues that the figure of Job illustrates one primary dimension of wisdom—his reactions to adversity in Job 1–2 present the right human response to God. The poem in Job 28, on the one hand, ascribes the "place" of wisdom to God. On the other hand, wisdom is accessible to humans, but only to those who display the appropriate qualities, thus reaffirming the piety of Job in Job 1–2.[69]

Recently, Julius Steinberg examined the place of wisdom in an Old Testament theology by using a thematic and structural-canonical approach. Steinberg chooses the canonical book order of Baba Batra due to its standing as the oldest source of Jewish tradition, dated to about 200 CE. In accordance with that ordering of the Writings, he divides the books into two series: the wisdom series and the national-historical series. The former includes Ruth, Psalms, Job, Proverbs, Ecclesiastes, and Song of Songs. The latter includes Lamentations, Daniel, Esther, Ezra-Nehemiah, and Chronicles. The first series represents the house of David, whereas the second series points to the house of God. Thus, the wisdom series reflects the way of the individual with God from sorrow to joy, whereas the second series reflects the way of the nation back to God from sorrow to joy. In terms of the place of wisdom in Old Testament theology, Steinberg follows Perdue, connecting wisdom with creation theology and anthropology. He sees Song of Songs as a wisdom book and situates it as a follow-up to Ecclesiastes, elaborating on the love between a man and a woman in Ecclesiastes 9:9, "to enjoy life with the wife of your youth."[70] Steinberg's research

---

[67]John Goldingay, *Old Testament Theology*, vol. 2, *Israel's Faith* (Downers Grove, IL: IVP Academic, 2006), 576-96.

[68]John Kessler, *Old Testament Theology: Divine Call and Human Response* (Waco, TX: Baylor University Press, 2013), vii, 447.

[69]Moberly, *Old Testament Theology*, 243-77, esp. 243, 271.

[70]Steinberg defines a "structural-canonical" approach as one that addresses the level of individual books but also the larger literary horizon of small collections of books and the canon of the

provides a helpful link in perceiving the interconnectedness within the books of the Writings, particularly the two series, with two varied themes and focuses. Yet these two ways and two houses do not take into account the absence of God's name in Song of Songs and Esther. In Baba Batra's arrangement of the books in the Writings, the canonical connection between Song of Songs and Esther with the other books in the same category suggests their affiliation.

Burnett devotes a whole chapter to the theology of divine presence and absence in wisdom books. Like Perdue, he grounds the theology of wisdom in God's creation of the world. Because the nature of wisdom has to do with universal concerns of daily life and not with national events or crises, Burnett stresses that divine presence and absence are difficult to distinguish. Wisdom confronts divine hiddenness in the world and humanity's need to search for divine presence. For wisdom, divine presence often appears as divine absence. As Burnett suggests, "Wisdom is concerned with discerning the difference between the two." He also offers another vital observation that wisdom accentuates the moral implications of divine presence in the created order and in mundane human lives. In such a context, divine absence goes hand in hand with the problem of theodicy. In wisdom books, the issue of innocent suffering creates a relational crisis marked by divine absence.[71] Among the three traditional books in wisdom, Job receives the most attention in regard to the theology of divine absence compared to Proverbs and Ecclesiastes.[72]

In a festschrift to Walter Brueggemann, *God in the Fray*, the editors arrange the structure of the book according to the three divisions of the

---

Hebrew Bible. See Julius Steinberg, "The Place of Wisdom Literature in an Old Testament Theology: A Thematic and Structural-Canonical Approach," in *The Shape of the Writings*, ed. Julius Steinberg and Timothy J. Stone with the assistance of Rachel Marie Stone, Siphrut 16 (Winona Lake, IN: Eisenbrauns, 2015), 97, 150, 153, 160-67.

[71]Burnett, *Where Is God?*, 85-86.

[72]The wisdom personified in Proverbs has been taken as a medium or a hypostasis of God. In Ecclesiastes, God is present in the world, but his presence is beyond human reach. See Burnett, *Where Is God?*, 101-14. In an article, Pleins articulates divine silence during Job's suffering as God listening to him. God's silence gives way to the terrifying reality of God's presence, and God's speeches at the end of Job balance and answer the silence of God. The silence of Job during God's speeches also balances out his previous vocal remarks to God. See J. David Pleins, "Why Do You Hide Your Face? Divine Silence and Speech in the Book of Job," *Interpretation* (July 1994): 229-38.

Hebrew Bible: God in the Torah, God in the Prophets, and God in the Writings. In the section on God in the Writings, two of the six chapters are devoted to Job. For the other chapters, two of four discuss prayers and complaints. Both of these two chapters make references to Job.[73] Within Israel's wisdom tradition, the predicament of innocent suffering directly challenges theodicy as well as divine absence. David Clines says Job's complaint about God's allowing wrongs to continue unchecked and being absent in governing the world is a serious theological problem. He focuses on Job 23–24, where Job intends but fails to find God (Job 23:8-9). For Job, not only can God not be found, but God is also not obliged to listen to the protests of human beings, because whatever God desires, he does (Job 23:13). In addition, Job criticizes God for being absent and for not carrying out the judgment for which God alone is responsible. From the beginning of the book to the end, God remains "above the fray," while human beings are caught "in the fray."[74] God's hidden presence in creation—the personified wisdom as divine presence in Proverbs—and the transcendent yet elusive presence of God in Ecclesiastes cannot balance out or explain away the reality of innocent suffering in Job as well as divine silence during Job's suffering. In this sense, the book of Job is similar to the lament psalms in that the experience of divine silence and absence is deeply felt and the issue of theodicy persists.[75] Melton's research on the aspects of divine presence and absence in wisdom books is helpful. She identifies the close affinity between wisdom and the presence of God and

---

[73]Miller, "Prayer and Divine Action," and Claus Westermann, "The Complaint Against God," trans. Armin Siedlecki, in Linafelt and Beal, *God in the Fray*. The other two chapters include one about Lamentations and one about Ecclesiastes.

[74]David J. A. Clines, "Quarter Days Gone: Job 24 and the Absence of God," in Linafelt and Beal, *God in the Fray*, 242-58, esp. 242, 250. Various research has addressed the issue of innocent suffering, theodicy, and rhetoric in the book of Job. A few among the many who place the issue of theodicy at the forefront of their book include Carl G. Jung, *Answer to Job*, trans. R. F. C. Hull (Princeton, NJ: Princeton University Press, 1969); Saadiah Ben Joseph Al-Fayyumi, *The Book of Theodicy: Translation and Commentary on the Book of Job*, trans. L. E. Goodman (New Haven, CT: Yale University Press, 1988); James L. Crenshaw, *Reading Job: A Literary and Theological Commentary* (Macon, GA: Smyth & Helwys, 2011).

[75]Crenshaw's summary of literature on the Wisdom corpus provides an overview of recent scholarship on wisdom theology. He concludes that the attempt to define wisdom yields little consensus among wisdom scholars, as he predicted two decades ago. See James L. Crenshaw, *Sipping from the Cup of Wisdom* (Macon, GA: Smyth & Helwys, 2017), 1:141-55, esp. 153.

concludes that "God and wisdom are accessible in Proverbs, beyond grasp in Ecclesiastes, and elusive in Job."[76]

Megilloth. In addition to the significance of the place of Wisdom in Old Testament theology, an emergent interest in the study of the Megilloth as a coherent canonical collection has also blossomed in recent years, with attention given to the individual books within this collection, the interconnectedness among the five scrolls, and their respective links with the other books in the Writings.[77] The reason for its neglect in past scholarship is primarily the lateness of the Megilloth as a collection, since most scholars consider texts that are "early" or "original" to be more authoritative. The earliest attestations of the Megilloth as a group come from the Tiberian manuscripts of the tenth and eleventh century CE but may be earlier.[78] However, the tide has shifted in recent years due to the growing recognition among scholars that the later uses of Scripture are also an essential component of its interpretation. Therefore, the lateness of the Megilloth does not preclude how its interpretive tradition has been shaped.[79]

Although his primary research focus is on the compilational history of these five scrolls, in examining the macrostructure of the Megilloth, Timothy Stone observes that in four out of five scrolls, the motif of a prominent female set in relationship to a male character emerges. For example, Ruth and Naomi are the dominant characters in Ruth, complemented by Boaz; the female character in Song of Songs is complemented by her male protagonist; in Lamentations, Daughter Zion is complemented by a man of affliction in Lamentations 3; and Esther is complemented by Mordecai in the book of Esther. Ecclesiastes is an exception in this collection of scrolls. Stone also notes that the absence of God constitutes another dominant

---

[76]Brittany N. Melton, "'Oh, That I Knew Where I Might Find Him': Aspects of Divine Absence in Proverbs, Job and Ecclesiastes," in *Interpreting Old Testament Wisdom Literature*, ed. David G. Firth and Lindsay Wilson (Downers Grove, IL: IVP Academic, 2017), 215.

[77]A program unit "Megilloth" has formed at the annual meeting of the Society of Biblical Literature, first as a consulting group for three years (2014–2016) and since 2017 as a formal meeting session.

[78]Timothy J. Stone, *The Compilational History of the Megilloth* (Tübingen: Mohr Siebeck, 2013), 102-17.

[79]Amy Erickson and Andrew R. Davis, "Recent Research on the Megilloth (Song of Songs, Ruth, Lamentations, Ecclesiastes, Esther)," *Currents in Biblical Research* 14, no. 3 (2016): 298-318, esp. 298.

motif among the Megilloth, where God is not mentioned in Song of Songs
and Esther. In Ecclesiastes, God is in heaven, and human beings are on
earth. In Lamentations, Daughter Zion pours out her grief, but God does
not appear. In Ruth, God gives bread and a baby but remains behind the
scenes throughout the whole narrative. However, Stone also mentions that
although the Megilloth has these common motifs, the books are characterized more by their diversity than by their unity. The books are arranged
in such a way that each has conversational partners with the other books in
the Writings, and none stands alone.[80]

In researching the current scholarship and trends of the Megilloth, Amy
Erickson and Andrew Davis discern "the relative absence of God as an
active presence in the five books."[81] They summarize past scholarship that
has responded to this issue in two ways: (1) ignored it or (2) argued for a
robust theology of divine providence. The first response is reflected in
standard theologies of the Old Testament. The second response can be seen
in theological treatments of the books of Ruth and Esther, where "divine
absence has proven not a challenge but an opportunity to assert God's constant but imperceptible oversight of human affairs."[82] Erickson and Davis
observe that divine activities in Ruth and Esther seem to shape the understanding of divine activities in other books of the Megilloth.

These two heretofore prevalent responses seem to have shifted recently.
For instance, two chapters from a recent monograph, *Megilloth Studies: The
Shape of Contemporary Scholarship*, which came from papers read in a con-
sultation group on the Megilloth at the Society of Biblical Literature, offer
a more nuanced understanding of divine absence in the Megilloth. Among
the issues that emerge in the book are gender, thematic frame, ethnicity and
identity, and theology.[83] For instance, Garrett Galvin's chapter examines the
horizontal theology in the Megilloth through four themes: female, narratives, wisdom, and suffering. These themes on female concerns may be
overlooked in nonnarrative sections of the Hebrew Bible.[84] Galvin also

---

[80]Stone, *Compilational History*, 205, 207.
[81]Erickson and Davis, "Recent Research," 307.
[82]Erickson and Davis, "Recent Research," 308.
[83]Embry, *Megilloth Studies*.
[84]Garrett Galvin, "Horizontal Theology in the Megilloth," in Embry, *Megilloth Studies*, 125. By
  "horizontal theology," Galvin refers to the kind of theology that takes a character's experience,

places Song of Songs under the tradition of Wisdom literature in the vein of Proverbs.[85] Stone considers the Megilloth to be held together by the gravitational pull exerted by the Wisdom corpus, which starts with Proverbs, just before the Megilloth, and Galvin furthers this argument by proposing that this gravitational pull does not stop with Ecclesiastes but includes Lamentations and Esther. Esther then becomes a figure of applied wisdom and functions as the counterpart to Joseph, only at a different geographical end of the diaspora. In sum, Galvin asserts that the theology of the Megilloth is a horizontal one that privileges human actors, who have to try to understand human suffering and see its connection to God, where meaning is found in human relationships and in the incarnation. This then forces human characters to reconsider how God acts in the world. Although I largely agree with Galvin's assessment of the horizontal theology, the part on human suffering does not seem to receive the same treatment in Song of Songs as in the other four books within the Megilloth.

In the same monograph, Megan Fullerton Strollo joins the discussion about the theology of the Megilloth by first distinguishing Christian biblical theology from the Jewish way of doing biblical theology. She argues that Jewish theologians have paid more attention to the books within the Megilloth. The incorporation of the annual Jewish feasts associated with the Megilloth demonstrates this phenomenon. She concludes that the theology presented in these five scrolls is one of a God who is distant and people who are capable of partnering with God. Thus, at the center of the theology of the Megilloth is divine absence and human responsibility.[86] While Strollo quotes from Marvin Sweeney's understanding of Jewish theologies as tending to focus on human responsibility, the text in question is Esther and not Song of Songs. The place of Song of Songs in the Megilloth and its contribution to biblical theology remains an area for further investigation and reflection. We may also add Andrew Davis's chapter in the same volume

---

praxis, and incarnation into consideration. It is a theology of everyday life, focusing on the concrete particularity of a lived experience within Scripture, as opposed to vertical theology, which emphasizes immutable concepts, timeless problems, and eternal arguments (see 126-27, 131).

[85]Galvin, "Horizontal Theology," 133.

[86]Megan Fullerton Strollo, "Initiative and Agency: Towards a Theology of the Megilloth," in Embry, *Megilloth Studies*, 150-60.

on not construing the divine hidden hand behind the narratives of Ruth and Esther but instead focusing on the experiences of human characters. The theology of the Megilloth is "not so much a common theology but a common way of doing theology."[87]

As I finish a draft of this book, Brittany Melton's newly published *Where Is God in Megilloth?* brings a welcome change of perspective to the current scholarship of the subject in question. Some of my literary reviews inevitably overlap with hers but her focus is more on the whole Megilloth, whereas my focus is on the two scrolls within the same corpus. Melton's research concerns understandings of divine presence and absence through the atrocities of history, particularly the Holocaust, and literature as well as through a survey of scholarship on God in the Megilloth. She concludes that there is a lack of consensus among the scholarship on divine presence and absence in the Megilloth, and she attempts to rectify this by a dialogical reading of the five scrolls, which she names a "theological-literary approach" in the format of a "table conversation" based on Mikhail Bakhtin's dialogism.[88] In regard to Song of Songs and Esther, Melton therefore establishes a table conversation with the two scrolls by defending God's literary absence on the one hand, and God's ambiguous presence on the other hand. What is illuminating for me is her use of the text "who is that coming up from the wilderness" in Song of Songs 3:6 to consider the "who knows" passage in Esther 4:14. Her conclusion is that divine presence and absence in both books reflect a theological ambiguity and that these two aspects of God are held in tension with each other.[89] Melton's book contributes to the discussion of the role of God in the Megilloth and creatively brings all five scrolls into an interlocking relationship with one another. Her work is a significant resource for future studies of divine presence and absence in the Megilloth.

Summary. McEntire challenges the notion of Old Testament theology when it is examined from the beginning of the biblical narrative, because

---

[87]Andrew R. Davis, "Ruth and Esther as the Thematic Frame of the Megilloth," in Embry, *Megilloth Studies*, 7-19, esp. 10, 17.

[88]Melton, *Where Is God*, 13-38, 44. In this "table conversation," Melton asks: Who is there? What is said? What is for dinner? The seats of the table are occupied by the canonical books. Some speak, and some remain silent. See Melton, *Where Is God*, 54-55.

[89]Melton, *Where Is God*, 82-83.

these narratives tend to focus on God's presence while less attention is given "to the parts of the Old Testament theology where God recedes into the background and becomes a subtle influence in various ways, rather than participating in the story as an active character."[90] Therefore, he proposes moving these latter biblical texts to the center of Old Testament theology in order to present a dynamic God. The Writings, which include the corpus of wisdom series and the Megilloth, belong to the texts in which God recedes to the background but exerts subtle influences as a character in the biblical stories. While one runs a risk by privileging the presence of God in the early biblical texts over the latter texts, where God recedes to the background, one also runs a risk by going in the other direction and privileging the latter texts over the earlier texts. In actuality, Scripture presents both portraits of God. He is both present and absent, transcendent and imminent, active and passive.

---

[90]McEntire, *Portraits of a Mature God*, 2.

2

ABSENCE

WISDOM *and* COUNTERTEXTS

Oh that I knew where I might find Him.

JOB 23:3

IN THE ENTIRE OLD TESTAMENT, Song of Songs and Esther stand out as two books that do not make explicit reference to the name of God. Both books belong to the Writings as well as within the collection of the Megilloth. In past scholarship, the theology of absence in Esther has long been noticed and tackled in various ways. However, the same theology receives less attention in Song of Songs. David Blumenthal has written an article addressing the issue of the absence of God in Song of Songs and Esther. However, his approach is more linguistic than theological. His study focuses exclusively on the linguistic territory of the name of God and its various forms rather than on the themes, motifs, and theology of these two books.[1]

In what follows, I first summarize past research on the theology of absence in Song of Songs and Esther. By absence, I do not mean nonexistence. Rather, absence refers to an aspect of God that escapes human comprehension. Here I borrow from Anthony Godzieba's phrase "absence signals

---

[1]David R. Blumenthal, "Where God Is Not: The Book of Esther and the Song of Songs," *Judaism* 44, no. 1 (1995): 81-92.

the otherness of God."[2] Then, I argue that Song of Songs and Esther share close affinity with Israel's wisdom, namely, the search for the order of things in God's created world. This affinity with wisdom in turn illuminates our understanding of the theology of absence in these two books.

The theology of absence in Song of Songs. The relationship of the lovers in the Song has been perceived as an "ideal love." Many interpreters over the course of time have construed the lovers' relationship allegorically as depicting how Christ loves the church or as representing the love between God and Israel.[3] In recent decades, following the prevalence of the historical-critical method, the allegorical or typological interpretations of Song of Songs have begun to fade into the background, although some interpreters persist in treating the Song figuratively or mystically as typifying a believer's inner communion with God.[4] Even in literal interpretations of the Song, the notion of a harmonious, mutual, reciprocal, and egalitarian relationship of the lovers often dominates the interpretation landscape, as we see in Phyllis Trible's groundbreaking study on redeeming the lost love in Eden.[5] Many feminist interpreters follow in Trible's footsteps and present the lovers in the Song as a paradigm shift from the male-dominated model.[6] Among them are Kathryn Harding, Elie Assis, and Jonathan Kaplan.

---

[2]He further defines *absence* as "God's excess that outruns our human ability to adequately 'name' and conceptualize the characteristics of the personality of God." Anthony J. Godzieba, *A Theology of the Presence and Absence of God* (Collegeville, MN: Liturgical Press, 2018), 38. Godzieba traces the history of development of the "God problem" in Western culture from a dialectical view on divine presence and absence to the rise of the extrinsic view, and then to the understanding of "God as love" in Christian theology.

[3]Allegorical interpretations have dominated the interpretative history of Song of Songs for over two thousand years. For an overview of references in both the Christian and Jewish allegorical interpretations, see Chloe Sun, *Oxford Bibliographies: Song of Songs* (Oxford: Oxford University Press, 2016), www.oxfordbibliographies.com/view/document/obo-9780195393361/obo-9780195393361-0215.xml ?rskey=XjUbjK&result=1&q=Song+of+Songs#firstMatch. See also R. Beaton, "Song of Songs 3: History of Interpretation," *DOTWPW* 760-69. See also Ilana Pardes, *The Song of Songs: A Biography*, Lives of Great Religious Books (Princeton, NJ: Princeton University Press, 2019), 22-58.

[4]For figurative interpretations, see articles in Annette Schellenberg and Ludger Schwienhorst-Schönberger, eds., *Interpreting the Song of Songs: Literal or Allegorical?*, Biblical Tools and Studies 26 (Leuven: Peeters, 2016). For a mystical interpretation, see, M. Basil Pennington, *Song of Songs: A Spiritual Commentary* (Woodstock, VT: Skylight Paths, 2004). An older classic is St. John of the Cross, *Dark Knight of the Soul*, trans. E. Allison Peers (New York: Doubleday, 1959).

[5]Phyllis Trible, *God and the Rhetoric of Sexuality* (Philadelphia: Fortress, 1978), 144-65.

[6]For example, Athalya Brenner, ed., *A Feminist Companion to the Song of Songs*, FCB (Sheffield: Sheffield Academic Press, 1993); Athalya Brenner and Carole R. Fontaine, eds., *A Feminist Companion to the Song of Songs*, FCB 2/6 (Sheffield: Sheffield Academic Press, 2000).

Harding remarks, "Though the theme of absence recurs, overtly, on at least two occasions in the Song of Songs, the attention that this theme has received in the scholarly literature is somewhat scant and perfunctory." Harding develops her thesis along the lines of seeking and finding the one who is absent. This absent lover is a gendered one, since in the Song it is always the female lover who does the seeking and finding in her male lover's absence. This yearning for her lover in his absence, then, creates a moment of crisis in the woman's perception of her relationship. It expresses her perceived vulnerability and anxiety, a feeling that she cannot endure, and that compels her to overcome his absence by going out to search for him. The underlying anxiety lurks in her mind: Could she love more than she is loved?[7] In one sense, the lover's absence makes the woman's heart grow fonder. In another sense, the woman retains her own identity. While searching for her lover, she refuses to be merged with him. Such is the paradox of absence and presence.

In light of this paradox, Harding argues that the boundaries between absence and presence in the poem are blurred, hazy, and unstable. Therefore, while the theme of absence can be discussed, it is also veiled by other aspects of the poem. In her lover's absence, the woman is able to conjure his presence through her words and dreams. Harding concludes with the statement that the locus of the Song's endless appeal is precisely its vision of love that is both beautiful and vulnerable.[8]

Harding's reading of the absent lover is a literal one. Nevertheless, the theology of absence bears astounding similarities to the theology of divine absence in lament psalms where one party yearns and searches for the presence of the other in his absence. As William Goodman's study shows, the idea of "yearning for you" and "yearning for You" are often overlapped in respect to certain psalms and Song of Songs. He observes that both Psalms and the Song of Songs share the theme of longing for the intimate other and that this theme is often expressed in the language of yearning and desire. Although the psalmists do not use the erotic language to address God, the intensity of their passion to God parallels the intensity of the

[7]Kathryn Harding, "'I Sought Him but I Did Not Find Him': The Elusive Lover in the Song of Songs," *Biblical Interpretation* 16, no. 1 (2008): 43-59.
[8]Harding, "'I Sought Him,'" 57, 59.

lovers in the Song. The blurring of distinction between human erotic relationships and encounters with the divine has been a persistent phenomenon
throughout the history of interpretation of the Song.[9] The idea of the absent
lover also resonates with the conceptual image of divine presence in absence in Ezekiel, where the notion of presence and absence reflects a more
complicated relationship than simply a dichotomy. It is in his absence that
the female lover uses other ways to invoke his presence, just like in Ezekiel,
where an aniconic tradition during exile does not prevent the prophet from
invoking divine presence through his prophecy—the written word.

In analyzing the literary structure of Song of Songs, Assis proposes
combining a thematic approach with form criticism. One of the dominant
themes of the Song he observes is the woman's longing for union with the
beloved. According to the form of the Song, he recognizes four major
types: poems of adoration, poems of yearning, descriptive poems, and
poems that are an invitation to a rendezvous. The poems of adoration and
poems of yearning express the woman's longing to be in her lover's
presence. Every poem of the invitation to a rendezvous becomes the climax
of the other poems that precede it. The variation between each unit of the
Song and the characters' lack of knowledge of the next stage constitutes
the driving force for the lovers. Assis argues that if every step of the lover's
relationship were foreseeable, then the interest of the poem would be lost.
The continuity among different units suggests an emotional development
of the lovers or arrangement of various highlights of their inner psyche.[10]
Although the theology of presence and absence is not at the forefront of
Assis's thesis, the way in which he distinguishes the themes of the Song and
the manner of his arrangement of each unit reveal a similar dynamic between theology of presence and absence. In each other's absence, the
feelings of yearning intensify. In other words, every incidence of absence
of the lover conjures the other lover's desire to have a rendezvous and to
be intimate with the other.

---

[9]See Goodman's detailed discussion of the various nuance in regard to "yearning for you" and
"yearning for You," in William Goodman, *Yearning for You: Psalms and the Song of Songs in
Conversation with Rock and Worship Songs*, Bible in the Modern World 46 (Sheffield: Sheffield
Phoenix, 2012), 187-208.

[10]Eliyahu Assis, *Flashes of Fire: A Literary Analysis of the Song of Songs*, LHBOTS 503 (New York:
T&T Clark, 2009), 25.

However, Assis departs from Harding in that while Harding sees the theology of absence as a gendered one, that is, only the woman does the seeking and finding of her beloved, Assis recognizes that both lovers are doing the seeking and finding of the other party in the other's absence. This is reflected by his division of the poems.[11] If the various rendezvous of the lovers form the climax of the Song in the emotional as well as relational development of the lovers, then it follows that the absence of the lover, whether that lover be male or female, is necessary in creating the climax for them to be united and reunited. The absence of the lover then becomes a natural element in the course of their relationship. It is precisely the absence of the lover that causes the longing to be united. Such is also the lingering appeal of the Song.

In *My Perfect One*, Jonathan Kaplan devotes one chapter to the theology of absence in Song of Songs. Building on Harding's article, Kaplan titles his chapter "Absence Makes the Heart Grow Fonder? Domesticating the Elusive Lover of Song of Songs."[12] As early as the Tannaim period in the second century CE, Jewish scholars were dealing with the themes of absence and desire in the Song. Rather than identifying the genre of the Song as love poetry, the early Tannaim scholars saw it as epic poetry that chronicles events, portraying Israel's idealized national history. In their interpretation, the female lover in the Song symbolizes Israel, and the male lover depicts God or the Shekinah.[13] Kaplan cites several examples in the literature of the Tannaim to demonstrate how they subvert the theology of absence of the male lover in the Song to redirect its focus to the presence of the male lover/God. In the two night visions of the woman, she fears for the absence of her lover and searches for him on the street. These visions in the Tannaim version have transformed into stressing the presence of the Shekinah with Israel.[14]

---

[11]For example, in Song 2:8-17, the man attempts to make a rendezvous, and the woman refuses. In Song 7:1-10, it is the man's description of the woman ending with his yearning for her. In Song 8:13-14, it is again the man's attempt to make a rendezvous, and the woman refuses. Assis, *Flashes of Fire*, 202-4, 256-62.

[12]Jonathan Kaplan, *My Perfect One: Typology and Early Rabbinic Interpretation of Song of Songs* (New York: Oxford University Press, 2015).

[13]*Shekinah* is the Hebrew for "glory," substituting for God.

[14]Kaplan, *My Perfect One*, 164-68.

After the experience of the exile, the early Jewish exegetes place strong emphasis on the certainty of divine presence with Israel. They reassure the Jewish people that God hears Israel in exile because God is with Israel. Kaplan writes, "The tannaitic subversion of the themes of absence in Song of Songs recasts exile as a space for renewal of relationship with God, space God shares with Israel. Exile, then, is like the wilderness. It is a place for restoration of relationship, for the bridegroom to renew his relationship with the bride before they return from exile to the Temple." Kalplan understands the frequent mentions of Lebanon to evoke the motif of the temple (Is 14:13; 60:13; Ps 48:3; 92:13-14).[15] Therefore, the theology of absence in the Song has been altered to become the presence of the male character, who is cast as a figure of God. In the tannaitic experience of exile and foreign subjugations, this typology provides reassurance of the ongoing and unbreakable presence of God with Israel. Although Kaplan's chapter deals with the theology of absence in the Song, the outcome of his analysis of the early Jewish exegetes presents instead a theology of presence. He does not take the theology of absence in the Song at face value, that is, on the plain meaning of the Song. Rather, the Jewish exegetes have altered the original theme of absence to fit their own theological agenda.

Recently, Marvin Sweeney deals with the theme of divine absence in Song of Songs. He posits that an approach that presupposes the "hiddenness of G-d" obscures the reality of the text. He argues that Song of Songs presupposes the human sexuality apart from the presence of G-d. Therefore, one aspect of the Song is about the procreativity of the human lover in the absence of G-d.[16]

Overall, the theme of absence in Song of Songs has received little attention until recently and warrants further exploration. By contrast, the same theme of absence in Esther has attracted far more attention.

---

[15]Kaplan, *My Perfect One*, 171, 174.

[16]See Marvin A. Sweeney, "What Is Biblical Theology? With an Example on Divine Absence and the Song of Songs," in *Theology of the Hebrew Bible*, vol 1, *Methodological Studies*, ed. Marvin A. Sweeney (Atlanta: SBL Press, 2019), 48-51. When the Song is read as an intertext of Eden, it shows the innerbiblical allusion that the Song is a part of the whole Scripture and thus presupposes the presence of God, albeit in different ways. See chap. 6.

The theology of absence in Esther. Compared to Song of Songs, the theology of absence in Esther in the Hebrew Masoretic Text has generated vast amounts of literature, and on this topic receives far more attention than any other book in the Bible. Commentators on Esther often point out that the absence of the reference of the name of God constitutes one of the book's distinctive features. Some take this feature as a literary one. Others take it as a theological issue. In my opinion, the absence of the divine name serves as a literary feature that intends to send a theological message.

Past research on the theology of absence in Esther generally falls at two ends of a continuum. At one end of the continuum stands the position of complete absence of God, with human beings as the sole actors in achieving their salvation. At the opposite end of the continuum stands divine hiddenness, that God works behind the scenes of history and that God works through the actions of the human beings, as shown below:

Position 1		Position 2
Divine Absence		Divine Hiddenness
Human Responsibility		Human Responsibility

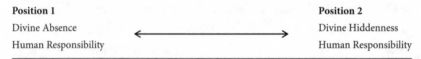

Figure 2.1

The difference between position 1 (divine absence) and position 2 (divine hiddenness or veiled divine presence) is that the former denies the presence of God and his involvement in the book, whereas the latter affirms divine presence but frames or perceives it in the notion of God hiding or working behind the scenes. In the first case, human beings take complete responsibility for their fate, while in the latter case, human responsibility is accentuated because of the hidden presence of God. Both positions stress the significance of human responsibility. Yet, they differ in the degree of divine involvement and the manifestation of divine presence in the face of evil.

One example of a prime advocate for position 1 is Sweeney. In discussing the unique literary features of Esther, Sweeney observes that both Jewish and Christian scholars seem to recoil from the book because it does not conform to the expected norms of what a biblical book should be. The book does not mention God or his involvement in human affairs. There are no religious observances, nor does it appeal to divine mercy or peace.[17] It also seems to promote violence and vengeance. Sweeney asserts, "This is precisely the point. The absence of G-d must be recognized as a fundamental premise of the book." He further elaborates that any attempts to read God into the book violate the integrity of its message and must be rejected categorically.[18] His are strong words defending the position of a complete absence of God in Esther. Sweeney concludes that in times of crisis, the presence of God is not always evident, and human beings are obliged to act when God fails to do so.

Using the absence of God in Esther as a springboard, Sweeney also highlights the contribution and significance of the absence of God for Christian theology and the biblical interpretation after the Shoah. Christian theology must take account of the Jewish character of the Scripture and not subordinate it under the enterprise of Christian theology.[19] When reading Esther at face value (that is, without reading God into the text), Sweeney's points are well taken, that any reference to God indeed is absent in the book and that human responsibility is indeed all there is. Imposing one's faith onto the text would affect the integrity of the text. What Sweeney does not stress is that Esther shares many affiliations with other biblical books in both the Jewish and the Christian canons, and such affiliations justifiably affect the way in which we read the text in a canonical dialogue with other texts of similar genre. In chapter six of this book, I will address the issue of Esther and the canon. Reading Esther in light of other biblical books yields a different reading from reading it as an isolated book.

An example of position 2 is Sandra Berg, whose dissertation, later published as a monograph under the title *The Book of Esther*, has greatly influenced later scholarly literature on the motifs and the significance of the book. Berg stresses the idea of human responsibility in Esther. She raises the profound implication for the Jewish people that each individual Jew who is in a position of power must use it to assist the people of Israel. She

---

[17]The book of Esther does mention the religious ritual of fasting.

[18]Marvin A. Sweeney, "Absence of G-d and Human Responsibility in the Book of Esther," in *Reading the Hebrew Bible for a New Millennium: Form, Concept, and Theological Perspective*, ed. Wonil Kim et al. (Harrisburg, PA: Trinity Press International, 2000), 269.

[19]Sweeney, "Absence of G-d," 272.

cites the story of Joseph and the actions of Esther and Mordecai as examples
to illustrate the dynamics between the use of power and inviolability.[20] According to Berg, the central passage of Esther is Esther 4:13-14, because it
points to Mordecai's complete confidence that assistance for the Jewish
people is imminent. Berg casts doubts on the source of assistance in this
passage in terms of "another place" being a veiled reference to God. She
focuses instead on Mordecai's belief in that assistance and his assurance that
Esther's attainment of royal position is for "a time such as this."

Berg sees the work of the narrator as intentionally weaving the story to
have both a surface meaning, as a reader reads the text, and a hidden
movement behind the occurrence, order, and implications of everyday life.
She identifies this as a "two-pronged thrust of the scroll's 'theology.'" In
this sense, Berg asserts, "The book of Esther, then, does not ignore the
presence of divine activity; rather, it points to the hiddenness of Yahweh's
presence in the world." She goes on to say that because Yahweh's control
of history is not easily discernible in everyday events, therefore the shape
and direction of history shifts to being under humans' control. Rather than
seeing the complete absence of God and his activities in Esther, Berg sees
the presence of God as hidden and working behind the appearance of
everyday events. For Berg, the purpose of the lack of any reference to God
in the book is to accentuate the role of human responsibility in shaping
history. Human beings, then, are partners with God in shaping the direction of human history.[21]

The positions of other scholars fall in between these two poles of this
continuum. For example, Frederic Bush advocates for a divine-providence
view, that "God acts through the coincidences and the remarkable reversals
that advance the plot."[22] Karen Jobes concurs with this view and adds con-
fidently that from a Jewish and Christian canonical point of view, the
unseen power present in the book of Esther is God.[23] Michael Fox proposes

---

[20]Sandra Beth Berg, *The Book of Esther: Motifs, Themes, and Structure*, Society of Biblical Literature
  Dissertation Series 44 (Missoula, MT: Scholars Press, 1979).
[21]Berg, *Book of Esther*, 178-79.
[22]Frederic William Bush, *Ruth, Esther*, WBC 9 (Dallas: Word Books, 1996), 325, 334.
[23]Karen H. Jobes, "Esther 1, Book of," *DOTWPW* 164. Lau uses "the Hidden King" to refer to God's
  hidden providence behind the Persian king. See Peter H. W. Lau, *Esther*, Asia Bible Commentary
  (Carlisle, UK: Langham Global Library, 2018), 20-21.

a "theology of possibility" in regard to the absence of the divine name in Esther. He thinks that the response to the question "Where is God?" in Esther is that "the matter cannot be decided." The indeterminacy lies not in the lack of information or lack of interest on the part of the author, or in the slipperiness inherent in the language. Fox asserts that this indeterminacy is due to the author's uncertainty—the author intends to convey uncertainty about divine activity and place in the events that emerge in the book, and more broadly that there is no definitive knowledge of the workings of God in history. On the other hand, this uncertainty does not mean that the Jews should lose faith. The author of Esther has faith in the survival of the Jews, but how this will come about remains unknown.[24]

Linda Day follows Fox's proposition and argues for a "theological ambiguity" when speaking of the absence of God in the book of Esther. Readers do not know for sure whether God is involved or whether it is chance at work in ensuring the salvation of the Jews. It is impossible for human beings to know whether God is working behind the scenes or is completely absent. Day claims, "The book of Esther does not attempt to convert skepticism into faith but permits actions to remain in their theological ambiguity."[25] After a thorough examination of the literary absence of God in Esther, Melton observes the theological ambiguity inherent in the book and claims that the book displays "permanent gapping" about God's role.[26] She also concludes that "it cannot be determined whether God is present or absent in God."[27] Aaron Koller considers Esther to be a story of desacralized redemption, while the story of Exodus serves as a display of sacred redemption through heavy involvement of God in the people's midst. Koller sees the story depicted in Esther as a "life without God" or a "history [that] operates without God." God even seems to be replaced by the king, the Jews, and the leaders of the Jews. The temple is replaced by the palace, and Jerusalem as the center has also been replaced by Persia. But the absence of God does

---

[24]Michael V. Fox, *Character and Ideology in the Book of Esther*, 2nd ed. (Grand Rapids, MI: Eerdmans, 2001), 246-47.

[25]Linda Day, *Esther*, Abingdon Old Testament Commentaries (Nashville: Abingdon, 2005), 18.

[26]The idea of narrative "gapping" comes from Meir Sternberg on the relevance of absence. The reader fulfills the function of filling the gaps of the story when it seems to have gaps. see Melton, *Where Is God*, 66.

[27]Melton, *Where Is God*, 74.

not induce defeat and despair. Such is the remarkable aspect of the book, he argues.[28]

Without the author of Esther's forthright explanation or evaluation of divine activity, the responsibility of interpretation falls solely to the reader. On the one hand, if one is to be honest about the text, the text does present a story that lacks mention of the name of God and his overt activities. This is undeniable. On the other hand, one's faith does influence the outcome of the reading. Those who read God into the text cannot help but interpret the story through the lens of faith. Taking the book of Esther at face value, its theological ambiguity perhaps is precisely its point. As Terence Fretheim asserts, "Too direct a divine presence would annul human existence as a flame kills a butterfly. God must set people at a certain distance from God; whatever the intensification of presence, there must be an element of ambiguity."[29] Others attempt to explain the reason for the absence of God's name. For example, Jewish rabbis understood Deuteronomy 31:16-18 as the theological reason behind the absence of God in Esther:

> The Lord said to Moses, "Behold, you are about to lie down with your fathers; and this people will arise and play the harlot with the strange gods of the land, into the midst of which they are going, and will forsake Me and break My covenant which I have made with them. Then My anger will be kindled against them in that day, and I will forsake them and hide My face from them, and they will be consumed, and many evils and troubles will come upon them; so that they will say in that day, "Is it not because our God is not among us that these evils have come upon us?" But I will surely hide My face in that day because of all the evil which they will do, for they will turn to other gods.

The rabbis often use the sound or the spelling of a Hebrew word and read it "intertextually," associating its meaning in light of the appearance of the same spelling of the same or different words in other biblical texts.[30] In this

---

[28]Aaron Koller, *Esther in Ancient Jewish Thought* (Cambridge: Cambridge University Press, 2014), 96-104.

[29]Terence E. Fretheim, *The Suffering of God: An Old Testament Perspective*, Overtures to Biblical Theology 14 (Philadelphia: Fortress, 1984), 67.

[30]Due to the fluidity of the understanding of *intertextuality*, we will just say that the rabbis have their own interpretive trajectory, which differs from that of contemporary theorists and exegetes. Kaplan considers the early rabbinic interpretation of Song of Songs in terms of typology (*My Perfect One*, 21).

case, the Hebrew consonants of the word "I will hide" (אסתיר) in Deuteronomy 31:18 are the same consonants in the name Esther (אסתר). Hence, the
rabbis combine the two texts and conclude that because of Israel's sin, God
hides his face from his people in the events unfolded in the book of Esther
concerning his people. Esther then is a book where God hides in plain sight
(Talmud Hullin 139b).

Lewis Bayles Paton proposes another reason for the absence of God's
name, a ritual matter. He thinks that the divine absence is tied to the festival
of Purim. In the annual feast of Purim, people are to drink until they cannot
distinguish between "blessed be Mordecai" and "cursed be Haman." Because on such an occasion people may easily profane the name of God, the
author omitted the divine name altogether.[31] While Adele Berlin follows
this view, Carey Moore rejects it, reasoning that while this view may explain
the absence of God's name, it does not explain the absence of other religious
elements such as Torah, covenant, dietary regulations, and so forth.[32] Moore
therefore opts for a "veiled wisdom theology" explanation, which I will
address shortly.

Gregory Goswell raises yet another possible reason for the absence of
God's name—a literary reason. He thinks that the absence of the divine
name is the author's deliberate literary strategy to place human action and
initiative in the foreground. He identifies several deliberate acts of the
author, who intends to suppress the "intrusion" of God in the story. For
instance, (1) in Esther 4:3, sackcloth, ashes, and mourning rites are mentioned, but prayer is suppressed by the author; (2) the casting of lots was
viewed as a way to discern the will of God, but there is no mention of a
cultic ritual such as meditation by a priest or an act of purification, as in
other biblical stories; and (3) rejoicing and feasting activities are often associated with religious contexts, as in Nehemiah 8:10-12, but such is not the
case in Esther. He also recognizes other elements in the book that point to
the author's intentional omission of the divine name so as to center human

---

[31]Lewis Bayles Paton, *The Book of Esther: A Critical and Exegetical Commentary*, International
Critical Commentary (Skokie, IL: Varda Books, 2016), 95. The earliest version was published in
1908.

[32]Adele Berlin, *Esther: The Traditional Hebrew Text with the New JPS Translation*, JPS Bible Commentary (Philadelphia: Jewish Publication Society, 2001), xvi; Carey A. Moore, *Esther*, AB (Garden City, NY: Doubleday, 1971), xxxiii.

actors. Goswell concludes with a positive notion that "the book of Esther encourages believers to live out their faith in a non-Christian environment with intelligence, resourcefulness and courage."[33]

Still others attempt to find God and his activities or suggest his mysterious presence in the book. For example, Jon Levenson notes that the fact that God is unnamed does not mean that he is uninvolved. The presence of coincidences in the book is an explicit indicator of divine presence.[34] David Beller uses the "divine passive" in Esther 9:1, 22 as an indicator that "God was at work among the scattered Jews." The juxtapositions and startling contrasts in the story also serve as an indication of divine presence.[35] Examples of linguistic implications that point to divine presence include the presence of the divine name YHWH in a hidden form. The Masoretic Text contains acrostics of the divine name YHWH in Esther 1:20; 5:4, 13; 7:7.[36] Some read the initial letters of the verse from left to right, while other verses read from right to left, as if God is hidden behind these verses, or the author of Esther is using God's name to play "hide and seek" with the reader. This argument has been rejected by John Manguno, who has researched other passages in the Masoretic Text and found similar acronomy of the divine name YHWH; in those other contexts, the acronomy bears no meaning related to the presence of God. Therefore, he dismisses the notion that the author of Esther intentionally hid the name of God in the text.[37]

Understandably, many scholars lean toward Berg's position of a hidden presence of God in Esther. In actuality, this hidden presence is an alternative way of saying "divine presence in absence."[38] For those who consider Scripture as the authority of the Christian faith, one common way of

---

[33]Gregory R. Goswell, "Keeping God Out of the Book of Esther," *Evangelical Quarterly* 82, no. 2 (2010): 100-101, 110.

[34]Jon Douglas Levenson, *Esther: A Commentary*, OTL (Louisville, KY: Westminster John Knox, 1997), 18-19.

[35]David Beller, "A Theology of the Book of Esther," *ResQ* (1997): 8-9.

[36]Paton, *Book of Esther*, 8.

[37]John M. Manguno Jr., "Accident or Acronomy: The Tetragrammaton in the Masoretic Text of Esther," *Bibliotheca Sacra* 171 (October–December 2014): 440-51. Manguno concludes, "Instead of being a rhetorical device, they are merely a coincidence seized by an audience that already perceives God's hand in the narrative and wishes to find his name there" (444).

[38]Other scholars in defense of the presence of God in the book of Esther include Forrest S Weiland, "Literary Clues to God's Providence in the Book of Esther," *Bibliotheca Sacra* 160 (2003): 34-47; William W. Grasham, "The Theology of the Book of Esther," *ResQ* 16, no. 2 (1973): 99-111.

reading Esther is reading through the book's interconnectedness with other biblical books, that is, reading Esther in relation to the canon, whether the Jewish or the Christian canon. Since the motif and plot of Esther share striking similarities with the stories of Joseph and Daniel, and also that of Saul and the Amalekites in 1 Samuel, it follows, they say, that the "theology" of Esther and divine activity fall into a similar trajectory. Here it is useful to recall that the implied author and the audience were people of faith whose religious context would have included God as its premise.[39] Additionally, the book of Esther is included as an integral component of Scripture. Reading it in isolation from the larger context of Scripture would violate its integrity.

In sum, literatures regarding the absence of God in Esther have been abundant when compared with that of Song of Songs. The majority of scholars likely agree on the significance of human responsibility in the story, but how each individual perceives the manner and the degree of divine presence differs. On one end of the continuum are those who see a complete absence of God, while those at the other end see a veiled presence of God behind history. Future generations will no doubt continue to discuss and wrestle with the theology of the absence of God in the book of Esther. While the same motif of absence receives far less attention in Song of Songs, I intend to rectify this by stressing the theology of absence in both Song of Songs and Esther and their place in Old Testament theology.

THE WISDOM ELEMENT IN SONG OF SONGS AND THE BOOK OF ESTHER

Having provided an overview of the literature on the theology of absence in Song of Songs and Esther, one way to confront the issue of absence is to read both books in the broader context of wisdom. However, the understanding of wisdom and wisdom texts is increasingly fuzzy in the scholarly discussions, as reflected in Will Kynes's "obituary" for the category "wisdom literature."[40] He contends that the traditional understanding of "wisdom

---

[39]Francisco-Javier Ruiz-Ortiz, *The Dynamics of Violence and Revenge in the Hebrew Book of Esther*, Supplements to Vetus Testamentum 175 (Leiden: Brill, 2017), 41.

[40]Will Kynes, *An Obituary for "Wisdom Literature": The Birth, Death, and Intertextual Reintegration of a Biblical Corpus* (Oxford: Oxford University Press, 2019).

literature" cannot be isolated from the other books in the Hebrew Bible because wisdom appears in other texts as well, including the historical and the prophetic texts. Therefore, Kynes proposes a multidimensional approach to wisdom, which results in a more dynamic, intertextual network of relationship with the rest of Scripture.[41] While we acknowledge the category of "wisdom literature" has its limits, it nevertheless presents one way to group Proverbs, Job, and Ecclesiastes in terms of their overlapped subjects. Technically speaking, both Song of Songs and Esther do not belong to the wisdom texts, if we understand "wisdom text" as a proverb-like text with didactic instructions on moral order. Song of Songs is best identified as an example of lyric poetry, while Esther could be a farce, a historical novella, an example of diasporic literature, or something else altogether, but Esther is not first and foremost a wisdom text.

Although Song of Songs and Esther are not wisdom texts per se, they do share overlapped thematic elements with wisdom. Here, I find Dell's family analogy helpful. Dell perceives wisdom as a family, and so identifying "family resemblances" helps to categorize a wisdom text.[42] In this case, Song of Songs can be seen as a "cousin" of wisdom on the lessons of *eros*, whereas the book of Esther can be categorized as a "second cousin" of wisdom, a court tale of applied wisdom in times of evil.[43] Therefore, both books are about the appropriation of wisdom in the real world: *eros* in Song of Songs, and human responsibility in Esther. If we can establish this broader context of wisdom for the two books, it will help to unravel the matter of God and his absence in them.

---

[41]Kynes identifies three major conceptual blends (Solomonic books, Misfortune, Wisdom Literature), together with the degrees of similarities and differences in Proverbs, Job, and Ecclesiastes, to create a "universe of texts" (Kynes, *Obiturary*, 131-39). For more discussions on the pitfalls of the wisdom category, see Mark R. Sneed, "'Grasping After the Wind': The Elusive Attempt to Define and Delimit Wisdom," in *Was There a Wisdom Tradition? New Prospects in Israelite Wisdom Studies*, ed. Mark R. Sneed (Atlanta: SBL Press, 2015), 39-67; Stuart Weeks, "The Place and Limits of Wisdom Revisited," in *Perspectives on Israelite Wisdom: Proceedings of the Oxford Old Testament Seminar*, ed. John Jarick (London: Bloomsbury T&T Clark, 2016), 3-23.
[42]Katherine J. Dell, "Deciding the Boundaries of Wisdom: Applying the Concept of Family Resemblances," in Sneed, *Was There a Wisdom Tradition?*, 145-60.
[43]This is particularly apparent when Song of Songs and Proverbs are read together. See Andruska's study on juxtaposing Song of Songs and Proverbs in teaching wise and foolish love: J. L. Andruska, *Wise and Foolish Love in the Song of Songs*, Oudestamentische Studiën 75 (Leiden: Brill, 2019).

Wisdom theology and divine presence. To date, there has been a lack of general consensus regarding how to define wisdom theology. Pertaining to our interest in wisdom theology is the understanding of divine presence and absence. Walter Zimmerli sees a dichotomy existing between wisdom and history, and thus he frames wisdom theology on creation.[44] In *The Tree of Life*, Roland Murphy stresses the nature of wisdom theology as (1) the understanding of reality in light of trusting God and embracing his mystery; (2) the search for order, which is comparable to the Egyptian concept of *maʿat* (rendered as "justice, truth, or order"); (3) wisdom theology as creation theology; and (4) wisdom as a faith experience in dialogue with God.[45] Building on Murphy's research, James Crenshaw articulates the notion of divine presence in Israel's wisdom thinking. He asserts (1) wisdom theology is creation theology, (2) wisdom thinking is a search for order, (3) wisdom is trust in and openness to the world, and (4) order derives from divine presence.[46] Perdue organizes wisdom thought under two broad categories: anthropology and cosmology, building on Zimmerli's idea that the objective of a wise person is "to master life" by means of coming to a knowledge of the world and applying that knowledge to one's circumstances in life. In this sense, Perdue advocates that anthropology is about human beings as active agents who seek out their place in God's world and find order in reality, whereas cosmology is about human beings seeking "a cosmic order that integrate[s] into a harmonious whole the various components of reality."[47]

In his chapter on Wisdom literature and divine presence, Burnett keenly perceives that "from wisdom's perspective, divine presence often appears as divine absence. Wisdom is concerned with discerning the difference between the two."[48] He also stresses that wisdom presupposes the moral implications of divine presence in the created order and in

---

[44]Walter Zimmerli, "The Place and Limit of Wisdom in the Framework of Old Testament Theology," *SJT* 17 (1964): 146-58.

[45]Roland E. Murphy, *The Tree of Life: An Exploration of Biblical Wisdom Literature*, Anchor Bible Reference Library (New York: Doubleday, 1992), 112-26.

[46]James L. Crenshaw, "In Search of Divine Presence: Some Remarks Preliminary to a Theology of Wisdom," *Review and Expositor* 74, no. 3 (1977): 353-69.

[47]Perdue, *Wisdom and Creation*, 35-40.

[48]Burnett, *Where Is God?*, 86.

mundane human existence.[49] John Kessler states that wisdom theology emphasizes "the careful observation of life in all its dimensions, diligent reflection on what one has observed and attentiveness to the teachings of a wise person." As such, Kessler conceives wisdom theology as a cord of four strands: (1) learning wisdom from the way God has made the world, from wise teachers, and from God's law; (2) applying wisdom's precepts to the complexities of life; (3) choosing the path dictated by wisdom and the "fear of the LORD"; and (4) reflecting wisely on the imponderables and contradictions that characterize earthly existence.[50] Tremper Longman draws the connection between wisdom and creation order in terms of the right time (Prov 15:23, 25:11) and observes that wisdom "does not naively assert that wisdom will always work."[51] Richard Belcher Jr. also advocates wisdom's emphasis on creation and the created order.[52] While scholars may not agree on using creation as the common element undergirding wisdom texts, it is nevertheless one of the dominant themes in wisdom texts.

The question "Where can wisdom be found?" (Job 28:12, 20) persists throughout humanity's search for wisdom. If the core of wisdom theology is human beings' search for meaning, order, pattern, principle, and the presence of God in all aspects of life in earthly existence, then the search for wisdom and the search for divine presence in times of his seeming absence are to be held in creative harmony. Since a major strand of wisdom theology is rooted in God's creation (but not limited to it), which encompasses two primary facets of cosmology and anthropology, as Perdue proposes, then both the created world and the created beings reveal the Creator. As the psalmist proclaims, "The heavens are telling of the glory of God; And their expanse is declaring the work of His hands. Day to day pours forth speech, And night to night reveals knowledge" (Ps 19:1-2). In regard to those who refuse to acknowledge the presence of God in the cosmos, the apostle Paul asserts that God's invisible attributes, his divine power and

[49]Burnett, *Where Is God?*, 86.
[50]Kessler, *Old Testament Theology*, 449.
[51]Tremper Longman III, *The Fear of the Lord Is Wisdom: A Theological Introduction to Wisdom in Israel* (Grand Rapids, MI: Baker Academic, 2017), 136, 145.
[52]Richard P. Belcher Jr., *Finding Favor in the Sight of God: A Theology of Wisdom Literature*, NSBT 46 (Downers Grove, IL: IVP Academic, 2018), 4-9.

divine nature, have been revealed through what he has made, so no one has the excuse of saying that God is absent (Rom 1:20). For the ancient Near Eastern mind, human life and the world people inhabited were ordered by the divine, as Fretheim states: "God is present and active wherever there is world."[53] The search for the order of things in reality follows the application of wisdom. This application can be framed as *ethics*. Wisdom incorporates the interlocking connectivity among creation, anthropology, and ethics. The cosmic order manifested in the created world forms the basis for moral order, as reflected in Proverbs 3:19-20; 8:1-36.[54] Therefore, wisdom is the vehicle through which human beings orient their actions toward the divine order in the world. As such, wisdom invites human beings to enter into the journey of wonder—a sense of marvel at the unexpected, an astonishing emotion mixed with unsettled sentiment, as well as a profound curiosity.[55] In human beings' perception of the seeming absence of God, we as the creatures of God are to reflect and apply wisdom in the complexities of life, in its most exotic dimension of sexuality as well as in the face of evil. Therefore, Song of Songs and Esther overlap with two intertwined strands of wisdom theology: creation theology and applied wisdom. Both books are grounded in the search for the order of things and the application of wisdom in one's circumstances. Below I explore the wisdom element in the two books and their significance in contemplating divine presence and absence.

Wisdom and Song of Songs. The connection between wisdom and Song of Songs falls into two primary trajectories. One is about the association of King Solomon, a symbol of Israel's wisdom tradition, with Song of Songs. The other is the intertextual connection between Song of Songs and Proverbs 1–9, for Proverbs has been firmly recognized as a wisdom text in the biblical canon.

---

[53]Terence E. Fretheim, *God and World in the Old Testament: A Relational Theology of Creation* (Nashville: Abingdon, 2005), 23.

[54]Christopher B. Ansberry, "Wisdom and Biblical Theology," in *Interpreting Old Testament Wisdom Literature*, ed. David G. Firth and Lindsay Wilson (Downers Grove, IL: IVP Academic, 2017), 174-93.

[55]William P. Brown, *Wisdom's Wonder: Character, Creation, and Crisis in the Bible's Wisdom Literature* (Grand Rapids, MI: Eerdmans, 2014), 20-21. Though, in the book of Ecclesiastes, the sense of wonder presents itself differently in Qoheleth's search for meaning.

Building on the work of her predecessors, such as Michael Sadgrove, Roland Murphy, and Brevard Childs, Katherine Dell has thoroughly investigated whether Song of Songs has any connection to wisdom. First, she distinguishes Wisdom literature as a genre from Wisdom in Proverbs 1–9. Based on form-critical definitions, Song of Songs is not to be categorized as "Wisdom literature." The genre "love songs" itself is already a distinct form or category, like Egyptian love poetry. Dell draws several connections between the Song and Solomon, such as the numerous wives of Solomon (1 Kings 11:1-3; Song 6:8-9), his interest in flora and fauna (1 Kings 4:32-33), exotic spices from abroad (1 Kings 10:10), and images of wealth and luxury (1 Kings 9–10), as well as Solomon's connection with wisdom and songs (1 Kings 4:32). She states that this internal evidence may represent a deliberate attempt to associate the Song with Solomon, the symbol of wisdom.[56]

Second, Dell unpacks the layers of redaction of the Song that are connected with the wisdom corpus, using Song of Songs 8:6-7 as an example that moves the language of love to a cosmological level, with personified forces of love against chaos and death. Love as an intrinsic part of the human experience places the Song alongside the didactic purpose of the sapiential tradition. In this sense, love songs can be incorporated within a broad definition of wisdom.[57]

Third, Dell identifies links between the wisdom motif in the Song and female configuration in Proverbs, such as a woman calling a young man to love her, the shared motifs in married love and sex outside marriage, and imagery of Wisdom as a tree of life (Prov 3:18) with the woman in the Song as the palm tree (Song 7:7-8). Dell also finds links between the woman in the Song and the loose woman in Proverbs, noting that the motif of seeking, finding, and kissing are present in both books (Prov 7:10-15; Song 3:1-4; 5:6; 8:1). At the same time, Song of Songs and Proverbs also differ in many aspects, such as in the theme of death, the animal imagery, and the treatment of family and house. Dell concludes that the link between the Song of Songs and wisdom is closer than most readers would have thought. From a

[56]Katherine J. Dell, "Does the Song of Songs Have Any Connections to Wisdom?," in *Perspectives on the Song of Songs*, ed. Anselm C. Hagedorn, Beihefte zur Zeitschrift für die Alttestamentliche Wissenschaft 346 (Berlin: de Gruyter, 2005), 10-13.
[57]Dell, "Does the Song of Songs," 14-16.

form-critical perspective, Song of Songs is not Wisdom literature, though its association with Solomon is a fact that cannot be dismissed. The presence of various facets of wisdom in the Song, according to Dell, may be due to the development of the preliterary stage, namely, the oral stage. It is at this oral stage that the love imagery in the Song could have provided the author of Proverbs with ideas for his description of the lady Wisdom and her counterpart, the loose woman. In other words, the Song has informed Proverbs in the latter's dealing with choosing wisdom and forsaking folly, as exemplified by the loose woman.[58]

Contrary to Dell, Martin Hauge sees Proverbs 2–9 as a dramaturgic frame for Song of Songs, rather than the other way around. In Proverbs 2–9, the strange-woman tradition interweaves two literary modes: admonishment and scenario. In the admonishment mode, King Solomon instructs a male, "my son," whom he addresses as "you." In the scenario mode, Proverbs presents a paradigmatic situation of a strange woman and a young man. In Song of Songs, the poet dissolves the blending of virtually identical scenes in Proverbs 2–9 and returns to a combination of two distinct literary modes. In the Song, the Shulamite instructs the daughters of Jerusalem in the admonishment, while the Shulamite and Solomon function as the two protagonists in the scenario. Consequently, admonishment and scenario become two separate entities. Therefore, Hauge perceives Song of Songs as a reinterpretation of the Proverbs tradition.[59]

However, since the respective dating of these two books is debatable, their exact relationship cannot be proven with absolute certainty. Many scholars place the dating of Proverbs to the Persian period, in the third century, but the internal evidence suggests the writing of some proverbs occurred as early as the Solomonic period and as late as the time before Ezra.[60] Song of

---

[58]Dell, "Does the Song of Songs," 23-24.

[59]Martin Ravndal Hauge, *Solomon the Lover and the Shape of the Song of Songs*, HBM 77 (Sheffield: Sheffield Phoenix, 2015), 158.

[60]Perdue suggests that the collection of Proverbs occurred over an extended period of time, that the prologue and the woman of worth in Prov 31 were inserted during the Persian period, and that the lack of any references to the temple suggests the dating was prior to the time of Ezra in the late fifth century. Leo G. Perdue, *Wisdom Literature: A Theological History* (Louisville, KY: Westminster John Knox, 2007), 47. Some scholars date the book early; for example, Clifford dates the book from 1000 BCE to the end of the sixth century BCE. See Richard J. Clifford, *The Wisdom Literature* (Nashville: Abingdon, 1998), 42. For an example of dating Proverbs to the

Songs may have existed even earlier, at the time when Tirzah was at its height, in the ninth century BCE, but it also contains late Biblical Hebrew in the Masoretic Text, which points to a later date. Dell's view that the oral tradition of Israelite wisdom was present earlier than the written texts would likely explain the intertwined and overlapping imageries in Proverbs and Song of Songs. It is also possible that both books used the same stock of literary and cultural images from their surroundings, and then adapted those images for their own purposes. Whichever is the case, the association between Song of Songs and Proverbs is quite close, if not intimate.

Kenton Sparks designates Song of Songs as originally being a wisdom composition, compiled to teach young Jewish women propriety in matters of love and sexuality. He too notes the Song's affiliation with Solomon as the first and foremost reason for considering the Song as a wisdom book. He also cites other reasons—including the didactic nature of the Song, the name and character of the Shulamite as the counterpart of Solomon on love, and the two opposing perspectives on love and sex, which resemble the framing of Proverbs on wisdom and folly—as evidence of the Song of Songs being a wisdom composition. In addition, Sparks proposes the *Sitz im Leben* of the Song as being composed through female eyes. The dreamy wedding scene in Song of Songs 3:6-11, the two dream sequences in Song of Songs 3:1-5 and Song of Songs 5:2-7, and Song of Songs 8:1-2 all describe female fantasy or frustrations of love. This female perspective aims to instruct young women on how to avoid being hurt and disappointed in the world of young love.[61] While Proverbs was written originally for young boys on matters of life, of choosing wisdom and forsaking folly, Song of Songs becomes its counterpart, advising young women in the art of choosing love wisely and forsaking the folly of premature love. Sparks thus offers another innovative perspective on identifying Song of Songs as a "female" wisdom text, corresponding to the "male" wisdom of Proverbs.

In her discussion on Song of Songs as a wisdom book, Edmee Kingsmill categorizes Song of Songs as Wisdom literature in its spirit and language.

Persian period, see James L. Crenshaw, *Old Testament Wisdom: An Introduction*, 3rd ed. (Louisville, KY: Westminster John Knox, 2010), 5.
[61] Kenton Sparks, "The Song of Songs: Wisdom for Young Jewish Women," *CBQ* 70, no. 2 (2008): 277-99.

The Song's connection with Solomon as the builder of the temple further reinforces this wisdom connection. As Dell and other scholars note, the Song's links with Proverbs in various motifs suggest their close affinity with wisdom, though there are differences inherent in both books. Kingsmill also draws attention to the wisdom elements in Sirach 24 and the Song of Songs, and advocates for the Song's association with the wisdom tradition. She concludes that she agrees with the Song's designation as a wisdom book.[62] Rosalind Clarke asserts that the Song of Songs has a long history of connection with wisdom, going as far back as the Septuagint, which groups the Song together with other wisdom books. As a result, she structures her chapter around four subtitles, which aptly summarize the connection between wisdom and Song of Songs. These four subtitles are (1) seeking wisdom in the genre of the Song, (2) seeking wisdom for women in the Song, (3) seeking woman Wisdom in the Song, and (4) Solomon, the wisdom seeker in the Song.[63] Marlene Oosthuizen's dissertation has made quite a convincing argument that Song of Songs should be read as a wisdom book. Her research centers on the literary and thematic patterns of wisdom books as a way to examine the literary and thematic motifs of the Song.[64] Likewise, J. L. Andruska's study also argues for the affinities of Song of Songs with wisdom while acknowledging the fluidity in the concept of genre.[65]

In sum, is Song of Songs a wisdom book? The answer is both yes and no. Song of Songs is a wisdom book for all the reasons mentioned above. At the same time, speaking from a form-critical perspective, Song of Songs is not entirely a wisdom book. Here I borrow from Tremper Longman III's statement that the identification of Song of Songs as belonging to Wisdom literature should be in addition to, but not in place of, its identification as

---

[62]Edmee Kingsmill, "The Song of Songs: A Wisdom Book," in *Perspectives on Israelite Wisdom: Proceedings of the Oxford Old Testament Seminar*, ed. Oxford Old Testament Seminar and John Jarick, LHBOTS 618 (London: Bloomsbury T&T Clark, 2016), 314-32.

[63]Rosalind Clarke, "Seeking Wisdom in the Song of Songs," in *Interpreting Old Testament Wisdom Literature*, ed. David G. Firth and Lindsay Wilson (Downers Grove, IL: IVP Academic, 2017), 100-112.

[64]Marlene Oosthuizen, "Reading Song of Songs as Wisdom Literature: An Interpretive Approach Integrating Sexuality and Spirituality" (PhD diss., University of the Free State, 2014).

[65]Andruska, *Wise and Foolish Love*, 15-18.

love poetry.[66] While we understand the Song of Songs first and foremost to be love poetry, it nevertheless falls under the broad trajectory of wisdom. This understanding is significant when we reflect on the absence of God in the book. I will address this theme shortly in reading Song of Songs as a countertext to Old Testament theology.

One aspect of wisdom theology is the application of wisdom in all aspects of human earthly existence. In this regard, Song of Songs intersects with two wisdom books: Proverbs and Ecclesiastes. In Proverbs 30:18-19, the sage seeks to understand four things that are too "wonderful" for him and that he does not understand. One of those four things is "the way of a man with a maiden." Song of Songs describes precisely "the way of a man with a maiden," as if to understand how this way works in real life. In Ecclesiastes 9:9, Qoheleth charges his male audience "to enjoy life with the woman whom you love all the days of your fleeting life which He has given to you under the sun; for this is your reward in life and in your toil in which you have labored under the sun." Song of Songs portrays the man listening to the sage's admonition and enjoying life with the woman whom he loves. Thus, Song of Songs exemplifies applied wisdom in human relationships.

Wisdom and the book of Esther. While the wisdom element in Song of Songs is contested, the wisdom element in Esther is even more complex and the subject of far less consensus. At first glance, the book of Esther is anything but a wisdom book. In the canonical arrangement of the Masoretic Text, Song of Songs is close in proximity to the Wisdom books. Proverbs and Job precede Song of Songs, whereas Esther is in close proximity to the historical narratives, since it is immediately followed by Daniel, Ezra, and Nehemiah. However, since Esther is preceded by Ecclesiastes, we cannot preclude any association of the book with wisdom by its proximity in the canonical arrangement. What we can say is that in content the book of Esther shares more similarities with the historical books that follow it than with Ecclesiastes, which precedes it. Scholars diverge in their positions concerning whether to subsume the book of Esther under the broader category of wisdom. Occupying the two ends of the spectrum are Shemaryahu

---

[66]Tremper Longman III, *Song of Songs*, New International Commentary on the Old Testament (Grand Rapids, MI: Eerdmans, 2001), 48.

Talmon, who advocates for reading Esther as a wisdom book, and James Crenshaw, who strongly objects. There are also those who fall somewhere in between.

Based on the book's enactment of standard wisdom motifs with other biblical texts of a similar nature, Talmon provides a thorough treatment on the subject. He defines Esther as a "historicized wisdom-tale." He was the first raise the possible connection between Esther and Wisdom literature. Talmon identifies the wisdom in Esther as an "applied wisdom," which means that the plot of the narrative and its central characters demonstrate the theme of wise people in action. Their success derives from the proper execution of wisdom, such as what Proverbs or even Ecclesiastes advises. Talmon further notes that the absence of the divine name and religious rituals such as prayer in Esther reflects a typical wisdom tradition that also appears in other ancient Near Eastern wisdom teachings. The reason behind this phenomenon is the nature of wisdom texts, which are intended for a universal human condition rather than any specific political or national contexts. The lack of mention of history or the Jewish community outside Persia in Esther further demonstrates this aspect as the nature of wisdom. Therefore, Talmon argues for seeing Esther as a wisdom tale. In his words, the book depicts the "timeless theme of intriguing courtiers whose battle is viewed against the background of the Persian court at the beginning of Ahasuerus' rule."[67]

In the story, both Mordecai and Haman fit the pattern of court scribe in the wisdom tradition. They are advisers to the king. The ascent of Esther at a foreign court reflects another wisdom motif, similar to the plot development of Joseph and Daniel. Her relationship with Mordecai, as adopter and adoptee, comprises yet another wisdom element, reminiscent of the story of Ahiqar but with some twists. Additionally, the three major characters exemplify a traditional wisdom triangle: the powerful but witless dupe (Ahasuerus), the righteous wise person (Mordecai), and the conspiratorial schemer (Haman). While the two contrasting characters of Mordecai and Haman reflect the polarity between good and evil (one of the common motifs of wisdom), Esther, on the other hand, embodies a wise courtier who

---

[67]Shemaryahu Talmon, "'Wisdom' in the Book of Esther," *VT* 13, no. 4 (1963): 419-55.

achieves success by finding favor with both men and the king, as Proverbs
3:4 indicates (Esther 2:9, 17). Talmon concludes by saying that the book of
Esther is "the author's endeavor to present a generalizing wisdom-tale and
traditional wisdom-motifs in a specific historical setting." Recently, Rebecca Hancock has identified Esther as a figure of the female royal counselor, and thus she affirms the wisdom element inherent in the story.[68]

Talmon's proposal, though plausible, does encounter some opposition.
Crenshaw criticizes Talmon's propositions and refutes them one by one. For
instance, Crenshaw says that Talmon takes his cue from similarities in situations and general trends and ideas from Esther and wisdom, rather than
from literary parallels such as the Joseph or the succession narratives. The
absence of Jewish history and religious sentiment, the concept of a remote
deity, the presence of an anthropocentric stance, a fondness for court life,
and typological characters all suggest a broad connection with wisdom. But
to conceive of Esther as Wisdom literature would be an alien concept, he
says. Crenshaw further repudiates Talmon's identifying of "another source"
in Esther 4:14 as a wisdom notion of a remote deity. He also thinks that the
typology of Ahasuerus as a witless dupe is unconvincing, since the text only
presents it very subtly. Mordecai also does not appear as all wise. Crenshaw's most convincing argument is that Talmon fails to reckon with the
nonwisdom elements in Esther. Additionally, national fervor does appear
in Esther, contrary to Talmon's claim. Overall, Crenshaw sees Talmon's interpretation as limiting "his study to broad themes and ideas, falling prey
to the appeal to ideas common to literature other than wisdom."[69] While
Crenshaw offers keen objections to Talmon's arguments, he misses a significant point, namely, that although Esther may not strictly be identified
as Wisdom literature, it does possess wisdom elements, as Talmon attempts
to demonstrate.

Fox seconds Crenshaw's sentiments. He states that "Esther is not affiliated with Wisdom by even the broadest definition and that few—if any—of
its elements are derived from Wisdom." According to Fox, Wisdom

---

[68]Rebecca S. Hancock, *Esther and the Politics of Negotiation: Public and Private Spaces and the Figure
    of the Female Royal Counselor*, Emerging Scholars (Minneapolis: Fortress, 2013).
[69]James L. Crenshaw, "Method in Determining Wisdom Influence upon Historical Literature,"
    JBL 88, no. 2 (1969): 129-42.

literature does not conceive of God as vague or remote. God is after all mentioned in other wisdom books, such as Proverbs. Also, Jewish or national concerns are at the center of the book of Esther, contrary to what Talmon suggests. Fox also disagrees with Talmon's stereotypical category of identifying Haman as a fool and Mordecai as an ideal sage, since the language of typical wisdom text, such as the wicked man or the righteous man, is lacking in Esther. The practice of adoption also is not a dominant feature of wisdom thought.[70] Overall, Fox dismisses Talmon's proposition entirely, and in this is followed by Francisco-Javier Ruiz-Ortiz, who favors the view that Esther has no wisdom influences due to its lack of wisdom language and images.[71]

Kevin McGeough goes beyond the wisdom debate. He sees a transformation of Esther from a wise courtier conformed to the character type in Wisdom literature to someone who goes beyond this category and emerges as a hero who saves her people. McGeough argues against Talmon concerning the plot development of Esther, noting that the plot does not fit into the genre of wisdom motifs. Rather, he considers Esther an instance of storytelling that reflects the prominence of wisdom values in exilic and postexilic audiences. Employing Murphy's idea, McGeough goes further by observing the upside-down world of the postexilic context in a world of liminal space and time, and notes that some elements in Esther find similarities with wisdom values, while others do not. The story of Esther both diverges from and converges with wisdom values while being consistent with folk stories.[72] McGeough sees Esther as one who transcends the character norms reflected in Wisdom books. He describes Esther as a hero.[73] For him, the strongest connection between Esther's story and wisdom lies in the "subcharacters," such as the king, Haman, and Mordecai, who conform to the typical character types in wisdom texts. Therefore, McGeough concludes by saying that wisdom reflects normative behavior for

---

[70]Fox, *Character and Ideology*, 143.

[71]Ruiz-Ortiz, *Dynamics of Violence*, 23-24.

[72]Kevin M. McGeough, "Esther the Hero: Going Beyond 'Wisdom' in Heroic Narratives," *CBQ* 70, no. 1 (2008): 44-65.

[73]Many scholars would agree with this point. For example, Sidnie White Crawford, "Esther: A Feminine Model for Jewish Diaspora," in *Gender and Difference in Ancient Israel*, ed. Peggy Lynne Day (Minneapolis: Fortress, 1989).

everyday life, but when this norm is threatened, as in the time of exile, it calls for heroic actions. Hence the story of Esther reflects wisdom values but also supersedes them.[74]

In light of the above discussion, is Esther a wisdom book? The answer is no. Wisdom is not its primary literary form. But does the book of Esther have any connection to wisdom? Yes. McGeough's insight regarding the difference between a normative context and a crisis situation is especially illuminating. As Fox asserts, the character of Esther progresses from passivity to activity to authority.[75] Rebecca Hancock also identifies Esther as a female royal counselor as well as a politician.[76] In an article on Ruth and Esther, I observe that both figures undergo character development and emerge as wise women in their own cultural and political contexts. Esther's tactful and calculated invitation to the king, along with her courage in risking her life for the sake of her people, places her among other wise courtiers in the Hebrew canon such as Joseph and Daniel.[77] Though first and foremost Esther does not belong to the wisdom category, it nevertheless includes wisdom elements in its character portrayal. This differentiation is significant with respect to the theology of divine absence in the book. Since wisdom involves discerning the moral order of the world, the literary absence of God in Esther invites readers to discern divine activity and human responsibility in the midst of injustice. Similar to the Song of Songs, Esther belongs to the category of applied wisdom, where human beings in their search for the order of things apply wisdom in the face of evil. In Esther's case, wisdom is embodied in the action of God's people. In light of the understanding of wisdom as the Egyptian concept of *ma'at* (which combines justice, truth, and order), the wisdom element in Esther can be rendered as a wisdom that seeks and exercises a just order in confronting the evil of her world.

---

[74]McGeough, "Esther the Hero," 57-61, 64.

[75]Fox, *Character and Ideology*, 196.

[76]Hancock, *Esther and the Politics*, 113-14.

[77]Chloe Sun, "Ruth and Esther: Negotiable Space in Christopher Wright's *The Mission of God*?," *Missiology* 46, no. 2 (2018): 157.

SONG OF SONGS AND ESTHER AS COUNTERTEXTS
TO DIVINE PRESENCE IN HEBREW SCRIPTURE

Why is it that the Song of Songs and Esther lack explicit references to God? Is this a deliberate literary device intending to communicate a different aspect of the nature of God, or does it occur for other reasons?

From the perspective of canonical and theological interpretation, I suggest that Song of Songs and Esther serve as two countertexts in Old Testament theology, particularly regarding the theology of divine presence and absence. Underlining the countertexts is wisdom, which complements and supplements Israel's salvation history. In doing so, these two scrolls complement and supplement what is lacking in Old Testament theology in regard to the transcendent and mysterious nature of God. Therefore, these two books contribute to a fuller picture of who God is and how human beings relate to this God. Rather than remaining in the periphery as two small, festive scrolls, these two books push the boundaries, moving to the center of Old Testament theology, contesting, challenging, or even protesting the loud voices of divine presence in human history.

Although the notion of a countertestimony is advocated eloquently by Brueggemann in his Old Testament theology, his countertexts exclude Song of Songs and Esther. Here I echo McEntire's sentiment on the current landscape of biblical interpretation that "the voice from the earlier portions of the story is still too loud. The voice at the end of the story must eventually be allowed to speak alone, or it will not be adequately heard."[78] This book does just that, moving the end of the story, that is, Song of Songs and Esther, to the center. I believe this "minority report" will become essential evidence in rethinking God and reconstructing Old Testament theology and biblical theology.[79]

---

[78]McEntire, *Portraits of a Mature God*, 21. For McEntire, his "end of the story" is Ezra-Nehemiah, whereas my end of the story is Song of Songs and Esther.

[79]The movie *The Minority Report* was set in a fictional futuristic context where majority reports on potential murder cases are taken to a crime-prevention agency to prevent the projected murders from happening. Yet there are a few cases in which they point to a different direction, suggesting a different profile for identifying the potential murderers. At the end of the movie, the minority report becomes actualized as the real murder cases, contrary to the expected majority report.

By *countertext*, I refer to those texts in the Scripture whose contents, ideology, and theology diverge from the main trajectory revealed in the majority portion of the Scripture. Alicia Ostriker defines a countertext as one that "resists dominant structures of authority, divine and legal, as defined by the Bible as a whole and by the history of interpretation." She goes on to say that Job, Ecclesiastes, and gynocentric books such as Ruth, Esther, and Song of Songs—and, in fact, all the Writings—stand at diverse, odd angles to the Law and the Prophets.[80] To see the Bible as presenting a consistent portrayal of God in every book would be an act of reductionism and oversimplification. It is not sufficient to say that God is present when a mother loses her child in her womb, or a grieving father mourns the loss of all his children at a school shooting, or a life is cut short by a car accident, or a family member dies alone during the COVID 19 pandemic. There are times when God seems absent. There are also times when theology fails to provide adequate answers to manifold facets of the human predicament.

Song of Songs presents an applied wisdom in the area of love and sexuality, whereas Esther exemplifies an applied wisdom in times of evil. Both books center on humans and accentuate human capabilities when God is absent. At the same time, both books are essentially distinct in genre, mood, motifs, literary features, and theological concerns. To place them together as a pair may risk flattening their differences. The fact is that Song of Songs and Esther display drastic literary and theological differences, but these differences do not and should not obscure their commonalities, particularly on the theology of absence.

The idea of divine presence in absence as well as the divine presence in the created order will guide our discussion below. With that in mind, I will treat both books separately first and then group them together as a pair in functioning as two countertexts on the theology of divine presence in the rest of the Old Testament and its implications for doing and thinking about Old Testament theology.

Song of Songs as a countertext. The Song's association with wisdom is reflected in its lack of explicit national concerns, such as Israel's history,

---

[80]Alicia Ostriker, "A Holy of Holies: The Song of Songs as Countertext," in Brenner and Fontaine, *Feminist Companion to the Song of Songs*, 43.

God's covenant with Israel, and the experience of the exile.[81] Divine presence exists in covert forms such as in the idea of love as a fierce flame or the flame of Yh(wh) in Song of Songs 8:6 (שַׁלְהֶבֶתְיָה), and in the adjuration formula, where "gazelles" (צְבָאוֹת) and "hinds of the field" (אַיְלוֹת הַשָּׂדֶה, Song 2:7; 3:5) in Hebrew sound like "hosts" or "armies," as in "Lord of Hosts" (צְבָאוֹת), and "almighty," as in "Lord Almighty" (אֵל שַׁדַּי), an association the original audiences would have made.[82] In the world of the Song, there is no overt presence of God in the forms of divine appearance, speech, or action, not even an evaluation of divine involvement from the mouth of the poet. In fact, some scholars have argued that the Song is a result of a compilation of multiple songs into an anthology of love poetry.[83] At the center of the Song are two human beings who express their love, desires, yearning, and praise for one another. Although there are times when the two lovers share this mutual admiration, the woman's search for her lover often dominates the song, as revealed in her two dream accounts, where she looks for him but cannot find him, and at the end of the Song, where she yearns for his return. The way in which the woman relates to her lover becomes a way for the reader of the Song to imagine and envision what an individual's interaction with God may have looked like and that there are times when God's presence is elusive and his actions are unfathomable.[84]

Perhaps it is precisely this literary absence of God in Song of Songs that makes it a countertext to the presence of God in the rest of the Old Testament Scripture, where God appears, speaks, and acts. Even when God does not act directly, like in the other scrolls of the Megilloth, he is present in the mouths of the characters, as in Naomi's laments (Ruth 1:8, 13, 21), Daughter Zion's protest (Lam 1:11-15; 2:1), Qoheleth's posed meditations

---

[81]Jewish exegetes would disagree with this sentiment. See chap. 4.

[82]Sarah Zhang has provided a beautiful description of Song 8:6 from a Hebrew sonic perspective, which attempts to demonstrate the trace of God in the Song. See Zhang, *I, You, and the Word God: Finding Meaning in the Song of Songs*, Siphrut 20 (Winona Lake, IN: Eisenbrauns, 2016), 117-25.

[83]E.g., Longman, *Song of Songs*.

[84]Numerous commentators, past and present, Jewish and Christian, have elevated the plain meaning of the text to the spiritual level. Fishbane's commentary, for example, uses four levels of meanings to explain each verse of the Song. For example, in the first, *derash* level, the reader would identify the Song's female protagonist as a personification of Israel and her lover as God. In the fourth level, *sod*, the text's surface meaning would hint at the divine realm. See Fishbane, *Song of Songs*.

(Eccles 3:11; 5:2), and in the voice of the narrator (Ruth 1:6; 4:13). By rendering divine presence covertly, the poet of Song of Songs presents an alternative vision of divine presence—God's presence does not conform to human expectations or even to his own norms of presence. God remains transcendent and mysterious. He does not appear or act according to human expectations. Consequently, the wisdom element in the Song reminds the reader that God's presence is grounded in creation, in humans' endeavor in searching for one another and in their openness to the unknown in the realm of human sexuality. In the Song, the garden setting is where love can be found and blossom. This garden imagery brings us back to the Garden of Eden—the creation scene. The human lovers in the Song exemplify the figures of Eve and Adam, though they also differ from them.

In Eden, the descriptions of male and female relationships are functional. The man is to cultivate and keep the garden, whereas the woman is his helper (Gen 2:15, 18). In the Song, the descriptions of the lovers are based purely on love and affection. The functional aspects of childbearing or rearing and of doing domestic chores are absent. The creation account centers on the man. It is the man who speaks and acts (Gen 2:23-24), while in the Song, the central character is the woman. It is her speech and action that permeate the whole poem. In Eden, God's presence is explicit in the creation of man and woman. The text even reveals his inner resolve—"It is not good for the man to be alone" (Gen 2:18). Also, it is God who brings the woman he created to Adam. In the Song, however, God does nothing. His conspicuous absence may be intentional, so as to let the human characters take center stage. As Sweeney says, the absence of God in the Song allows the human characters to play fully as actors and powers in creation.[85] His silence may also indicate that he purposely leaves the human couple alone and does not want to intrude on their privacy. His absence and silence may also be a deliberate act of the composer, who leaves God out of the text for a purpose unknown to the reader. As chapter six will demonstrate, Song of Songs both resonates with the Eden narrative and deviates from it. In this

---

[85]Marvin A. Sweeney, *Reading the Hebrew Bible After the Shoah: Engaging Holocaust Theology* (Minneapolis: Fortress, 2008), 206.

sense, Song of Songs works as a countertext to make the reader reassess, rethink, and reflect on the theology of *eros* and the theology of absence.

Some scholars have noticed and understood the presence of *eros* in Song of Songs as a representation or embodiment of God's presence. For example, Aren Wilson-Wright draws on the Northwest Semitic combat myth of the Baal Cycle and other mythic combat elements from the Hebrew Bible. He notes that the root "love" (אהב) appears eighteen times in the Song. In Song 8:6-7, love is a counterpoint to death, Sheol, mighty waters, and rivers. Love is likened to fire, flame, and jealousy. All these cosmic images appear in the combat myths from the ancient Near East. In the Baal Cycle, Baal challenges his enemies Yamm (Sea) and Mot (Death). In the Hebrew Bible, the Leviathan symbolizes the mythic element of chaos, whereas Yahweh's jealous love for Israel often emerges as his divine nature and also appears in combat narratives (Ex 20:5; Deut 5:10; Is 42:13; Zeph 1:18). Therefore, Wilson-Wright asserts that Song 8:6 identifies love with God's role as a divine warrior.[86] This notion of love as God incarnate rather than as an attribute of God counters the portrayal of divine presence elsewhere in Scripture.

Song of Songs presents an alternative vision of divine presence. Rather than overtly stating the name of God and his activities in the world of human beings, Song of Songs presents an absent male lover (God), or, at best, a hidden God in the guise of a fierce love and an ascetic garden. As wisdom is rooted in creation theology, so God's presence is implicated in the natural world, in his creation, in flowers, trees, fruits, and animals. In his created world, there is order and disorder, just as *eros* is both rational and irrational. *Eros* can make one jubilant and awakened, but it can also make one drunk and sick. If order is associated with divine presence and chaos is associated with divine absence, then both notions are present in the Song. The enigma of the male lover's elusive presence makes room for the woman to desire him, long for him, and search for him. In the desire of the woman, she is searching for the order of things in her beloved. As a countertext, Song of Songs defies simple resolution to the theology of

---

[86] Aren Wilson-Wright, "Love Conquers All: Song of Songs 8:6b-7a as a Reflex of the Northwest Semitic Combat Myth," *JBL* 134, no. 2 (2015): 333-45.

absence. Instead, it affirms humans' dilemma of living in a world of complexity and ambiguity, and the search for the order of things, of people, and of love in times of uncertainty.

Esther as a countertext. The complete absence of God and his involvement in human affairs at a time of crisis in the book of Esther forms a stark contrast to the presence of God and his interventions in times of crisis in the other texts in Scripture, such as Exodus, Ezekiel, and even many of the lament psalms. Within the Megilloth, there are traces of God, such as in Song of Songs 8:6 in the disguise of love. In the Hebrew text of Esther, there is no such trace. This absence, in and of itself, makes Esther a countertext. Although all scrolls in the Megilloth function in big or small ways as countertexts, the book of Esther most deserves the appellation.[87]

Although scholars, commentators, and exegetes have noted the coincidences that occur in the story, the dramatic reversal of fortunes in its key characters, and the phrase "salvation will arise from another place" in Esther 4:14 as indications of divine deliverance, one cannot deny the complete absence of the divine name and reference to the divine in the book. The confessional stance of reading God or his providence into Esther is typical of the Christian reading. Yet, the deliberate absence of God in the book may well be the author's intentional way of heightening human responsibility in times of crisis.

There are many counterelements inherent in Esther, such as that the book is named after a woman. The only other book in Scripture named after a woman is Ruth. The central male character, Mordecai, is from the tribe of Benjamin rather than the esteemed tribe of Judah. Mordecai takes Esther as his adopted daughter rather than the more usual and expected taking her as a wife, as in the book of Ruth. Mordecai, an older father figure, obeys Esther, a woman and his inferior. The Persian palace in the city of Shushan is the central location of the book rather than the temple in Jerusalem. The Jews in Shushan show no intention of returning to Jerusalem, contrary to other postexilic books such as Ezra, Nehemiah, and Chronicles. Esther

---

[87]Queen-Sutherland sees Ruth as countering law, Qoheleth as countering wisdom, and Esther as countering the absence of God. See Kandy Queen-Sutherland, "Ruth, Qoheleth, and Esther: Counter Voices from the Megilloth," *Perspectives in Religious Studies* 43, no. 2 (2016): 227-42, esp. 242.

writes law, contrary to the idea that only men write law. Esther also marries a Gentile, contrary to the strong sentiments expressed in Ezra and Nehemiah. There are no religious rituals such as worship or prayer. However, the absence of God in the book surpasses all these counterelements in setting the scroll apart from every other book in the Bible.

Many scholars have compared the story of Esther to those of Joseph and Daniel. In all three stories, all central characters rise from a lowly status to occupying a high place at a foreign court. All characters face death threats at a time of national crisis, and all display tremendous wisdom to save their kindred. All are beautiful, young, and of the Jewish race. The glaring difference between Esther and the other two narratives lies precisely in the presence and absence of God. While the reference to God is present in the stories of Joseph and Daniel, he is absent in Esther. Therefore, to place the three stories side by side results only in revealing Esther as a countertext to other courtroom tales or stories of wise courtiers in the Bible.

Some also juxtapose the story of Esther with the events in Exodus. Both stories recount the salvation of God's people. Both stories involve an impending threat to the lives of the Jewish race. Both stories include writing law. However, the story of Esther counters the Exodus narrative in achieving salvation without the explicit presence and actions of God. While we may be uncertain whether it is fair to say that human beings are replacing God or on a par with God in Esther, what is certain is that the salvation history in Esther counters the salvation history described in Exodus.

Additionally, the wisdom element in Esther suggests that in times of divine absence, human beings should exercise their wisdom in order to avert evil. This runs completely counter to the stories of God saving his people, as in Exodus, or God being present with his people in exile, as in Ezekiel 1, or God listening to the pleas of his people, as in some lament psalms. Here I quote Sweeney again regarding divine hiddenness and human initiative in Wisdom literature. He notes, "The wisdom literature of the Hebrew Bible calls upon human beings to act, that is, to discern wisdom and order in the world and to act on that knowledge, however limited it might be, to ensure a stable and productive order in creation and life in the world."[88] The book of Esther, indeed, is a form of applied wisdom in time of crisis, however limited that wisdom may be.

MOVING THE MARGINAL VOICES TO THE CENTER

Song of Songs and Esther embody the marginal voices in Old Testament theology and have often been overlooked or suppressed. This marginality is due to the dominance of the historical framework of God's salvation history in the history of interpretation as well as in biblical theology. Another reason is the perception that narratives are more significant than the poetic books and wisdom texts, where the national aspect of Israel and the covenantal relation between God and Israel are downplayed. In addition, the late shaping of the Megilloth also renders it less "authoritative" than the Torah and the Prophets.

Recent scholarship has taken note of the emerging significance of the Megilloth, in which human responsibility is highlighted and the role of God recedes into the background. Jewish theologies place more emphasis on these five scrolls and their contribution to the place of human responsibility in the larger scheme of biblical theology, where human beings can exert their voices in protest, lament, wails, and shouts.[89] Queen-Sutherland asserts, "The five (scrolls) cross the full range of human experience and call God's people to live life as party and prayer. Ruth celebrates kindness and Song of Songs revels in love. For all its randomness, Qoheleth celebrates life, while Lamentations honors loss. Esther celebrates justice, a fitting conclusion to the Megilloth."[90] Indeed, in contrast to the vertical theology of straightforward doctrinal teachings of the Torah or prophetic oracles, the theology of the Megilloth is one of "horizontal theology"—one that centers on women, narratives, wisdom, and suffering, and on the particularity of an incarnational or lived experience of human characters. Galvin sees the books of the Megilloth as privileging human actors who attempt to comprehend human suffering in light of their understanding of God. Meaning is found in human relationships, and this forces humans to grapple with the

---

[88]Sweeney, *Reading the Hebrew Bible*, 207.
[89]Strollo, "Initiative and Agency," 154.
[90]Queen-Sutherland, "Ruth, Qoheleth, and Esther," 242.

nature of God and how he acts in the world.[91] Without this horizontal axis, Old Testament and biblical theology would only present a partial theology, without a dialogic character and a multiplicity of voices.

The main characters in Song of Songs express the intricacy of *eros*, articulate their desire, and highlight the created beauty of human bodies. The lovers live in the natural world of God's creation, where animals, plants, and fruits all participate in conjuring a world of erotic love. God's name is obscured in the Song, yet his presence is subtly and artfully expressed through his creation and through the force of love between the woman and the man, which is as fierce as the flame and as strong as death, comparable to the flame of God. In Esther, the complete and conspicuous absence of God's name presents human beings with an opportunity to act on their wisdom to execute justice in the face of evil.

These two books were compiled and included in the Hebrew canon after the cruel experience of the exile. In times of exile, the question of the presence of God comes to the fore for the people of God. Where is God in exile? Where is God when his people need him the most? Has God abandoned his people, as the elders of Judah perceive him to have done (Ezek 8:12; 9:9)? Has God hidden his face as he said he would (Deut 31:17-18)? Is God tired or powerless? Did he lose the war to the Babylonian deities? These questions were lurking and gnawing in the minds and hearts of the postexilic Jewish community. As Goldingay observes, the lack of emphasis on God and his acts in the Megilloth and in the Writings reflect the books' historical background in the postexilic period, by which time the mighty acts of God were perceived as belonging to the distant past, the early days of Israel's history.[92] In the seeming absence of God, the actions of the human characters define the stories of exile and diaspora. In the contemporary world, the actions of God and his lack of intervention in crises and in times of evil compel his people to question and to challenge his theodicy. In this regard, Esther is nearer to the contemporary world in its portrayal of reality than the visible presence of God and his miraculous activities in the book of Exodus.

---

[91]Galvin, "Horizontal Theology," 125, 138. Song of Songs is a minor exception, since it is not a narrative or about suffering, unless one construes the female protagonist's search for her lover, whom she cannot find, or her lovesickness as a form of suffering.
[92]John Goldingay, "Hermeneutics," *DOTWPW* 274.

In sum, Song of Songs and Esther present two different but equally important trajectories of human experiences: the search for love and the search for justice in the created world. The theology of absence in these books is not to be taken lightly or relegated to the margins. Rather, the two books, even without explicit reference to God's name, exert their voices in conversation with the rest of the Scripture—that the absence of God is a serious theological issue. These two books contribute to Old Testament theology and biblical theology in that God's absence and silence is an integral part of his divine nature, countering his presence and active participation in human history.

The way in which God works in these two books differs from that of the Torah and the Prophets. God's presence is not confined to the dominant models as in Exodus. Therefore, these two scrolls complement and supplement what the rest of the biblical canon lacks, and therefore they offer insight into the larger question of the nature of God and how believers should respond in times of his perceived absence. The absence of God in these two biblical books is a theological necessity because it helps to align theology with real life, in which there are times when the people of God hear the echoes of the psalmist's voice, "My God, my God, why have You forsaken me" (Ps 22:1), in their own lived experiences.

The subsequent chapters will focus on four aspects of Song of Songs and Esther, namely: time, temple, feasts, and canon, as ways to rethink and reflect on the significance of the theology of absence in Old Testament theology and how it contributes to a fuller picture of God, and of human beings in relation to him so that we can live with wisdom in the midst of divine absence.

3

TIME

SONG *and* NARRATIVE

A time to search and a time to give up as lost.

ECCLESIASTES 3:6

TIME IS A HUMAN CONCERN. If time defines human experiences, then timelessness defines God. If God is eternal, then he does not live within the realm of time, nor is he subject to it. Rather, he works as he pleases both outside time and from within. We clearly see this different treatment of time in the two books discussed in this chapter, the Song of Songs and Esther. Due to their difference in genre—the first poetry, the second prose—these two books perceive time in different ways. Therefore, this chapter is about a deep meditation on how these two books portray time and how this understanding of time contributes to the understanding of the theology of absence.

While the genre of poetry in the Song of Songs resists a rational analysis of time, contemplation of it may assist readers in appreciating the Song as lyric poetry. Poetry does not follow a formal structure, with introduction, plot, and conclusion, like narratives do. Poetry has a structure of its own, which is often signaled by soundplay, wordplay, or other literary features.[1]

---

[1]Lyric poetry tends to direct its mimesis inward rather than outward. The concern of the lyric is more about the inner life and emotion rather than characterization and actions. However, Linafelt notes that the Song of Songs displays literary features beyond the confine of poetry. It contains dramatic and narrative elements in order to create a richer mix for a complex lyrical experience and thus it is "pseudonarrative." Tod Linafelt, "Lyrical Theology: The Song of Songs

It tends to change time and space abruptly from one scene to another, in contrast to prose, where there is usually a linear development of the plot from past to present to future. Poetry also tends to express emotional experience, whereas prose tends to simulate reality.[2] "Lyric poetry," in short, refers to a nonnarrative lyric structure that is characterized by rhythm, sounds, rhymes, and other verbal features.

In the Song of Songs, time is fluid and always in-between times, or going back and forth across time. This nature of time warns readers not to bring their own understanding of time into reading the Song. Questions such as "Is the author telling a story with plot and character development?" may reflect readers' concerns, but they may not be the Song's concern. The Song obviously has dramatic elements, such as the two night scenes, but it is largely poetry. How does each scene of the Song connect to the others chronologically? Are they supposed to be connected into a coherent whole at all? Is each scene independent from one another? If so, should we see the Song as an anthology of love poetry without a discernible plot? Or should the reader fill in the gaps between the scenes and create countless versions of the story, as many commentators have done?[3] Scholars have attempted to make sense of the sequence and divisions of the Song for over two thousand years. The range of the division varies from five to fifty-two songs, and rarely do two scholars agree.[4] The fluidity of time in the Song defies human logic and reason. Yet, the timelessness

---

and the Advantage of Poetry," in *Toward a Theology of Eros: Transfiguring Passion at the Limits of Discipline*, ed. Catherine Keller and Virginia Burrus (New York: Fordham University Press, 2006), 291-305, esp. 292-93.

[2] Eliyahu Assis, *Flashes of Fire: A Literary Analysis of the Song of Songs*, LHBOTS 503 (New York: T&T Clark, 2009), 9-10.

[3] For instance, Delitzsch considers six scenes for the Song of Songs: (1) mutual love by the lovers (Song 1:2–2:7); (2) mutual seeking by the lovers (Song 2:8–3:5); (3) wedding and marriage (Song 3:6–5:1); (4) love lost and found (Song 5:2–6:9); (5) the Shulamite's beauty and humility (Song 6:10–8:4); and (6) the covenant in the house of Shulamite (Song 8:5-14). See Franz Delitzsch, *Commentary on the Song of Songs and Ecclesiastes*, trans. M. G. Easton (Edinburgh: T&T Clark, 1891), 8-10. Michael Goulder suggests that the Song contains a semicontinuous plot. He proposes there are fourteen songs in the Song of Songs, with Solomon and his Arabic princess as the main characters of the story. See Michael D. Goulder, *The Song of Fourteen Songs*, JSOTSup 36 (Sheffield: University of Sheffield Press, 1986), 2-4. Those who discern a plot in the Song often interpret the Song historically, as if the characters in the Song correspond to historical figures at the time when the Song was composed.

[4] See Tournay's list as an example of scholars who understand the number of songs in the Song of Songs differently. Raymond Jacques Tournay, *Word of God, Song of Love: A Commentary on the Song of Songs*, trans. J. Edward Crowley (New York: Paulist, 1988), 31.

of love described in the Song reflects the immortality of love that transcends the boundary of time.

By contrast, in Esther, characters and events are constrained within the boundary of time. Time progresses linearly, from past to present and then from present into the future. Reading Esther for the first time, there is always the element of the unknown and suspense regarding what the future may hold for the characters. By contrast, the narrator is omniscient, knowing the story's past, present, and future while designing the pace of the story to create a dramatic effect. The story of Esther reflects an earthly experience of "time and narrative," where time advances chronologically through human experiences. The merging of times, through specific timing and coincidences in the story, points to the presence of God, who, though unseen and unnamed, is working miracles for his people.[5] Although time progresses mostly in a linear fashion, the installation of Purim carries the past to the present and into the future. Ritual and its repetition create continuity in time, connecting past memory with the present reality, which in turn heads forward into the future.

When the Song and Esther are read together, the two books share the explicit absence of God's name.[6] Additionally, the sometimes absence of the male lover in the Song parallels the absence of God in the book of Esther, although they differ in degree. In the Song, the male lover is not entirely absent throughout the Song, whereas the name of God is completely absent in Esther. In both books, the absence of the male protagonist and of God heightens the desire to think of them even more. In the Song, the female protagonist is sick with love in the absence of her beloved, whereas in the book of Esther, the reader is often placed in a position to seek traces of God's activities in his literary absence. In the Song, absence makes the heart grow fonder. Yet, in Esther, absence makes the mind ponder. Both books

---

[5]Walton puts it this way: "Thus the great cycle of time was put in place by the Creator. As his first act, he mixed time into the features of the cosmos that would serve the needs of the human beings he was going to place in its midst." John Walton, *The Lost World of Genesis One: Ancient Cosmology and the Origins Debate* (Downers Grove, IL: InterVarsity Press, 2009), 56.

[6]Although in Song 8:6, the ending *yâ* may suggest a shorter form of God's name. Also, Wilson-Wright's article identifies love in the Song as YHWH, based on the Northwest Semitic combat myth expressed in Song 8:6-7. See Aren Wilson-Wright, "Love Conquers All: Song of Songs 8:6b-7a as a Reflex of the Northwest Semitic Combat Myth," *JBL* 134, no. 2 (2015): 333-45. In any case, divine presence in the Song is implicit and not explicit.

have something to say about the theology of absence, which contrasts sharply with God's presence in the rest of the Scripture.

THE SONG OF SONGS

In the Song of Songs, time does not progress chronologically, with causes and effects, or with a distinct sequence from past to present to future. In the Song of Songs, time refuses to be defined or fixed in any form. Time is perceived subjectively, from the perspective of the lovers, rather than objectively. The past, present, and future are all swirled together with an ending pointing toward the future, which in turn echoes back to the beginning of the Song. Although the concept of time is fuzzy, elements of time are discernible in the Song and create an intricate dynamic with the timelessness of love, which permeates the whole poem.

Time and song. In reading the Song of Songs, one quickly discovers that the movements of the scenes do not follow a sequential pattern. The couple is apparently married in Song of Songs 4, where the man addresses the woman as "my bride" (Song 4:8) for the very first time. Later, the bride invites her beloved to "come into her garden" (Song 4:16). The beloved responds by saying, "I have come to my garden" (Song 5:1), which may suggest erotic union in the context of marriage. However, in Song of Songs 8 the couple seems to describe a premarital state, where the woman wishes that she could kiss her beloved without being despised by others (Song 8:1). Here, the social strain in their relationship suggests they are not married. Even at the end of the Song, the woman is still yearning for the return of her beloved (Song 8:14), suggesting they are not together physically. Therefore, the flow of the Song defies linear movement from premarital to married life but rather jumps from one scene to another.

The anticipation of seeing the beloved lingers to the end, which flashes back to the beginning of the Song. The Song opens with a woman's desire for her beloved's kiss, "Let him kiss me with the kisses of his mouth" (Song 1:2) and ends with the longing for the lover's presence, "Come, my beloved, and be like a gazelle or a young stag on the mountains of spices" (Song 8:14). This ending does not seem like a closure but echoes back to

Song of Songs 2:17. Cheryl Exum calls this resistance to closure the Song's most important strategy for immortalizing love.[7]

F. W. Dobbs-Allsopp identifies lyric poetry in terms of its musicality, which originates from an oral form and later develops into "a sung word."[8] As a song, it refuses to be read as a narrative. Exum highlights the temporal aspect of the Song by stressing that love is forever in progress. This nonlinear but meandering progression is in fact a feature of lyric poetry, which moves forward and then backward while continuously repeating this cycle of conjuring and reissuing its invitation to readers to participate in the lovers' relationship.[9] While a nonunilateral movement is apparent in the Song, pauses or disjunctives are also present. One of the characteristics of lyric poetry is that it sometimes includes refrains after every stanza. Simply put, a refrain is "a group of words which recurs several times."[10] Refrains are usually repetitions of a single word or phrase, or even an entire stanza, used to assert something of importance while enhancing the meter or rhythm of the literary work itself.[11] Another function of the refrain is to create a circular motion or a literary symmetry.[12] In the Song, notable refrains are discernible by the repetition of phrases, with some variations, such as:

His left hand is under my head, and his right hand embraces me. (Song 2:6; 8:3)

I adjure you, daughters of Jerusalem, by female gazelles or by hinds of the field, do not stir up and do not arouse love until it desires. (Song 2:7; 3:5; 5:8; 8:4)[13]

My beloved is mine, and I am his. (Song 2:16; 6:3; 7:10)[14]

---

[7]J. Cheryl Exum, *Song of Songs: A Commentary*, OTL (Louisville: KY: Westminster John Knox, 2005), 12.

[8]F. W. Dobbs-Allsopp, *On Biblical Poetry* (Oxford: Oxford University Press, 2015), 182-83.

[9]Exum, *Song of Songs*, 3-4. "Lyric poetry" is a lyric that is intended to be sung. It expresses the thoughts and especially the feelings of a speaker. See Leland Ryken, *How to Read the Bible as Literature* (Grand Rapids, MI: Zondervan, 1984), 109.

[10]Roland E. Murphy, "The Unity of the Song of Songs," in *Poetry in the Hebrew Bible: Selected Studies from Vetus Testamentum* (Leiden: Brill, 2000), 148-55, esp. 148.

[11]Tremper Longman III, "Refrain," *DOTWPW* 641.

[12]Robert Alter, *The Art of Biblical Poetry* (New York: Basic Books, 1985), 118-19.

[13]The latter part of the refrains in Song 5:8 and Song 8:4 are different from Song 2:7 and Song 3:5. A refrain with some variation is common among lyric poetry.

[14]Song 7:10 is a variation on Song 2:16 and Song 6:3. "I am my beloved's and for me is his desire."

These refrains not only add emphasis and rhythm to the Song, but also make the reader pause. Time halts at the refrains. The function of these refrains is similar to that of the *selah* in the Psalms, making the reader stop and reflect on the previous strophe. "His left hand is under my head, and his right hand embraces me" (Song 2:6; 8:3) is an action of the male lover at the present moment, while it also implies actions to come. Twice that refrain is followed by the adjuration formula, "Do not stir up and do not arouse love until it desires."[15] Here, "until" (עַד) marks a rupture in time.[16] It points to a future where the time is right. The adjuration temporarily interrupts the time sequence and the expected actions, as if the woman is saying to readers, "Now is not the right time for love." Love (אַהֲבָה) in the Song has its time, but this time is not in the objective sense but in a felt sense that marks the readiness or ripeness of love. It is a force (עַז) to be reckoned with (Song 8:6). It functions as if it has a will of its own. Several times in the Song, love is personified with a definite article, "the Love" (Song 2:7; 3:5; 8:4, 7). Hauge states, "Love is a superhuman power that is asleep and is not to be awakened until the proper time, when it itself desires."[17] Thus, cycles of continuous movements with periodic moments of pause depict one aspect of time in the Song.

On the one hand, love continues in spite of repeated interruptions. On the other hand, the moments of pause enhances the erotic aspect of love. They slow down love until it reaches the right time to blossom. It teases the desire in the dynamic relationship of the human couple. In other words, there is a time for love and a time to abstain from it, as the book of Ecclesiastes observes: "A time to embrace and a time to shun embracing" (Eccles 3:5). The continuity of love together with periodic pauses so as not to stir up love carries the Song forward in a spiral motion until its

---

[15] A different interpretation of "Do not stir up love" is that it means "Do not disturb." If this is the case, then the time for love is now rather than in the future. See Brian P. Gault, "A 'Do Not Disturb' Sign? Reexamining the Adjuration Refrain in Song of Songs," *JSOT* 36, no. 1 (2011): 93-104. The problem with this interpretation is that we are uncertain regarding when the woman utters this adjuration to the daughters of Jerusalem. Is it before her marriage or after? If it is before her marriage, as in Song 2:7, then it would be problematic as regards the rest of the biblical teachings.

[16] See the detailed analysis of the uses of *until* in the Song by Martin Ravndal Hauge, *Solomon the Lover and the Shape of the Song of Songs*, HBM 77 (Sheffield: Sheffield Phoenix, 2015), 39-64. Hauge links *until* to other images that appear in the Song to suggest a conceptual structure that is part of the Song's compositional movements.

[17] Hauge, *Solomon the Lover*, 61.

crescendo in Song of Songs 8:6-7. This suggests that an intricate relationship exists between the opportune time for love and the inopportune time for love. What stays unchanged in between is the significance and the timelessness of love.

Another aspect of time is conveyed through seasons. Love has its specific season. In the Song of Songs, spring is the season for love, while winter is not. The imagery of nature in the Song, particularly the botanical world, all responds to the beginning of the spring season. However, the way the woman recounts the beloved's invitation in this spring season blurs the specificity of time. The reader is uncertain when the following events take place.

> The voice of my beloved, look! This (he) is coming, leaping over the mountains and springing over the hills.
>
> Like, my beloved, to a gazelle to a young stag, look! This (he) is standing behind our walls, gazing through the windows, peering through the lattices.
>
> My beloved spoke and he said to me, "Arise for yourself! My darling, my beautiful, and come away yourself!
>
> For look! The winter has passed. The rain has passed through and gone.
>
> The blossoms appear in the land. The time of pruning has arrived. The sound of the turtle doves is heard in our land.
>
> The fig tree has ripened her early fig and the vines in blossom have given forth fragrance. Arise for yourself! My darling, my beautiful, and come away yourself." (Song 2:8-13)

From the first-person perspective, the woman describes her beloved coming, leaping, and springing over the hills. The sequence of participles denotes the actions of the man, which are occurring in front of her right at that moment. Then he stands behind the walls and gazes through the windows to see her. She hears him say, "Arise and come!" Then he invites her to come out, because the winter has gone and spring has come. The season of spring is characterized by the blossoming of flowers, the ripening of figs, the sound of turtledoves, and the fragrance of vines. The sensuous ambience of spring nature imagery provides the fitting time for love. As nature responds to the refreshing and blooming spring, so does love. Jill Munro observes, "Not only does the advent of spring confirm that the time for love has come . . .

it also provides the setting for the lovers' meeting."[18] The budding of the vines, the blooming of the pomegranates, the fragrant mandrakes, and the choice fruits together create an opulent mood for the woman finally to declare to her beloved: "There, I will give my love to you" (Song 7:13). Spring is indeed the season for love.

The timeliness of love in the spring stands in contrast to the uncertainty of time in this poem as a whole. Is the poem in the present or in the past? Does the poem describe a reality or a mere fantasy in the mind of the woman? Exum observes that the poem creates a sense of immediacy through the actions of the lovers, as if their actions were taking place in the present moment, in front of the reader.[19] When a reader reads the Song, there are no narratives, comments, evaluations, or asides from the composer. The entire Song presents the lovers through direct speech. We know the characters through what and how they speak to each other. The whole poem of Song of Songs 2:8-13 is a direct speech. This puts the speaker in the present. As Paul Ricoeur notes, "To have a present, someone must speak."[20]

The frequent uses of the particle "Look!" (הִנֵּה) plus a participle create a sense of urgency. These invite the reader to look in the same way or the same direction as the speaker is looking: "Look! He is coming!" "Look! He is standing behind our walls!"[21] "Look" helps the hearer focus on a particular person or event.[22] Here, the angle is from the perception of the woman. She is attempting to draw attention to the object she is seeing, as if to take a snapshot of that specific moment. In doing so, the woman subconsciously tries to stop time. "Look" conveys the sense of "now." This "now" will soon be gone, because time moves forward. However, the mental snapshot that she has taken preserves the memory of "now" in her

[18]Jill M. Munro, *Spikenard and Saffron: A Study in the Poetic Language of the Song of Songs*, JSOTSup 203 (Sheffield: Sheffield Academic Press, 1995), 118.

[19]Exum, *Song of Songs*, 11.

[20]Paul Ricoeur, *Time and Narrative*, trans. Kathleen Blamey and David Pellauer (Chicago: University of Chicago Press, 1985), 3:109.

[21]The construction of "look [*hinnēh*]" plus a participle (the "ing" form, equivalent to the present continuous tense) of seeing or discovering is frequently used in making the narrative graphic and vivid while enabling the reader to enter into the surprise or satisfaction of the speaker (*BDB* 244). Although the genre of the Song of Songs is that of lyric poetry, the uses of *look* plus participles also convey the idea of surprise and immediacy.

[22]Adele Berlin, *Poetics and Interpretation of Biblical Narrative* (Winona Lake, IN: Eisenbrauns, 1994), 91.

consciousness. Then the man also calls out from his own point of view: "Look! The winter has passed." Both parties are inviting the other to see from their perspective.[23] Twice, the man calls using imperatives: "Arise for yourself [קוּמִי לָךְ]! And come along yourself [וּלְכִי־לָךְ]!"[24] The poem invites the reader to be present with the characters in the present moment. Just as the woman hears the man's voice reaching out to her, so too does the reader hear that voice.

The lyrics are abrupt in movement, usually because the verses before and after are emotional and psychological rather than logical.[25] We are uncertain as to whether Song of Songs 2:10 immediately follows Song of Songs 2:9 in context, or whether Song of Songs 2:10 begins a new scene. If Song of Songs 2:10 follows Song of Songs 2:9 in logical and chronological sequence, then "My beloved spoke and he said to me" can be understood in the present tense as "My beloved speaks and he says to me," putting the timeframe, "then," in the immediate present.[26] It is also possible that the poem of Song of Songs 2:8-13 happened in the past and that the woman recounts it by using direct speech to convey that to her it seems as if it is happening right now. If so, she fuses the past with the present.

It is also possible that the entire poem of Song of Songs 2:8-13 is a piece of fantasy or imagination. In this case, it would refer to the future.[27] The woman imagines her beloved coming to her and asking her to go out. In other words, the whole invitation may occur only in her own mind, revealing her desire to be invited to go out with her beloved. Daphna Arbel proposes that the nonlinear and nonsequential plot of the Song with its various scenes suggests that the Song is the result of a woman's inner dreams, emotions, and thoughts. The woman takes on different roles and places herself in numerous locations, and then pictures herself in manifold situations while predicting social and cultural reactions to her acts. In this case,

---

[23]"Look" (*hinnēh*) conveys point of view. Its basic function is to be an attention getter. Although Berlin's work is primarily on biblical narrative, the term *look* applies to poetry. In a way, Song 2:8-13 can be taken as a mininarrative. See Berlin, *Poetics and Interpretation*, 91.

[24]The combination of *go* plus *for yourself* also appears in Gen 12:1; 22:2. In the latter cases, they are in the masculine form. Here in Song 2:10, 13, they are in the feminine form.

[25]Ryken, *How to Read the Bible*, 111.

[26]The verbs "answer" (עָנָה) and "say" (אָמַר) in Hebrew are in the perfect tense, which can be translated as either present or past tense depending on the context.

[27]Munro raises this possible interpretation. See *Spikenard and Saffron*, 121.

the Song of Songs would be a vehicle of self-expression because it reflects a woman's inner and personal discourse. The woman frequently uses the word "my soul," which describes her inner realm of emotions, feelings, and thoughts. In Song of Songs 6:12, she says, "My soul set me over the chariots of Ammi-nadib."[28] This verse suggests that the woman's soul takes her to a world of fantasy. Is it possible, then, that other places in the Song also describe her fantasy?

If the poem in Song of Songs 2:8-13 describes the woman's imagination rather than reality, then it places the question of time in the possible or wishful future. While the season for love is in the spring, the exact timing of the invitation from the beloved is unclear. The reader is uncertain whether the incident is a description of a real account, or whether it is merely an illusion. Time is a fuzzy concept in this poem of invitation. Time may not appear to be essential for the poet of the Song, but it may be for the ordinary reader. A linear understanding of time, however, should be resisted when one attempts to read the Song in its own right. What remains unchanged is the *eros* and emotions expressed between the two lovers.

Dream vision and time. Two night scenes appear in the Song of Songs (Song 3:1-5; 5:2-8). Their inclusion leads some commentators to construe the whole song as a dream. For instance, Solomon Freehof considers Song of Songs 5:2, "I am sleeping but my heart was awake," as the key to interpreting the Song. He thinks that "heart" refers to intelligence and mind, and that "For the body to be asleep and the mind to be active means simply to dream."[29] If we read what follows Song of Songs 5:2, it makes sense to consider it as a dream rather than as reality.

> I am sleeping but my heart was awake. The voice of my beloved is knocking,
> "Open! To me, my sister, my darling, my dove, my perfect one, for my head
> is full of dew, my locks (with) the drops (fragments) of the night."
>   I have stripped my tunic, how can I put it on? I have washed my feet, how
> can I soil them?

---

[28]Daphna V. Arbel, "'My Vineyard, My Very Own, Is for Myself,'" in *The Feminist Companion to the Song of Songs*, ed. Athalya Brenner and Carole R. Fontaine, FCB (Sheffield: Sheffield Academic Press, 2000), 90-92.

[29]Solomon B. Freehof, "The Song of Songs: A General Suggestion," *Jewish Quarterly Review* (1948): 399.

My beloved extended his hand from the hole, and my inward part growled upon it.

I arose, I, to open to my beloved, and my hands dripped (with) myrrh, and my fingers passing myrrh upon the palms (handles) of the bolt.

I opened, I, to my beloved, but my beloved turned away and passed. My soul went out as he spoke. I sought him, but I did not find him. I called him but he did not answer me.

The watchmen, the ones patrolling the city, found me, they struck me, they bruised me; they lifted up my shawl from upon me, the watchmen of the walls.

I adjure you, daughters of Jerusalem, if you find my beloved, what will you tell him? I am being sick of love. (Song 5:2-8)

What frequently occurs in dreams (such as nakedness, running through streets and fields, and the sudden movements from one scene to another, from palace to Mount Gilead, from inner chamber to vineyards) may seem surreal in real life. It is thus understandable that scholars such as Freehof see the entire Song of Songs as a sequence of dreams. He understands "the dream [to be] the outcome of longing and desire expressed in symbolic scenes and actions." In the ancient world, dreams were the medium through which the human and the divine communicated. In the story of Joseph, the two dreams he has foretell of his relationships with his family members, and the dreams of Pharaoh are the means through which God speaks to him (Gen 37:5-11; 41:1-8). Likewise, the dreams of Nebuchadnezzar are given from God, who speaks to him in regard to future empires (Dan 2:1; 4:10-18). Therefore, Freehof interprets Song of Songs 5:2-8 as the lover and beloved being lost and separated from each other, and then turning to seek each other out. In the same way, God seeks after Israel, but Israel seems to be far from his presence. Then Israel seeks after God, but now God seems far away. Finally, they find each other because "many waters cannot quench love," and Israel is forever united with God as "I am my beloved and he is mine."[30]

In this dream interpretation, dream and allegory are not divorced from each other but go hand in hand. As Harold Fisch posits, there is no "literal meaning" in a dream, because by definition a dream implies symbolic

---

[30]Freehof, "Song of Songs," 401-2.

meaning on multiple levels. The shifting movements of a dream, with its merging stories and identities, make the dream interpretation an "allegorical imperative."[31] By that Fisch means a dream must be interpreted allegorically to do justice to this poetic genre. Whether the two night scenes belong to the genre of dream is a matter of debate; poetry, by definition, includes imagination, which lends space to ambiguity. Such is precisely the appeal of poetry.

What about time? How do we discern time in a dream? In Song of Songs 3:1-5, the dream appears during the night, but its contents may reflect past, present, and future:

> Upon my bed at nights, I sought the one my soul loves. I sought him but I did not find him.
>
> Let me rise and let me go around in the city, in the streets, and in the broad places; I sought the one my soul loves. I sought him but I did not find him.
>
> The watchmen, the ones patrolling the city found me, "Have you seen the one my soul loves?"
>
> Just a little I passed from them until I found the one my soul loves. I seized him, I would not let him slacken (go) until I brought him to the house of my mother, to the chamber of her who conceived me.
>
> I adjure you, daughters of Jerusalem, by female gazelles and by the hinds of the field, do not stir up and do not arouse love until it desires. (Song 3:1-5)

The poem clearly indicates that the woman is on her bed at "nights." Here, *nights* in Hebrew is in the plural from, reflecting not just one night but many nights. Some translators render it "night after night," which means it is a regular nocturnal occurrence.[32] Dreams usually take place when one is asleep at night. The imagery that appears in dreams reflects the dreamer's lived experience in the past, in the waking life, in the daytime. Therefore,

---

[31]Harold Fisch, *Poetry with a Purpose: Biblical Poetics and Interpretation* (Bloomington: Indiana University Press, 1988), 89.

[32]See, for example, Duane Garrett, *Song of Songs*, WBC 23B (Nashville: Thomas Nelson, 2004), 169-70. Exum translates it "nightly," meaning "night after night" (*Song of Songs*, 122). However, some commentators translate it as in the singular "night," among them Falk, Murphy, Bloch and Bloch, Longman, and Pope. Pope thinks that the plural for nights here does not indicate successive nights but rather a plural of composition designating nighttime. See Marvin H. Pope, *Song of Songs*, AB 7C (Garden City, NY: Doubleday, 1977), 415.

time continues in a dream; but it is not the same kind of time as real time, actual time, daytime, or world time. Dreams have their own pace of time. Sometimes one dreams of a recent event, reliving the past in some way.[33] But real time keeps moving forward as the dreamer sleeps. The past influences the present and carries on to the future.

Twice in the night scenes, the woman has images of the watchmen in the city. They appear to be distant and hostile, especially in the second scene. She recounts, "They found me, they struck me, they bruised me; they lifted up my shawl from upon me" (Song 5:7). Marcia Falk suggests that the watchmen represent the public domain. They are outside the love relationship, so they represent the real world.[34] What is interesting is that this real world appears in the dream world, and thus obscures real time and imagined time. This interconnectedness between the night scenes and reality is intriguing. The two realms of time, real time and the imagined time, intersect and overlap the realms of past and present.[35] Tod Linafelt sees the watchmen as those who keep the lovers apart, and so they function to intensify erotic desire by protracting absence.[36] Harding too considers the beating and stripping scene as the psychological manifestation of the protagonist's inner anxieties about her relationship.[37] If this anxiety exposes what is hidden in the subconscious mind of the

---

[33]Freud quotes Haffner's research on dreams that "The dream continues the waking life. Our dreams always connect themselves with such ideas as have shortly before been present in our consciousness." Sigmund Freud, *Interpretation of Dreams* (Sioux Falls, SD: NuVision, 2007), 17.

[34]Marcia Falk, *Love Lyrics from the Bible: The Song of Songs* (New York: HarperSanFrancisco, 1990), 147.

[35]Exum questions the notion of reality in the dream sequence. She sees the whole Song as a literary construction of the poet, and thus to ask the question about reality is to confuse literary creation as something real (*Song of Songs*, 45). Meredith surveys major contributors and thoughts in dream interpretation and points out its pitfalls, which is to write out the violence in Song 5:7. Christopher Meredith, *Journeys in the Songscape: Space and the Song of Songs*, HBM 53 (Sheffield: Sheffield Phoenix, 2013), 35-38.

[36]Tod Linafelt, "The Arithmetic of Eros," *Interpretation* (2005): 253.

[37]Kathryn Harding, "'I Sought Him but I Did Not Find Him': The Elusive Lover in the Song of Songs," *Biblical Interpretation* 16, no. 1 (2008): 49n17. Black, on the other hand, provides an alternative reading of the beating scene in Song 5:6-7. She thinks that the beating of the woman represents "border-crossing," thus moving the woman from the center to the margin and so forcing her to conform to social expectations. The scene is intended to make the reader unsettled, she thinks, and challenges a cohesive reading of the text. See Fiona C. Black, "Nocturnal Egression: Exploring Some Margins of the Song of Songs," in *Postmodern Interpretation of the Bible: A Reader*, ed. A. K. M. Adam (St. Louis: Chalice, 2001), 93-94.

woman, then what is on her mind and what is reality are indeed fused in terms of time.

Another aspect in both night scenes is timing. His time and her time do not mesh. In the first night scene (Song 3:1-5), she searches for her lover, but he is nowhere to be found. She asks the watchmen, and their response is not recorded. But just as she passes them, she finds him. "I sought him but I did not find him" reflects that, although the timing for the lovers to see each other is off, the scene will eventually end on a happy note. In the second night scene (Song 5:2-8), the timing for the lovers to see each other is even worse. When he knocks on the door, she is not ready to open it. But when she is ready to open it, he is no longer there. When she searches for him, he has vanished and is nowhere to be seen. His time and her time crisscross, so the two lovers do not get to see each other. As a result, she is compelled to live in his absence and so becomes "sick of love."

The recurring night scenes of similar content indicate these dreamlike encounters' continuing effect from the past to the present. In both scenes, the theme of seeking and finding emerges. In both scenes, she goes out and looks for him, but she cannot find him (Song 3:1; 5:6). In the Song of Songs, the city and streets symbolize hostility, whereas the countryside and the field connote safety and lovemaking. In the city, in the streets and the broad places, she cannot find him and is beaten by the watchmen. By contrast, the countryside is where the couple enjoys each other's presence. The vineyards and the gardens are where they find love (Song 1:17; 2:12-15; 6:11; 7:11-13). This theme of seeking and finding reveals the woman's inner fear and anxiety. Her desire is to be with her lover at all times. But there are times in the "actual life" within the Song when he is nowhere to be found, leaving her distressed to the point of feeling sick. Living in his absence constitutes her greatest dread.

It is also possible that in the "actual life" of the Song, the lovers are always together, but the woman fears that this will not last forever and that one day she will lose him. The apprehension of losing him surfaces in her inner psyche. Harding sees these night scenes as the woman's moments of crisis in her perception of the relationship with her lover. They express her vulnerability in love and her attempt to come to terms with these moments and to deal with them. One of these anxieties is the question, "Could she love more than she is loved?"[38] If this is indeed the case, it would challenge the mutual love and harmony between the lovers in the Song as some commentators have perceived it in the past.[39]

If the two night scenes are dreams or involve dreamlike visions, it is notable that sometimes dreams appear otherworldly, with foreign images that are beyond the dreamer's earthly experience. In this sense, dreams may become prophetic, saying something new to the dreamer about events that will take place in the future. Dreams can also be psychological or symbolic. The images and events that transpire in dreams reflect how the dreamer feels about a particular situation in life. Going out into the city at night to seek her beloved appears to be absurd in reality. Yet, as Munro remarks, "In a dream, anything is possible."[40] It is likely that the woman's dreamlike occurrences of going out into the city at night to seek her beloved are actually a reflection of her psychological state. Rather than describing actual events, the two night scenes express how she feels about her beloved. In his absence, her soul goes out. She searches for him, but he is nowhere to be found (Song 5:6). Sarah Zhang explicates this state of emotion: "The felt intensity of these lines springs from thematic and generic ambiguities that bathe poetic meaning in the nocturnal night."[41] In such emotional state, time is not linear or logical. Rather, time appears in many forms, with the past, present, and future all fused together. What remains significant are the impressions or feelings that the contents of the night scenes leave with the dreamer, and how these impressions and feelings reflect her psychological state and emotional being in his absence.

Desire and time. In the woman's dreamlike visions, seeking and not finding her beloved reveals her desire to be in his presence. The dream describes her intense feelings for him with vivid imagery. When he

---

[38]Harding, "'I Sought Him,'" 49, 53.

[39]Trible, for example, thinks that the relationship of the lovers in the Song reflects mutuality, equality, and harmony. There is no male dominance or female subordination. The female character is independent, fully equal with the man. See Phyllis Trible, *God and the Rhetoric of Sexuality* (Philadelphia: Fortress, 1978), 161.

[40]Munro, *Spikenard and Saffron*, 120.

[41]Sarah Zhang, *I, You, and the Word God: Finding Meaning in the Song of Songs*, Siphrut 20 (Winona Lake, IN: Eisenbrauns, 2016), 88.

"extended his hand from the hole, her inward part growled upon it."[42]
"Inward part" (מֵעֶה) refers to belly, stomach, intestines, and womb. For the
Hebrews it was the seat of emotion.[43] Paul Griffiths states that "belly" has
three levels of meanings: (1) womb, (2) a place of digestion, and (3) the most
receptive part of the body. He thinks that when her belly trembles because
of him, she is fully engaged and profoundly responsive to him.[44] The word
"growled" (הָמָה) describes a dog's growl or sexual desire.[45]

Davis points out that "growl" appears also in the book of Jeremiah, where
it describes God's feelings for Ephraim:[46]

> "Is Ephraim My dear son?
> Is he a delightful child?
> Indeed, as often as I have spoken against him,
> I certainly *still* remember him;
> Therefore My heart yearns for him;
> I will surely have mercy on him," declares the LORD. (Jer 31:20)

Here "my heart" in Hebrew is "my inward part" or "my womb"; and "yearn"
is the exact same word for "growl" in Song of Songs 5:4. The parallel between God's feelings for Ephraim and the woman's feelings for her beloved
is evident in the author's deliberate choice of words. The woman desires the
man, and at the hint of his movement toward her, her inward part growls.
She responds fully to his attempt to connect. However, when she opens to

---

[42]The "hand" refers either to the man's hand or his private parts. In the Ugaritic poem "The Birth
of the Gracious God" or "Shahar and Shalim," El's "hand" refers to his private parts. See Simon
B. Parker, ed., *Ugaritic Narrative Poetry*, Writings from the Ancient World (Atlanta: Scholars
Press, 1997), 210. The "hole" can refer to the opening of the door or be a euphemism referring
to a woman's private parts. The poet may purposely be using these erotic words to suggest a
double entendre.

[43]*BDB* 588.

[44]Paul J. Griffiths, *Song of Songs*, Brazos Theological Commentary on the Bible (Grand Rapids, MI:
Brazos, 2011), 121.

[45]*BDB*, 242. Other English translations:
"My beloved extended his hand through the opening, and my feelings were aroused for him"
(NASB).
"My lover thrust his hand through the latch-opening; my heart began to pound for him" (NIV).
"My beloved thrust his hand into the opening, and my inmost being yearned for him" (NRSV).
"My beloved put his hand to the latch, and my heart was thrilled within me" (ESV).
"My beloved took his hand off the latch, and my heart was stirred for him" (JPS).

[46]Ellen F. Davis, *Proverbs, Ecclesiastes, and the Song of Songs*, Westminster Bible Companion
(Louisville, KY: Westminster John Knox, 2000), 277.

her beloved, he turns away and passes. "Passed" (עָבָר), on the one hand, reflects that he left quickly. On the other hand, it reveals her painful disappointment that he has vanished before her eyes.

The following verse records her response: "My soul went out" (Song 5:6). Elsewhere, the expression "my soul went out" describes the state of death (Gen 35:18; see Ps 146:4). In his absence, she feels as if she is at the brink of death. In Linafelt's words, "What is evoked in this passage (Song 5:2-8) is the genuine loss of self entailed in the experience of *eros*."[47] In her lover's absence, her sense of self as expressed by "my inward part" and "my soul" is no longer attached to her. Zhang captures this intense loss of self beautifully: "Her life force is emptied, and the color of all that is in her world is drained. Yet her soul is not poured into nothingness; rather, it follows the immense pull of the soul of her soul and the core of her enjoyment—the other who had intrigued her and is withdrawn."[48]

His absence indeed makes her heart grow even fonder of his presence. The woman's desire to be intimate, to be in his presence, lingers from the beginning to the end of the Song. The poem begins with her desire to be kissed by her beloved and the desire to be with him while he pastures his flock (Song 1:2, 7). At the end of the Song, she desires for him to come back to her (Song 8:14).[49] The open-endedness of the last verse portrays the continuation of this longing, which refuses to end. Through form-critical analysis, Assis discerns five units in the Song. In each of these units, there are combinations of poems of adoration, poems of yearning, and descriptive poems, all ending with an invitation to a rendezvous.[50] The desire to see each other, then, becomes the connecting thread to each unit. Its repetition not only expresses the main characters' actions, but also reflects their emotional development. In his absence, her desire to be with him heightens.

---

[47]Linafelt, "Arithmetic of Eros," 257. Linafelt construes the whole poem of Song 5:2-8 as a self-expression of the woman's inner world, framed by the "I" inclusio from Song 5:2, 8.

[48]Zhang, *I, You, and the Word "God,"* 89.

[49]Song 8:14 says, "Come, my beloved, and be like a gazelle or a young stag upon the mountains of spices." "Come" may also be translated as "flee." Elsewhere in the Song, "spices" refer to the woman's body (Song 4:10, 14). "Mountains of spices" may be paralleled with "mountains of Bether" (Song 2:17), also symbolizing the woman's body.

[50]Assis, *Flashes of Fire*, 19-20.

Carey Walsh sees desire for the lover as a central theme in the Song of
Songs. She speaks of the difference between desire and fantasy or dreams.
The latter is unrealistic, with little or no chance of being enjoyed within the
parameter of one's life. A desire, by contrast, is feasible in historical time but
missing in the here and now of life. This absence of the desired object then
fuels desire in the same way that absence inflames desire, just like selective
memory. She further clarifies that "desire is memory of an experienced
pleasure."[51] Desire, then, arises from pleasant memories from the past.[52] We
can see desire as a memory of past pleasure that leads to present yearning
to enliven that past pleasure in the foreseeable future. Dreamlike nocturnal
visions, along with desires, contribute to the blurring of time in the Song.
But then desire clearly points toward anticipation for the future, whether in
dreams or in reality.

Much ink has been spilled trying to account for the fact that the one
seeking in both dreams is the female character, and the male character in
both dreams acts as an absent lover.[53] However, the male lover also looks
for her, as in Song of Songs 2:8-14. When we take the theme of seeking and
finding a step further, yearning for the presence of the significant other is
characteristic of the human experience. One of the ultimate examples of
this significant other is God. Nobel Prize–winning poet Octavio Paz declares: "Eroticism is first and foremost a thirst for otherness. And the supernatural is the supreme otherness."[54] The Bible contains examples of
people longing to see God, thirsting for his presence, and wanting to hear
his voice. The psalmist cries out,

As the deer pants for the water brooks,
So my soul pants for You, O God. (Ps 42:1)

My tears have been my food day and night,

---

[51]Carey Ellen Walsh, *Exquisite Desire: Religion, the Erotic, and the Song of Songs* (Minneapolis:
Fortress, 2000), 22.
[52]Walsh distinguishes erotica from pornography by noting that erotica is about wanting and
pornography is about power. Erotica uses allusions and metaphors to slow down the reader and
make them feel, whereas pornography moves quickly and with little or no prelude to the act of
intercourse. See Walsh, *Exquisite Desire*, 44-45.
[53]Harding, for example, considers this seeking and finding theme to be a gender issue. The woman
desires, but the man is elusive. Harding, "'I Sought Him,'" 49; see also Linafelt, "Arithmetic of
Eros," 244-58.
[54]Octavio Paz, *The Double Flame: Love and Eroticism* (San Diego: A Harvest Book, 1993), 15.

> While *they* say to me all day long,
> "Where is your God?" (Ps 42:3)

> My soul thirsts for You, my flesh yearns for You,
> In a dry and weary land where there is no water. (Ps 63:1)

> [Job in his suffering pleads to God,] Oh that I knew where I might find Him,
> That I might come to his seat! (Job 23:3)

Whether the absence is of God or of a person, that absence exacerbates the desire for the other's presence. Sometimes it exacerbates it to the point of feeling sick, as with the woman's agony. Her agony in her lover's absence also demonstrates that he is present in her consciousness at all times, even on countless nights. The core of her whole being is consumed with him, whether in his presence or absence.

Paz recounts an ancient Greek love poem in the *Symposium* that describes how once upon a time there were three sexes: male, female, and androgynous. In order to subjugate them, Zeus decided to split each in two. Ever since then, the separate halves wander around searching for their complementary pieces. Through this myth, Paz conveys that we are all incomplete beings and that our desire for love is a "perpetual thirst for completion."[55] This story resonates with the creation account of Adam and Eve. Adam is created first, and then Eve is taken from his rib. "Rib" (צֵלָע) in Hebrew is also the word for "side," suggesting they were originally one.[56] On a spiritual level, this incompleteness suggests that we are all incomplete without God and that we are all constantly seeking that significant someone or something we believe will complete us. I wonder whether this is what Eve is attempting to do when she desires "to be like God" in Genesis 3.

Just like the woman who has trouble finding her beloved in her night scenes, especially in Song of Songs 5, there are times when believers have trouble finding God, albeit while seeking him earnestly and continuously. While one of God's attributes is omnipresence, God can choose when to be present and when to be absent, as evident in the experiences of the psalmists and in Job. This absence, however, is perceived from the perspective of believers. Just like the beloved's absence is perceived from the perspective

---

[55]Paz, *Double Flame*, 43.
[56]Linafelt also makes this point. See "Arithmetic of Eros," 246.

of the woman in her inner psyche, it is possible that divine absence is also perceived by believers in their psyche as a subjective feeling.

The poet of the Song of Songs does not reveal why the male beloved has turned away and gone. Perhaps he had tried to reach out to the woman and been rejected. Perhaps he had an emergency to attend to. Perhaps he did not understand what was going on with the inner world of the woman and misunderstood her intentions or her coyness. In the same way, when God chooses to be absent in believers' lives at times, the reasons may elude us. Connecting the beloved's absence to divine absence, Walsh sums it up in this way: "A Song about delayed or frustrated desire in the form of two lovers is a necessary and adroit adaptation to a subtle theological condition. It captures in part what it has felt like to live without the felt presence of their beloved God."[57] Whether divine absence is psychological or logical, it is nevertheless a felt reality in the experience of many believers. The desire to be in the presence of God, however, expresses a sense of hope toward its possible realization in the future. The question is, Are we seeking God with intensity like the woman in the Song seeking for her beloved in his absence?

Landscapes and time. In the Song of Songs, the lovers move effortlessly through a poetic landscape of vineyards, gardens, palaces, houses, rocky cliffs, wilderness, and Lebanon. This suggests that they inhabit a world of bliss, without the weariness of the world impinging on them.[58] Indeed, the lovers live in a world of their own, a world that is delightful and enchanting. They appear to be teleporting from one place to another without any hint of transition or difficulty. Interpreting this from the perspective of cartography and phantasmagoria, Christopher Meredith suggests that spaces in the Song merge and meld together. For instance, the lovers' bedroom becomes a royal chamber (Song 1:4), then a forest abode with a green daybed (Song 1:16), and then a shady bower surrounded by wild forest (Song 2:3), followed by a fruity house erected in the vineyards (Song 2:4). It becomes a latticed house (Song 2:9) and a city surrounded by watchmen (Song 3:1-5). Then the bed becomes a royal palanquin, and the watchmen are

---

[57] Walsh, *Exquisite Desire*, 97.
[58] Exum, *Song of Songs*, 5-6.

transformed into a circle of royal guards (Song 3:6-8). The blurring of contexts and imagery creates both continuity and discontinuity through the poet's reimagining.[59] Meredith sees the literary landscape appearing in the Song as a map, but he also acknowledges the fusing as well as the confusing of the spatiality both in the Song and in the reading process.[60] As one reads the Song, the fluidity of its landscapes becomes a part of the Song's "beauty and enigma."[61]

Elaine James's study on the landscapes of the Song of Songs also demonstrates a close connection between human beings and their natural environments and how these physical sites shape the desire and experience of the lovers in the Song. For instance, a place evokes yearning, memory, and knowledge, as in one's mother's house, which forms intimate memory of childhood experiences and nurture (Song 8:1-2), or the woman brings the man to the vineyard to see whether the pomegranates are in bloom (Song 7:12).[62]

Since time and space are inseparable, time shifts, skips, and merges abruptly from one scene to another in the same way that spaces do throughout the Song. Sometimes, time in the Song is reminiscent of the staccato in a musical note. The player jumps quickly from one note to another without smooth transitions. The mood is often jubilant and joyful. Elsewhere, time in the Song appears to be overlapping and converging, and it is difficult to tell "from time to time." This fluid pattern is the same with the landscapes in the Song. James sees the landscapes in the Song as fragmentary, episodic, and evocative, and so difficult to be "put on a map."[63] Although time in the Song of Songs does not advance linearly, the portrayal of the time for nature and the time for love do merge. Nature and the lovers

---

[59]Meredith, *Journeys in the Songscape*, 51-54. Another must-read monograph on the spatiality of the Song is by Yvonne Sophie Thöne, *Liebe zwischen Stadt und Feld: Raum und Geschlecht im Hohelied* (Berlin: LIT Verlag, 2012). She identifies the gender of each place in the Song and categorizes them into groups.

[60]Meredith, *Journeys in the Songscape*, 2-3. Regarding the relationship between text and the reader, Meredith thinks that the Song confuses this relationship by turning love into poetry. There is no narration, only discourse between two lovers (*Journeys in the Songscape*, 60-62).

[61]I borrow this phrase from Francis Landy, "Beauty and the Enigma: An Inquiry into Some Interrelated Episodes in the Song of Songs," *JSOT* 17 (1980): 55-106.

[62]Elaine T. James, *Landscapes of the Song of Songs: Poetry and Place* (New York: Oxford University Press, 2017), 16.

[63]James, *Landscapes of the Song of Songs*, 16.

are in a harmonious relationship that reflects an Edenic delight. Just as the man in the Garden of Eden delighted in the presence of the woman whom God created, and just as the man lived harmoniously with nature in the garden, so too do the lovers in the Song.[64]

When the woman praises her beloved, "Ah you are beautiful, my beloved, Oh pleasant! Oh our couch is luxuriant. The beams of our house are cedars, cypresses the rafters" (Song 1:16-17), they are outdoors in the countryside, in the midst of nature. The lovers make the grass their couch, and the cedars and cypresses become the supporting beams of their imaginary house. She further describes herself as "the rose of Sharon and the lily of the valleys" (Song 2:1), and her beloved to her is like "an apple tree among the trees of the forest" (Song 2:3). While various spatial images meld together, the woman and man also merge into various spatial contents. She is a lady with dark skin, a vineyard, a rose of Sharon, a locked garden, and a fountain spring, whereas he is a shepherd, a king, an apple tree, and a reverent statue.[65] In the Song's enchanting world, these two characters constantly shape-shift as the Song progresses.[66] This "blending and shifting" of the landscape in the Song is precisely its poetic strategy to create a rich world for meditation on love.[67] Falk identifies the countryside as one of the four basic contexts appearing in the Song where love dialogues and many love monologues take place.[68] Not only do the lovers use nature as their setting for love, but they also use nature imageries as their love language. He is to her a "pouch of myrrh" (Song 1:13) and "a cluster of henna blossoms in the vineyard of Engedi" (Song 1:14); and she is to him as "honey and milk" (Song 4:11) and "a well of a water of life" (Song 4:15).

---

[64]See chap. 4.

[65]In Song 5:11-15, the woman describes the man with language descriptive of a statute, "His head, gold, refined gold, his locks of hair, black like the raven. His eyes, like doves, upon (by) the streams of water, washing in milk and sitting upon the rim. His cheeks, like beds of spices, towers of perfume, his lips, lilies dripping flowing myrrh. His hands, rods of gold, are being filled with yellow jasper; his belly, an ivory plate, being covered (with) sapphires. His legs are like pillars of alabaster, being founded upon a pedestal of refined gold. His appearance is like the Lebanon, being chosen like cedars."

[66]There is one *Star Trek* episode in which a character named Shapeshifter transforms into anyone and anything, including another known person, a stranger, a table, and even water.

[67]James, *Landscapes of the Song of Songs*, 16.

[68]The other three include the remote landscape, interior environments (houses, halls, rooms) and city streets. Falk, *Love Lyrics from the Bible*, 139.

He reciprocates her love and invites her to journey from Lebanon, from the summit of Amana, Senir, and Hermon (Song 4:8). Then he lavishes her with images of fragrance, choice fruit, and a garden spring to laud her supreme value:

> How beautiful, your love, my sister, (my) bride! How better is your love than wine! the fragrance of your oil than all the spices
>
> Flowing honey dripped (from) your lips, (my) bride; honey and milk under your tongue; the fragrance of your robes like Lebanon.
>
> A garden locked, my sister, (my) bride; a fountain locked, a spring sealed;
>
> Your shoots, orchard (parks) of pomegranates, with choice fruit, henna with nards.
>
> Nard and saffron, reed and cinnamon, with all the trees of frankincense, myrrh and aloes, with all the top (heads, choice) spices.
>
> A spring, gardens (garden spring), a well of water of life, and the ones flowing from Lebanon. (Song 4:10-15)[69]

Then she conjures the north and the south winds to blow into her garden, and she invites him to come to her garden: "Arise! North (wind) and come! South (wind), breathe (into) my garden, let its spices spread. Let my beloved come to my garden, and let him eat its choice fruit" (Song 4:16). Nature and the lovers in the Song appear to be on the same timeline regardless of the fluidity of space. This harmony between the lovers and nature contrasts with the scenes described in the book of Ecclesiastes.[70] In Ecclesiastes, although nature and humans share the same earthly space, they are not equal in the realm of time. While nature is ongoing, cyclical, and repetitive, the lives of human beings are finite and exist only in the here and now. The sun rises, sets, and returns to where it rises. The wind blows in circular motions.

---

[69]The word translated "fountain" here is literally "stone heap." NASB: "A rock garden."

[70]Qoheleth's unique view of creation is unlike any other book in the Bible. In the opening poem of the book (Eccles 1:2-11), nature goes into perpetual cycle, as if it is a world without past and future, a world without telos and purpose. The concluding poem (Eccles 12:1-7) describes the death of the cosmos in that as the cosmos darkens, so does human life. See William P. Brown, *The Seven Pillars of Creation: The Bible, Science, and the Ecology of Wonder* (Oxford: Oxford University Press, 2010), 177-84. Seow also interprets this last poem as the dying of the cosmos. See Choon Leong Seow, "Qoheleth's Eschatological Poem," *JBL* 118 (Summer 1999): 209-34. Others, however, see this poem as either allegorical or literal regarding the death of an individual. See Michael V. Fox, *Ecclesiastes*, JPS Bible Commentary (Philadelphia: Jewish Publication Society, 2004), 76.

The rivers flow into the sea and to the place where the rivers flow, where they flow again (Eccles 1:5-7). In these verses, Qoheleth frequently uses verbs of going (הָלַךְ, Eccles 1:6 [2×], Eccles 1:7 [3×]), coming (בּוֹא, Eccles 1:5), circling (סָבַב, Eccles 1:6 [3×]), and returning (שׁוּב, Eccles 1:6-7) to express the repetitive phenomenon of nature. A strong dichotomy, then, is established between the sun, wind, and rivers' cyclical movements through time; and the linear, noncyclical, and ephemeral life of individual human lives.[71] This relationship with nature is not evident in the Song of Songs.

In the Song, the time for nature to blossom and the time for love to blossom are in a parallel relationship. In Ecclesiastes, time renders human existence transitory. In the Song, time lingers as long as love remains. In the Song, time does not move unilaterally. Rather, time moves forward, backward, and then forward again with the lovers. This is reflected in the opening and the closing of the Song. The Song opens without a definite beginning point of time. The reader does not know when the woman's passionate cry, "Let him kiss me with the kisses of his mouth," happens or where it takes place. When we reach the ending of the Song, the woman calls her beloved to come to the mountains of spices. Again, the question of time escapes the reader. Although there is a destination named, the precise meaning of this location remains cryptic.[72]

There is, however, another aspect of nature that is not always charming, enthralling, or agreeing with the lovers: nature's wild, dangerous, and mysterious side. As Falk points out, there are forces that attempt to quench love, forces such as the wilderness, the dens of lions, the mountains of leopards, the seas, and the rivers. These elements of nature suggest overwhelming forces that evoke anxiety, mystery, and a sense of urgency. Unlike the countryside, where love occurs, this environment does not support intimacy.[73] As the springtime and the countryside are receptive to the blossoming love,

---

[71]Mette Bundvad, *Time in the Book of Ecclesiastes* (Oxford: Oxford University Press, 2015), 59. If we see the whole human race in terms of generations, then it is cyclical, as in "a generation goes and a generation comes" (Eccles 1:4). However, if we see human beings as individuals, then each human life progresses linearly through time without returning. Here *goes* and *comes* are the same verbs used to describe the going and coming of elements in nature. The earth, however, stands still and does not progress in a circular motion like the sun, the wind, and the rivers.

[72]Meredith, *Journeys in the Songscape*, 58n96.

[73]Falk, *Love Lyrics from the Bible*, 140.

so too there are forces of nature that challenge this harmony. The opposition from within the nature imageries echoes the motif of seeking and not finding, as well as the absence of the beloved. It appears that lovers unite when their space and time merge, and lovers separate when their space and time are split apart. If the space and time between God and human are not within the same realm, then the experience of divine absence is to be expected rather than a peculiar one-time phenomenon.

In summary, time in the Song of Songs is mingled with a plethora of sensual experiences as well as nature. It is not linear or rational. First, there is a paradoxical relationship between the timelessness of love and the blurring of time in the Song's world. On the one hand, love is forever in process. On the other hand, there are moments of pause where there is a temporary break of time in love, such as when the woman gives the adjuration not to arouse love until it desires. Second, spring is the season for love. However, it remains uncertain whether this spring-love season describes a poetic reality or a fantasy in the mind of the woman. Do the descriptions of the spring-love season recall a past experience, or are they happening at the present time as the poet speaks? Third, the two night scenes of the woman reflect a conflation of past and present, as well as the real world and the dreamlike world. The contents of the dreamlike visions, especially the one in Song of Songs 5:2-8, reveal that her time and his time fail to converge, resulting in her seeking and not finding him. The theme of "seeking and not finding" constitutes a common religious experience, which suggests that there is (will be) a time when he (God) cannot be found. Fourth, the fluidity in the Song's landscapes matches its fluidity of time. As landscapes shift from one to another, so does time. The forever fluidity of time and space in the Song of Songs reflects its genre of lyric poetry, on the one hand, and invites the reader to experience its mood and contemplate the elusive presence of the divine, on the other hand.

Although nature and the lovers are on the same timeline, there is an aspect of nature that poses a danger and a threat to their relationship, which parallels the theme of *eros*: she loves him, but there are times when she seeks him and cannot find him. The difference between his and her space and time informs us that there is also a vast difference between the time and space of human and divine. While God is omnipresent and unbound in time, humans are not. Humans think of their experiences in the boundaries of time. Therefore, our sometimes-felt divine absence captures a common religious experience across time and culture. Rather than a factual truth or an objective phenomenon, this felt divine absence reflects emotional, subjective, and psychological sentiments on the part of the believer in search of the ultimate Other—God, in his seeming absence. Thinking of time in the Song reinforces the notion of a God who is free of human's conceptualization of time and space. Any experience of divine absence may only remain in the realm of human beings' subjective consciousness. Thus, a meditation on time in Song of Songs compels us to contemplate on the divide between human and God and to cope with the reality that "I sought him but I did not find him."

THE BOOK OF ESTHER

The genre of the book of Esther has been construed by different scholars as having various forms, such as comedy, carnivalesque literature, burlesque, satire, a diaspora story, a festive etiology and a festive lection, a short story, a historical novella, and a testimony.[74] Some scholars tie the book together

---

[74]On Esther as carnivalesque literature, see Andre LaCocque, *Esther Regina: A Bakhtinian Reading* (Evanston, IL: Northwestern University Press, 2008), 4-5. Burlesque is defined as "an artistic composition . . . that, for the sake of laughter, vulgarizes lofty material or treats ordinary material with mock dignity." See Adele Berlin, *Esther: The Traditional Hebrew Text with the New JPS Translation*, JPS Bible Commentary (Philadelphia: Jewish Publication Society, 2001), xix. In the book of Esther, the Persian Empire and the Persian court are the objects of vulgarization. See also Kenneth Craig, *Reading Esther: A Case for the Literary Carnivalesque* (Louisville, KY: Westminster John Knox, 1995). On Esther as a diaspora story, see W. Lee Humphrey, "A Life-Style for Diaspora: A Study of the Tales of Esther and Daniel," *JBL* 92 (1977): 211-23; Michael V. Fox, *Character and Ideology in the Book of Esther* (Grand Rapids, MI: Eerdmans, 1991), 233-34. Kah-Jin Kuan has addressed the issue of diaspora by using his own experience as a doubly diasporic person to read the book of Esther. See Jeffrey Kah-Jin Kuan, "Diasporic Reading of a Diasporic Text: Identity Politics and Race Relations and the Book of Esther," in *Interpreting Beyond Borders*, ed. Fernando F. Segovia (Sheffield: Sheffield Academic Press, 2000), 161-73. The diasporic nature of Esther has been challenged by Stern. On the one hand, Stern acknowledges Esther as a diasporic story, but, on the other hand, argues that the intended audience of Esther was Hebrew, using Esther as a satire for the Jewish diaspora. See Elsie R. Stern, "Esther and the Politics of Diaspora," *Jewish Quarterly Review* 100, no. 1 (Winter 2010): 25-53. On Esther as a short story, see for example, Frederic William Bush, *Ruth, Esther*, WBC 9 (Dallas: Word Books, 1996), 309. Moore sees the book as a historical novel. Carey A. Moore, *Esther*, AB (Garden City, NY: Doubleday, 1971), lii. Levenson sees it as a historical novella within the Persian Empire. See Jon Douglas Levenson, *Esther: A Commentary*, OTL (Louisville, KY: Westminster John Knox, 1997),

with wisdom books.[75] Berlin asserts that the comic aspects of the book are not incidental but are the very essence of the book. She then narrows it down to a more specific genre within the general idea of comedy: farce with a carnival-like festival. She quotes M. H. Abrams's definition of farce: "Farce is a type of comedy designed to provoke the audience to simple, hearty laughter. To do so, it employs highly exaggerated or caricatured character types, puts them into impossible and ludicrous situations, and makes free use of broad verbal humor and physical horseplay."[76] In ancient Persian, Greek, and Roman cultures, carnival was characterized by drinking, costumes, carousing, masks and disguises, parades, and mock battles, even violence. This genre fits the contents of Esther, where secret identities, gross indulgence, sexual innuendoes, madness, and violence all appear concurrently.[77] Broadly speaking, the book of Esther is a prose narrative as opposed to poetry. As a prose narrative, the book is subject to literary conventions that befit its genre, including plot and character development, point of view, repetition, type scenes, and dialogues. The Song of Songs is full of dialogue without narration, contrary to the book of Esther, which relies more on narration and less on speech.[78] Their literary differences could not be more conspicuous.

As prose narrative, the way the book of Esther perceives time is fundamentally different from that of the Song of Songs. In Esther, there is a clear sense of general movements from past, to present, and to future. Many scholars have noted the presence of coincidence in the story. A coincidence is essentially the unexpected meeting of the two realms of time. Another significant aspect of time in Esther is that it perceives "right timing" as an opportunity—an opportune time. The rise of Esther from a Jewish orphan

---

25. Wills identifies Esther as an evolvement from court legend to a novella. See Lawrence M. Wills, *The Jew in the Court of the Foreign King: Ancient Jewish Court Legends*, Harvard Dissertations in Religion 26 (Minneapolis: Fortress, 1990), 153. On Esther as a testimony, see introduction in Berlin, *Esther*, xvi-xxii. Reid proposes seeing the book as a testimony of Esther and/or her people. Debra Reid, *Esther*, Tyndale Old Testament Commentaries 13 (Downers Grove, IL: IVP Academic, 2008), 20.

[75]Shemaryahu Talmon, "'Wisdom' in the Book of Esther," *VT* 13, no. 4 (1963): 426.

[76]M. H. Abrams, *A Glossary of Literary Terms*, 4th ed. (New York: Holt, Rinehart and Winston, 1981), 26.

[77]Berlin, *Esther*, xix, xxii.

[78]A fact noted by Levenson: "The book relies more on narration and less on quoted speech than most comparable biblical material" (*Esther*, 1).

to the Persian queen is for "such a time as this" to save her own (Esther 4:14). When her time in the narrative and the historical time of the narrative meet, opportunity is the result. In other words, when the time of her narrated story and the circumstances of the narrated history meet, it creates the opportunity for history making. Although the narrative recounts past events retrospectively, its institution of the Purim festival anticipates future remembrance of this past story. In this respect, documenting and ritualizing the past is for the purpose of the future, while the future is already rooted in the past. Throughout the narrative, the name of God is absent. This unsettling absence connects the book to the absence of the beloved sometimes in the Song of Songs, although for different purposes.

Time and story. Speaking about narratives, Sternberg remarks that narrative has to fall into a timeline: "For a narrative to make sense as narrative, it must make chronological sense."[79] In *Time and Narrative*, Paul Ricoeur distinguishes between two conceptions of time. The first one is cosmological time: time is experienced as linear succession from birth to death.[80] The other is phenomenological time: time is experienced in terms of the past, present, and future. These two conceptions of time, according to Ricoeur, are not mutually exclusive but are both aspects of human experience.[81] In Esther, both conceptions of time appear. The linear progression of time is indicated by the specific naming of time sequence, such as "after these things" or "on the seventh day." Esther 1:1-9 demonstrates cosmological time, while the rest of the chapter describes phenomenological time within cosmological time.

The story opens with a vague temporal statement: "And it was, in the days of Ahasuerus, he, Ahasuerus, was the one who reigned from India to as far as Cush, 127 provinces" (Esther 1:1). The narrator does not provide a specific year of the reign of Ahasuerus, such as 450 BCE. He simply notes that it was "in the days of," as if to place the reign of this king into a distant past without a definite time, which implies the book's historicity is of a lesser concern for

---

[79]Meir Sternberg, "Time and Space in Biblical (Hi)story Telling: The Grand Chronology," in *The Book and the Text: The Bible and Literary Theory*, ed. Regina M. Schwartz (Oxford: Basil Blackwell, 1990), 81.
[80]Sternberg calls this "the world time" ("Time and Space," 88).
[81]Ricoeur, *Time and Narrative*, 112-13.

the narrator. Berlin understands the phrase as the opening of a folktale, reminiscent of the standard opening phrase "Once upon a time."[82] This opening sets the narrative in the distant past. The next verse follows by saying "in those days," another deliberately vague reference to time. The statement "In those days when King Ahasuerus sat upon the throne of his kingdom which was in Shushan the fortress" (Esther 1:2) directs readers' focus to this past event rather than the exact time of its occurrence. Then the third verse zeroes in on the specificity of time: "In the third year of his reign, he made a banquet to all his officials and his servants" (Esther 1:3). "In the third year" gives the reader a specific time frame as a reference point to develop the plot of the story. Everything that happens afterward starts from here, the third year of Ahasuerus's reign.

Then Esther 1:4 states: "When he displayed richness, glory of his kingdom and honor, beauty of his greatness many days—180 days." The reference "180 days" indicates the duration of time and the length of the event. Although it is expressed in a short phrase, "180 days," the banquet lasts six months, a long period in actual physical time! Here we see a disparity between the narration time and the narrated time. The narration time is the time required to tell or to read the narrative, whereas the narrated time is the literary time, the subjective time.[83] The mention of the length of time indicates that this fact is important to the narrator and to the reader. As a farce, a banquet that lasts 180 days is meant to convey exaggeration and impossibility, and to suggest a sense of humor or irony.

Then Esther 1:5 continues, "And when these days were full, the king made for all the people, the ones who can be found in Shushan the fortress, from old as far as young, a banquet, seven days in court of the garden of the house of the king." "And when these days were full" refers back to the previous banquet that lasted 180 days. The seven-day banquet for all the people of Shushan forms a stark contrast to the 180-day banquet for all the officials and servants of the court, both in scope and in duration. This also reveals where the interests of the king and the narrator lie.

---

[82]Berlin, *Esther*, 5.
[83]Shimon Bar-Efrat, *Narrative Art in the Bible* (London: T&T Clark, 1989), 142. Sternberg calls this "the text time" ("Time and Space," 88).

Then in the next verses, the narrator provides a detailed account regarding the exquisite palace decorations and drinking vessels (Esther 1:5-8). These details temporarily suspend the narrated time, while external actual time continues to progress.[84] Then comes Esther 1:9: "Also, Vashti the Queen made a banquet (for the) women, (in the) house of the kingdom which belongs to King Ahasuerus." Here "also" (גַּם) can mean "in addition," "immediately following," or "even," providing emphasis or introducing a climax.[85] It is uncertain whether Vashti holds the banquet of her own at the same time that King Ahasuerus has his banquets or holds it immediately after his banquets have concluded. The Hebrew subject-verb reversal "Vashti made" (וַשְׁתִּי הַמַּלְכָּה עָשְׂתָה) suggests that what is happening here is not a usual practice.[86] It is possible that Vashti made a banquet simultaneously with the king's banquet. But since the duration of her banquet is not given by the narrator, the focus of this verse is not so much on the time frame as it is on the event itself. It is interesting to note that while Vashti asserts her authority as a queen by holding a banquet for the women, the location of the banquet is within the royal house belonging to King Ahasuerus. Her power, though remarkable, is still limited. So far, the narrative proceeds linearly from the first banquet to the third banquet in chronological order within cosmological time.

Then the narrator recounts a momentous event on the seventh day of the banquet, on which the subsequent course of the story hinges. The seventh day is singled out by the narrator both by its proportion to the rest of the chapter and by its way of narrating through direct speech. As the story unfolds, we learn that Vashti refused to appear before the king. A dreadful fear explodes in outrageous proportion as one person's defiance extends to the whole Persian Empire, followed by a decree deposing Queen Vashti from her royal position, which will be given to another better than her (Esther 1:12-19). Vashti's refusal and its consequence are documented in the form of a dialogue between the eunuch Memucan and the king (Esther

---

[84]Bar-Efrat observes that time stops in two situations: when the narrator gives an explanation, evaluation, or conclusion, and when depictions are given within the narrative. Esther 1:5-8 falls under second category (Bar-Efrat, *Narrative Art in the Bible*, 146).

[85]*BDB* 169.

[86]In Hebrew syntax, the normal word order is verb-subject. When the subject comes before the verb, it usually indicates an emphasis or a somewhat unusual circumstance.

1:15-20). The dialogue portrays the event as if it were happening in the present moment right in front of the reader. The duration of the dialogue does not take long in actual time, but its details are meticulously narrated. The dialogue slows down the story for the purpose of presenting the issue at hand in a more entertaining manner, while giving the reader a close-up view of the scene.

Through Memucan's speech to the king, the narrator exposes the seemingly hilarious and inconceivable fear of the Persians in that all the women in the Persian Empire will show contempt to their husbands by modeling themselves according to Queen Vashti's example. The narrator also discloses the extreme measures the Persians take to avert this fear, which are to depose the queen and to find a replacement for her. While the king displayed his riches and honor for 180 days, as indicated in one verse (Esther 1:4), the events that transpired on the seventh day are described in thirteen verses (Esther 1:10-22), with six verses conveyed through direct speech (Esther 1:15-20). Therefore, this "seventh day" marks a phenomenological time in a cosmological time, where it signifies a specific day that happened in the past, while it is also occurring in the present as the reader reads it. At the same time, the effect of the edict that all wives should honor their husbands carries forward to the future. Without this fateful day, Esther the queen, the enmity between Haman and Mordecai, the annihilation of the Jewish race, and the institution of Purim would cease to exist. There would be no book of Esther, period. The seventh day is the key to the whole story. Although the seventh day happened in the past, its effects linger into the future.

Later, "after these things," when the anger of the king has subsided, the king has a flashback of this past incident. He remembers Vashti, what she had done, and what had been decreed against her (Esther 2:1). "Remembered" implies an idea that occurred in the past but is now resurfacing in the present. Thus, memories are vehicles through which the past enters the character's present. The events on the seventh day of the banquet occurred in the past, were expressed in the present through the dialogue between the king and Memucan, and were remembered in the future by the king. This seventh day is understood in the past, present, and future, and then back to the past through the king's memory, while its effects continue into the future.

While the past enters characters' present through memories, the future enters characters' present through expectations and intentions.[87] As the story advances to the aftermath of the king's remembrance of Vashti, it points to the future. Sensing that the king might be missing his queen, his servants suggest that he seek a new queen in place of the deposed Vashti. The king gladly agrees. Then the narrator inserts a side story to introduce new characters, Mordecai and Esther (Esther 2:5-7). This insertion stops narrated time momentarily, taking the reader into the past of the new characters to get acquainted with them, then resuming the previous narration. Here we see that the narrator is omniscient. Although the story progresses along a linear timeline, his knowledge about the story's past as well as its future is immense. He has the freedom to insert new information, either to introduce the past or to prepare for the future, at his own discretion. He also paces the story line with a different rhythm. Sometimes the narration is slow, other times it is fast.

This insertion starts a new strand of narration, which will then join the main strand of the narrative in Esther 2:8.

> A man of the Jews was in Shushan the fortress, and his name was Mordecai, son of Jair, son of Shimei, son of Kish, a man of Benjamin.
>
> Who had been exiled from Jerusalem, with the exile, who had been exiled with Jeconiah, King of Judah, who had been caused to be exiled by Nebuchadnezzar, King of Babylon.
>
> He was the foster father of Esther. That Esther, was the daughter of his uncle, because she had no father and mother. The girl was beautiful of form and good appearance, and when her father and her mother died, Mordecai took her for him as (his) daughter. (Esther 2:5-7)

The way the narrator introduces Mordecai is by presenting his ancestry through a series of "son of" clauses, followed by a succession of relative clauses, "who" (אֲשֶׁר). The word *exile* appears four times in Esther 2:6 to highlight where Mordecai came from. He is the descendant of an exile. The sequence of "son of" and "who had been" places Mordecai's lineage in the

---

[87]Bar-Efrat, *Narrative Art in the Bible*, 184.

historical past with the names of his fathers and the names of kings of Judah and Babylon. Then the narrative introduces Esther through her relationship with Mordecai. Mordecai is her foster father. He took her as his daughter when her parents died. Their relationship and the deaths of Esther's father and mother apparently happened in the past, long before the three banquets in Esther 1. Here we see that narrative in the Bible does not always progress linearly from past, to present, to future. Sometimes it goes back in time to introduce the past of new characters and to explain how their past connects with the present. Another insertion within this insertion is the disjunctive clause "The girl was beautiful of form and good appearance" (Esther 2:7).[88] This phrase temporarily brings the story to a halt by giving the reader an aside, a crucial piece of information for what is about to be unraveled in the story.

From the perspective of narrated time, Esther 2:8 resumes right after Esther 2:4. "When the word of the king and his law was heard" (Esther 2:8) immediately follows "The word was good in the eyes of the king and he did so" (Esther 2:4), therefore continuing the same narrative strand. The story then progresses linearly to recount how Esther is among the women who are brought to Shushan, how she found favor with Hegai (the guardian of the women), and how the king provides for her sustenance as well as for the maids (Esther 2:8-9). Then the narrator steps into narrated time once again and inserts another aside to the reader: "Esther did not tell her people and her kindred about her Jewish identity because Mordecai commanded her not to tell" (Esther 2:10). Although this piece of information does not move time forward, it is vital for the development of the plot. If Esther had made her people known at that time, then Haman would not have dared to annihilate the entire Jewish race. There would have been no story to tell. The beginning of Esther 2:11 provides another time marker: "On every single day, Mordecai would walk to and fro before the courtyard of the house of women in order to know the peace of Esther and what was done to her."[89]

---

[88]The *waw* before "the girl" is a disjunctive *waw*. It stops the narrative by introducing supplemental or circumstantial information to the reader. Robert Chisholm Jr., *From Exegesis to Exposition: A Practical Guide to Using Biblical Hebrew* (Grand Rapids, MI: Baker Books, 1998), 124-25.

[89]The verb "do" is in *niphal* stem (נַעֲשֶׂה בָּהּ). It can be understood as either passive voice or reflexive. If passive, then it means "what was done to her." If reflexive, it means "how she was doing with herself."

The temporal marker "on every single day" literally is "on every day and day" (וּבְכָל־יוֹם וָיוֹם), referring to the days when Esther was taken into the royal house. This temporal marker reflects the caring and perhaps anxious disposition of Mordecai in regard to the well-being of Esther.

The next paragraph (Esther 2:12-14) provides background information concerning how the maidens are treated with cosmetics and spices within the harem to prepare them to go into the king's palace, and how they are chosen by the king. In other words, it explains how things work in choosing a queen. As for the time frame, it seems to coincide with Mordecai's daily walk in front of the harem.

> When the turn for each girl arrived to go in to King Ahasuerus from the end of twelve months, according to the law of the women, for thus the days were filled with beautifying them: six months with oil of myrrh and six months with spices and with cosmetics of the women.
>
> And in this (way), the girl came to the king. All which she said will be given to her to go with her from the house of the women to the house of the king.
>
> In the evening she would go, and in the morning she would return to the house of the women the second time, to the hand of Shaashgaz, the eunuch of the king, the guardian of concubines. She would not go again to the king unless the king delighted in her and she was called by name. (Esther 2:12-14)[90]

Again we see several temporal markers in these verses. "The turn," "evening," "morning," and "the second time" indicate the intervals of time. Each maiden lives her life within the boundaries of these intervals. The phrases "twelve months" and "six months" specify the duration of time. It takes one year for each maiden to prepare herself before she can be seen by the king. Again, the length of time is a form of exaggeration, which is one aspect of this genre. One year is long enough to include many stories and dramas regarding these women. Some of them may want to compete with one another, or some may feel jealous toward Esther. Some may look forward to being the queen of Persia, while others may fear being in that position. Some may even consider escaping from the palace or sneaking out to see the outside world. Esther may have had a hard time adjusting to life in the palace. When

---

[90]The word translated "beautifying" literally means rubbing or using cosmetics.

other maidens ask her about her ancestry, what does she tell them? What does she think about herself, a Jew, sleeping with a Gentile king? Does she have any friends among these maidens, or is she always alone? Apparently, these possible scenarios and questions did not concern the narrator. In his sweeping faction, the narrator reveals only the necessary facts about the situation while veiling the characters' thoughts and emotions from the reader. Up to this point, the narrator has not given Mordecai and Esther an opportunity to speak a word. They remain "flat characters."[91] Although the period of beautification of the maidens lasts for a whole year, it is recorded in sweeping fashion in three verses. This sped-up version of three verses sets the stage for the coming paragraph: Esther's turn has arrived.[92]

The details concerning her one-night stand with the king are not given. Only that "she found favor with all who saw her" and that "she was taken to the house of the king" are provided. Here the narrator reveals another specific time frame with month and year, suggesting this time frame is significant to the story. Its significance is compounded with elaborations: in the tenth month, the month of Tebeth, and in the seventh year of the king's reign. Earlier, a specific time frame was given in Esther 1: "In the third year of his reign, he made a banquet for all his officials and his servants" (Esther 1:3). From the king's first banquet for his officials and from the time when Queen Vashti was deposed to the time when Esther was chosen as her replacement has taken four years! Of these four years, one year was devoted to the beautification of the maidens. An uncertain time period had passed for each maiden to go see the king. Since the reader does not know the exact number of the maidens, it is impossible to guess. Supposing there were 365 maidens, it would take a whole year for all the girls to finish their turns, given that the king would see one girl per night. Then there is a time lapse between Esther 1 and Esther 2. "After these things" (Esther 2:1) can refer to a short or a relatively long period of time. If this time period is short, then the time for each maiden to see the king must be long. If this time period is long, it would suggest that it takes a long time for the anger of the king to subside and that the time period for the maidens to be seen would be

---

[91] Berlin, *Poetics and Interpretation*, 11.

[92] "Arrive" (נגע) is also the word for "touch," "strike," or "hit" (2 Sam 5:8; Jon 3:6; Ezra 3:1; Neh 7:73; Eccles 12:1; Song 2:12; Ezek 7:12).

correspondingly shorter. Ambiguities abound even in these specific time frames.

The narrative then progresses linearly and swiftly, describing how Esther wins the favor of the king so that he throws her a banquet, and how Esther conceals her ancestry in obedience to Mordecai (Esther 2:17-20). Then the narrator introduces another strand of story with a distinct time marker: "in those days."

> In those days, Mordecai was sitting by the gate of the king, Bigthan and Teresh, two of the eunuchs of the king, the ones who guarded the threshold, were angry. And they sought to send hand against the King Ahasuerus.
>
> The matter was known to Mordecai and he told Esther the queen and Esther spoke to the king in the name Mordecai.
>
> The matter was sought and found. Then the two of them were hanged upon a tree and it was recorded in the book of the words of the days in the presence of the king. (Esther 2:21-23)

"In those days" (בַּיָּמִים הָהֵם), followed by a *waw* disjunctive with subject-verb reversal "Mordecai was sitting (וּמָרְדֳּכַי יֹשֵׁב)," aims to draw attention to the subsequent event.[93] "In those days" echoes "in those days" in Esther 1:2. This temporal phrase refers to none other than the event in the previous context above, namely, Esther 2:19, "When the virgins were gathered the second time, Mordecai was sitting by the gate of the king." Esther 2:21 continues with "Mordecai was sitting by the gate of the king," thus connecting the two accounts. The event centers on how Mordecai uncovers a plot of two eunuchs attempting to harm the king. As a result, the two perpetrators are hanged on a tree, and the matter is documented in the book of chronicles in the presence of the king. A reward for Mordecai, however, is not mentioned. The significance of this event will not be revealed until Esther 6, when the king has insomnia and asks for this exact book to be read. It is then that he inquires about the reward for Mordecai (Esther 6:1-9).

Consequently, that night sealed the fate of both Mordecai and the Jewish people, as well as of Haman and his sons. Thus far, the narrative moves forward from past toward future, anticipating future events while bringing

---

[93]The Hebrew reverses the normal word order, verb-subject (was sitting Mordecai). Reversing it (Mordecai was sitting) to show emphasis. This is not apparent in the English translation.

different strands of the story to form a coherent whole. The narrator sometimes slows down the story by inserting necessary background information, such as direct speech and asides. Other times, the narrator speeds up the story by simply stating the facts and the time that has elapsed. For the narrator and the reader, the pace of time in the story is largely subjective and psychological.

Likewise, our lived time is also subjective and psychological, whereas objective time passes evenly and predictably. For example, when we experience happy and pleasant events, time flies by quickly. When we go through mundane or boring chores, time seems to slow down. Fast and slow are subjective perceptions. We all know that every human being has twenty-four hours in each day without discrimination. If time tells stories, all human beings, whether real or fictional, live within the boundaries of time. This is in contrast to God, who resides outside time and who is not bound by time. For him, is there such a thing as "time running out" or "time being too slow"? No. When considering human time and divine time, Moses says: "For a thousand years in Your sight Are like yesterday when it passes by, Or as a watch in the night" (Ps 90:4). Peter also remarks how Jesus sees time: "With the Lord one day is like a thousand years, and a thousand years like one day" (2 Pet 3:8).

Therefore, our time and God's time exist in two different dimensions. As we live our lives through time, we move linearly from present toward the future while reliving the past through memories. God, on the other hand, exists in an entirely different dimension of time. God and human beings are on two different timelines. It follows that our felt experience of divine absence happens only in the human understanding of time. This reflects a psychological perception of time. This is why we say things such as, "God should have intervened at the time when I needed him the most" or "Why is God not there when I call on him?" or "Why is he silent when the situation demands his action?" In an objective view of time, God is omnipresent. He is always there, whether we perceive his presence or not. What we perceive as God's absence does not negate his presence, because his absence only occurs in humanity's psychological perception of time. Time is indeed a human concern.

The merging of times. When speaking about such synchronic narratives in the Bible, Shimon Bar-Efrat makes four observations: (1) Time is not reversed even when the narrative splits up into two parallel story lines. Time passes by only once. (2) The transitions from one story line to another are usually smooth and natural. (3) The two story lines are connected by runners acting as messengers who relay information from one place to another. (4) In certain cases, there is synchronization between events within the two story lines of the plot.[94] All four elements appear in Esther. What Bar-Efrat does not mention is that when two story lines meet, their two timelines also merge. The merging of timelines, on the one hand, draws attention to the major points of the narrative. On the other hand, it indicates crucial timing that alters the course of the story. In the book of Esther, the merging of time appears at several places, and this calls for theological reflection: Could such merging of time suggest mere coincidence without any supernatural forces or divine providence underlying it?

Scholars such as Arndt Meinhold consider Esther 4:14 to be the heart of the entire book.[95] Previously in the narrative, one story line is about the hostility between Haman and Mordecai. This storyline morphs into Haman's plot to kill all the Jews, which then results in a royal edict to execute that plot. Another timeline is about Esther, how she becomes the queen of Persia, and how she hears about the edict to annihilate all the Jews. The two storylines become joined by messengers who convey the messages of the edict, thus merging the two story lines on the same narrated timeline.[96] Then the narrative slows down by presenting the moment at which the two timelines intersect through direct speech (Esther 4:11, 13-16). Esther gives Mordecai two reasons to express her hesitation to go to the king: First, there is a Persian law that penalizes with death anyone who appears before the kind unsummoned, that is, without the king extending his golden scepter. Second, Esther is currently out of favor with the king since she has not been summoned by the king for thirty days (Esther 4:11-12). Then Mordecai utters the following words to Esther, which change not only her life but the

[94]Bar-Efrat, *Narrative Art in the Bible,* 173.
[95]See, for example, Meinhold, who considers Esther 4:14 as the center (*mitte*) of the book. Arndt Meinhold, "Zu Aufbau und Mitte des Estherbuches," *VT* 33 (1983): 435-45.
[96]The messengers include Esther's maids and her eunuchs, particularly Hathach (Esther 4:4-12).

history of the entire Jewish people: "Do not think that your soul would escape the house of the king from all the Jews. Because if you remain silent at this time, relief and deliverance will arise for the Jews from another place, but you and the house of your father will perish, and who knows if for a time as this, you arrive as royalty?" (Esther 4:13-14).[97]

By this time, Esther has been married to King Ahasuerus for five years. She became the queen of Persia in the seventh year of his reign (Esther 2:16), and it was in the twelfth year of the king's reign that the edict was issued (Esther 3:7). The narrator provides these specific time frames, suggesting that they are significant to the story. Having been married for five years, Esther has become more or less accustomed to life in the Persian court, as well as life with the Persian king. Throughout this time, she has concealed her ethnic roots as a Jew because Mordecai told her to do so (Esther 2:10, 20). Esther has been silent about her ethnicity for all this time, but now Mordecai is telling her that it is time to reveal her Jewish identity. If she continues to remain silent, relief and deliverance for the Jews will arise from another place, he says, and she and her father's house will perish. What Mordecai sees in the current circumstances is the merging of times: the timing of the edict to annihilate the Jews and the timing for Esther to become the queen of Persia. For him, the intersecting of the two timelines at this particular moment in time cannot be accidental; it must be providential. Mordecai's rhetoric hinges on two other key words: "another place" and "who knows."

What exactly does Mordecai mean when he says "another place"? Some would say the word *place* is a veiled allusion to God, which then affirms God's providential care for his people.[98] Fox states that in Rabbinic Hebrew, "the place" is used as a designation of God.[99] If this is so, it would have to read "another God," which would not make sense in the context of the

---

[97]The word translated "silence" appears twice (infinitive absolute + imperfect) for emphasis. "Arise" is literally "stand." Previously the word translated "arrive" appears in Esther 2:15, "when the turn of Esther to come to the king arrived."

[98]See for example, Moore, *Esther*, 50, 52. Moore cites the Alpha Text (an earlier text than MT Esther), Josephus, and 1–2 Targums to demonstrate that their reading of seeing "another place" is a veiled allusion to God. Moore also indicates that "mercy" is a veiled allusion to God in 1 Maccabees 16:3 and "the kingdom of heaven" in Matthew is a surrogate for "the kingdom of God."

[99]Fox, *Character and Ideology,* 63.

narrative.[100] Did Mordecai intend to enlist help from another deity if Esther remained silent? He could have named God openly here without resorting to such an ambiguous phrase. Since Mordecai is speaking directly to Esther as a potential human agent, "another place" can also refer to help from another source, possibly another human source. Therefore, he is most likely suggesting a human agent other than Esther. Clines thinks that "another place" may refer to Jews holding high offices in the realm, or that the Jews themselves would rise up in revolt, or even that the Persians who are sympathizers of the Jews would come to their aid.[101] These proposals, though possible, remain mere speculation.[102]

Still, the phrase "another place" can also refer to an unspecified or uncertain source, just as the expression "somewhere else" conveys. Mordecai is saying that if Esther refuses to act, relief and deliverance will arise from somewhere else. Mordecai might not know exactly what that "somewhere else" is. What he does know is that help will come regardless of Esther's action. "Another place" has a range of meanings, with an allusion to God on the one end of the spectrum and an uncertain source of help on the other end. This ambiguity places the burden of interpretation on the reader.

In the Hebrew Bible, the expression "who knows" (מִי יוֹדֵעַ) appears ten times (2 Sam 12:22; Ps 90:11; Prov 24:22; Eccles 2:19; 3:21; 6:12; 8:1; Joel 2:14; Jon 3:9; Esther 4:14). Sometimes it refers to a skeptical stance toward something perplexing or unknown, as the following verses demonstrate:

---

[100]P. R. Ackroyd, "Two Hebrew Notes," *Annual of the Swedish Theological Institute* 5 (1966–1967): 83.

[101]David J. A. Clines, *The Esther Scroll: The Story of the Story*, JSOTSup 30 (Sheffield: University of Sheffield Press, 1984), 42-43.

[102]Wiebe proposes another solution. He sees the clause "relief and deliverance will arise to the Jews from another place" as a rhetorical clause with a rhetorical question, which anticipates a negative answer, thus, "Will relief and deliverance arise from another place?" The answer is no, implying that Esther was the only source of the deliverance for the Jews. Although there is no interrogative particle in the Hebrew text of this verse, Wiebe argues that in Biblical Hebrew, interrogative clauses need not be introduced by an interrogative particle at all. When the context allows it, one can construe the clause as an interrogative clause. He cites examples from Job, Malachi, and Mishnaic Hebrew to strengthen this argument. See John M. Wiebe, "Esther 4:14: 'Will Relief and Deliverance Arise for the Jews from Another Place?,'" *CBQ* 53 (1991): 413-15. Wiebe's proposal, though attractive and probable, requires the reader to supply an interrogative meaning. How can one be sure whether this clause should be understood as a rhetorical question?

And who knows whether he will be a wise man or a fool? Yet he will have control over all the fruit of my labor for which I have labored by acting wisely under the sun. This too is vanity. (Eccles 2:19)

Who knows that the breath of man ascends upward and the breath of the beast descends downward to the earth? (Eccles 3:21)

For who knows what is good for a man during *his* lifetime, *during* the few years of his futile life? He will spend them like a shadow. For who can tell a man what will be after him under the sun? (Eccles 6:12)

Sometimes, "who knows" serves as a rhetorical question, probing for more. The answer to the question is usually negative, as the following examples show:

Who is like the wise man and who knows the interpretation of a matter? A man's wisdom illumines him and causes his stern face to beam. (Eccles 8:1)

Who knows the strength of your anger, and your fury like your fear? (Ps 90:11)[103]

For their calamity will rise suddenly, And who knows the ruin *that comes* from both of them? (Prov 24:22)

Other times, "who knows" expresses a hopeful aspiration. The following three texts all appear in the context of fasting.

He said, "While the child was *still* alive, I fasted and wept; for I said, 'Who knows, the LORD may be gracious to me, that the child may live.'" (2 Sam 12:22)

Who knows whether He will *not* turn and relent
And leave a blessing behind Him,
Even a grain offering and a drink offering
For the LORD your God? (Joel 2:14)

Who knows, God may turn and relent and withdraw His burning anger so that we will not perish. (Jon 3:9)

When the child with Bathsheba becomes sick, David inquires of God and fasts while lying on the ground all night (2 Sam 12:16). In Joel, God urges the Israelites to return to him with all their heart with fasting, weeping, and

---

[103]My translation. ESV and NRSV translate this as "who considers," and NASB translates "who understands?"

mourning (Joel 2:12). The people of Nineveh, upon hearing Jonah's message, respond by fasting and putting on sackcloth, from the greatest to the least of them (Jon 3:5). All three contexts involve threats of destruction, repentance, and besieging God for mercy through fasting, contrition, and mourning. It is in this context of "who knows" that Esther fits in: "Who knows if for a time as this, you arrive as royalty?!" (Esther 4:14). Mordecai recognizes the merging of two realms of time as an indicator of none other than divine providence. "Who knows" expresses a hopeful possibility that the reason and purpose for Esther's attained royalty is for such a time as this. The intersecting of time cannot be a mere coincidence or accident. We don't know how confident Mordecai is when he speaks these words. Nevertheless, it is a positive affirmation of the high possibility that Esther's royalty serves a greater purpose in such a time as this.

Mordecai perceives the unusual merging of times as an opportunity for Esther to take action. "Time" in the phrase "for a time as this" connotes opportunity. It has a similar meaning in "for time and chance overtake them all" (Eccles 9:11). The winner does not always win, nor does the battle always belong to the warriors. The wise may not have bread to eat, and the man of ability does not always get what he wants, precisely because there is the factor of time and chance. I take "time and chance" here as a hendiadys, that is, two different words expressing a singular meaning, as opposed to two different words expressing two different ideas. Clines goes a step further and says that "to the religious believer 'chance' is a name for God."[104] The merging of times indicates a rare opportunity or chance for Esther to save her people. Mordecai's rhetoric aims to urge Esther to act on this very opportunity as a Jew who has become the queen of Persia.

Fox proposes another possible reading in his discussion of the phrase "who knows." He argues that the author uses the phrase to carefully create and maintain a sense of uncertainty. The author was uncertain of God's involvement in history, and so he left the phrase "who knows" in the mouth of Mordecai to convey the idea of indeterminacy. The faith of the author is not so much in God per se, but in the confidence that the Jewish people will survive despite divine absence. Therefore, Fox construes the phrase "who

---

[104]Clines, *Esther Scroll*, 153.

knows" as expressing an attitude both of faith and doubt. What the author teaches is a theology of possibility.[105] These statements sound sensible and even persuasive when we take the book of Esther out of the canonical context. Sometimes a biblical book adheres to the theologies of other books in the canon. Other times a biblical book may stray from its canonical context and assert its own theology as a part of the whole of biblical the-ology.[106] We do not know which of these is the case for the book of Esther.[107] Here lies a theological ambiguity, and here the burden of proof falls on the shoulder of the reader: to choose faith or doubt, divine providence or inde-terminacy, or somewhere in between.

The merging of times occurs again in the episode of the king's insomnia and its aftermath. Before this episode, the narrative has recounted the story through two synchronized timelines: the timeline of Esther and the timeline of Haman. In Esther's timeline, she responds to Mordecai's plea, deter-mined to go to the king unsummoned, asks the Jews in Shushan to fast for her, goes to appear before the king on the third day, and then invites both the king and Haman to her banquet (Esther 4:15–5:8). In Haman's timeline, he successfully persuades the king to issue the edict to annihilate all the Jews in Shushan. He also responds to Esther's invitation and gladly comes to her banquet. On the same day of the banquet (בַּיּוֹם הַהוּא), Haman be-comes enraged after he sees Mordecai refusing to bow down to him. He then goes home, consults his wife and friends, and then sets up a gallows for Mordecai, intending to hang him (Esther 5:4-14).

It is this time that the narrative specifically refers to as "on that night" (בַּלַּיְלָה הַהוּא), namely, on the exact night Haman makes gallows for Mordecai. Retrospectively, this is also the exact day on which Haman sees the unbowed Mordecai, and the exact day on which both the king and Haman go to Esther's banquet. This day also happens to be on the third day after

---

[105]Fox, *Character and Ideology*, 246-47.

[106]For example, the book of Ecclesiastes is very different from the rest of the biblical canon on the idea of creation, life, and death. The book of Job also is very different from the theology of Proverbs in how it portrays the concepts of retribution and divine justice.

[107]Crenshaw distinguishes two broad uses of the expression "who knows." One is an "open door," where human beings can still hope for divine intervention on behalf of themselves. The other is a "closed door," where the expression "who knows" is equal to "no one knows." See James L. Crenshaw, "The Expression *MÎ YÔDĒA'* In the Hebrew Bible," *VT* 26 (1986): 279-85.

the Jews in Shushan fasted for Esther (Esther 5:1). Therefore, the phrase "on that night" in Esther 6:1 refers to the evening of the third day. If the king had not extended his golden scepter to Esther on that day, history would have to have been rewritten. If Haman had not seen Mordecai unbowed on that day, he would not have become so enraged as to build gallows for him. It was on this fateful night that the king had insomnia and gave orders to have the chronicles read to him.

The two timelines merge on this very night; but there is yet a third timeline occurring earlier in the story about the heroic deed of Mordecai in Esther 2:21-23, in which he uncovered a plot against the king but was unrewarded. It occurred "in those days" (בַּיָּמִים הָהֵם, Esther 2:21), referring to the days when Esther became queen, which was five years ago (Esther 2:16; 3:7). Hence, three strands of timeline merge at the same exact moment on the night when sleep deserts the king. What are the odds that everything would come together like this? The suggestion of divine providence underlying here is not outrageous.

The Hebrew expression "sleep deserted the king," or "sleep fled from the king" (Esther 6:1) sounds comical, as if sleep were personified and she were playing "hide and seek" with the king.[108] We do not know whether it was customary for the king to have sleepless nights, or whether this night was unusual. The Septuagint inserts the book's reference to God in this insomnia: "On that night, the Lord took away the sleep from the king," attributing the king's sleeplessness to an act of God (Esther 6:1 LXX). In the Septuagint, the insomnia, then, is not habitual but intentional. On a night like this, the king could have done many other things, such as have a snack or take a short walk. But of all the options he could have chosen, he chose to have the chronicles read to him, as if listening to something mundane would help put him to sleep. Even then, his reader could have read about another of the numerous events that occurred during his reign. It so happens that he reads the account about Mordecai's saving act, which in turn arouses the king's curiosity regarding the reward due to Mordecai.

---

[108]The word "deserted" (נָדַד) also means "retreat," "depart," "stray," "wander," and "flutter." A similar expression, "sleep fled from my eyes," appears in Gen 31:40. See *BDB* 622.

This late-night reading episode takes the narrative retrospectively back five years in the past, when Esther had just became queen, and in those days when Mordecai saved the king. Here we see how the effect of past events carries on to the present and how the present returns to the past in order to correct the wrongs of the past. The narrative flows from the past to the present, and then back again to the past, through the king's and the reader's memories, recalling the past events of the narrative. The timeline of when Mordecai saves the king continues advancing forward until it meets the timeline of the king's insomnia.

However, there is more.

Just when the servants have replied to the king, and before anything has been done to Mordecai, the text takes us to the next verse: "And the king said, 'Who is in the courtyard?' And Haman came to the outer courtyard of the house of the king to speak to the king about hanging Mordecai on the tree which was prepared for him" (Esther 6:4). Earlier that day, Haman had consulted with his wife and friends, and later built gallows for Mordecai. His wife and friends advised him to go see the king in the morning and ask him to hang Mordecai from the gallows (Esther 5:14), and Haman shows up in the middle of the night at the same time the king has just asked about Mordecai's reward.[109] In that split second, another merging of times occurs. The subsequent story diverges into two strands, one on Haman's inner thoughts regarding his honor, and the other on the king's intention to honor Mordecai. As it turns out, the king adopts Haman's own idea to honor a person favored by the king and confers it on Mordecai instead—a reversal of fortunes.

There is yet another merging of times in Esther. During Esther's second banquet, she reveals to the king that Haman is the person responsible for the edict to annihilate her people. Then Haman becomes terrified, and the king goes out from the banquet as if he does not know how to respond to this astonishing news. Just as the king returns to the banquet house after his rage subsides, he sees Haman falling onto the couch on which Esther is sitting (Esther 7:7-8). The scene could not be more comical, and the timing

---

[109]In Hebrew, there is disjunctive *waw* with a subject-verb reversal (וְהָמָן בָּא), indicating that the timing of Haman's coming is peculiar.

could not be more remarkable. Upon hearing the news that Haman is the enemy of the Jews, the king might have not known what to do with him. But now, seeing Haman falling on the couch while Esther is sitting on it prompts the king's decision to hang him. "To subdue the queen with me in the house" implies that Haman's action ranged from inappropriate touching to a violent assault.[110]

So far, we have seen that the merging of times occurs when the crisis of the annihilation of the Jews and the timing for Esther to attain royalty intersect, when sleep deserts the king and he reads the chronicles regarding Mordecai's saving act just as Haman appears before the king, and when the king returns to the banquet house to find Haman falling on the couch that Esther is sitting on. Are these merging of times simply accidental or coincidental? If they are coincidence, then why do they all tilt in favor of the Jews? Sternberg observes, "Whether the characters meet or miss each other, whether the happenings manage or just fail to coincide and intersect, depends on precision work that is not so much the narrator's as God's."[111] The merging of times and the split-second timing suggest something supernatural is at work in favor of the Jews. Sternberg takes this as pointing to God's omnipotence. The narrator of the book could have used words of chance, such as "happen" (קרה), to connote the idea of coincidence; that he refrains from using such words suggests that the miraculous timing unfolded in Esther is not coincidental.[112] Therefore, coincidence opens up the possibility for faith. One can take it as an accidental or chance event without any supernatural influence, or one can see it as an indication of divine providence behind human affairs. The theological ambiguity inherited in the text offers an opportunity for the reader to decide where faith should lie or not take faith into consideration at all. As such, reading Esther then becomes an interpretive journey for the reader.

---

[110]Hebrew כָּבַשׁ means "subdue," "dominate," "bring into bondage," "tread down" (Gen 1:28). In late Biblical Hebrew, it means "force," as in Esther 7:8. See *BDB* 461.

[111]Sternberg, "Time and Space," 107-8.

[112]Such as in Ruth 2:3, "She happened to come to the portion of the field belonging to Boaz." Melton construes the understanding of *miqreh* as a retrospective point of view where human beings perceive human experience as fate with the incomprehensible ways of God while acknowledging the presence of God behind the chance events. See Brittany N. Melton, "Miqreh in Retrospect: An Illumination of Miqreh," in *Megilloth Studies: The Shape of Contemporary Scholarship*, ed. Brad Embry (Sheffield: Sheffield Phoenix, 2016), 30-42.

Purim as past, present, future. In his book *About Time*, Mark Currie sees narrative not just as a retrospective but also as an anticipation of the future. For him, narrative is both anticipation and retrospection, because it structures the present as the object of a future memory just as much as it records the past.[113] Currie's theory applies not only to narrative in general but specifically to the ritual element in narrative. In the book of Esther, the installation of Purim as a national festival climaxes the story. The word *Purim* appears five times in Esther 9, the penultimate chapter of the book, stressing its significance to the design of the story (Esther 9:26, 28, 29, 31, 32). It is no wonder that scholars see the establishment of Purim as the ultimate purpose of the book.[114]

As a national holiday, Purim commemorates the deliverance of the Jews through Esther's heroism. The author recorded the dates for its observance precisely. First, the opening of the chapter prepares the reader for the date of Purim: "In the twelfth month, that is, the month of Adar, on the thirteenth day," which was also the date set for the Jews to kill their enemies (Esther 9:1). Then the dates for observing the Purim festival are set for two groups of Jews. The Jews who are located within the rest of the king's provinces kill their enemies on the thirteenth day of the twelfth month, and then rest and feast on the fourteenth day (Esther 9:16-17, 19). The Jews in Shushan kill their enemies on two days, on both the thirteenth and the fourteenth, and then rest and feast on the fifteenth day (Esther 9:18). This careful reiteration of the dates fixes the incident on a specific timeline in history. Yet, Purim is not just a festival to be celebrated in the past. It was instituted as a perpetual holiday by which to remember the past. The past is relived through memory, and the annual reenacting and reciting of the story of Esther in the form of a festival is the means to accomplish that.

Certainly, Purim happened in the past. However, its institution as a national holiday carries the past to the present and into the future. Purim serves as another example of Ricoeur's phenomenological time, where time is perceived as past, present, and future. At the same time, this past event is remembered in the present through its annual enactment and is anticipated in the future through future reenactments. Purim is for every generation of

---

[113]Mark Currie, *About Time: Narrative, Fiction, and the Philosophy of Time* (Edinburgh: University of Edinburgh Press, 2007), 11.
[114]See, e.g., Berlin, *Esther*, xv.

the Jewish people and for their descendants for all eternity. In Esther, time progresses linearly for the most part. Yet, with the institution of Purim, time keeps progressing beyond the text. The narrated time ends with the last verse of the book, but the effect of Purim extends far beyond the story itself. Therefore, phenomenological time occurs within the linear cosmological time, or world time. As Exum claims, if resistance to closure is how the ending of the Song of Songs immortalizes love, then the institution of Purim in the book of Esther immortalizes Esther's heroism to save the Jews.

In sum, the narrator tells the story through time, progressing linearly, and at times gives a different emphasis to various events. For 180 days of the banquet, the narrator simply mentions them. But on the seventh day of the banquet, he elaborates on events with tremendous detail, demonstrating where his interest lies. Sometimes the narrator writes retrospectively to introduce new characters. Other times he anticipates future events through the intentions and expectations of the characters. Specific dates are given to stress their significance to the plot. The pace of time allotted to diverse strands of the story reflects how the narrator conceives them. Therefore, the narrator's perception of events through time is largely subjective and psychological, and this forms a stark contrast to God's time, where time is always objective and constant.

The many examples of the merging of time in the story hint at divine providence, but they may also raise the possibility for doubt. "Could all be mere coincidence without God's help?" The burden of interpretation then falls on the shoulders of the reader to decide whether coincidences are adequate evidence to suggest God's presence, or whether they are merely accidental. Last but not least, the institution of the Purim festival carries the past into the present and future. The narrative ends, but the memory of the story of Esther lives on. Therefore, cosmological and phenomenological time coexist in the book of Esther.

TIME: IN THE ABSENCE OF GOD

The Song of Songs and Esther both share the theology of absence, albeit in different degrees. In the Song, the woman seeks her beloved in his absence. In Esther, the reader seeks the presence of God in his literary absence. The seeking-and-finding theme the woman experiences in the Song parallels the seeking-and-finding theme in Esther. Only, in the latter case, it is the readers who become the subject of seeking and finding. In both scrolls, the absence of the male lover and of God makes the desire to seek their presence grow more intensely.

How do we understand the nature and the work of God in these two books without explicit reference to his name? In the Song, we learn that in the absence of the beloved, the woman's desire for him grows even fonder. Absence does not negate the beloved's presence altogether. On the contrary, it enhances the desire of the woman to be in his presence. She seeks him in other ways, such as through two nocturnal, dreamlike visions, through her friends, and through the guards of the city. The elusiveness of the beloved in the Song creates an analogy for believers to conceive their relationship with God. Sometimes God is visible, as in the time of the exodus or when he called the prophets Isaiah, Jeremiah, and Ezekiel. Other times he is hidden and cannot be found, as in Job's experience (Job 23:3, 8-9). That does not mean that this state of being absent is permanent. The implication is that there are times and there will be times when we feel that God is absent because God does not subject himself to human beings' timeline, nor does he live inside the confinement of human time. In that sense, God's presence is elusive from humanity's experience. In Esther, we observe that God's presence is not overt. Because of his covert presence in the text, some readers attempt to seek his presence even more, whether through unlikely coincidences in the timing of events or through dramatic reversals of fate. Still others attempt to read Esther without reading God into it. As a result, God becomes an absent character in the book, which leads to the possibility of his noninvolvement in the book of Esther.

Given these approaches to time in Song of Songs and Esther, how should we think about how to live our lives in the absence of God?

First, the absence of God is a real, lived human experience. To deny its existence is to deny reality and reduce God to one-dimensionality. When catastrophe happens and innocent people die, we ask, "Where is God?" When injustice occurs, we ask, "Why didn't God intervene?" Sometimes when we pray, we do not feel any divine assurance or sense of direction, and we wonder, "God, are you there?" The experience of the absence of God captures a part of humanity's encounter with the divine, and this absence should be acknowledged rather than suppressed.

Second, human time and God's time are not in the same realm. Human beings are timebound. Human beings live within the boundary of twenty-four hours a day, whereas God is not bound by this constraint. God is eternal and timeless. There are times when human time and God's time do not meet, and so people do not or cannot feel his presence. Ingolf Dalferth perceives presence in terms of humanity's understanding of time. Presence is a term of humanity's scheme of orientation in time. Therefore, we relate to events and things and people in the temporal frame of past, present, and future, whereas God relates to human beings in his divine mode of time, which may obscure our comprehension.[115] In this sense, the absence of God remains incomprehensive to human consciousness.

Third, the experience of divine absence is a subjective, psychological feeling on the part of believers and is not an objective truth. There is the reality of the psychological time, in which it feels as if time is moving slowly in the absence of the significant other. As Fretheim observes, "Issues relating to divine absence are best understood within the context of varying intensifications of presence."[116] The feeling of divine absence is the loss of the intensity of presence in one's experience. Therefore, the absence of God is a perceived absence rather than a structural absence.

Fourth, when God is silent, it does not mean that he is also absent. God can be present in silence. Sometimes he is simply there, watching human beings taking action. Other times he may choose not to "show up" so as to give us more options to do whatever it takes to avert the situation, or simply is there listening to the cry of his people and giving them space to reflect, as in the book of Lamentations.

Fifth, in the absence of God, we can discern his presence through nature, erotic love, mysterious timing, coincidences, and miraculous circumstances. God can be present in his absence.

---

[115]Ingolf U. Dalferth, "God, Time, and Orientation: 'Presence' and 'Absence' in Religious and Everyday Discourse," in *The Presence and Absence of God: Claremont Studies in the Philosophy of Religion, Conference 2008*, ed. Ingolf U. Dalferth, RPT 42 (Tübingen: Mohr Siebeck, 2009), 1-20, esp. 7-9.

[116]Terence E. Fretheim, *The Suffering of God: An Old Testament Perspective*, Overtures to Biblical Theology 14 (Philadelphia: Fortress, 1984), 65.

The way time works in human lives is similar to the way time works in the story of Esther. As time progresses chronologically, our lives move forward in the human timeline. We remember the past through memory. We commemorate specific holidays to remember the past here in the present and to continue remembering it into the future. We anticipate the future through expectations and desires. Sometimes we experience the mysterious merging of times. These are the times when we think beyond the visible to the invisible God. We are like characters in a story, living in the present and not knowing what the future will hold. This uncertainty is especially pertinent in the wake of a global pandemic such as COVID-19. We do not know how long the pandemic will last or whether it will return or whether other forms of calamity will befall us in the future.

Most of us do not experience the God of the exodus in our daily lives. The God of the exodus is visible and vocal, and appears through fire and smoke. But the God of our lives is mostly silent, and many times we may feel as if he is unresponsive to our calls. Although there is no reference to the name of God in the book of Esther, many readers cannot help but think of him as present. In the same vein, in the absence of the beloved, the woman in the Song of Songs desires even more intensely than in his presence to be with him. She so longs to be with him that she is sick with longing. From the beginning to the ending of the Song, she continues to yearn for him. She oscillates between her lover's presence and absence. She repetitively yearns for him, but this results in "I sought him but I did not find him" (Song 3:1; 5:6, 8). Still, she continues her seeking.

In the absence of God, it is easy to feel distressed, lost, and even sick; but we have a choice to continue hoping and yearning for his presence in the foreseeable future, just as the woman in the Song who keeps on seeking. In the end, she declares in her beloved's absence, "Come, my beloved" (Song 8:14). We too have the choice to believe that divine presence and deliverance will come eventually, because the alternative is to deny God's presence and goodness, which is a far more miserable option for the human soul. In times when we feel as if God is absent, an opportunity opens up before us for hope and faith.

4

TEMPLE

GARDEN *and* PALACE

And her wilderness He will make like Eden,
And her desert like the garden of the Lord.

ISAIAH 51:3

IF TIME EXPRESSES THE INVISIBLE REALITY of human existence, as we saw in the previous chapter, then space becomes its natural counterpart. The question "Where is God?" reflects not only a temporal question but also a spatial notion that the God of the Bible is a God who is known and sought in life in this world.[1]

The garden-temple is the shared theme between the Song of Songs and the book of Esther. In the Song of Songs, the temple theme is by possible allusion, whereas in Esther, it is by imagination and association. Temple stands at the center of Jewish theology. Marvin Sweeney asserts that the temple is the holy center of the Hebrew canon and of God's creation. In fact, the three division of the Hebrew canon testify to this significance of the temple theology.[2] Song of Songs and Esther imagine space in different but

---

[1]Joel S. Burnett, *Where Is God? Divine Absence in the Hebrew Bible* (Minneapolis: Fortress, 2010), 5.

[2]Marvin A. Sweeney, "Foundations for a Jewish Theology of the Hebrew Bible: Prophets in Dialogue," in *Jewish Bible Theology: Perspectives and Case Studies*, ed. Isaac Kalimi (Winona Lake, IN: Eisenbrauns, 2012), 161-86, esp. 166-73.

complementary ways. The dominant image of space in the Song is the garden. This garden is reminiscent of an Edenic garden-temple, with fountains, water streams, trees, fruits, jewelry, and animals. In the ancient Near East and the Hebrew Bible, temple symbolizes divine presence. Although God appears to be invisible in the Song, the presence of the garden-temple imagery indirectly suggests his presence. While the male lover in the Song is endowed with regal imagery as the king, the female lover experiences a transformation from a Cinderella character to a royal figure. Together the garden-temple imagery reflects an Edenic paradise, an Edenic couple, a garden of bliss and love. If we see the garden in the Song in light of the Garden of Eden, then the Song's garden is no longer a mere garden for the human lovers but a garden of God, in which he invites the human couple to enjoy each other as well as to enjoy his creation. In this sense, the garden imagery evokes creation theology, in which God's presence is fused with his creation and creature.

In the book of Esther, the Babylonians have already destroyed the physical temple in Jerusalem and exiled most of the Jews to Babylon. Those who remained in Persia live in a "templeless age," with the Persian palace as the only space to conceive of kingship, royalty, and the divine sphere.[3] This earthly palace represents the human domain, where a Gentile king rules. The descriptions of the Persian palace form a striking overlap with Israel's temple imagery. The powerlessness and incompetence of the Persian king radically contrast with the heavenly king, who, although invisible and silent, works wonders for his people. At the end of Esther, Mordecai advances from being merely a descendant of an exile to becoming a person with royal status in the Persian court. His noble clothing reflects the decorations of the Persian palace as well as Israel's priestly garment. In a Gentile territory that prides itself on ostentatious and luxurious palace decorations and drinking parties, possible allusions to temple imagery suggest there is more to the text. Perhaps the author, by introducing the Persian palace and its shared

---

[3]Middlemas coined the term "the templeless age" to designate the period between 587 and 515 BCE, in between the period of the two temples. With the prevalence of the image of the temple in Jewish theology, "the templeless age" captures well all the sufferings and unspeakable trauma of the exile and beyond. See Jill Middlemas, *The Templeless Age: An Introduction to the History, Literature, and Theology of the "Exile"* (Louisville, KY: Westminster John Knox, 2007), 3-6.

lexical terms with the temple, intends to convey the lost temple in Jerusalem in the mind of the audiences, so as to solicit a certain response from them. Perhaps the author, by connecting the palace and temple imagery, attempts to form a contrast between a Gentile kingdom and God's kingdom. Perhaps the author suggests that, at the time of exile, God's presence has shifted from being in a physical temple to being among his people, as evidenced by the ascension of Mordecai and the symbolism of his clothing. These interpretative possibilities demonstrate the theological ambiguity and possibilities when God is absent literarily in the text.

While the image of the temple in the Song of Songs is reflected in the garden, the idea of the temple in Esther is aniconic and remains a probable possibility. In the literary absence of God, while both books are connected in some degree to Israel's temple imagery, they serve different purposes and manifest divine presence differently.[4]

THE SONG OF SONGS

Many scholars have observed the centrality of the garden imagery in the Song of Songs. Phyllis Trible was one of the first scholars to notice the relationship between the Eden narrative and the Song of Songs. She sees that the Edenic *eros* was first created, and then contaminated and condemned through human disobedience. However, in the Song of Songs, *eros* is redeemed through the couple's mutuality and harmony. The garden (גן) in the Song echoes the garden in Eden (Song 4:12; Gen 2:8). The garden imagery unites person and place, since the woman in the Song is also metaphorically a garden (Song 4:16; 5:1). The sensuality of the garden in the Song expands and deepens when compared to the Garden of Eden. What is more, the divine absence in the Song parallels the withdrawal of God in Genesis 2, when the *eros* of the first couple emerged. Therefore, Trible considers Genesis 2–3 the hermeneutical key to unlock the garden of the Song of

---

[4]The connection between Song of Songs and the temple imagery had long been noticed by early rabbis, as shown in Song of Songs Rabbah. The themes of temple, Torah, and exodus are at the heart of early rabbinic interpretation of the Song. The major difference between their exegesis and contemporary interpretation is that the former correlates images in the Song to other parts of Scripture that may not reflect a parallel context to the Song, whereas the latter attempts to correlate Scripture in context.

Songs.[5] What Trible has neglected is the connection between the two gardens with the temple imagery.

Francis Landy also notes the presence of these two gardens in the Hebrew canon: the Garden of Eden and the garden in the Song of Songs. He resonates with Trible in that he also sees the close relationship between the two gardens, but he departs from Trible in that he takes the garden in the Song as an inverted image of the Garden of Eden. The two gardens have similarities but also differences.[6] Therefore, he envisions the garden in the Song and the Garden of Eden as "two versions of paradise."[7] What I would like to reinforce is that the temple imagery not only reflects the royal identity of the couple in the garden but also suggests divine presence in the garden.[8]

Two royal gardens. The similarities between the garden in the Song of Songs and the Garden of Eden are striking. In the Song, the word *garden* has multiple meanings. On the one hand, there is a literal garden, to which the man goes to pasture his flock and gather lilies (Song 6:2). On the other hand, there is also a metaphorical garden that symbolizes the woman's body (Song 4:12-15). She is the "locked garden." Oftentimes, these two images of the garden converge to create a double entendre. Thus when the man goes down to pasture his flock, it may infer that he goes down to her body.[9] The poet employs the garden imagery to characterize the woman, her body, and her sexuality. Therefore, the garden invokes a sense of beauty, delight, and

---

[5]Phyllis Trible, *God and the Rhetoric of Sexuality* (Philadelphia: Fortress, 1978), 144, 152-53, 161.

[6]Francis Landy, *Paradoxes of Paradise: Identity and Difference in the Song of Songs*, 2nd ed. (Sheffield: Sheffield Phoenix, 2011), 178-99; Landy, "The Song of Songs and the Garden of Eden," *JBL* 98, no. 4 (1979): 513-28.

[7]Landy, *Paradoxes of Paradise*, 172. Although most scholars consider the image of a garden as positive metaphor, Meredith, on the contrary, provides a more negative connotation of the garden imagery as an expression of human manipulation of nature and exerting power over the environment. See Christopher Meredith, *Journeys in the Songscape: Space and the Song of Songs*, HBM 53 (Sheffield: Sheffield Phoenix, 2013), 73-76.

[8]Melton juxtaposes Song of Songs and Lamentations as dialogical partners. While Lamentations mourns for the loss of the temple, Song of Songs takes up the same theme and offers hope to the restoration of the temple. See Brittany N. Melton, *Where Is God in the Megilloth? A Dialogue on the Ambiguity of Divine Presence and Absence* (Leiden: Brill, 2018), 129-34.

[9]See the explanation of Falk, who considers the garden as both a location and a metaphor for the female body. Marcia Falk, *Love Lyrics from the Bible: The Song of Songs* (New York: HarperSanFrancisco, 1990), 156. Bloch and Bloch see an erotic double entendre in the expression "the one who pastures among the lilies" as both pasturing a flock of sheep and "pasturing" the woman's body, since the woman's body is associated with lilies (Song 4:5; 5:13; 7:3). See Ariel Bloch and Chana Bloch, *The Song of Songs* (New York: Random House, 1995), 157.

invigoration. The garden, by definition, is enclosed. It is private, and only invited guests have the privilege to enter. In the Garden of Eden, God planted a garden toward the east in Eden (Gen 2:8). The same word "garden" (גַּן) is used in the Song of Songs 4:12, suggesting that the two gardens are connected and can be read in light of each other.

> In the garden of the Song, there are trees, plants, fruits, spices, water, and love:
> A garden locked, my sister, (my) bride; a fountain locked, a spring sealed;
> Your shoots, orchard of pomegranates, with choice fruit, henna with nards.
> Nard and saffron, reed and cinnamon, with all the trees of frankincense,
> myrrh and aloes, with all the top spices.
> A garden spring, a well of water of life, and the ones flowing from Lebanon.
> (Song 4:12-15)[10]

The orchard or "park" (פַּרְדֵּס) in Song 4:13 is a Persian loanword, appearing also in Ecclesiastes 2:5, referring to the royal orchard or park. This word further suggests the garden metaphor in the Song as a royal garden. This metaphorical garden echoes the imagery in the first garden, where God, out of the earth, caused to grow every tree that is pleasing to the sight and good for food (Gen 2:9). The details of these trees are not given, because attention is focused on the two trees that are in the middle of the garden (Gen 2:9).[11] By contrast, in the Song, the names of the trees are provided. They are used metaphorically to describe both the woman and the man. There are cedars (Song 1:17), cypresses (Song 1:17), an apple tree (Song 2:3; 8:5), a fig tree (Song 2:13), trees of frankincense (Song 4:14), an orchard of nut trees (Song 6:11), and a palm tree (Song 7:7-8). The Song uses the fruits from the fruit trees extensively to connote the image of sustenance, delight, and sensuality. The woman says "his fruit is sweet to my palate" (Song 2:3), and then, "support me with apples, for sick of love I am" (Song 2:5).

Nature also responds to the season of love. The man invites the woman to go out, mimicking nature: "The fig tree has ripened her early fig and the vines in blossom have given forth fragrance. Arise! For yourself, my darling,

---

[10]The word translated "fountain" is literally "stone heap"; NASB: "a rock garden." The word translated "top" can be "heads," "choice." "Garden spring" is literally "a spring, gardens."
[11]Ezekiel, when he speaks of the demise of the king of Tyre, describes Eden as the garden of God with precious stones and jewelry within it (Ezek 28:13). The Garden of Eden also contains precious jewelry such as gold, bdellium, and onyx stone (Gen 2:11-12).

my beautiful, and come away yourself" (Song 2:13). When describing the woman's temple, the man says to her, "Like a split pomegranate is your temple from behind your veil" (Song 4:3; 6:7).[12] The detailed descriptions of the garden in the Song along with the extensive employment of nature imagery make a garden an exquisite paradise, especially when it is compared to the Garden of Eden, the garden of delight.[13]

Another dominant imagery of the garden is its connection to the spring. The woman in the Song is a "spring sealed up" (Song 4:12), a "garden spring," "a well of water of life," and "flowing from Lebanon" (Song 4:15). In the ancient world, gardens were closely connected with springs. Horticulture and water are inseparable, especially in royal palaces. Whether the palace of Ashurbanipal in Nineveh, the hanging gardens of Nebuchadnezzar, the palace of Versailles in Paris, or the Summer Palace in Beijing, the royal court always has a grand garden that often has a fountain or a spring. This image of a royal setting is part of a long tradition.[14] In ancient Near Eastern literature, the dwellings of the gods are associated with a watery abode. The Ugaritic El dwells at the source of two rivers. The Mesopotamian god Enki/Ea also dwells by a water source.[15] The residences of the kings in the ancient Near East were patterned after the temple. Othmar Keel, who specializes in ancient Near Eastern iconography, states, "One of the most beautiful things and one of the greatest pleasures known to the ancient Near East was a garden—a carefully enclosed and heavily watered plot of ground planted with fragrant plants, blooming bushes, and trees filled with choicest fruits."[16]

This is precisely how the garden is portrayed in the Song of Songs. This image of a royal garden is also reflected in Qoheleth's autobiography, "I made gardens and parks for myself and I planted in them all kinds of fruit trees; I made ponds of water for myself from which to irrigate a forest of growing

---

[12]Pomegranates appear in the orchard of nut trees and the vineyards as well (Song 6:11; 7:12).

[13]*Eden* means "delight."

[14]Meredith states that the lovers' garden in the Song models itself on a very particular tradition, a royal tradition that is rooted in the processes of political control. This reading, although sensible, does not agree with the mood of the Song. Meredith, *Journeys in the Songscape*, 81.

[15]John J. Walton, "Eden, Garden of," in *Dictionary of the Old Testament: Pentateuch*, ed. T. Desmond Alexander and David W. Baker (Downers Grove, IL: InterVarsity Press, 2002), 202.

[16]Othmar Keel, *The Song of Songs*, Continental Commentary (Minneapolis: Fortress, 1994), 169.

trees" (Eccles 2:5-6).[17] "Parks" (פַּרְדֵּסִים) and "orchard" (פַּרְדֵּס) in Song of Songs
4:13 are the exact the same word, only the former is plural, whereas the latter
is singular, which suggests they share a similar royal context.[18]

In the Garden of Eden, the water source is a mist that arises from the
earth and waters the whole surface of the ground (Gen 2:6). In addition, a
river is flowing out of Eden to water the garden, and from there, the water
is divided into four other rivers (Gen 2:10). These four rivers flow in different directions and cover various regions of the land (Gen 2:11-14).[19] The
Garden of Eden contains not only a luxurious garden with trees and lus-
cious fruits but also a well-watered irrigation system with flowing rivers
that sustain the land and the people. This garden-river imagery parallels the
garden-spring imagery in the Song. The two gardens conjure a sense of awe
and delight that enlivens whoever enters them.

What is more, both gardens have animals. In the Song of Songs, there are
both literal and metaphorical animals. However, oftentimes the literal and the
metaphorical meanings coalesce. For instance, the sound of the turtledove indicates the arrival of the spring season (Song 2:12), whereas the little foxes in
the vineyards (Song 2:15) may be either literal, metaphorical, or both. The faunal
images are used for both the woman and the man. The woman is likened to the
man's mare among the chariots of Pharaoh (Song 1:9).[20] Her hair is compared
to the flock of goats descending from Mount Gilead (Song 4:1; 6:5). She is also
associated with the dens of lions and mountains of leopards (Song 4:8).[21] As for

---

[17]Qoheleth, the preacher, is believed to take on the persona of King Solomon when he probed into
the meaning of life under the sun.

[18]The word "parks/orchard" is a Persian loanword. Another Persian loanword in the Ecclesiastes is
"command" (פִתְגָם; Eccles 8:11). Seow indicates that Persian names in the Bible are found in the
late books such as Chronicles, Ezra, Nehemiah, Esther, and Daniel. They are not found in earlier
books. See Choon-Leong Seow, *Ecclesiastes: A New Translation with Introduction and Commentary*,
Anchor Yale Bible (New Haven, CT: Yale University Press, 1997), 12. The presence of Persian loan
words in Ecclesiastes and the Song of Songs may point to their late date, but this is not conclusive.

[19]Only two of the named rivers can be identified historically: Tigris and Euphrates. The existence
of the other two rivers, Pishon and Gihon, is uncertain.

[20]The image of a mare is an interpretive enigma. Most commentators cite Pope's remarks that a mare
used in the context of war would thwart the whole army by way of distraction, but no consensus has
been reached. See Marvin H. Pope, *Song of Songs*, AB 7C (Garden City, NY: Doubleday, 1977), 336-41.

[21]Myers sees the imageries of lions and leopards as a reflection the deities of ancient Near Eastern
goddess of love and war, whose iconography depicts them holding implements of war or surrounded by ferocious animals such as lions. Carol Myers, "Gender Imagery in the Song of
Songs," in *A Feminist Companion to the Song of Songs*, ed. Athalya Brenner, FCB 2/6 (Sheffield:
Sheffield Academic Press, 2001), 212.

the man, the blackness of his hair is compared to a raven (Song 5:11). The way
he leaps and bounds is like a gazelle or a young stag (Song 2:9, 17; 8:14). The
woman's breasts are likened to a gazelle (Song 4:5; 7:3), the eyes of both the
woman and the man to a dove (Song 1:15; 4:1; 5:12), as is the woman herself, as
the man addresses her as "my dove" (Song 6:9). These literal and metaphorical
animals are specifically named. This brings us back to the first garden.

In the Garden of Eden, out of the ground God formed every beast of the
field and every bird of the sky, and God brought them before the man.
Whatever the man called a living creature, that became its name (Gen 2:19).
In the garden of the Song, the named animals, whether literal or metaphorical, correspond to the beasts of the field in the Garden of Eden.

Although the two gardens share similar natural settings, there is an even
more conspicuous similarity: the presence of two lovers, male and female.
The main lovers of the garden in the Song of Songs are the woman and the
man. They express mutual love and lavish praise after praise on one another.
In the Garden of Eden, we meet the first couple, the man and the woman.
The man is created first, and then the woman is created from his rib or side.
When God brings the woman to the man, the man shouts joyfully, "This
time! Bone from my bones and flesh from my flesh" (Gen 2:23).[22] Then God
retreats from the scene. The following verses describe the union of the first
couple and note that they are naked but not ashamed (Gen 2:24-25). This
picture of purity and innocence of the first love has echoes in the garden of
the Song, where the couple offer praises for the beauty of their respective
bodies (Song 4:1-7; 5:10-16; 7:1-8) and likewise are naked but not ashamed.

Despite shared images of the garden, trees, fruits, water, animals, and
even the lovers, if there is no king in its midst, it remains a beautiful garden
and not a temple. Only the presence of God in the Garden of Eden renders
it a garden-temple where God, the king of heaven, resides.[23] In the Song of
Songs, the explicit reference to God is absent. Yet, all the other elements in

---

[22]My translation. "This time" (זֹאת הַפַּעַם) expresses the excitement of the man. It reflects a joyful
proclamation, as if to say, "At last!"

[23]Morales's study has made a strong case for identifying the Garden of Eden as the holy of
holies through the idea of the cosmic mountain, the gate liturgy, and humanity as priesthood.
If the Garden of Eden is the holy of holies, it is God's residence par excellence. See L. Michael
Morales, *The Tabernacle Pre-figured: Cosmic Mountain Ideology in Genesis and Exodus*, Biblical
Tools and Studies 15 (Leuven: Peeters, 2012), 51-119.

the garden suggest his presence in absence. As we discussed in chapter two, wisdom theology reflects creation theology. Nature evokes divine presence.

The following table summarizes the two royal gardens:

Table 4.1

	The Garden in the Song of Songs	**The Garden of Eden**
Garden	a locked garden (Song 4:12)	a locked garden (Gen 2:8)
Trees	named trees: cedars (Song 1:17), cypresses (Song 1:17), apple tree (Song 2:3; 8:5), fig tree (Song 2:13), trees of frankincense (Song 4:14), orchard of nut trees (Song 6:11), palm tree (Song 7:7-8)	unnamed trees: God causes to grow every tree that is pleasing to the sight and good for food (Gen 2:9)
Fruits	named fruits: apples (Song 2:5), figs (Song 2:13), pomegranates (Song 4:3; 6:7)	unnamed fruits: God causes to grow every tree that is pleasing to the sight and good for food (Gen 2:9)
Water	the woman is a "spring sealed up" (Song 4:12), a "garden spring," "a well of water of life," and "flowing from Lebanon" (Song 4:15)	a river is flowing out of Eden to water the garden, and from there, the water is then divided into four other rivers (Gen 2:10)
Animals	named animals: turtledove (Song 2:12), little foxes (Song 2:15), mare (Song 1:9), a flock of goats (Song 4:1; 6:5), dens of lions and mountains of leopards (Song 4:8), raven (Song 5:11), gazelle or a young stag (Song 2:9, 17; 4:5; 7:3; 8:14), dove (Song 1:15; 4:1; 5:12; 6:9)	unnamed animals: God forms every beast of the field and every bird of the sky (Gen 2:19)
Eros	the couple are naked but not ashamed (Song 4:1-17; 5:10-16; 7:1-8)	the couple are naked but not ashamed (Gen 2:24-25)
God	absence of God (except for the possible hint of God in Song 8:6)	explicit presence of God before the union of the couple; absence of God after the union of the couple

As the table demonstrates, the two gardens have similarities on multiple levels. The most glaring difference is the presence of God in Eden and the explicit literary absence of God in the Song. If the composer of the Song intends the setting of the garden to echo the Garden of Eden, then the two gardens should be read in light of each other. It follows, then, that the presence of God is implied and suggested in the Song, even though the explicit name of God is absent. Trible observes that the absence of God in the Garden of Eden occurs precisely when *eros* between the human lovers emerges.[24] This divine withdrawal parallels the divine physical absence in the entire Song of Songs, precisely since love captivates the man and the woman from the beginning to the ending of the Song. God retreats to the background and leaves them alone to enjoy their private times and space together.

Eden as the garden-temple. We have already established some correlation between royal gardens and temple and palace imagery. What we have not yet said explicitly is that the Garden of Eden is the temple of God. More precisely, it is the holy of holies in the cosmic temple complex of God, as scholars have understood.[25] Genesis 1 portrays the cosmos as God's holy temple, where God dwells. In the ancient world, God only dwelled in his temple. Therefore, Sabbath rest for God substantiates the idea of the cosmos as God's temple.[26] If Genesis 1 deals with sacred time, then Genesis 2 deals with sacred space.[27] The identification of the Garden of Eden with the temple is confirmed by later texts, especially Ezekiel and Revelation. G. K. Beale asserts that "the Garden of Eden was the first archetypal temple, and that it was the model for all subsequent temples."[28] In Genesis 2, the river is going out of Eden to water the garden, which then divides to become four rivers (Gen 2:10). Applying visualization to the text of Eden, Lifsa Schachter sees the Garden of Eden situated on top of a mountain from which rivers flowed downward.[29] This corresponds to the water that is flowing from under the threshold of the temple in Ezekiel's temple vision. There Ezekiel sees the water flowing toward the east (Ezek 47:1-2). Wherever the water reaches, there creatures swarm and live. Later the text indicates that this water originates from the sanctuary: "By the river on its bank, on one side and on the other, will grow all *kinds* of trees for food. Their leaves will not wither and their fruit will not fail. They will bear every month because their

---

[24]Trible, *God and the Rhetoric of Sexuality*, 145.

[25]Morales, *Tabernacle Pre-figured*, 51-119.

[26]John Walton, *The Lost World of Genesis One: Ancient Cosmology and the Origins Debate* (Downers Grove, IL: InterVarsity Press, 2009), 72.

[27]Walton, "Eden, Garden of," 205.

[28]G. K. Beale, *The Temple and the Church's Mission: A Biblical Theology of the Dwelling Place of God* (Downers Grove, IL: InterVarsity Press, 2004), 26.

[29]Lifsa Schachter, "The Garden of Eden as God's First Sanctuary," *Jewish Bible Quarterly* (2013): 74.

water flows from the sanctuary, and their fruit will be for food and their leaves for healing" (Ezek 47:12).

On the one hand, the scenes of the life-giving water, trees for food, and leaves that heal point backward to the Edenic paradise. On the other hand, they point forward to the eschatological temple in Revelation. There the apostle John witnesses a river of the water of life, clear as crystal, coming from the throne of God and of the Lamb (Rev 22:1). Then the text says, "On either side of the river was the tree of life, bearing twelve *kinds of* fruit, yielding its fruit every month; and the leaves of the tree were for the healing of the nations" (Rev 22:2). The similarities between Ezekiel's temple vision and the eschatological temple in the book of Revelation suggest that their model is the temple in Eden. Just as Eden has the source of the river and the trees for food, so do Ezekiel's and John's vision of the temple. When describing the righteous man, the psalmist likens him to a palm tree planted in the house of God: "The righteous man will flourish like the palm tree, He will grow like a cedar in Lebanon. Planted in the house of the LORD, They will flourish in the courts of our God. They will still yield fruit in old age; They shall be full of sap and very green" (Ps 92:12-14). This image of the righteous man flourishing in the house of God like an evergreen tree takes its cue from the images in the Garden of Eden. This image of a tree of life appears also in the form of a menorah in the tabernacle. God instructs Moses to make a lampstand with six branches going out from the lampstand. "Three cups *shall be* shaped like almond *blossoms* in the one branch, a bulb and a flower, and three cups shaped like almond *blossoms* in the other branch, a bulb and a flower" (Ex 25:33). This forms an image of a flowering tree with seven protruding branches from a central trunk, three on each side, with the central branch going straight up from the middle of the lampstand.[30]

Additionally, gold, precious metals, and onyx (שֹׁהַם) are present in the Garden of Eden (Gen 2:12). The materials for building the tabernacle and the temple and for decorating the priestly garment include both gold and onyx. Gold is used to build the inner and outer linings of the ark of the covenant (Ex 25:11), the mercy seat (Ex 25:17), and the golden lampstand (Ex 25:31). Gold is also used extensively in the building of the temple in

---

[30]Beale, *Temple and the Church's Mission*, 71.

Jerusalem, in covering the floor and the inner sanctuary and in making the altar, the lampstand, and the table of showbread (1 Kings 6:20-35; 7:48-51; 1 Chron 29:2). Onyx stones are used to decorate the ephod and the breast-plate (Ex 25:7; 28:9; 35:9). When referring to the Garden of Eden, Ezekiel also indicates the presence of gold, onyx, and other precious stones there (Ezek 28:13), suggesting the tabernacle and the temple originate from and share the same source—the Garden of Eden. This garden imagery becomes the primary source to conceive of the paradise as a garden of delight.

Lebanon. If the setting of the garden in the Song of Songs reflects, echoes, and evokes the Garden of Eden, and if the Garden of Eden serves as the archetype of God's temple, then the garden imagery in the Song of Songs is also a reflection of the temple—a boundless and shapeless yet visible and enchanting garden-temple of God.[31] In the ancient worldview, this identification of the Edenic paradise with the sanctuary of God was well-established. The frequent appearance of Lebanon in the Song also suggests its connection with the temple imagery, specifically the temple in Jerusalem.[32] Lebanon is a wooded mountain range on the northern side of Israel. The word *Lebanon* itself means "white," perhaps referring to the whiteness of cliffs.[33] In the Hebrew Bible, Lebanon evokes the image of forests and especially cedars. In the biblical tradition, Lebanon and cedar are closely linked (Is 2:13; 14:8; 37:24; Jer 22:23; Ezek 17:3; 27:5; Hos 14:5). Because King Solomon chose cedar as the building material for the temple in Jerusalem (1 Kings 5:6), the word *Lebanon* often evokes the image of the temple; as Isaiah indicates, "The glory of Lebanon will come to you, The juniper, the box tree and the cypress together, to

---

[31]Lyke provides a succinct and helpful study on the interconnectedness between the temple, women, and wombs in the prophetic books. Larry L. Lyke, *I Will Espouse You Forever: The Song of Songs and the Theology of Love in the Hebrew Bible* (Nashville: Abingdon, 2007), 29. In the Song of Songs, the identification of the woman with the royal city of Tirzah and the temple in Jerusalem demonstrates the centrality of woman-temple in the mind of the composer.

[32]Ellen F. Davis, *Proverbs, Ecclesiastes, and the Song of Songs*, Westminster Bible Companion (Louisville, KY: Westminster John Knox, 2000), 267. See also Smith's chapter on the idea of the temple in the Ugaritic Baal Cycle, where Lebanon, Eden, and Ezekiel 28 all derive from the same ancient Near Eastern concept of the temple. Mark S. Smith, "Like Deities, Like Temples (Like People)," in *Temple and Worship in Biblical Israel*, ed. John Day, LHBOTS 422 (London: T&T Clark, 2005), 3-27, esp. 8-9.

[33]In the Targums, half of the uses of *Lebanon* appear to be metaphorical, referring to the temple. See Edmee Kingsmill, *The Song of Songs and the Eros of God: A Study in Biblical Intertextuality* (Oxford: Oxford University Press, 2009), 102-3.

beautify the place of My sanctuary; and I shall make the place of My feet glorious" (Is 60:13). Keel remarks, "Lebanon was regarded in large parts of the Near East as a prototype of the gardens of the gods."[34] Terje Stordalen's research shows Lebanon as a symbol for Zion—the Jerusalem temple. Davis also asserts, "Lebanon became a code word for Jerusalem's glory as God's dwelling place."[35]

Coincidentally, *Lebanon* appears seven times in the Song of Songs. It is used to describe the sedan chair of Solomon, which is made from the timber of Lebanon (Song 3:9). Twice the groom invites the bride to come with him from Lebanon (Song 4:8), suggesting she is at Lebanon at the time when the groom invites her. The groom describes the fragrance of her robes as being "like the fragrance of Lebanon" (Song 4:11). By metonymy, this refers to the fragrance of the cedars of Lebanon. The description of the woman in the Song reminds one of Israel's tabernacle and the temple. The groom also uses "a well of water of life" (Ezek 43; Rev 22) and the ones "flowing from Lebanon" as a metaphor for her as a garden spring (Song 4:15). In his temple vision, Ezekiel sees water was flowing from under the threshold of the temple (Ezek 47:1). Wherever the water goes, it heals and invigorates everything it passes (Ezek 47:8-9). In the eschatological future, John describes his vision of the new heaven and new earth as that of a river of water of life, coming from the throne of God and of the Lamb (Rev 22:1).

Lebanon, then, is not merely a place. It also subtly symbolizes the temple in Jerusalem. Lebanon appears two more times in the Song, once in Song of Songs 5:15 to depict the groom, whose appearance is described as "like the Lebanon, being chosen like cedars." Here Lebanon and cedar are closely

---

[34]Keel, *Song of Songs*, 170. In Ezek 31:3-9, Assyria was metaphorically depicted as a cedar in Lebanon with beautiful branches and forest shade. The cedars in God's garden could not match it, and no trees in God's garden could compare with its beauty. God further stresses, "I made it beautiful with the multitude of its branches, And all the trees of Eden, which were in the garden of God, were jealous of it" (Ezek 31:9). Although the prominence of the garden of God, which appears three times in this periscope, fades in comparison with the beauty of Assyria, it nevertheless presupposes the notion that both Lebanon and Eden are associated with the temple of God.

[35]Terje Stordalen, *Echoes of Eden: Genesis 2–3 and Symbolism of the Eden Garden in Biblical Hebrew Literature*, Contributions to Biblical Exegesis and Theology 25 (Leuven: Peeters, 2000), 163, 307-10; Davis, *Proverbs, Ecclesiastes, and the Song of Songs*, 268.

connected. The last occurrence of Lebanon is in Song of Songs 7:4, where the groom describes the woman's nose as "like the tower of Lebanon." This sevenfold appearance of *Lebanon* parallels the sevenfold presence of the name Solomon (Song 1:1, 5; 3:7, 9, 11; 8:11-12).

We have established that the image of the garden in the Song of Songs evokes the image of Eden. Both are associated with royalty as well as with the temple of God. The garden imagery of the Song reflects a boundless, luxurious, and beautiful temple, reminiscent of God's dwelling place. Although God is not explicitly present in the Song, the Edenic image begs readers to see that God's presence is implicit and assumed. With that in mind, we turn to the identity of the human lovers in the garden of the Song of Songs.

Two royal lovers. In the Song of Songs, the male lover appears to be the king. In ancient times, king and shepherd were synonyms. The king was also the shepherd of his people.[36] Imagery of both king and shepherd surfaces in the first chapter. The woman says: "The king brought me to his chambers" (Song 1:4); "Tell me! whom my soul loves, where do you pasture?" (Song 1:7); "While the king is on his couch, my nard gave forth its fragrance" (Song 1:12).[37] From a literary perspective, when the woman calls her lover "king" or "shepherd," she may be using terms of endearment to express her affection and respect.[38] In her mind, he is like a king and a shepherd. It is also possible that these terms reflect the actual identity of her lover. The male lover's association with King Solomon further reinforces his royal identity, albeit with blurring of the actual and the metaphorical images (Song 1:1; 3:9, 11).

Munro observes that the banner motif is sufficient to evoke a regal milieu. A banner is raised to mark capture. It is also a sign to the one it represents. The banner suggests that the banner bearer is not just her captor but also

---

[36]For instance, the "shepherds of Israel" in Ezek 34 are understood as the kings of Israel, and God will be the shepherd of his people. In Ps 23:1, David proclaims, "The LORD is my shepherd." In Hammurapi's inscriptions, he addresses himself as the "shepherd." See William W. Hallo, ed., *The Context of Scripture: Monumental Inscriptions from the Biblical World* (Leiden: Brill, 2003), 2:257.

[37]However, some commentators construe the king and the shepherd as two different characters.

[38]Tremper Longman III, *Song of Songs*, New International Commentary on the Old Testament (Grand Rapids, MI: Eerdmans, 2001), 16.

her king. He is proud to raise a banner to declare his love for her.[39] Along
with the image of a banner, oils, fragrance, and food are also associated with
the regal image.[40] Thus we learn that he brought her to a wine house, that
his love is better than wine, and that she wants to be sustained by raisin
cakes because she is lovesick (Song 1:4, 12; 2:4-5).

When the women of Jerusalem ask the female protagonist of the
Song, "How is your beloved better than others?" (Song 5:9), she responds
with a *waṣf* (praise song) praising his appearance and body. When the
woman describes her lover's body, she employs royal images and even a
godlike description:

> My beloved is dazzling and ruddy, more prominent than ten thousand.
>
> His head, gold, refined gold, his locks of hair, black like the raven.
>
> His eyes, like doves, upon the streams of water, washing in milk and
> sitting upon the rim.
>
> His cheeks, like beds of spices, towers of perfume, his lips, lilies dripping
> flowing myrrh.
>
> His hands, rods of gold, are being filled with yellow jasper; his belly, an
> ivory plate, being covered (with) sapphires.
>
> His legs, are like pillars of alabaster, being founded upon a pedestal of
> refined gold, His appearance is like the Lebanon, being chosen like cedars.
>
> His palate is sweetness, and all of him is pleasant. This is my beloved. This
> is my darling, O Daughters of Jerusalem. (Song 5:10-16)[41]

She describes his body as if he were an extravagant statute of a divine
being or an esteemed king. He is like a banner raised high and far above
everyone else.[42] From head to toe, he is made of refined gold, which is the
purest form of gold (Song 5:11, 15). His eyes match hers; both are like

---

[39]Jill M. Munro, *Spikenard and Saffron: A Study in the Poetic Language of the Song of Songs*, JSOTSup
203 (Sheffield: Sheffield Academic Press, 1995), 36. The banner imagery for the king also appears
in Song 5:10, when the woman praises her lover as "more prominent than 10,000." In Song 6:10,
the woman is also associated with the image of a banner ("dreadful like banners"). There it is a
military image and evokes a sense of awe.

[40]Munro, *Spikenard and Saffron*, 36. Munro further states that oils and spices are used to bridge
between the natural and the courtly imagery in the Song (*Spikenard and Saffron*, 68).

[41]"Refined gold" appears also in Song 5:15. "Washing" could also be translated "bathing." "Flowing"
is literally "passing." Compare "lilies dripping flowing myrrh" here to "my fingers passing (NASB
'liquid myrrh') myrrh upon the palms (handles) of the bolt" (Song 5:5). For "yellow jasper," NASB
and JPS have "set with beryl." "All of him" could also be translated "every part of him."

[42]"Prominent" is "banner."

doves. His lips are like lilies, dripping with flowing myrrh, corresponding to her as the lily of the valley and her hands dripping with myrrh (Song 2:1; 5:5). His hands are rods of gold, and his belly is like an ivory plate. Both hands and belly are filled with precious metals. He is, in a nutshell, "gold from top to bottom."[43]

When describing his legs, the writer uses temple-palace imagery: "His legs are like pillars of alabaster" (עַמּוּדֵי שֵׁשׁ; or "marble"). The other place in the Hebrew canon where the phrase "pillars of alabaster" appears is in Esther 1:6, depicting marble pillars of the Persian palace. Not only is his body like the statute of a divine being or a king; it is also likened to a temple-palace structure. The mention of Lebanon and cedar further evokes the image of the temple in Jerusalem as well as the palace of Solomon; both are made from the cedars of Lebanon (1 Kings 6–7). Whether a poetic or a literal portrayal, in the garden the male lover in the Song is endowed with royal status in a god-like language.

What about the woman in the Song? At the beginning of the poem, the woman appears as a Cinderella figure. Her brothers were angry with her. They made her work in the vineyard, and the sun darkened her skin. She addresses the daughters of Jerusalem:

> Dark, I am but lovely, daughters of Jerusalem, like the tent of Kadar, like the curtains of Solomon.
> Do not gaze upon me, (because) I am dark. The Sun looked at me. The sons of my mother were angry with me. They set me as the keeper of the vineyards. My own vineyard, I did not keep. (Song 1:5-6)[44]

The reasons for her brothers' anger are not given. What is certain is that she and her brothers are not on good terms. She is also not happy with the way her skin looks. However, as the Song progresses forward, the woman is transformed from this lowly Cinderella figure to nobility. The man compares her to the cities of Tirzah and Jerusalem: "Beautiful, you are, my darling, like Tirzah; comely like Jerusalem" (Song 6:4). Tirzah was the capital of the northern kingdom of Israel during the reign of Omri (1 Kings

---

[43]J. Cheryl Exum, *Song of Songs: A Commentary*, OTL (Louisville: KY: Westminster John Knox, 2005), 209.

[44]"But lovely" could also be translated "and lovely."

16:17, 23), and Jerusalem was the city of King David. The name Tirzah means "pleasing" or "lovely." It conjures a sense of beauty. Jerusalem is known for its beauty, as the psalmists have declared: "Beautiful in elevation, the joy of the whole earth" (Ps 48:2); "Out of Zion, the perfection of beauty" (Ps 50:2).[45]

Not only is the woman identified with the two royal cities, but she is also endowed with cosmic attributes: "Who is this, the one who looks down like dawn? Beautiful like the moon, pure like the Sun, dreadful like banners" (Song 6:10).[46] Dawn, the moon, and the sun are all cosmic elements. Here they are associated with the woman. Munro sees a contrast between the woman's former pleading with the daughters of Jerusalem, "Do not gaze upon me," in Song of Songs 1:6, whereas now she becomes the one who looks down and is identified with the sun. She was despised but now is blessed by the maidens. Even the royal family, the queens and the concubines, praise her (Song 6:9).[47] Her ascent to nobility does not stop here. At the beginning of Song of Songs 7, the man acclaims: "How beautiful are your feet (steps) in your sandals? O Daughter of nobles" (Song 7:1 [Hebrew 7:2]). "Daughter of nobles" (בַּת־נָדִיב) can also be understood as "daughter of princes."[48] Here he endows her with noble status, matching his royal identity. In his eyes, she is no longer a peasant girl working in the vineyard but a daughter of nobility, being praised by other courtly members and by him, a kingly figure.

The man continues his compliment: "Your head upon you is like an orchard; and the hair of your head is like red purple, a king is being confined in the troughs" (Song 7:5 [Hebrew 7:6]).[49] An orchard here is a plantation or a garden. It is the word *Carmel*, as in Mount Carmel (כַּרְמֶל). In Israel, Mount Carmel was associated with dominating height, for the Carmel

---

[45]Keel indicates that Tirzah is also a name for a woman (Num 26:33; 27:1). She is one of the five daughters of Zelophehad. See Keel, *Song of Songs*, 213, 215. Zion is a poetic name for Jerusalem.

[46]"Pure" also appears in Song 6:9: "Pure, she, to the one who bore her."

[47]Munro, *Spikenard and Saffron*, 39.

[48]See *BDB* 622. NASB, NKJV, and NIV translate this as "prince's daughter"; RSV, NRSV, and NLT translate it as "queenly maiden." Scholars who translate it as "the prince's daughter" include Keel, *Song of Songs*, 230; Tom Gledhill, *The Message of the Song of Songs* (Downers Grove, IL: InterVarsity Press, 1994), 204; Duane Garrett, *Song of Songs*, WBC 23B (Nashville: Thomas Nelson, 2004), 236n2a.

[49]Or "A king is held captive in the tresses" (JPS).

range rises abruptly to 1,640 feet (500 meters) above sea level and is comparable to the Lebanon range. Thus, when the man says her head is like an orchard, he is saying that she carries her head high.[50] Her hair is like red purple, the exact color of the chariot of Solomon's palanquin in Song of Songs 3:10, which is also the color of the hangings of the tabernacle and of the ephod for the priestly garment (Ex 25:4; 26:1, 31, 36; 35:25; 39:3), as well as the hangings for the temple in Jerusalem (2 Chron 3:14).[51] What is more, red purple is the color of the hangings of the Persian palace (Esther 1:6). In the ancient world, this red purple fabric was associated with dignity and honor. By attributing this royal color to her hair, he elevates her to the status of royalty and even queenship. Because of her dignified beauty, the king is captivated by her as if he were confined to the valleys and admires her high above him.

The name Shulamite (הַשּׁוּלַמִּית) first appears in Song of Songs 6:13 (Hebrew 7:1). It is a feminine form of šālôm (שָׁלוֹם), which means "peace." Coincidentally or not, the name Solomon (שְׁלֹמֹה) also comes from the word šālôm and means "peace." Poetically, the two names suggest they are a matching couple, corresponding to one another. If Solomon is associated with the regal images, so is the Shulamite. As the Song progresses, the Cinderella figure has transformed into a queenly figure. Her ascent forms a striking parallel to the ascent of Esther, who was once an orphan but will become a queen, corresponding to the king. Close to the end of the Song of Songs, the lovers emerge as two royal lovers, inhabiting the garden-temple of God.[52]

Divine presence and the garden. In wisdom theology, creation and wisdom are intertwined. Wisdom is the tree of life, planted in a fertile garden, which yields fruit in its season. The world as depicted in Genesis 2–3, when viewed with wisdom, presents "an environment teeming with life,

---

[50]Keel, *Song of Songs*, 236, 238.

[51]Other references to red purple used in building the tabernacle include Ex 27:16; 28:6, 8, 15, 33; 35:6, 23; 36:8, 35, 37; 38:18; 39:2, 5, 8; 24, 29. Mordecai's clothing is also red purple, suggesting his noble status (Esther 8:15).

[52]Smith's research suggests the relationship between temple and eroticism. He cites Song 1:2 as an allusion of a cuneiform text from Ugarit where Baal is enthroned on his mountain; the text ends with "his mouth like two clouds [?] . . . like wine is the love of his heart" (1.101). Though the lines are missing, the ending is suggestive of his lips kissing. See Smith, "Like Deities, Like Temple," 19.

made possible and nurtured by divine providence."[53] Roland Murphy states, "The world is the showcase for divine activity."[54] Thus, divine activity can be discerned through observing the world and its inhabitants as well as the order behind his creation.

The garden setting of the Song, with fountains, water streams, trees, fruits, jewelry, and animals, echoes the Edenic paradise with blessing and luxuriance. The garden in the Song is not just a garden but a garden-temple, where divine presence is assumed and where love and bliss occur. This garden-temple conjures images of the tabernacle and royal figures as well as the cedars of Lebanon. Yet, unlike Israel's tabernacle and the temple in Jerusalem, the garden-temple in the Song has no clear boundary or shape, nor an identifiable physical structure. It is meant for readers to imagine and to envisage its enchanting effect on one's mind and soul. Nature is God's temple. In this boundless and shapeless temple, love abides. Creation is infused with human *eros* and divine presence. Just as the garden in the Song is unrestricted by a fixed construction, the presence of God is unhampered and is intended to be felt rather than stated in the enthralling environ of the poetic world. In the garden of the Song of Songs, God is present in absence.

THE BOOK OF ESTHER

In "The Temple Theme in the Book of Daniel," Greg Goswell argues that one of the major themes of the book is its temple theme and that this theme unifies the whole narrative of Daniel.[55] While the text of Daniel includes temple-related objects and explicit reference to the sanctuary, such as temple vessels (Dan 1:2; 5:2), and while it describes the overthrow and the restoration of the sanctuary (Dan 8:11-14), the book of Esther includes no such explicit remarks. While Daniel makes numerous references to the presence of God, Esther makes none. In Esther, there is no mention of Israel, covenant, prayer, or worship; nor is there any concern with the land,

---

[53]Leo G. Perdue, *Wisdom and Creation: The Theology of Wisdom Literature* (Nashville: Abingdon, 1994), 338.

[54]Roland E. Murphy, *The Tree of Life: An Exploration of Biblical Wisdom Literature*, Anchor Bible Reference Library (New York: Doubleday, 1992), 119.

[55]Greg Goswell, "The Temple Theme in the Book of Daniel," *Journal of the Evangelical Theological Society* 55, no. 3 (2012): 509-20.

Jerusalem, or aspiration for an eternal kingdom.[56] Although the setting of both books is a foreign court during the reign of a Gentile monarch, their references to divine activity could not be more different.

Since in the Hebrew Scriptures, divine presence is often conveyed through the presence of the temple, when the temple in Jerusalem was destroyed in 586 BCE, the question of divine presence remained at the heart of the Jewish faith. In the exilic and postexilic period, the loss of the temple equated with the abandonment of God.[57] Besides the temple, in the ancient Near East, divine presence was construed and represented also through cultic objects, statues of gods, divine symbols, and cult stelae; but none of these is present in Esther.[58] If read apart from the Hebrew canon, the book of Esther seems rather "secular" or nonreligious. However, as Goswell indicates, "The temple as a theme may be present even when the temple as an object or image is absent, namely by means of various associated cultic and non-cultic motifs.[59] To identify the temple as a leading theme is to assert that it embodies an important aspect of the fundamental value system expressed in Daniel as a literary work."[60] I believe this "fundamental value system" applies to the book of Esther as well in the absence of a physical temple.

This section of the chapter attempts to suggest that the temple theme is hidden in Esther but may be present in the mind of the readers who are conscious with the idea of the temple. The common vocabulary shared between the Persian palace and Israel's tabernacle and temple imagery hints at their possible connections, which further probes for the implications of divine presence and absence. The ascension of Mordecai the Jew, with his royal and priestly clothing resembling Israel's priestly garment, further

---

[56]Fasting occurs in Esther. The book of Daniel includes elements of prayer and worship (Dan 3:16-18; 6:10).

[57]This can be seen through lament psalms on the loss of the temple, such as Ps 74, or Lamentations. The loss of the temple as a sign of the abandonment of the gods is a widespread notion in the ancient Near East. See "Lamentation over the Destruction of Sumer and Ur," in Hallo, *Context of Scripture*, 1:535-39; Christopher B. Hays, *Hidden Riches: A Sourcebook for the Comparative Study of the Hebrew Bible and Ancient Near East* (Louisville, KY: Westminster John Knox, 2014), 375-90.

[58]Regarding representations of divine presence, see Pekka Pitkanen, "Temple Building and Exodus 25–40," in *From the Foundations to the Crenellations: Essays on Temple Building in the Ancient Near East and Hebrew Bible*, ed. Mark J. Boda and Jamie Novotny (Münster: Ugarit-Verlag, 2010), 259.

[59]For example, the temple vessels in Dan 5.

[60]Goswell, "Temple Theme," 510.

suggests that divine presence may have shifted from a physical temple to God's chosen people at the time of the exile. However, due to the explicit absence of God's name and the lack of any credit given to God, the real intent of the author in making such links (if there are indeed such links) remains a theological ambiguity.

Julia Kristeva coined the term *intertextuality*. Inspired by Mikhail Bakhtin's idea that literary structure is not a fixed entity but is always in relation to another structure, the "literary word" serves as an intersection of textual surfaces rather than as a single point. It is a dialogue among several writings, which includes the writer, the addressee (or the character) and the contemporary or earlier cultural context. For Bakhtin, "any text is constructed as a mosaic of quotations; any text is the absorption and trans-formation of another. The notion of intertextuality replaces that of inter-subjectivity, and poetic language is read at least double." Kristeva further articulates and develops Bakhtin's idea, asserting that "each word (text) is an intersection of word (texts) where at least one other word (text) can be read." Each word in and of itself represents a minimal textual unit that func-tions as a mediator, linking structural models to a cultural and historical environment. At the same time, it acts as a regulator, preventing mutations from diachrony to synchrony. Therefore, the word is spatialized and func-tions in three dimensions—subject, addressee, and context.[61] We may also consider this intertextuality as a form of innerbiblical allusion, dialogue, or interpretation. That is, the words in Esther allude to, dialogue, and interact with other texts in the Hebrew Scripture.

Since Kristeva, scholarly discussions on intertextuality, innerbiblical exegesis, and innerbiblical allusions are complex. For example, Russel Meek considers *intertextuality* a broad term to determine the relationship between texts. "Innerbiblical exegesis" attempts to make a case that later authors used an earlier text to expand, transform, or apply to a new context, whereas "innerbiblical allusion" is simply to demonstrate that a later text is in some way making references to an earlier text.[62] Geoffrey

---

[61]Julia Kristeva, "Word, Dialogue and Novel," in *The Kristeva Reader*, ed. Toril Moi (New York: Columbia University Press, 1986), 36-37.

[62]Russell L. Meek, "Intertextuality, Inner-Biblical Exegesis, and Inner-Biblical Allusion: The Eth-ics of a Methodology," *Biblica* 95, no. 1 (2014): 280-91, esp. 280, 288-89.

Miller distinguishes two kinds of intertextuality: synchronic and dia-chronic. A synchronic approach juxtaposes two or more texts without resort to authorial intent. Thus, the burden of interpretation falls on the reader, while a diachronic approach involves determining which text pre-dates the others and influences them. This second approach is author-oriented. The reader is trying to see how the author shapes the perception of the reader.

There are also questions concerning the criteria of determining the in-tertextual relationships such as shared lexical similarities, motif, genre, and structural features.[63] The understanding of shared textual resemblances is another contested issue, since lexical, thematic, or structural similarities may be due to coincidences, or the authors may use common languages or literary devices of their time in their writings. Therefore, Paul Noble pro-poses using "type-narratives" to identify the plot of the stories among dif-ferent texts as a means to delineate a proper intertextual relationship.[64] Although Jeffrey Leonard formulates eight principles for intertextual allu-sions, at the end, he concludes that the process of identifying and deter-mining the allusions is "often more art than science."[65] Miller also concurs with this sentiment by saying that the practice of intertextuality is "very much in the eye of the beholder."[66]

---

[63]Geoffrey D. Miller, "Intertextuality in Old Testament Research," *Currents in Biblical Research* 9, no. 3 (2010): 283-309.

[64]Noble's study nuances the methodology on determining resemblances between texts. He asserts that these texts should not be random similarities or "half-similarities" that do not contribute to the meanings of each narrative. See Paul R. Noble, "Esau, Tamar, and Joseph: Criteria for Identifying Inner-biblical Allusions," *VT* 52 (2002): 219-52.

[65]The eight principles include: (1) Shared language is the single most important factor in establish-ing a textual connection. (2) Shared language is more important than nonshared language. (3) Shared language that is rare or distinctive suggests a stronger connection than does language that is widely used. (4) Shared phrases suggest a stronger connection than do individual shared terms. (5) The accumulation of shared language suggests a stronger connection than does a single shared term or phrase. (6) Shared language in similar contexts suggests a stronger con-nection than does shared language alone. (7) Shared language need not be accompanied by shared ideology to establish a connection. (8) Shared language need not be accompanied by shared form to establish a connection. See Jeffrey M. Leonard, "Identifying Inner-biblical Allu-sions: Psalm 78 as a Test Case," *JBL* 127, no. 2 (2008): 246. Lyons also suggests two ways to tell allusions from mere coincidences: (1) inversion of elements and (2) splitting and redistribution of elements. See Michael A. Lyons, "Marking Inner-biblical Allusion in the Book of Ezekiel," *Biblica* 88 (2007): 245-50.

[66]Miller, "Intertextuality in Old Testament Research," 298.

Given this fluid understanding concerning *intertextuality*, I will use it loosely by adopting Kristeva's notion of "each word as an intersection of other words" as a working principle in exploring the Persian palace and Israel's temple imagery.[67] In fact, ancient Jewish exegetes already discovered the temple theme in the book of Esther, as demonstrated by Midrash Rabbah Esther.[68] As we will see, words and phrases in the book of Esther, such as "Shushan the fortress," "house," "garden," "royalty," "banquet of wine," "spices and myrrh," "hanging," "red purple," and "gold and silver vessels," are not fixed literary points. Rather, they form a "double" or dialogue with another text—in this case texts involve Israel's temple imagery. In such reading, it is indeed more art than science.

The portrayal of the Persian palace. The book of Esther begins with a statement introducing the King of Persia and offers a sneak peek into the Persian palace with its drinking parties, royal members, ostentatious decorations, and extravagant lifestyle. Below I will draw attention to several lexical terms that may intersect and overlap with Israel's temple imagery, though there may be more than these.

Shushan the fortress. The term "Shushan the fortress" (שׁוּשַׁן הַבִּירָה) can be translated as "Shushan the castle" or "Shushan the citadel." The word *fortress* is precisely understood as "temple" in 1 Chronicles 29:1; 29:19, where it specifically refers to the temple in Jerusalem. For example,

> Then King David said to the entire assembly, "My son Solomon, whom alone God has chosen, is still young and inexperienced and the work is great; for the temple [הַבִּירָה] is not for man, but for the LORD God." (1 Chron 29:1)

> And give to my son Solomon a perfect heart to keep Your commandments, Your testimonies and Your statutes, and to do *them* all, and to build the temple [הַבִּירָה], for which I have made provision. (1 Chron 29:19)

"Shushan the fortress" connects this physical locale to the image of the temple of Israel. The word *Shushan* in Hebrew means "lily." When describing the temple of Solomon, it refers to the capitals on the tops of the

---

[67]By "loosely," I mean I do not distinguish the author-oriented or the reader-oriented approach so sharply. I read Esther with both approaches in mind.

[68]Midrash Rabbah Esther interprets the text through the rabbis' intertextual reading, linking specific elements in Esther to what they thought were the related texts in the rest of the Hebrew Bible.

pillars in the porch being of a lily design (1 Kings 7:19). In Hosea, *lily* comes to be associated not only with Israel but also with the temple, since the parallel reference to *lily* is Lebanon, which is often identified with the temple in Jerusalem (Hos 14:5), as noted above. Shushan also appears as the Persian capitol in Nehemiah and Daniel (Neh 1:1; Dan 8:2). Elsewhere, Shushan as the lily appears frequently in the Song of Songs to describe the female protagonist and her physical attributes (Song 2:2, 16; 4:5; 6:2-3; 7:2), and once describing the male protagonist's lips (Song 5:13). The association of Shushan with Israel, and *fortress* with the temple in Jerusalem, may conjure the memory of the temple in Jerusalem.

One cannot miss that Esther and Chronicles were written around the same period.[69] In the Hebrew canon, Esther is placed at the end of the Megilloth, followed by Daniel, Ezra-Nehemiah, and then Chronicles. Esther's canonical position and association with Daniel are apparent through their sharing similar themes, especially with Daniel 1–6. Esther's canonical affinity with Ezra-Nehemiah may suggest their similarity given their shared historical period and their emphasis on Jewish identity.

The place of Chronicles at the end of the canon seems to make it a conclusion to the Writings. The suggested dating of Chronicles ranges from 527–500 BCE to 166 BCE.[70] The intermediary date, around 400 BCE, has the most supporters. In regard to the dating of Esther, there is no conclusive evidence and thus no real agreement. Moore suggests that the book was composed in either the late Persian (539–332 BCE) or early Hellenistic periods (331–168 BCE) in light of its sympathetic attitude toward a Gentile king. Jon Levenson places the date of composition some time after the reign of Xerxes but before the watershed of the mid-second century BCE. Michael Fox argues that Esther's language is a mixture of early and late Biblical Hebrew. He suggests a third-century dating for the book.[71]

---

[69]Both books are considered postexilic and likely were written after the third century BCE.

[70]Kalimi proposes three possible dates—an early, a late, and an intermediary one. See Julius Steinberg and Timothy J. Stone with the assistance of Rachel Marie Stone, *The Shape of the Writings*, Siphrut 16 (Winona Lake, IN: Eisenbrauns, 2015), 215-18.

[71]See Carey A. Moore, *Esther*, AB (Garden City, NY: Doubleday, 1971), lix; Jon Douglas Levenson, *Esther: A Commentary*, OTL (Louisville, KY: Westminster John Knox, 1997), 26; Michael V. Fox, *Character and Ideology in the Book of Esther* (Grand Rapids, MI: Eerdmans, 1991), 139-40.

Although the dating for Chronicles and Esther is not definitive, the books fall into a relatively similar historical period, and therefore the use of *fortress* as a double entendre, referring to both an earthly location and a heavenly abode, is probable. It is likely that the word *fortress* is a late Hebrew word from the postexilic period or an Akkadian or Persian loanword.[72] Intriguingly, in Esther, "Shushan the fortress" seems to replace the temple in Jerusalem as the center of action. Those who are conscious of Israel's temple may wonder, "Where is God now?" Therefore the phrase conjures up images of familiarity as well as foreignness.

Garden. In Esther, the garden (גִּנָּה) is closely connected to the courtyard in the house of the king. *Garden*, in the context of the ancient Near East, is associated with a palace or a temple.[73] Later in the book of Esther, the king in his rage goes out to the palace garden (Esther 7:7-8). Mohammad Gharipour's study on Persian gardens provides both textual and visual illustrations of gardens at that time. They were usually enclosed and designed as a "micro-paradise" with a pleasant environment including shady areas, fountains and water channels, a pavilion, and a wall separating it from the outside world.[74] Ezekiel confirms this garden-temple imagery. When addressing the king of Tyre, Ezekiel compares his supreme status to the Garden of Eden: "You were in Eden, the garden of God" (Ezek 28:13).

The word *house* is a double entendre. In the ancient world, a house was a palace as well as a temple.[75] From archaeological finds we know that the boundary between ancient palaces and temples was often blurry. Michael Roaf's study on palaces and temples in ancient Mesopotamia reveals that Mesopotamian palaces were not just residences but also included temples and other functionary buildings. In addition, gardens were often constructed

---

[72]*BDB* 108. In Nehemiah, the word בִּירָה refers to a fortress near the temple (Neh 2:8; 7:2).

[73]Widespread attention has been given to the connection between garden and temple and the idea that the earthly temple reflects the heavenly temple. See, for instance, Beale, *Temple and the Church's Mission*, 31-44.

[74]Mohammad Gharipour, *Persian Gardens and Pavilions: Reflections in History, Poetry and the Arts* (London: I. B. Tauris, 2013), 1.

[75]"House" appears in Esther 1:5, 8-9, 22. In the ancient world, temple and palace originate from similar concepts. This is evident in the shared vocabulary between palace and temple. In Akkadian, *ekallu* comes from the Sumerian *é.gal*, which means a "big house." Another Akkadian word, *bītu*, refers to a semantic range that includes a house, a palace, or a temple. In the same way, in Hebrew הֵיכָל refers to either a palace or a temple. In the Aramaic of Dan 4:4, "house" and "palace" are used synonymously and parallel to each other.

alongside the palace-temple complex.[76] Likewise, in ancient Iran, the distinction between buildings where religion was practiced and buildings that served as palatial compounds was anything but rigid.[77]

Therefore, in the cultural world of Esther, "the courtyard of the garden of the house of the king" indicates an earthly, Gentile palace, but the shared semantics between the palace structure and Israel's sacred space enable the reader to relate the earthly palace with the temple of God—only in this case, the temple of God is nowhere to be seen.

Royalty. The root "royalty" (מֶלֶךְ) appears in Esther 1 with great frequency, along with its variations, such as in "his royal throne" (Esther 1:2), "his reign" (Esther 1:3), "the riches of the glory of his kingdom" (Esther 1:4), "by the hand of the king" (Esther 1:7), "royal house" (Esther 1:9), "King Ahasuerus" (Esther 1:1-2, 9) and "Queen Vashti" (Esther 1:9). In fact, the root "royalty" (מֶלֶךְ) appears no fewer than forty-five times in Esther 1. Such frequent occurrences of the root "royalty" on the one hand convey the image of the king, his palace, and its royal activities. On the other hand, they reflect the temple setting. Only here, the kingly language projects into an unknown space and prompts questions such as: Where is God? Where is the temple? Is there a heavenly temple that is unseen but present in disguise? As Iain Duguid observes, the phrase "royal glory" (כְּבוֹד מַלְכוּתוֹ), describing the kingdom of Ahasuerus in Esther 1:4, also appears in Psalm 145:11, where it depicts God's glorious kingdom (כְּבוֹד מַלְכוּתְךָ). Only here the glorious kingdom of Ahasuerus is visible, but God's glorious kingdom is unseen.[78] This reality of the unseen kingdom, which extends to the whole earth, is expressed elsewhere in the Psalms:

> The Lord reigns, He is clothed with majesty;
> The Lord has clothed and girded Himself with strength;
> Indeed, the world is firmly established, it will not be moved. (Ps 93:1)

---

[76]Michael Roaf, "Palaces and Temples in Ancient Mesopotamia," in *Civilizations of the Ancient Near East*, ed. Jack M. Sasson (Peabody, MA: Hendrickson, 1995), 1:427, 433, 439-40.

[77]Margaret Cool Root, "Palace to Temple—King to Cosmos: Achaemenid Foundation Texts in Iran," in Boda and Novotny, *From the Foundations*, 175. In the biblical account, Solomon built his own palace and a house for his queen, the daughter of Pharaoh, after he built the temple (1 Kings 6–7), suggesting the close affinity between palace and temple.

[78]Iain Duguid, "But Did They Live Happily Ever After? The Eschatology of the Book of Esther," *Westminster Theological Journal* 68 (2006): 88.

The LORD reigns, let the earth rejoice;
Let the many islands be glad. (Ps 97:1)

The LORD reigns, let the peoples tremble;
He is enthroned *above* the cherubim, let the earth shake! (Ps 99:1)

Therefore, in the ancient mind, earthly royalty are connected to heavenly royalty. The earthly king links to the heavenly king. The unseen God does not preclude his presence entirely. Early Jewish exegetes were familiar with this earthly-heavenly connection when they read Esther. For example, in Esther Rabbah, concerning the phrase "on the throne of his kingdom" (Esther 1:1), Rabbi Aibu says,

> It is written, "For the kingdom is the Lord's; and He is the ruler over the nations" (Ps 22:29), and yet you say here (that Ahasuerus sat) on the throne of his kingdom? The truth is that formerly sovereignty was vested in Israel, but when they sinned it was taken from them and given to the other nations, as the biblical text says, "And I will give the land over into the hand of evil men" (Ezek 30:12).[79]

In the worldview of Rabbi Aibu, God reigns, and his dominion is over all earthly rulers. When a Gentile king sits on the throne, it means that his authority is given by God. The frequent appearance of royal vocabulary in Esther connects it to the divine realm. One is likely to form two images in mind—the earthly king and the heavenly king.

Wine and drinking vessels. Scholars have long noted the prominence of the banquet theme in the book of Esther.[80] Sandra Berg asserts, "Banquets provide the settings for several significant plot developments. As such, they form an important motif in Esther."[81] Over the course of the book, nine banquets are described, three of them in Esther 1.[82] In this first

---

[79]Maurice Simon, trans., *Midrash Rabbah: Esther* (London: Soncino, 1939), 29.

[80]For instance, Sandra Beth Berg, *The Book of Esther: Motifs, Themes, and Structure*, Society of Biblical Literature Dissertation Series 44 (Missoula, MT: Scholars Press, 1979), 31-37; David J. A. Clines, *The Esther Scroll: The Story of the Story*, JSOTSup 30 (Sheffield: University of Sheffield Press, 1984), 36-37; Fox, *Character and Ideology*, 156-58; Levenson, *Esther*, 5-6; Young Lee Hertig, "The Subversive Banquets of Esther and Vashti," in *Mirrored Reflections: Reframing Biblical Characters*, ed. Young Lee Hertig and Chloe Sun (Eugene, OR: Wipf & Stock, 2010), 15-29.

[81]Berg, *Book of Esther*, 31.

[82]There are ten banquets if one counts the one in Esther 3:15, where the king and Haman drank after selecting the date to annihilate the Jews. However, the word "banquet" (משתה) is not used here.

chapter, two banquets are held by King Ahasuerus and one by Queen Vashti. All three of them take place at the Persian palace, in the house of the king (Esther 1:5, 9). The purpose of the first two banquets is to display the king's glory, whereas Queen Vashti's banquet portrays ambivalence toward the king and his royal power. A separate banquet held by the queen, targeted at the female guests, attempts to demonstrate the queen's royal power. But the location of the banquet sends a different message. The narrator specifically draws attention to the fact that where Queen Vashti holds the banquet is "in the house of the kingdom which belongs to King Ahasuerus" (Esther 1:9; בֵּית הַמַּלְכוּת אֲשֶׁר לַמֶּלֶךְ אֲחַשְׁוֵרוֹשׁ), suggesting that she is under the authority of the king regardless of her own assertion of power. Therefore, all three banquets are carried out under the king's seemingly absolute monarchy.

Following ancient Near Eastern tradition, these banquets are drinking parties with wine and goblets.[83] The vessels of gold and the varied designs of the vessels (Esther 1:7) once again connect the king's drinking party to his ostentatious and luxurious lifestyle in order to display his standing and to elicit a sense of respect and honor in readers. Gold was a precious metal, often used in the construction of palaces as well as the tabernacle and the temple in Jerusalem. Golden vessels thus remind the reader of the vessels in the Jerusalem temple. In Midrash Rabbah Esther, the rabbi associates the vessels of gold in the Persian temple with the drinking vessels of Solomon: "All King Solomon's drinking vessels *were* of gold, and all the vessels of the house of the forest of Lebanon *were* of pure gold" (1 Kings 10:21).[84] In Daniel, the vessels of the house of God are brought to the house of Nebuchadnezzar, king of Babylon (Dan 1:2). King Belshazzar holds a banquet for a thousand of his nobles, and he is drinking wine with the gold and silver vessels Nebuchadnezzar brought from the temple in Jerusalem (Dan 5:1-2).[85] Moreover, wine appears in Song of Songs as a way to express intoxicated love (Song 1:2; 4:10). The presence of "wine house" suggests a palace or court

---

[83]In a Ugaritic text, the chief god El has a drinking party at which he gets drunk and has to be carried away. See Theodore J. Lewis, trans., "El's Divine Feast," in *Ugaritic Narrative Poetry*, ed. Simon B. Parker, Writings from the Ancient World (Atlanta: Scholars Press, 1997), 193-96.

[84]Simon, *Midrash Rabbah: Esther*, 40.

[85]See also Goswell, "Temple Theme," 515.

setting (Song 2:4).[86] It appears that drinking parties, golden vessels, and kings are closely associated in the palace and royal context.

Wine in Esther almost exclusively designates the king's realm. In the opening chapter, which describes the second banquet held for the people in Shushan, drinks with vessels of gold and vessels of varied design are offered; and royal wine is abundant, as befits the bounty of the king (Esther 1:7). The golden vessels together with the abundance of the royal wine serve as status symbols to display the king's wealth and generosity. It is when the king's heart is merry with wine that he orders Queen Vashti to come forward as a trophy to be displayed (Esther 1:10-11). The other three occurrences of the word *wine* are at Esther's two banquets. The king and Haman drink wine at both banquets, and it is during the drinking of wine at the second banquet that the king asks Esther about the content of her request (Esther 5:6; 7:1, 2). In the context of these drinking banquets, Esther reveals Haman's plot to annihilate all the Jews in Persia. The king, although possessing wealth and power, has been in the dark about this until then. When the king hears this news, he arises from his anger and from drinking wine (Esther 7:7), and then returns from the palace garden to the place where they were drinking wine (Esther 7:8). The king does not know what to do with what he has just heard and has to go away for a while to think and compose himself before returning to the wine banquet.

Wine in Esther forms an interesting paradox in regard to the king of Persia. On the one hand, wine symbolizes the king's bounty, wealth, and power. Royal wine is given out to all the people in Shushan. A law is even established there will be no restraint when it comes to the amount one can drink. Each man can drink as much as he wishes (Esther 1:8). This indulgence in wine further demonstrates the king's generosity. On the other hand, wine exposes the impotence and the comic nature of the king. He is clueless about Haman's plot and has no sense of how to respond to the crisis. For the king, drinking parties are events at which to display his power, but for Esther they are places at which to negotiate and assert power. Thus wine becomes a vehicle through which the author ridicules the both powerful

---

[86]"Wine house" is often translated as "banquet hall" (NASB, NIV, NLT) or "banqueting house" (ESV, NRSV, NKJV). Arabic poetry in medieval times often associated wine with a courtly celebrations. See Pardes, *Song of Songs*, 65-66.

and powerless king of Persia. That there are seven occurrences of wine in the book of Esther thus makes this farce all the more perfect and complete. Hence, banquets of wine at the Persian palace are associated with the other types of royal-wine banquet scenes as well as the temple vessels in Jerusalem and their subsequent journeys after the exile.

Myrrh and spices. The presence of myrrh and spices in connection with the women in the book of Esther forms another intersection of words with Israel's temple imagery, but not limited to it. Upon the dethronement of Queen Vashti, King Ahasuerus listens to the advice of his eunuchs and organizes a search for her replacement through a beauty pageant. It is at this time that Esther is taken to the palace and placed in the custody of Hegai, who is in charge of the women in the harem. Then the text says, "When the turn for each girl arrived to go in to the King Ahasuerus at the end of twelve months according to the law of the women, for thus the days were filled with rubbing them: six months with oil of myrrh and six months with spices and with cosmetics of the women" (Esther 2:12). Each woman, before being summoned to meet the king, has to undergo a yearlong beauty-treatment regimen. The length of time alone suggests an improbable situation, one that likely aims to invoke a laugh from the reader. This extensive beauty treatment involves six months with oil of myrrh and six months with spices. Presumably, the oil of myrrh and the spices are applied to the bodies of the women. Myrrh (מֹר) is an Arabian gum derived from the bark of a tree, the *Balsamodendron Myrrha.*[87] Here it functions as an aromatic ointment that is meant to make the women smell good.

One of the most significant images associated with myrrh is that of anointing, especially in the context of setting apart vessels and priests for services of the sanctuary. So, for example, God instructs Moses, saying: "Take also for yourself the finest of spices: of flowing myrrh five hundred *shekels*, and of fragrant cinnamon half as much, two hundred and fifty, and of fragrant cane two hundred and fifty" (Ex 30:23). "Flowing myrrh" is the best, finest, choicest myrrh. It was carefully prepared by pressing and mixing.[88] The holy oil is a perfume mixture. With it Moses is to anoint the

---

[87] BDB 600. *Balsamodendron Myrrha* means "spiced myrrh."
[88] BDB 600.

tent of meeting, the ark of the testimony, the table and all its utensils, the
lampstand and its utensils, the altar of incense, the altar of burnt offering
and all its utensils, and the laver and its stand (Ex 30:25-28). The oil mixture
is also used to anoint Aaron and his sons, consecrating them to minister as
priests to God (Ex 30:30).[89]

Myrrh, in and of itself, may suggest merely a perfume or an ointment
for nonreligious uses.[90] However, when myrrh is associated with the
anointing oil used in God's sanctuary, it takes on a different meaning,
pointing to the temple and priestly imagery. In Esther, myrrh is used for
the women preparing themselves to see the king. The word may suggest a
secular connotation, but its link with the myrrh in the Song of Songs as
well as the anointing oil in the book of Exodus points to its function as
setting persons apart for special functions. The women in the harem are
being set apart for the enjoyment of the king. Myrrh, then, becomes a part
of the ritual process that distinguishes the women in the harem from those
outside it.[91]

The beauty treatment of the women in the harem involves six months
with oil of myrrh and six months with spices. Here spices are used as a rite
of purification as well as a fragrance. Like myrrh, spices have their sacred
uses in the tabernacle. The finest of the spices are used with the sacred oil
to anoint the vessels in the tabernacle as well as the clothes of the priests
(Ex 30:23-33). The choice spices in Song of Songs 4:14 are listed in Exodus
30:23, 34: "myrrh, cinnamon, and calamus for the holy anointing oil, and
stacte, onycha, galbanum, and frankincense for the holy perfume."[92] The

---

[89]This exact nature of mixing the oil and its exclusive use for holy vessels and holy priests indicates
its sacredness and seriousness. Anyone who violates the above would have been cut off from his
people (Ex 30:33). See J. Hausmann, "*mōr*," in *Theological Dictionary of the Old Testament*, ed. G.
Johannes Botterweck and Helmer Ringgren, trans. John T. Willis et al. (Grand Rapids, MI: Eerdmans, 1974–2006), 8:559-60.

[90]In Proverbs, the adulteress uses myrrh to spice up her bed (Prov 7:17). In the New Testament,
myrrh is also used as an anesthetic (Mk 15:23) and to embalm the bodies of the dead (Jn 19:39),
as well as being offered as a gift (Mt 2:11). See Munro, *Spikenard and Saffron*, 49n18.

[91]Wetter, drawing from Timothy Beals's study on ritual, suggests that ritual plays a part in Esther's
ethnic identity. The twelve-month beauty treatment before the girls are introduced to the king
changes not only their bodies but also their identities. Therefore, the ritual serves to separate
the girls from their previous ties and incorporates them into the Persian court. See Anne-Mareike Wetter, "*On Her Account*": *Reconfiguring Israel in Ruth, Esther, and Judith* (London: T&T
Clark, 2015), 101-3.

[92]Kingsmill, *Song of Songs*, 161. Kingsmill also lists references to the spices in 1 Enoch.

presence of myrrh and spices in the Persian palace suggests a subtle connection with both their secular and their sacred functions.

In sum, Shushan the fortress, the garden of the Persian palace, the house of the king, royal images of the king, banquets of wine, drinking vessels, and myrrh and spices can be applied to both a royal cluster of images and to Israel's sacred space. Palace and temple are closely linked by their shared ambiance. By itself, each word or term might not suggest a temple connection, but together the shared vocabulary and their associations with the temple imagery may conjure a sense of suspicion on their possible affinities. The presence of various royal elements in the Persian palace makes God's absence even more pronounced. What could be the author's intentions of creating these subtle links (if they did)? The following are some possibilities:

1. The author may intentionally use the royal imagery in Esther as a way to hide or subvert the images' other meaning—namely, a divine kingdom that is unseen but is at work behind human eyes. To conceive these shared imageries as accidental and random is unreasonable.[93]

2. The author intends to turn his implied reader to anger and destruction, since the descriptions of the palace serve precisely as the antithesis of the temple in Jerusalem. The vivid colors of the feast in the Persian palace add majesty to the narrative at first, but then turn into "symbols of destruction for the Jewish people, a commemoration of the Temple and a condemnation of the Jews of Shushan."[94]

3. It is also conceivable that both the Persian palace and the temple in Jerusalem were constructed similarly according to the conventional design of the time and used the best possible materials available at the time to present their optimum value to the world.

4. The author may intend to evoke a sense of suspicion on the part of the reader: the Persian palace is here, but where is the temple? Where is divine presence that is often associated with the temple? The

---

[93]Duguid, "But Did They Live," 85-98.
[94]Jonathan Grossman, *Esther: The Outer Narrative and the Hidden Reading*, Siphrut 6 (Winona Lake, IN: Eisenbrauns, 2011), 24.

Persian palace seems to have replaced the temple as the center of world power. Where is God at this time of history?

All four possibilities are probable explanations for the subtle connections between palace and temple in Esther. The first position is common of Protestant Christians, who tend to read Esther through the lens of faith by reading God into the text. My response to this position is that this reading is valid for the Greek texts of Esther, where God indeed works behind the scenes, but the Hebrew Masoretic Text omits God's name for a reason. Any speculations about that reason remain probable readings and not a definitive reading. The second position is likely but conjectural. How can we be sure that this reading is the only reading? What is the purpose of inciting anger in implied readers? Is it to punish them for their ancestors' apostasy or motivate them to retaliate against the enemy? The third position is devoid of any further correlation between the Persian palace and the temple in Jerusalem and simply suggests they are buildings that share similar ambience.

The fourth position is what I propose: that audiences can generate various responses or even conflicting responses to the subtle palace-temple connection, but no one can be certain of its precise interpretation due to the absence of God in the text. The presence of the Persia palace forms a stark contrast with the absence of the temple. Consequently, the absence of the physical temple in Esther parallels the literary absence of God in Esther. Is the temple theme indeed hiding, as Esther is a "the book of hiding"?[95] Could Esther be a sort of palimpsest where an earlier text with the divine name or temple language was erased but their traces remain?[96] Since the book of Esther uses other veiled languages such as "another place" or "who knows" to convey its message, could it be possible that the shared royal ambience between the Persian palace and Israel's temple imagery suggest their theological connections? This uncertainty regarding the divine activity in Esther may be due to its setting in the time of exile, when the destruction of the temple placed doubt on the manifestation of divine presence.

---

[95]Timothy K. Beal, *The Book of Hiding: Gender, Ethnicity, Annihilation, and Esther* (London: Routledge, 1997).

[96]Palimpsest refers to a text written over an earlier, erased text. See Beal, *Book of Hiding*, x, 29.

After entertaining the notion of divine presence and absence in Esther, Melton concludes, "It cannot be determined whether God is present or absent in Esther."[97] I would take this sentiment further to say that God is absent literally in Esther, but this does not preclude his possible presence in other ways entirely, no matter how subtle or hidden it may be.

The following section takes a step further in probing the question of divine presence in absence through Mordecai's clothing.

The Persian palace and Mordecai's clothing. Esther 1:6 provides a detailed description of the Persian palace. It aims to showcase the ostentation, luxury, honor, and glory of the Persian Empire.

חוּר כַּרְפַּס וּתְכֵלֶת אָחוּז בְּחַבְלֵי־בוּץ וְאַרְגָּמָן עַל־גְּלִילֵי כֶסֶף וְעַמּוּדֵי שֵׁשׁ מִטּוֹת זָהָב וָכֶסֶף עַל רִצְפַת בַּהַט־וָשֵׁשׁ וְדַר וְסֹחָרֶת

White cotton, and violet fastened with cord of byssus and red purple to cylinder of silver and pillar of alabaster, couches of gold and silver upon pavement of porphyry and alabaster and pearl and stone.[98]

Esther 8:15 describes the clothing of Mordecai when he was promoted to royalty:

וּמָרְדֳּכַי יָצָא מִלִּפְנֵי הַמֶּלֶךְ בִּלְבוּשׁ מַלְכוּת תְּכֵלֶת וָחוּר וַעֲטֶרֶת זָהָב גְּדוֹלָה וְתַכְרִיךְ בּוּץ וְאַרְגָּמָן וְהָעִיר שׁוּשָׁן צָהֲלָה וְשָׂמֵחָה

Then Mordecai went out from the presence of the king in royal clothing violet and white, and a great golden wreath and robe of byssus and red purple. And the city of Shushan cried and rejoiced.

The detailed description of Mordecai's garment bears astounding resemblance to the descriptions of the Persian palace in Esther 1:6. This is reminiscent of the parallel connection between the decorations of Israel's temple and the decorations of the priestly garment. The high priest's clothing is made of "the blue and the purple and the scarlet material" (Ex 28:5). The ephod and the breastpiece of judgment are made from the same colors (Ex 28:6, 15). These colors are also the exact same colors as the

---

[97]Melton, *Where Is God*, 74.
[98]"White cotton" could also be translated "fine linen." "Pillar" could also be translated "columns." "Couches" could also be translated "beds." "Porphyry" could also be translated "marble." "Pearl" could also be translated "mother of pearl." "Stone" could also be translated "mosaics."

curtains, the veils, and the screen for the doorway of the tabernacle (Ex 25:4, 26:1, 31, 36), reflecting that Israel's priesthood symbolizes the cosmic temple. The jewels and the three sections of the priestly garment also point to the heavenly temple.[99] Carmen Imes's study on the priestly regalia in the ancient Near East suggests that the garments of similar quality and style to Aaron's priestly attire were "typically associated with royal, priestly or divine figures."[100]

Esther 1:6 begins with the decorations of the palace complex, focusing particularly on the hangings, marble columns, couches, and pavement. White cotton (כַּרְפַּס) can also be understood as "fine linen." This fine linen is made of white and violet thread or wool (תְּכֵלֶת). Elsewhere in the biblical text, violet thread is exclusively used in the decorations of the tabernacle and the temple. In the construction of the tabernacle, God instructs Moses to gather materials, which include violet thread (Ex 25:4; 35:6). Violet thread is used to make the curtains of the tabernacle (Ex 26:1), the clothing of the priests (Ex 39:29), and the reconstruction of the temple (2 Chron 2:6). "Cord of byssus" (בְּחַבְלֵי־בוּץ) also has temple connections. When the ark is brought back to Jerusalem, David wears a robe of byssus (1 Chron 15:27), as do all the Levitical singers, to celebrate the occasion (2 Chron 5:12). Interestingly, when Mordecai is promoted, he goes out from the presence of the king in a royal robe of byssus, the exact material of the Persian palace.

The cord of byssus is paired with red purple. Red purple (אַרְגָּמָן) reminds one of the major colors used in the tabernacle (Ex 25:4; 35:6, 23) and is used in Israel's temple tradition, as well as an esteemed noble color in the ancient Near East (Judg 8:26, Jer 10:9).[101] In the tabernacle, red purple is one of the colors of the curtains (Ex 26:1; 36:8), the veil (Ex 26:31; 36:35), the screen of the doorway of the tent (Ex 26:36; 36:37), the screen of the gate of the court (Ex 27:16; 38:18), the ephod of the priests (Ex 28:6; 39:2), the woven band

---

[99]For details of the connections between Israel's priestly garment to the cosmic temple, see Beale, *Temple and the Church's Mission*, 39-45. Imes also points out the parallel connection between Aaron's priestly clothing with the design of the tabernacle. Carmen Joy Imes, "Between Two Worlds: The Functional and Symbolic Significance of the High Priestly Regalia," in *Dress and Clothing in the Hebrew Bible: "For All Her Households Are Clothed in Crimson,"* ed. Finitsis Antonios, LHBOTS 679 (London: T&T Clark, 2019), 37.

[100]Imes, "Between Two Worlds," 39.

[101]Red purple appears in Prov 31:22, where it describes the clothing of the woman of noble character, and Ezek 27:7, where it addresses Tyre and describes its clothing of blue and purple from the coasts of Elishah.

of the shoulder pieces of the priests (Ex 28:8; 39:5), the breastpiece of judgment (Ex 28:15; 39:8), the pomegranates of the hem of the ephod (Ex 28:33; 39:24), and the tunics of the priests (Ex 39:29). Red purple is also one of the major colors of the veil of the second temple (2 Chron 3:14).

In addition, Aaron Koller observes that the combination of violet wool (תְּכֵלֶת), fine linen or byssus (בוּץ), and red purple (אַרְגָּמָן) appears nineteen times in the description of the tabernacle in Exodus 25–28; 35–40 as well as in the description of the temple in 2 Chronicles 3:14. Outside Esther, this combination only appears twice, once in Jeremiah 10:9 and once in Ezekiel 27:7. It is not surprising that Koller draws the conclusion that this combination of descriptions in Shushan the fortress "conjures up images of the Temple in the mind of the Jewish reader."[102] Together with byssus, red purple is also the major color of the royal robe of Mordecai (Esther 8:15).[103]

Esther 1:6 continues with the description of the white linen and violet thread, which are fastened with a cord of byssus and red purple to a cylinder of silver.[104] Silver and gold are precious metals. Not only are they used in the decorations of the Persian palace, but they are also used in the construction of the tabernacle and the temple (Ex 25:3). Gold is used extensively in overlaying the outside and the inside of the ark (Ex 25:11), the rings and the poles of the ark (Ex 25:12-13), the cherubim (Ex 25:18), the table of showbread and all its utensils (Ex 25:23-29), the hooks of the veil and the screen (Ex 26:32, 37), and the altar of incense (Ex 30:3-5). The clothing of the priest also mirrors the color and material of the tabernacle, with gold, blue, red purple, and scarlet (Ex 28:5). Silver is used in the sockets (Ex 26:19, 32) and in the hooks of the pillars and their bands (Ex 27:10-11, 17).

---

[102]Aaron Koller, *Esther in Ancient Jewish Thought* (Cambridge: Cambridge University Press, 2014), 100.

[103]Further indications of the combinations of blue and red-purple in Israel's temple imagery can be found in S. Busatta, "The Perception of Color," *Antrocom Online Journal of Anthropology* 10, no. 2 (2014): 317-19.

[104]The word "cylinder" (גָּלִיל) appears in the Song of Songs, where it refers to the hands or arms of the man (יָדָיו גְּלִילֵי זָהָב, Song 5:14). The woman's description of her beloved resembles that of a statue, worthy of adoration. Longman, while acknowledging that the language being used here is also used to describe the gods in the ancient Near East, also thinks that the woman is most likely using godlike language to describe the man as an expression of her vision of love. Longman, *Song of Songs*, 173.

Coincidentally or not, Mordecai's wreath is made out of gold as well. Just as the priests' clothing matches the color and the material used in the tabernacle, Mordecai's clothing matches that of the Persian palace. This parallel is so striking that one can't help but wonder: What does this mean? Berg thinks that Mordecai's robe, plus the fact that he issues his own edict, suggest that Mordecai is acting like a king.[105]

However, the crown (עֲטָרָה) that Mordecai wears is not the royal crown (כֶּתֶר) that Queen Vashti wears in Esther 1:11, nor the crown that Esther wears in Esther 2:17, nor the crown that Haman fantasizes about in Esther 6:8. This suggests that Mordecai is not a king but is endowed with royalty nevertheless. Clines indicates that Mordecai's clothing was possibly no different from Haman's everyday attire. His clothing not only serves as a reversal of his sackcloth in Esther 4, but also symbolizes the elevation of the Jews.[106] Levenson draws attention to the similarity between Mordecai's clothing and Daniel's clothing (Dan 5:7, 29) when he rules as the third in the empire. He also points out that the garments and colors mentioned in Esther 8:15 are reminiscent of the vestments of the priesthood in the Torah. With the overlapping offices of royalty and priesthood, Mordecai's clothing may suggest that he is perceived as a kind of secular priest celebrated for his service of saving his people.[107] Like Aaron as the mediator between the sacred and the profane, could Mordecai in his Persian royal regalia also suggest similar function and symbolism as the mediator between the Persian and the Jewish worlds?

---

[105]Berg, *Book of Esther*, 64.

[106]D. J. A. Clines, *Ezra, Nehemiah, Esther*, New Century Bible Commentary (London: Eerdmans, 1984), 318. Berlin also thinks that Mordecai's clothing was a typical fashion at the Persian court. See Adele Berlin, *Esther: The Traditional Hebrew Text with the New JPS Translation*, JPS Bible Commentary (Philadelphia: Jewish Publication Society, 2001), 79. Firth thinks that Mordecai's new clothing indicates that he now fills the old role of Haman. David G. Firth, *The Message of Esther* (Downers Grove, IL: InterVarsity Press, 2010), 118.

[107]Levenson, *Esther*, 116. Fried's study demonstrates the power dynamics between priest and king in the Persian Empire. She observes three models: (1) Self-governance: While the king ruled the Persian Empire, a high priest ruled its provinces, such as Yehud. Each province worked independently of the others. (2) Imperial authorization: as long as the central authority in Persia received tribute from its provinces, each province retained its own socioeconomic unit with its own social institutions, internal structure, laws, customs, and traditions. (3) Central control: The rulers controlled all the provinces. In Judah, this would include the Davidic descendant as well as the priesthood. See Lisbeth S. Fried, *The Priest and the Great King: The Temple-Palace Relations in Persian Empire* (Winona Lake, IN: Eisenbrauns, 2004), 2-4.

Indeed, the boundaries between priesthood and kingship, religious and imperial status, are often blurred in the ancient Near Eastern context.[108] The resemblance of Mordecai's clothing to the descriptions of the Persian palace reflects Persian identity and Israel's sacred space and priesthood, as well as wealth, honor, and nobility.[109] What might be the theological implications of this resemblance? Below are some possibilities:

1. That Mordecai's clothing bears a striking similarity to the decorations of the Persian palace suggests their close affinity. Just like Israel's priestly garment parallels the decorations of the tabernacle and thus reflects a heavenly temple, Mordecai's royal clothing also corresponds to and reflects the Persian palace and Persian identity. Mordecai the Jew attains a priestly status at the Persian court. This could be extreme irony and comedy. It celebrates the achievement of the Jews at the expanse of the Persians. If the genre of Esther is satire, ridiculing the Persian regime, then this reading is a likely one.

2. As a Jew, Mordecai represents Jewish identity, as the book frequently reinforces.[110] In light of this, Mordecai's Persian royal clothing takes on a different meaning. On the one hand, it demonstrates that a double identity, namely, a Jewish-Persian identity, coexists in Mordecai. On the other hand, that a diaspora Jew ascends to royalty at a foreign court suggests nothing short of a miracle. Could there be divine presence at work to ensure this outcome? Mordecai's clothing reflects a blending of Persian-Jewish identity and may suggest an ambivalent but dynamic reality between visible earthly power and the invisible heavenly reign.

3. That Mordecai's clothing resembles the Persian palace also suggests the outcome could all be credited to human responsibility without

---

[108]Root, "Palace to Temple—King to Cosmos," 169.

[109]Esther Rabbah correlates "beauty/splendor" (תִפְאֶרֶת) in Esther 1:4 to the "beauty/splendor" (תִפְאֶרֶת) of the garments of Aaron and his brothers (Ex 28:2), further demonstrating the shared semantics and conceptual world between palace and temple priesthood. See Simon, *Midrash Rabbah: Esther*, 33.

[110]The text repeatedly uses the signature phrase "Mordecai the Jew" (מָרְדֳּכַי הַיְהוּדִי) to highlight his Jewish identity (Esther 5:13; 6:10; 8:7; 9:29, 31; 10:3; see Esther 2:5; 3:4). Fox characterizes Mordecai as an ideal figure for the Jewish people living in the diaspora. His Jewishness is a necessary constituent of this ideal. He is identified first and last by his Jewishness (Fox, *Character and Ideology*, 185-86).

any intervention of God. Taking the text at face value, the lack of any reference to the divine name or God's involvement in any blatant way supports this notion.

4. It is also possible that the descriptions of Mordecai's clothing suggests that the materials and decorations were best available ones at the time, reminiscent of the priestly garments in Exodus in that they are made of the best materials at the time for the purpose of demonstrating the glory and beauty of priesthood (Ex 28:40).

5. Reading the story of Esther canonically, however, yields another possibility—that ascension to power in Esther can be credited to human beings alone without overt divine intervention. German scholar Martin Wahl von Harald has noted the motif of ascension in the book of Esther. He observes the shared motif of elevation among Joseph, Daniel, and Esther and notes that the setting of all three narratives is a foreign court during exile, and that as the stories unfold, all three characters ascend to power. Given the juxtaposition of the three texts, he concludes that all three stories testify to the salvation of God among exilic communities.[111] However, as I will discuss in chapter six, though the motif of ascension of Esther does resonate with Joseph and Daniel, at the same time it counters those stories. While God is with Joseph and Daniel, the name of God is absent in Esther, which means one should interpret the motifs in Esther differently from those in the narratives of Joseph and Daniel. The literary absence of God in Esther points to the book's subversive function, unlike its similar type-narratives, such as in Joseph and Daniel's stories.

---

[111]Martin Wahl von Harald, "Das Motiv des 'Aufstiegs' in der Hofgeschichte: Am Beispiel von Joseph, Esther und Daniel," *Zeitschrift für die alttestamentliche Wissenschaft* 112 (2000): 59-74. Other scholars who have noted the parallel ascension of Joseph and Esther include Berg, *Book of Esther*, 123-52; Susan Niditch, "Esther: Folklore, Wisdom, Feminism and Authority," in *A Feminist Companion to Esther, Judith and Susanna*, ed. Athalya Brenner, FCB (Sheffield: Sheffield Academic Press, 1995), 26-46; Klara Butting, "Esther: A New Interpretation of the Joseph Story in the Fight Against Anti-Semitism and Sexism," in *A Feminist Companion to Ruth and Esther*, ed. Athalya Brenner, FCB 2/3 (Sheffield: Sheffield Academic Press, 1999), 239-48; Berlin, *Esther*, xxxvii; Nathan Ward, *God Unseen: A Theological Introduction to Esther* (Chillicothe, OH: DeWard, 2016), 59-61.

In light of these interpretive possibilities, what is certain is that the outcome of the story of Esther reflects victory on the part of the Jews, and that Esther and Mordecai triumph over their enemies. This ending suggests that, whether God is present in Esther or not, God's chosen people will prevail eventually. This triumph of the Jews is conveyed in part through the symbolism of Mordecai's clothing at the Persian court. The clothing of Mordecai embodies both the Persian royal position as well as Israel's priestly status. A Jew's ascent to the height of a foreign court may be due to humanity's endeavor without God's help. It may also be due to divine providence. Such is the theological ambiguity inherited in a story with the literary absence of God. Through this theological ambiguity and possibilities, the story of Esther forms a conversation with the rest of the canon and directs readers' attention to the dialectic between divine incomprehensibility and human responsibility.

Divine absence in Esther. The book of Esther by itself can be read as an independent story, a historical novella, a diaspora story, or a farce ridiculing the king of Persia and the apparent discrepancy between power and incompetence. However, when read intertextually with Israel's temple imagery, the book suggests otherwise. The book was written with its original audience in mind, an audience that most likely was aware of or even lived in the reality of exile with foreign domination. In times like these, it was expected that one use encrypted language to veil the obvious. Is it possible that the original readers would have connected the earthly realm with the heavenly realm and that there is an inverse relationship between the literary absence of God in the book of Esther and his presence elsewhere in Israel's history?

For the author of Esther, the choice of words must be intentional and meant to elicit a response from its readers. Does the author intend the readers to reflect on matters that transcend what is seen and visible through what is unseen? The possibility of an unseen reality hovers over the description of the tangible Persian palace. One distinctive feature of Bakhtin's dialogism is that its ending is often open. Open-endedness is precisely what happens here. Readers do not know why the book of Esther does not mention the name of God even once, or whether the author is using the descriptions of the Persian palace as a way for readers to imagine an invisible temple. This unknowability and the possible intertextual connections create a sense of open-endedness, which makes the question of the absence of God linger.

Is it possible that in the absence of the physical temple, God is no longer bound by a physical location but transcends it? At the time of exile and Jewish diaspora, is it possible that God's presence has shifted from a physical temple to his people, as exemplified by Mordecai the Jew's ascension at the Persian court, and symbolized by his royal and priestly clothing resembling Israel's priestly garment? Scholars often draw attention to the hidden divine presence in Esther through the story's remarkable coincidences, dramatic reversals, and the final outcome of the story, with the edict against the Jews being revoked and the Jewish people being allowed to avenge their enemies.[112] When Esther is read through the lens of Israel's temple theme and priestly attire, it suggests the possibility that even in the absence of his name and his physical temple, the presence of God is with his chosen people, albeit with theological ambiguity.[113]

TEMPLE: IN THE ABSENCE OF GOD

In both the Song of Songs and Esther, the theme of garden-temple emerges. Both books have intertextual connections with Israel's temple imagery. In the Song, the garden-temple is reminiscent of the Garden of Eden. Both gardens have water streams, precious metals, animals, trees, and a human couple. The garden-temple in the Song is boundless and permeated with love. In Esther, the presence of an invisible and boundless temple is to be imagined through the visible Persian palace. The lexical terms associated

---

[112]For example, David Bland, "God's Activity as Reflected in the Books of Ruth and Esther," *ResQ* 24 (1981): 129-41; Berg, *Book of Esther*, 103-6; Frederic William Bush, *Ruth, Esther*, WBC 9 (Dallas: Word Books, 1996), 325; David Beller, "A Theology of the Book of Esther," *ResQ* 39 (1997): 1-15; Karen H. Jobes, *The NIV Application Commentary: Esther* (Grand Rapids, MI: Zondervan, 1999), 48; Ward, *God Unseen*, 100-109. The rhetorical question Duguid raises summarizes the sentiment of God's hidden work behind human eyes: "How could anyone possibly remember the turning of darkness into light and sorrow to joy without thinking about God?" ("But Did They Live," 94.)

[113]While Brittany Melton's recent work focuses more on the ambiguity of divine presence in the Megilloth, and both divine presence and absence are viable interpretive options, I contend that through a canonical reading of the Megilloth with the rest of the Hebrew Scripture, the Megilloth is intended to be read as Scripture and thus presumes the presence of God, but varies on the degree and manner of that presence.

with the decorations of the Persian palace suggest the language of Israel's sacred space. Although God is absent in the Song and Esther, the idea of the garden-temple-palace may convey his presence in subtle and hidden forms. Just as in the Song the woman's desire to see her beloved intensifies in his absence, in Esther the thought of the presence of God lingers in the mind of the informed reader in its absence. Thus, the association with the garden-temple brings Song of Songs and Esther together with a hint of divine presence in covert and imagined forms.

What do we do in the absence of God?

First, in the absence of God, nature conjures his presence. The whole earth is his temple. In the absence of God, we can go out to see and be in touch with his creation, with plants, trees, flowers, animals, gardens, streams, rivers, canyons, and mountains. All of God's creation declares his glory (Ps 19:1). Through nature, the presence of a divine creator is felt and evoked.

Second, in the absence of God, the love between the human couple also reflects his presence as in the Garden of Eden. The human couple in the garden is sealed by their mutual love for each other. If God is love, then the presence of love between the human couple reflects the presence of God. Though it is invisible and intangible, it is as strong as death.

Third, in the absence of God, the presence of the transitory kingdom with imperfect human rulers compels us to yearn for an invisible kingdom that will last forever. The visible earthly palace will be gone, but the invisible heavenly temple will be there from now until eternity. The theological notion of "already but not yet" can be applied in Esther—that God's people will prevail eventually in the face of evil, but the complete realization of God's kingdom on earth still lies in the future.

Fourth, the accentuation of Mordecai at a foreign court suggests that, in divine absence, God's people can exert wisdom to do what is just for God's people. This exercise of wisdom is grounded in human beings' search for just order in the world. In wisdom theology, a wise person is someone who "both creates order and brings his life into harmony with the established order of the universe."[114] This expresses the confidence that human beings

---

[114]Terence E. Fretheim, *God and World in the Old Testament: A Relational Theology of Creation* (Nashville: Abingdon, 2005), 201.

are capable of discerning what is right and just and to act on it. In the equi-
librium of God's world, there is no place for annihilation of any race, be it
Jewish or any other. Therefore, a dynamic relationship between a hidden
God who works wonders for his people and human responsibility without
divine help is held in tension. In the absence of God, the responsibility falls
on humans to search for justice and to do justice in the here and now.

5

FEAST

PASSOVER *and* PURIM

In the first month, on the fourteenth day
of the month at twilight is the LORD's Passover.

LEVITICUS 23:5

THIS CHAPTER LOOKS AT THE EARLY INTERPRETATIONS of Song of Songs and Esther and inquires into their theological connections through their liturgical functions. The five scrolls, also known as the Megilloth, are associated with five Jewish festivals. In the Jewish liturgical calendar, the Song of Songs is recited at Passover, Ruth is recited on Pentecost, Lamentations is recited on the ninth of Ab, Ecclesiastes is recited during the Feast of Tabernacles, and Esther is recited at Purim. Passover and Purim take place back to back in the spring.[1] Passover takes place during March–April, which is considered the first month of the year (Ex 12:2), and Purim takes

---

[1]Prosic's study on the symbolism of Passover generates a fascinating insight. She notes that according to the Mishnah, a judgment on grain is delivered on Passover. That is during the month when barley is ready to be harvested. Therefore, the time right before Passover was the hungriest time of the year, when supplies from the previous harvest were at their lowest and the new crops were yet to be harvested. She then quotes Song 2:11-12, "For lo, the winter is past, the rain is over and gone. The flowers appear on the earth, the time of singing has come." She further explains that the connection between the season of harvest and the idea of delivery from danger emerged in the exodus story, where the pharaoh and Egypt took on the symbol of the threatening aspects of the period preceding the harvest, Yahweh replaced the harvest, and the rescue from starvation turns into liberation from slavery. See Tamara Prosic, *The Development and Symbolism of Passover Until 70 CE* (London: T&T Clark, 2004), 93-94.

place in February–March, which closes out the liturgical year.[2] The development of the canonical order of these five scrolls is complicated; how the
order of the Megilloth came to its present form is a fascinating story, but
one that is beyond the scope of the chapter.[3]

Though the rabbinic Bible published in 1525 orders the books of the
Megilloth as Song of Songs, Ruth, Lamentations, Ecclesiastes, and Esther,
in practice at what time the five scrolls were used in the five festivals remains unclear.[4] Yet this biblical arrangement of the five scrolls to accord
with their respective festivals points to their likely order, with the Song of
Songs opening the Megilloth and the Esther scroll book ending the collection.[5] At first glance, this arrangement appears to be purely liturgical,
since the festivals occur back to back, ending the seasonal cycle of the year.
However, if one delves further into the arrangement, one can't help but
notice the theological connections behind this liturgical ordering.[6] The
following table presents the connection of the two festivals and their
respective elements.

---

[2] Passover is celebrated in the month of Nisan, which in ancient times was called Abib. Now it usually falls in the month of April. Purim falls in the month of Adar (Esther 3:7).

[3] Some scholars argue that the Megilloth are arranged liturgically, while others think that they are arranged chiastically. That the Talmud, the Masoretic Text, and the JPS Bible all have different arrangements demonstrates this point. Stone proposes that the Megilloth is arranged meaningfully with the books' various conversational partners within the Writings. Every book in the collection has at least one connection to another within the Writings, so none stands alone. See Timothy J. Stone, *The Compilational History of the Megilloth* (Tübingen: Mohr Siebeck, 2013), 207. See also B. C. Gregory, "Megilot and Festivals," *DOTWPW* 457-64.

[4] Christian M. M. Brady, "The Use of the Eschatological Lists Within the Targumim of the Megilloth," *JSJ* 40 (2009): 494.

[5] According to Steinberg, the grouping of the Megilloth occurred only after the sixth century CE. The book arrangements that do not have this group are considered "original," and Baba Batra can be said to be the mother of the family of manuscripts without a grouped Megilloth. See Julius Steinberg, "The Place of Wisdom Literature in an Old Testament Theology: A Thematic and Structural-Canonical Approach," in *The Shape of the Writings*, ed. Julius Steinberg and Timothy J. Stone with the assistance of Rachel Marie Stone, Siphrut 16 (Winona Lake, IN: Eisenbrauns, 2015), 152. Scholars often name Ruth and Esther as the bookends of the Megilloth. Based on similarities in genre, motifs, gender, ethnicity, and theological themes, these two books do present themselves to be read in light of one another. The recent study of the Megilloth that includes three chapters devoted to Ruth and Esther proves this point. See Brad Embry, ed., *Megilloth Studies: The Shape of Contemporary Scholarship* (Sheffield: Sheffield Phoenix, 2016). However, Song of Songs and Esther also bear striking similarities, especially in their liturgical order.

[6] Many scholars consider the lateness of the liturgical order of the Megilloth as discrediting its value for biblical interpretation. I would like to challenge that assumption, since the arrangement of the liturgical order reflects interpreters' perception of their theological connections.

Table 5.1

Religious Year	Hebrew Calendar	Western Correlation	Reading	Feasts
first month	Nisan	March–April	Song of Songs	Passover
	Sivan	May–June	Ruth	Pentecost
	Ab	July–August	Lamentations	Ninth of Ab
	Tishri	September–October	Ecclesiastes	Feast of Tabernacles
last month	Adar	February–March	Esther	Purim

That neither scroll includes the name of God but both are recited at Jewish feasts creates a curious irony. Why would the Song of Songs be chanted in a ritual that commemorates Israel's deliverance from the Egyptians yet do so without explicitly mentioning God once? How does the love between a man and a woman have anything to do with Israel's experience of exodus? Why would the book of Esther, which deliberately does not refer to God, be recounted annually at Purim? Is Purim a religious festival in any way, or does it merely celebrate human effort in achieving the salvation of the Jews? How is the celebration of Purim connected to Israel's deliverance in the exodus? Last but not least, how is Purim connected to Passover? These questions invite readers to put the two scrolls and their liturgical uses together and ask, "Why"?

Another key question pertaining to the order or arrangement of the books is, What sort of scriptural authority does it have in biblical interpretation? The neglect of the Megilloth in the past is precisely due to its lateness as a collection, since most scholars consider texts that are "early" or "original" to be more authoritative. The earliest attestations of the Megilloth as a group come from the Tiberian manuscripts of the tenth and eleventh century CE but may be earlier.[7] However, the tide has shifted in recent years due to growing recognition among scholars that the later uses of Scripture are also an essential component of its interpretation. Therefore, the lateness of the

---

[7]Stone, *Compilational History of the Megilloth*, 102-17.

Megilloth does not preclude how it has been shaped.[8] Steinberg states that throughout history people were thinking of how best to order the biblical books. Issues of genre, chronology, content, and theology are all part of the criteria for a meaningful arrangement of these books. Additionally, the different ways of arranging the books reflect various approaches and possibilities for integrating the biblical books into a greater whole.[9]

This chapter demonstrates that the Song of Songs and Esther, the books recited at Passover and Purim respectively, provide two varied responses to the event of the exodus. In other words, the two scrolls are composed and arranged as bookends in the liturgical order of the Megilloth to reveal the theology of God's presence in absence. In God's absence, especially during the postexilic time, the two feasts recall and commemorate God's faithfulness and deliverance all year round. This later development of the liturgical use of the scrolls testifies to the books' practical meaning to the community of faith throughout all generations, particularly the Jewish community.

THE SONG OF SONGS

How did the Song of Songs not only come to be associated with Passover but even be sung on this most significant Jewish festival, especially given that the word *Passover* is never mentioned in the text? Their association must be a development that occurred after the canonization process in the Council of Jamnia in 70 CE. If the plain sense of the Song of Songs does not mention Passover or the exodus event explicitly, early interpreters must have found a connection between them through a metaphorical or figurative reading of the text. Although Western scholarship has largely abandoned this kind of interpretation due to its incongruence with historical-critical methods, it has been the dominant mode of interpretation since the Song's inclusion in the canon.[10] Marvin Pope remarks that the

---

[8]Amy Erickson and Andrew R. Davis, "Recent Research on the Megilloth (Song of Songs, Ruth, Lamentations, Ecclesiastes, Esther)," *Currents in Biblical Research* 14, no. 3 (2016): 298-318, esp. 298.

[9]Steinberg, "Place of Wisdom Literature," 151.

[10]There are a few exceptions, that is, scholars who use allegory as an interpretive lens to read Song of Songs in the contemporary West. One such exception is Harold Fisch. He contends that the genre of dream itself implies that it contains many meanings, and there is no literal meaning of

allegorical approach has prevailed both in the synagogue and the church. This interpretation is reflected in the Talmud, spreading over the first half of the first millennium.[11] In fact, the reason the Song of Songs is accepted in the canon is primarily due to its metaphorical understanding as a song depicting the love between God and Israel, his chosen people, his bride. In ancient Jewish thought, there is a blurring of distinctions between what is literal and what is metaphorical. In this sense, "erotic language is religious, religious language is erotic."[12]

The Song of Songs and Ecclesiastes (Hebrew: Qohelet) are two of the few books that were considered disputed in the discussion of their inclusion in the canon. The issue had to do with uncleanness of hands and purification. Jacob Neusner explains this rabbinic tradition: if a person touches a document that is considered to be unclean, then that person has to go through a process of purification before eating food. When sages say that a document is unclean through having been touched by unclean hands, they mean that those words and the object (papyrus, manuscript, etc.) on which they are written must be handled with respect and care.[13] Below is the

a dream. He also cites many images that emerge in the Song to demonstrate its multifaceted symbolism. As of result of the nature of the Song, Fisch deems its key interpretative mode to be "the allegorical imperative." That is, the Song must be interpreted allegorically in order to make sense of its meaning. See Harold Fisch, *Poetry with a Purpose: Biblical Poetics and Interpretation* (Bloomington: Indiana University Press, 1988), 89-97. On another note, although the contemporary West has largely abandoned allegorical interpretation, it still persists in the Chinese Christian community due to its cultural and religious mentality, which elevates spiritual over sensual interpretations. See Chloe Sun, "As Strong as Death: The Immortality of Allegory in the Chinese Reception of the Song of Songs," in *Honoring the Past, Looking to the Future: Essays from the 2014 International Congress of Ethnic Chinese Biblical Scholars*, ed. Gale A. Yee and John Y. H. Yieh (Hong Kong: Divinity School of Chung Chi College, 2016), 217-46. What Western scholarship abandons, Chinese scholarship continues.

[11]Marvin H. Pope, *Song of Songs*, AB 7C (Garden City, NY: Doubleday, 1977), 89. Pope understands the term *allegorical* in a broader sense, without differentiating it from metaphorical, figurative, or typological senses as other scholars such as Boyarin and Kaplan do.

[12]Judith A. Kates, "Entering the Holy of Holies: Rabbinic Midrash and the Language of Intimacy," in *Scrolls of Love: Ruth and the Song of Songs*, ed. Peter S. Hawkins and Lesleigh Cushing Stahlberg (New York: Fordham University Press, 2006), 213. See also Ilana Pardes, *The Song of Songs: A Biography*, Lives of Great Religious Books (Princeton, NJ: Princeton University Press, 2019), 17.

[13]Jacob Neusner, *Israel's Love Affair with God: Song of Songs* (Valley Forge, PA: Trinity Press International, 1993), 2. Lim attempts to resolve the enigma regarding the interconnectedness between Holy Scripture and the cleanliness of hands. See Timothy H. Lim, "The Defilement of the Hands as a Principle Determining the Holiness of Scriptures," *Journal of Theological Studies* 61, no. 2 (2010): 501-15.

verbatim report of the discussion concerning the status of the Song of Songs
and Qohelet in the Hebrew canon:

> All sacred scriptures impart uncleanness to hands. The Song of Songs and
> Qohelet impart uncleanness to hands. Rabbi Judah says, "Song of Songs im-
> parts uncleanness to hands, but as to Qohelet there is dispute." Rabbi Yose
> says, "Qohelet does not impart uncleanness to hands, but as to Song of Songs
> there is dispute." Rabbi Simeon says, "Qohelet is among the lenient rulings
> of the House of Shammari and strict rulings of the House of Hillel." Said
> Rabbi Simeon ben Azzai, "I have a tradition from the testimony of the
> seventy-two elders, on the day on which they seated Rabbi Eleazar ben
> Azariah in the session, that the Song of Songs and Qohelet do impart un-
> cleanness to hands." Said Rabbi Aqiba, "Heaven forbid! No Israelite man ever
> disputed concerning Song of Songs that it imparts uncleanness to hands. For
> the entire age is not worthy as the day on which the Song of Songs was given
> to Israel. For all the scriptures are holy, but the Song of Songs is holiest of all.
> And if they disputed, they disputed only concerning Qohelet."[14]

This discussion reflects that the canonical status of the Song of Songs was
still in question in the second century CE. Rabbi Aqiba's statement on the
Song of Songs being the holiest of Holy Scripture is the strongest defense
in favor of its inclusion in the canon. In another statement, Rabbi Aqiba
says, "Had not the Torah been given, Canticles (Latin for Song of Songs)
would have sufficed to guide the world."[15] Thus he elevates the status of the
Song to the same level as that of the Torah. During the same time period,
Rabbi Aqiba also declares, "He who warbles the Song of Songs in a banquet
hall and makes it into a kind of love-song has no portion in the world to
come."[16] This statement rejects seeing the Song of Songs as a secular love
song while revealing that the Song was in fact treated as such by some
people at the time.

In discussing the Song of Songs and the Jewish religious mentality,
Gerson Cohen raises the question of why the Song of Songs came to be
interpreted allegorically as depicting the love between God and Israel,

[14]Mishnah Tractate Yadayyim 3:5, quoted in Neusner, *Israel's Love Affair*, 2-3. See also Maurice
Simon, trans. *Midrash Rabbah: The Song of Songs* (London: Soncino, 1939), 18.
[15]Pope, *Song of Songs*, 92.
[16]Babylonian Talmud, Sanhedrin 101a, in Jacob Neusner, *The Talmud of Babylon: An American
Translation*, vol. 23C, *Tractate Sanhedrin, chapters 9–11* (Chico, CA: Scholars Press, 1985), 152.

especially in the context of ancient Israel, where pagan worship and idola-
trous rites were so popular. His answer is directly linked to the first com-
mandment: "You have no other gods before Me" (Ex 20:3). Cohen says that
the metaphorical relationship of God as Israel's husband was not found in
any other religion of the ancient world. Therefore, infidelity to God is comparable to infidelity to a spouse in a marital covenant. In Israel's religious
language, observing the commandments became the concrete expression
of fidelity, and love became the language of the metaphorical relationship
between God and Israel.[17]

Two early documents that bear witness to the metaphorical reading of
the Song are Song of Songs Rabbah (Shir Hashirm Rabbah) and the Aramaic Targum to the Song of Songs. The exact dating of their composition
eludes many commentators, since the compilations of the two documents
draw on interpretations by interpreters in the first and second centuries
CE.[18] Nevertheless, these two documents not only reflect an earlier reception of the Song of Songs but also profoundly influenced the subsequent
interpretations of the book to the medieval period and beyond.

Song of Songs Rabbah: A parable for Exodus. To modern readers, the
Song of Songs is a love song between a man and a woman. However, in the
early centuries, this was not the case. Early Jewish interpreters perceived
the Song as a parable about God's love for Israel. In Song of Songs Rabbah,
the rabbis understand the Song as a parable for the book of Exodus and
regarded the Song as a "commentary" that unlocks the hidden meaning of
Exodus.[19] The association between the Song of Songs and Passover, then,

---

[17]Gerson D. Cohen, "The Song of Songs and the Jewish Religious Mentality," in *Studies in the Variety of Rabbinic Cultures*, ed. Gerson D. Cohen (Philadelphia: Jewish Publication Society, 1991), 1-17, esp. 3-7.

[18]Larry L. Lyke, *I Will Espouse You Forever: The Song of Songs and the Theology of Love in the Hebrew Bible* (Nashville: Abingdon, 2007), 66. While Alexander acknowledges that Song of Songs Rabbah and the Targum of the Song of Songs have overlapping interpretations, he also notes that the Targum of the Song of Songs displays details of which Song of Songs Rabbah is unaware, which shows that the Targum comes later than the Song of Songs Rabbah. See Philip S. Alexander, "Jewish Aramaic Translations of Hebrew Scriptures," in *Mikra: Text, Translation, Reading and Interpretation of the Hebrew Bible in Ancient Judaism and Early Christianity* (Peabody, MA: Hendrickson, 2004), 237.

[19]Broadly speaking, early rabbis considered the Song of Songs as a midrash or a commentary on the Torah, with Exodus as one of its major focuses. Torah serves as the medium through which to demonstrate the mutual love between God and Israel. See Jacob Neusner, *The Midrash: An Introduction* (London: Jason Aronson, 1990), 208.

results from this identification of the genre of the Song as a parable and not as love lyrics or love poetry.

A parable is known in Hebrew as a *mashal*. Jewish scholar Daniel Boyarin defines a *mashal* as "a story whose meaning is perfectly clear and simple, and because of its simplicity enables one to interpret by analogy a more complex, difficult, or hermetic text."[20] In contemporary scholarship, the genre of the Song of Songs is identified as lyric poetry. However, early interpreters did not see it the same way. For them, the understanding of the Song as a parable meant that it served as a hermeneutical key to interpret the Song not as poetry. In early rabbinic tradition, Solomon's writings, such as Proverbs, Ecclesiastes, and Song of Songs, were considered a source of light to illuminate the dark sayings of the Torah.[21] In fact, the whole Writings itself is understood as a *mashal*, a series of readings in figurative language of the text of the Torah. Therefore, the Song of Songs is perceived as a light to illuminate the dark places of the Torah, specifically as the hermeneutical key to Exodus.[22] Through this mode of thinking the Song of Songs came to be associated with Passover, unfolding the meanings of Exodus.

For the early Jewish interpreters, one typical way of making the connections between the Song of Songs and Passover was by reading the Song literally into a narrative context in Exodus. In other words, the figures in the Song are made concrete by being identified with particular situations, events, and characters from Exodus. Neusner further explains that the sages "set forth sequences of words that connote meanings, elicit emotions, stand for events, form the verbal equivalent of pictures, music, dance, or poetry."[23] Therefore, they read the Song as a sequence of statements of urgent love between God and Israel, the holy people. Michael Fishbane also remarks, "Solomon was inspired to render the sacred history of Israel found in the

---

[20]Daniel Boyarin, *Intertextuality and the Reading of Midrash* (Bloomington: Indiana University Press, 1990), 106.
[21]Simon, *Midrash Rabbah: The Song of Songs*, 10.
[22]Boyarin, *Intertextuality and the Reading*, 107, 110. Boyarin further explains that a parable is different from an allegory. An allegory works from the concrete to the abstract, whereas a parable such as a midrashic reading of the Song works from the abstract to the concrete (*Intertextuality and the Reading*, 108).
[23]Neusner, *Israel's Love Affair*, 1. Neusner deems the Song of Songs the greatest intellectual achievement of sages who read the Song as if it is about the love of God for Israel and Israel for God. See Neusner, *Midrash: An Introduction*, 197.

Torah into poetic images for the people. Through metaphor and simile, he transfigured earthly *eros* into tropes of tradition and memory. The rabbis thus place the Exodus and, particularly, the events at Sinai at the center of their national reading of the Song."[24]

A tenth-century medieval Jewish exegete, Saadia Gaon, coined a famous saying, namely, that the Song of Songs is "a lock to which the key has been lost."[25] Early Jewish commentators, however, did not perceive it to be so. Rather, understanding the Song as a parable, in and of itself, serves as a hermeneutical key to unlock the meanings of the Song. According to Boyarin, this reading method is not allegorical, which relates signifier to signified, but rather intertextual, which relates signifier to signifier.[26] Another Jewish scholar, Benjamin Scolnic, further remarks that if the Song was composed as an interpretation of the exodus, then to explain a verse of the Song of Songs as pertaining to the exodus event is not to allegorize but to explain what that verse really means.[27] Jonathan Kaplan proposes that what the early exegetes employed was actually typology, not allegory. Typology sees the figurations of ideal characters and events in the Song in Israel's scriptural history. In doing so, says Kaplan, the exegetes "historicized" the Song, and through this they intended to cultivate the social and hermeneutical space for piety, marked by affective devotion to God through the commandments. Therefore, in the Song, Israel is perceived as God's "perfect one" (Song 5:2; 6:9). She is the idealized portrait of divine-human relationship.[28] Kaplan advances the study of the early phase of reading Song of Songs as a divine love song, which helps the reader to connect it with how God loves Israel through the exodus event. A pivotal emblem to that event is Passover.

Although a direct connection between the rabbinic reading of the Song of Songs and Passover does not surface, numerous cases are found that

---

[24]Michael Fishbane, *The Kiss of God: Spiritual and Mystical Death in Judaism* (Seattle: University of Washington Press, 1994), 15. For the rabbis, the kiss in Song 1:2 symbolizes the intimacy between God and Israel at Sinai.

[25]Quoted from Pope, *Song of Songs*, 89.

[26]Boyarin, *Intertextuality and the Reading*, 115.

[27]Benjamin Edidin Scolnic, "Why Do We Sing the Song of Songs on Passover?," *Conservative Judaism* 48, no. 4 (1996): 60.

[28]Jonathan Kaplan, *My Perfect One: Typology and Early Rabbinic Interpretation of Song of Songs* (New York: Oxford University Press, 2015), 2.

correlate specific verses in the Song to the exodus event. The association of Passover with Song of Songs then becomes an extended one, in connection with events in Exodus. In summarizing how the rabbis do exegesis, Judith Kates puts it this way: "To read as the midrashist reads means to experience Scripture as an interwoven texture of texts. We can pick up a thread anywhere on sacred texts and it will lead us—by creative juxtaposition, by plays on sounds, by flowing from one possible meaning to another in the semantic range of a root, or by conceptual analogy."[29] Indeed, in this interwoven network of texts, Song of Songs becomes associated with Passover.

I will cite a few examples below from Song of Songs Rabbah and show how they became associated with Passover.[30] The selected texts are taken from different parts of the Song, serve representative purposes, and are not meant to be exhaustive.

Song of Songs Rabbah 1:2.

"Let Him kiss me with the kisses of his mouth!" Where was it said? Rabbi Hinnena ben Pappa said: It was said by the Red Sea, as it is written, "To a steed in Pharaoh's chariots" (Song 1:9). Rabbi Judah ben Rabbi Simon said: It was said at Sinai, as it says. "The Song of Songs (*shirim*): that is the song which was uttered by the chanting singers (*sharim*), as it says "The singers (*sharim*) go before, the minstrels follow after" (Ps 68:26). It was taught in the name of Rabbi Nathan: The Holy One, blessed be He, said it in the excellence of His majesty, as it says. "The Song of Songs which is Solomon," that is, of the King to whom belongs peace. Rabbi Gamaliel said: The ministering angels said it; "the Song of Songs"—that is, the song which the singers on high uttered. Rabbi Johanan said: It was said on Sinai, as it says, "Let Him kiss me with the kisses of His mouth."[31]

Hebrew text: "Let him kiss me with the kisses of his mouth!"

The usual pattern of a midrash is that it records dialogues between different rabbis, who discuss the meaning of a given text. In this case, the rabbis

---

[29]Kates, "Entering the Holy of Holies," 202.

[30]One may also consult Neusner's two-volume translation of the entire Song of Songs Rabbah. See Jacob Neusner, *Song of Songs Rabbah: An Analytical Translation*, 2 vols., Brown Judaic Studies 197 (Atlanta: Scholars Press, 1989).

[31]Simon, *Midrash Rabbah: The Song of Songs*, 20. For those who are not familiar with rabbinic writings, I have altered the original abbreviated "R. Hinnena b. Pappa" to the long form "Rabbi Hinnena ben Pappa" for purposes of clarity.

discuss the meaning of Song of Songs 1:2, "Let him kiss me with the kisses of his mouth." Instead of concerning themselves with the question of "who," that is, who are "he" and "me," the rabbis are more concerned with the issue of "where," because they already presuppose that the "he" symbolizes God, whereas the "me" symbolizes Israel. So, one rabbi asks, "Where was it said?"[32] Then another rabbi responds, "It was said by the Red Sea." Then he quotes another verse from Song of Songs 1:9 about a horse (steed) in Pharaoh's chariots. For a contemporary reader, Song of Songs 1:2 and the Red Sea are as good as a million miles away and unrelated to each other. How did the rabbi make a connection between them? As Boyarin observes, what the early interpreters did with Scripture was intertextual reading, which relates signifier to signifier.[33] In this case, the rabbi relates the signifier "Let him kiss me" to "a steed in Pharaoh's chariots," which then in retrospect relates to crossing the Red Sea. In ancient Jewish spirituality, crossing the Red Sea marked the climax of God's relationship with Israel. There God parted the Red Sea to enable the Israelites to walk on dry land while he overthrew the horses of Pharaoh's chariots in the midst of the sea, as described in Exodus 14. The kiss of God then symbolizes the crossing of the Red Sea, the most intimate moment of Israel's experience with God.

Another rabbi then confirms this interpretation by citing Psalm 68:26 in the Hebrew version (Ps 68:25 English), which says, "The singers go before, the minstrels follow after." Since the rabbis were familiar with the Hebrew Scripture, when they see "Song of Songs," which in Hebrew is *shir hashirim*, they correlate the signifier "songs" (*shirim*) with another signifier, "singers" (*sharim*), in Psalm 68:26, which they understand to be occurring at the time of Exodus.[34] In Exodus 15, after the parting of the Red Sea, Miriam takes the timbrel in her hand, and all the women go out after her with timbrels and with dancing. Miriam then tells them, "Sing to the LORD, for He is highly exalted; The horse and his rider He has hurled into the sea" (Ex 15:20-21). To the contemporary reader, the rabbis are taking Scripture out of context by relating two different genres of texts and forcing a meaning

---

[32]According to Neusner, this voice is the voice of the document or the author of the composition (*Israel's Love Affair*, 20).

[33]Boyarin, *Intertextuality and the Reading*, 115.

[34]In Hebrew, "songs" is שִׁירִים, and "singers" is שָׁרִים. The only difference is their first vowel.

the original author did not intend. In other words, they seem to commit the fallacy of "eisegesis," reading their own interpretation into the text without letting the text speak for itself. In the ancient Jewish mind, however, this is the way to interpret Scripture, as Boyarin explains.

The rabbis' dialogue about Song of Songs 1:2 does not end here. They continue for a few more pages, proposing, responding, and expounding the verse through various angles of Scripture such as through the Torah, the temple, Sinai, and Moses. How they come up with the correlations between "Let him kiss me with the kisses of his mouth" and other parts of Scripture, particularly in the Torah, is rather bewildering to the modern mind, but this nevertheless was the way interpretation occurred in early rabbinic tradition. Neusner summarizes that the midrashic commentary of Song of Songs 1:2 "refers in much more general terms to the Song of Songs, and hardly to Song 1:2 in particular." That the various opinions invoke other verses than the verse assigned demonstrates that the document was a result of a highly sophisticated work of compilation, involving layers of editorial intervention.[35]

Song of Songs Rabbah 1:9. Below is an excerpt of early rabbis' interpretations of Song 1:9 in Song of Songs Rabbah. The beginning part records a part of the conversation seemingly unrelated to Exodus. It is Rabbi Aqiba's response that steers the conversation back to Exodus.

> He (Rabbi Pappus) said to him (Rabbi Aqiba), "How then do you explain the words 'To my steed in the chariots of Pharaoh'?" He replied: 'Pharaoh rode first on a male steed, and, if one may say so, God showed Himself on a male steed, as it says, 'And he rode upon a cherub, and did fly' (Ps 18:11). Pharaoh thereupon said: 'Surely this male steed kills its rider in battle; I will therefore ride on a female steed.' Hence it is written: 'To my (female) steed in the chariots of Pharaoh.' Pharaoh then changed to a white horse, a red horse, a black horse, and, if one may say so, God appeared on a red, white, or black

---

[35]Neuser, *Israel's Love Affair*, 25. Lyke commends the early Jewish exegetes for their attentiveness to the specific language and imagery of the Song (*I Will Espouse You*, 102). Kaplan acknowledges the early Jewish interpreters' influence on later works such as the Song of Songs Rabbah and the Targum. He observes that the Tannaim do not dwell on Israel's failure or apostasy but instead focus on the "good times" with God. Through their retelling of Israel's good times with God, they intend to foster a renewal of relationship for the present (Kaplan, *My Perfect One*, 79). Kaplan understands the term *Tannaim* as referring to the first generations of rabbinic sages during the first centuries of the rabbinic era (*My Perfect One*, 2).

horse; hence it says, Thou has trodden the sea with the horses (Hab 3:15)—
diverse horses. Pharaoh the wicked went forth with breastplate and helmet,
and, if one may say so, the Holy One, blessed be He, did so also, as it says,
'And he put on righteousness as a coat of mail'" (Is 59:17).[36]

Hebrew text: "To a mare in the chariots of Pharaoh, I compare you, my darling."

From Rabbi Aqiba's response to Rabbi Pappus one can see that he uses his
own creative imagination in attempting to unlock the meaning of Song of
Songs 1:9. On the one hand, Aqiba is keenly aware from the Hebrew text
that the horse in Song of Songs 1:9 is a female horse, a mare. On the other
hand, he also connects the male horse with God as the rider when he quotes
Psalm 18:11 (Ps 18:10 English). Looking closely at Psalm 18:11, we find no
horse there, but a cherub. The only remote connection between Song of
Songs 1:9 and Psalm 18:11 is that both a horse and a cherub are meant to be
ridden on. In this case, God the rider engages in a battle with Pharaoh the
rider. Along the way, both change to a horse of a different color. This battle
keeps going, with verses taken from Habakkuk 3, where God is portrayed
as a warrior riding on a horse. Here Aqiba treats the Song of Songs as a
parable unlocking the supposed meaning of the Exodus text both through
its intertextual connections with other parts of Scripture and through his
own imagination.

Rabbi Aqiba's explanation of Song of Songs 1:9 meets with different responses. Paragraph six offers another explanation. Again, this opinion reflects Israel's experience in Exodus.

The Rabbis say: "The expression 'mare' is used" because the Israelites appeared like mares and the wicked Egyptians who pursued them were like
stallions eager with desire, and they ran after them until they were sunk in
the sea. Rabbi Simon said: Far be it from us to think that the Israelites were
like mares. No. It was the waves of the sea which looked like mares, and the
Egyptians are compared to inflamed stallions, and they ran after them till
they sank in the sea. The Egyptians would say to his horse: "Yesterday I
wanted to take you to the Nile and you would not come, and now you are
drowning me in the sea," and the horse would answer: "*Ramah bayam*—He

---

[36]Simon, *Midrash Rabbah: The Song of Songs*, 69.

had thrown into the sea": See what is in the sea (*re'eh mah yayam*)! An orgy
has been prepared for you in the sea. Rabbi Ishmael taught: And the Lord
overthrew the Egyptians in the midst of the sea (Ex 14:27): this informs us
that the horses threw their riders, and they went down with the horses on top
of them. Rabbi Levi said: It was like a man turning a dish over, so that what
was at the bottom goes to the top and what was at the top goes to the bottom.[37]

Here the rabbi once again correlates the mare of Pharaoh's chariot with the
horses of Pharaoh at the Red Sea. Only this time the Scripture reference is
not taken from Psalms and Habakkuk but directly from Exodus 14:27. Song
of Songs 1:9 then becomes a commentary describing how God overthrew
the Egyptian horses and their riders at the sea.

Song of Songs Rabbah 4:5. Altogether, there are three body praise songs
known as *waṣf* in the Song of Songs (Song 4:1-7; 5:10-16; 7:1-9). In regard to
the female body, breasts are mentioned. How do the early rabbis interpret
the breasts, and how are they related to Passover? Once again, the rabbis
associate a particular verse in the Song with an event or a character in
Exodus rather than with Passover in particular.

Thy two breasts. These are Moses and Aaron. Just as the breasts are the beauty
and the ornament of a woman, so Moses and Aaron were the beauty and
ornament of Israel. Just as the breasts are the charm of a woman, so Moses
and Aaron were the charm of Israel. Just as the breasts are the glory and pride
of a woman, so Moses and Aaron were the glory and pride of Israel. Just as
the breasts are full of milk, so Moses and Aaron were filled with Torah. Just
as whatever a woman eats helps to feed the child at the breast, so all the Torah
that Moses our master learned he taught to Aaron, as it is written, "And
Moses told Aaron all the words of the Lord" (Ex 4:28). The Rabbis say: "He
revealed to him the ineffable Name. Just as one breast is not greater than the
other, so it was with Moses and Aaron; for it is written, 'These are that Moses
and Aaron' (Ex 6:27), and it is also written, 'These are that Aaron and Moses'
(Ex 6:26), showing that Moses was not greater than Aaron nor was Aaron
greater than Moses in knowledge of Torah."[38]

Hebrew text: "Two of your breasts, like two young stags, twins of a female
gazelle, pasturing among the lilies."

---

[37]Simon, *Midrash Rabbah: The Song of Songs*, 71.
[38]Simon, *Midrash Rabbah: The Song of Songs*, 198-99.

In illuminating the "real" meaning of the two breasts in Song of Songs 4:5, the Rabbis understand them to mean Moses and Aaron in respect to their knowledge of the Torah. The beginning few sentences read like poetry, juxtaposing Moses and Aaron with the two breasts of a woman. Their common denominator lies in the sameness or evenness of the breasts. The aim is to demonstrate that Moses and Aaron are equal. None is greater than the other. In order to show this, verses from Exodus are quoted frequently.[39] Again, one can see that the rabbis are using the Song of Songs as a hermeneutical key to elucidate the meaning of Exodus. In this example, the two breasts in Song of Songs 4:5 become vehicles to unravel the equality of Moses and Aaron, the two main characters in Exodus. The rabbis are not concerned with quoting Scripture in context. Instead, they associate signifier with signifier rather than using a signifier to identify the signified.

Song of Songs Rabbah 5:1.

"I am come into my garden." Rabbi Menahem, the son in law of Rabbi Eleazar ben Abuna, said in the name of Rabbi Simeon ben Jusna: It does not say here, "I am come into the garden," but I am come into my garden (*ganni*): as if to say, to my bridal-chamber (*ginnuni*): to the place which was my real home originally; for was not the original home of the Shechinah in the lower realm, as it says, "and they heard the voice of the Lord God walking in the garden" (Gen 3:8)? . . . When did the Shechinah rest upon the earth? On the day when the Tabernacle was set up, "And it came to pass on the day that Moses had made an end of setting up the Tabernacle" (Num 7:1) . . . "I have come into my garden, my sister, my bride, I have gathered my myrrh with my spices": This refers to the incense of spices and the handful of frankincense. "I have eaten my honeycomb with my honey": this refers to the parts of the burnt-offering and the sacrificial parts of the most holy things. "I have drunk my wine with my milk": this refers to the drink-offerings and the sacrificial parts of the lesser holy things. "Eat, O friends": These are Moses and Aaron. "Drink, yea, drink abundantly, O beloved": These are Nadab and Abihu, who drank to their hurt.[40]

Hebrew text: "I have come to my garden, my sister, (my) bride; I have plucked my myrrh with my spices; I have eaten honeycomb with my honey, I have

---

[39]The above example is less than half of the whole commentary. For the rest, see Simon, *Midrash Rabbah: The Song of Songs*, 199.

[40]Simon, *Midrash Rabbah: The Song of Songs*, 228-30.

drunk my wine with my milk. Eat! O Friends, Drink! and get drunk! O Lovers."

In a literal reading of Song of Songs 5:1, the man comes into the "garden" of his bride inferring a sexual consummation of their marriage. In Song of Songs Rabbah of the same verse, the rabbis regard this as referring to the setting up of the tabernacle, thus placing its time frame in Israel's wilderness wanderings. In Song of Songs Rabbah, the union between a husband and a wife becomes a metaphorical reading of Israel's intimacy with her God. The garden alludes to the Garden of Eden (Gen 3:8), whereas Shechinah (Shekinah) refers to God's indwelling presence in the tabernacle.[41] In association with the tabernacle language, myrrh and spices symbolize the incense used in connection with the tabernacle (Ex 30:23); honey and honeycomb symbolize the burnt offering; wine and milk symbolize the drink offering. "Friends" is identified with Moses, Aaron, and Aaron's sons.

The tabernacle marks God's indwelling presence with his people, Israel, which forms the climax to Exodus. The setting up of the tabernacle then represents the high point in Israel's relationship with her God. Although no Passover is mentioned in this verse, this figurative reading of the spiritual union between God and Israel demonstrates the early rabbis' hermeneutical scheme of reading Song of Songs as an explanation to Exodus.

Song of Songs Rabbah 8:6.

"Set me as a seal (upon your heart)." Said Rabbi Meir: "Said the Israelites before the Holy One, blessed by He: 'Lord of the world, what you have thought in your heart to do for us, do!'" For said Rabbi Yohanan in the name of Rabbi Eliezer, son of Rabbi Yose the Galilean: "When the Israelites stood before Mount Sinai and said: 'We shall do and we shall obey' (Ex 24:7), at that very moment the Holy One, blessed be He, summoned the angel of death and said to him: 'Even though I have appointed you as executioner and world-ruler over all my creations, you have no business to do with this nation in particular.' That is in line with this verse: 'And it came to pass, when you heard the voice out of the midst of the darkness' (Deut 5:20). 'But is there such a thing as darkness on high?' And lo, it is written, 'And the light dwells with him' (Dan 2:22)? What then is the sense of 'out of the midst of the

---

[41]In Hebrew, shakan (שׁכן) means "dwelling."

darkness' (Deut 5:20)? This refers to the angel of death, who is called darkness. And so Scripture states, 'And the tablets were the work of God, and the writing was the writing of God, graven upon the tablets' (Ex 32:16). Do not read the letters of the word as graven but as freedom."[42]

Hebrew text: "Put me like a seal upon your heart, like a seal upon your arm because strong like death is love, severe like Sheol is jealousy, her flames are flames of fire, a blazing flame (or a flame of Yahweh)."

In contemporary Western academia, Song of Songs 8:6 has been perceived as the climax of the Song, because it is here that love is given a theological meaning. In the early rabbinic tradition, the whole Song of Songs was considered theological, since it is understood to describe the love between God and Israel. In Song of Songs Rabbah 8:6, again, the question is not the identity of the speaker who says "set me as a seal" but the timing and location of the saying. Rabbi Yohanan responds by connecting the utterance "set me as a seal" to the time when Israel stood before Mount Sinai, where they pledged to obey God's commandments delivered through Moses. Then he relates this utterance to the angel of death through an intertextual reading of Deuteronomy. How does the verse "set me as a seal" relate to the angel of darkness, and how does the angel of darkness relate to the writing of God on the tablets in Exodus? All this is confusing to the modern reader, but this was how rabbis used one passage in the Scripture and connected it to another until a new meaning emerged through this process of elucidating the meaning of the text. What is certain is that the rabbis do not take the phrase "set me as a seal" literally but rather use it as a hermeneutical key to explain the Torah in general and Exodus in particular.

In summary, the word *Passover* is nowhere to be found in Song of Songs Rabbah. However, references to the book of Exodus can be found everywhere. This is because the rabbis consider the Song of Songs a parable for Exodus, and Exodus symbolizes the most intimate time between God and Israel. They see the Song as a hermeneutical key that unlocks the mysteries of Exodus, and therefore almost every verse of it serves as a means to that

---

[42]Neusner, *Song of Songs Rabbah*, 2:220. For this passage, I am using Neusner's translation, since the typos and old English in Simon's translation make it difficult to read (Simon, *Midrash Rabbah: The Song of Songs*, 305-6).

end. To the contemporary reader, the early interpreters' use of intertextuality seems to take Scripture out of context, but how they connect the Song to Exodus does show the early rabbinic vision of an ideal portrait—love between God and Israel, his chosen people, his bride. The feast of Passover became associated with the Song of Songs precisely because the early rabbis envisioned recapturing the love between God and Israel, epitomized in the exodus experience.

Targum of the Song of Songs: Israel's salvation history. The Targum is an Aramaic paraphrase of the Hebrew Song of Songs. On the grounds of linguistic characteristics, Pope dates the Aramaic Targum to the Song of Songs to the latter part of the eighth century CE. He notes that the Aramaic Targum presents a generous mixture of Palestinian and Babylonian forms, which supports this eighth-century date. Another Targum scholar, R. Loewe, contends that the Targum should be dated after the beginning of the expansion of Islam, precisely after the conquest of Palestine in 636–638, that is, the seventh century CE.[43] The mystical interpretation of the Targum was derived from early tannaitic traditions, which Kaplan expounds brilliantly in his work. According to Kaplan, early tannaitic interpreters see the Song of Songs as an archetypical expression of Israel's national historical narrative, which chronicles Israel's ideal portrait of its relationship with God. In doing so, the Song of Songs serves the purpose of valorizing the past, describing Israel's present circumstances, and imagining Israel's future.[44]

---

[43]Pope, *Song of Songs*, 94. While De Moor quotes Philip Alexander's statement that the Targum to the Song of Songs seems to be the result of a single author given its sophisticated artistry, he also challenges this notion by saying that it must have undergone many centuries of editing. See J. C. De Moor, "The Love of God in the Targum to the Prophets," *JSJ* 24, no. 2 (1993): 259.

[44]Kaplan, *My Perfect One*, 2, 71, 82. The way in which the tannaitic interpreters do this is by correlating verses in Song of Songs to the book of Exodus. See the many examples in chap. 2, "Song of Songs and Israel's National Narrative," 47-93. In discussing Midrash exegesis, Avery-Peck notes that rabbinic biblical interpretation generally uses the Hebrew Bible as a foundation to explain and make sense of the contemporaneous experience of the Jewish communities so that biblical interpretation is not so much exegetical as polemical. It understands that Scripture speaks to an age other than the one in which it was written. Among the themes that emerge in rabbinic literatures are Israel's election, Israel's suffering, and Israel's final redemption. See Alan J. Avery-Peck, "Midrash and Exegesis: Insights from Genesis Rabbah on the Binding of Isaac," in *Method Matters: Essays on the Interpretation of the Hebrew Bible in Honor of David L. Petersen*, ed. Joel M. LeMon and Kent Harold Richards (Atlanta: Society of Biblical Literature, 2009), 442-44.

Targum expert Philip Alexander says, "The Targum of the Song of Songs was unquestionably one of the most popular and widely disseminated works of the Jewish Middle Ages." It survives in over sixty manuscripts throughout Judaica libraries all over the world. When compared to the Song of Songs Rabbah, which survives in only four complete manuscripts, the significance and the influence of the Targum to the Song of Songs cannot be underestimated.[45] The Targum recounts Israel's salvation history through ten songs from Adam to the return of the exiles.[46] Alexander states that the distinctive contribution of the Targumist is to read it systematically as a cryptic history of God's relationship to Israel. The rhythm of this relationship is marked by fellowship, estrangement, and reconciliation, which is reflected in the biblical portrayal of Israel's history. This history involves Israel's repetitive cycles of following God, sinning against God, being punished by God, and then returning to God.[47] He further remarks that the Targum of the Song of Songs is "one of the few truly systematic readings of any biblical book which treats the book as a whole from a unified hermeneutical standpoint."[48] Lyke also notes that the rabbis read the Song "not only with itself but also with other parts of the Hebrew Bible and, in particular, with the theology of love." For the Targumists, the exodus represents the origin of the relationship between Israel and God (Hos 2:16-25; Ezek

---

[45]Philip S. Alexander, "Tradition and Originality in the Targum of the Song of Songs," in *The Aramaic Bible: Targums in Their Historical Context*, JSOTSup 166 (Sheffield: Sheffield Academic Press, 1994), 318-19. Alexander also indicates that the Targum of the Song of Songs was included in the first Bomberg Rabbinic Bible, Venice, 1517, and then developed in subsequent versions.

[46]For the Aramaic Targum on the Song of Songs, see Philip S. Alexander, *The Targum of Canticles: Translated with a Critical Introduction, Apparatus, and Notes*, Aramaic Bible 17A (Collegeville, MN: Liturgical Press, 2003).

[47]Alexander, "Tradition and Originality," 332. Menn, however, challenges this notion and sees many other metaphors appearing in this same document, including relationships between male friends and scholarly colleagues, siblings, infants and nurses, fathers and sons, gardeners and plants, and farmers and animals. She argues that the Targum presents a multiplicity of additional metaphors, suggesting the intimacy between divine and human counterparts throughout their history together. See Esther M. Menn, "Thwarted Metaphors: Complicating the Language of Desire in the Targum of the Song of Songs," *JSJ* 34, no. 3 (2003): 237-73.

[48]Alexander, "Tradition and Originality," 334. In another article, Alexander compares Targum Song of Songs and the biblical Song of Songs and claims that while the biblical Song of Songs does not have a clear plot, Targum Song of Songs exceeds the former with a systematic hermeneutical scheme of Israel's salvation history. Thus, Targum Song of Songs is more coherent in content than the biblical Song of Songs. See Philip S. Alexander, "'Translation and Midrash Completely Fused Together?' The Form of the Targums to Canticles, Lamentations and Qohelet," *Aramaic Studies* 9, no. 1 (2011): 95-96.

16).[49] The association with Passover in connection with Exodus is only natural, since Passover marks the beginning of Israel's exodus experience. Alexander confirms this by saying that the Targum helps to reinforce the connection between Song of Songs and Passover.[50]

The Song of Songs is situated as the ninth song in the Targum. In these ten songs, Israel's salvation history is divided into five sections:[51]

> Introduction: The Ten Songs (Song 1:1)
> Section 1: The Wilderness (Song 1:2–3:6)
> Section 2: The Temple (Song 3:7–5:1)
> Section 3: Exile (Song 5:2–6:1)
> Section 4: The Second Temple (Song 6:2–7:10)
> Section 5: The Final Exile, Redemption, and Temple (Song 7:11–8:14)

The ten songs are all taken from the Hebrew Bible, and they all praise God's awesomeness. This reflects the Targumists' sensitivity to Scripture and their acute awareness of the themes of these songs, as well as the theological connections among the songs. By attributing the ten songs to Solomon the prophet, the creator of the Targum places the text in the tradition of wisdom and prophecies. The ten songs in the introduction are listed below:[52]

> The Song of Adam: Adam spoke at the time his guilt was forgiven and the Sabbath Day arrived and protected him. He opened his mouth and said, "A Psalm, a song for the Sabbath Day" (Ps 92).

> The Song of Moses: Moses said with the children of Israel at the time the Master of the World divided the Reed Sea for them. All of them opened their mouths together and spoke the song, as it is written: "Then sang Moses and the Israelites" (Ex 15:1).

> The Song of the Children of Israel: They spoke at the time the well of water was given to them, as it is written, "Then sang Israel" (Num 21:17).

---

[49]Lyke, *I Will Espouse You*, 68.

[50]Alexander, *Targum of Canticles*, 54.

[51]English translation by Jay C. Treat, "The Aramaic Targum to Song of Songs," August 12, 2004, http://ccat.sas.upenn.edu/~jtreat/song/targum/. The same five sections also appear in Loewe's work. See Pope, *Song of Songs*, 95.

[52]Treat, "Aramaic Targum." I have changed the original "YY" to "the Lord" and have shortened the scriptural references from the full name to the abbreviated reference, such as from "Exodus" to "Ex." See also Alexander's translation, Alexander, *Targum of Canticles*, 75-77.

The Song of Moses: When his time had come to depart from the world, and he reproved the people of the house of Israel, as it is written, "Give ear, O heavens, and I will speak" (Deut 32:1).

The Song of Joshua: He spoke when he waged war in Gibeon, and the sun and moon stood for him 36 hours and they ceased to utter the song (of their praise). He opened his mouth and sang the song, as it is written, "Thus sang Joshua before the LORD" (Josh 10:12).

The Song of Barak and Deborah: They said on the day the LORD delivered Sisera and his camp into the hands of the children of Israel, as it is written: "Then sang Deborah and Barak, son of Abinoam" (Judg 5:1).

The Song of Hannah: She said at the time she was granted a son from before the LORD, as it is written, "And Hannah prayed in the Spirit of prophecy and said" (1 Sam 2:1).

The Song of David: David, king of Israel, said because of all the miracles which the LORD had performed for him. He opened his mouth and spoke a song, as it is written, "And David praised in prophecy before the LORD" (2 Sam 22:1).

The Song of Solomon: Solomon, king of Israel, said by the Holy Spirit, before the Master of all the World, the LORD (Song 1:1-8:14).

The Song of the Exile: The children of the Exile are destined to say at the time they are redeemed from Exile, as it is written and explained by the hand of Isaiah the prophet, as it is written: "You shall have this song for joy, as on the night the feast of Passover is sanctified, and for gladness of heart, as the people who go to appear before the LORD three times a year with varieties of music and the sound of the drum, to come up to the mountain of the LORD and to worship before the LORD, the Strength of Israel" (Is 30:29).

In chronicling Israel's national history, the Targumist places Israel's historical figures in the context of Israel's national historical narrative, particularly where Scripture indicates someone "speaks" or "sings." The formula goes like this: "So and so utters this song, as it is written, 'he, she, or they sang,' followed by a scriptural reference." In accord with the early Jewish interpretive tradition, the Targumist did not have the same concept of intertextuality as contemporary interpreters do, but the way in which he perceives Song of Songs 1:1 as recounting Israel's salvation history through ten songs does reflect the author's creativity, sensitivity to Scripture, and piety in constructing the ideal relationship with his God.

Among these ten songs, the Song of Songs is in the ninth position, in between the Song of David and the Song of the Exile. This ninth song was not perceived merely as a secular love song but as a sacred song sung by Solomon, the king of Israel, and said by the Holy Spirit before the Lord. As we will see in the next section, the Song is read as commentary on Israel's salvation history. The association with Passover appears in Song of Songs 2:9. It also appears in the tenth song, where "the night of the feast of Passover" is mentioned specifically in connection with the returnees, who sang the song for joy as Isaiah uttered it in Isaiah 30:29, "You will have songs as in the night when you keep the festival, And gladness of heart as when one marches to *the sound of* the flute, To go to the mountain of the Lord, to the Rock of Israel."[53] Although the context of that verse does not precisely refer to the feast of Passover, the Targumist sees much more there than what appears.[54] The juxtaposition of the Passover and Exodus, together with the reunion with God at his mountain, makes this the future event of the restoration of relationship between God and Israel. For the Targumist, the Song of Songs represents the greatest song of redemption in the Hebrew Bible.[55]

In studying the lists in the Targum of Megilloth, Christian Brady makes use of Etan Levine's research and notes the symbolic nature of the idea "ten events in history, the tenth being eschatological," as shown in Targum Ruth.[56] Coincidentally, Targum Song of Songs also contains ten songs, with the last song pointing toward the messianic age. Alexander names the tenth song "The Song of the World to Come," in which all of

---

[53]"The songs" here in Hebrew is singular, "a song."

[54]In fact, an earlier rabbinic source indicates that the first song is the First Passover and the last song ends with the world to come. Targum Song alters this order and places the Song of Adam first. Alexander proposes that the Targumist aims for completeness, which begins with Adam and Eve, and from them comes the salvation history needed for Israel. Brady, "Use of Eschatological Lists," 500-501.

[55]Lyke, *I Will Espouse You*, 71.

[56]The list of ten appears frequently in Targumim. In Targum Megilloth, there are four lists of ten, including the Ten Songs in Targum Song, the Ten Famines in Targum Ruth, and the Ten Kingdoms in Targum Esth. All of them have the following elements in common: (1) they include ten items, (2) each end with an eschatological figure/event, and (3) each list serves as a prologue to the Targum in question. See Brady, "Use of Eschatological Lists," 496.

Israel will return to Zion to worship before the Strength of Israel. He states that this is the overarching theme of the Targum.[57]

Below, I will evaluate the same four examples as in the section on the Song of Songs Rabbah. In addition, I will include Song of Songs 2:9 due to its explicit reference to Passover, and Song of Songs 8:1-2 due to its reference to the Messiah. My own translation of the corresponding verses in Hebrew will follow to illustrate how the Targum of the Song of Songs portrays itself as a chronicle of Israel's salvation history.[58]

Targum Song of Songs 1:2.

Solomon the prophet said: "Blessed be the name of the Lord who gave us the Torah at the hands of Moses, the Great Scribe, (both the Torah) written on the two tablets of stone, and the Six Orders of the Mishnah and Talmud by oral tradition, and (who) spoke with us face to face as a man kisses his friend, out of the abundance of the love wherewith He loved us more than the seventy nations."

Hebrew text: "Let him kiss me with the kisses of his mouth! Because your love is better than wine."

This verse falls into the first section of Targum Song of Songs—the wilderness (Song 1:2–3:6). In Israel's experience with her God, the wilderness wandering was the "honeymoon" period, as God speaks to Jeremiah regarding Israel, "I remember concerning you the devotion of your youth, The love of your betrothals, Your following after Me in the wilderness, through a land not sown" (Jer 2:2). Kaplan remarks, "It is as if the rabbis are filling in the back story of this verse by correlating Song of Songs to the Exodus, the Sinai theophany, and the wilderness wanderings." Through this correlation, the early rabbis attempt to shape rabbinic piety in terms of obedience animated by love and affection.[59] In this verse, the author of the Targum understands the kiss metaphorically to be the kiss between God and Israel through the medium of the Torah. God converses face to face

---

[57] Alexander, *Targum of Canticles*, 77-78.

[58] The examples are taken from Alexander's translations. See Alexander, *Targum of Canticles*, 78-79.

[59] Kaplan, *My Perfect One*, 121. Although the Kaplan uses texts from the Tannaim period, much earlier than that of the Targum, the understanding of the Targum is derived from this earlier tannaitic interpretive tradition.

with Israel as a man who kisses his companion.[60] This act demonstrates the
great love that God has for Israel, whom he treasures more than the seventy
nations. Here we see on the one hand the role of the Torah in symbolizing
God's love for Israel, and on the other the unique and special place of Israel
in God's heart when compared with the seventy Gentile nations. The giving
of the Torah happens in Exodus, after God appears to Israel on Mount Sinai
(Ex 19–24). That event marks Israel's betrothal to God as his bride.

Targum Song of Songs 1:9.

> When Israel went out from Egypt, Pharaoh and his hosts pursued them with
> chariots and horsemen, and the way was barred to them on their four sides.
> To the right and left were deserts full of fiery serpents. Behind them was
> wicked Pharaoh with his hosts, and in front of them was the Red Sea. What
> did the Holy One, blessed be He, do? He revealed Himself in the power of
> His might by the Sea and dried up the water, but the mud He did not dry
> up. The wicked, the mixed multitude, and the strangers who were among
> them said, "He is able to dry up the waters, but the mud He is not able to
> dry!" At that hour, the wrath of the Lord waxed hot against them, and He
> would have drowned them in the waters of the sea, just as Pharaoh, his
> mares, chariots, and horsemen were drowned, had it not been for Moses the
> prophet, who spread out his hands in prayer before the Lord, and turned
> back from them the wrath of the Lord. He and the righteous of that gen-
> eration opened their mouths, recited the songs, and passed through the
> midst of the sea on dry land, on account of the merits of Abraham, Isaac,
> and Jacob, the beloved of the Lord.[61]

Hebrew text: "To a mare in the chariots of Pharaoh, I compare you, my darling."

The male protagonist in the Song praises the woman and likens her to a
mare in the chariots of Pharaoh. The Targumist correlates this one verse to
the whole event of Pharaoh pursuing the Israelites at the Red Sea and how

---

[60]Lyke provides a detail behind the association of "face to face" with the kiss of God. He indicates
that according to Mishnah Avot 1:1-18, the rabbis could trace the generations through which the
Torah passed from Moses to their own time. In their understanding, the Torah was not the only
literature that God communicated to Moses on Mount Sinai. There was also the oral Torah,
which Moses did not have time to write down. It was written down later and comprised the
Mishnah and Talmud. The Targum, by associating the kisses with Moses' face-to-face meeting
with God, presumes that the Song of Songs celebrates the original meeting between God and
Moses (Lyke, *I Will Espouse You*, 72).
[61]Alexander, *Targum of Canticles*, 86-87.

God saved them. The event is recounted in great detail, but not all of the details are based on Exodus 14–15. The Targumist added his own imagination to dramatize the event of exodus. The passage begins by stating when this comparison to a mare in Pharaoh's chariot occurred: when Israel went out from Egypt. Just like Song of Songs Rabbah, here the interpreter is not concerned with the identity of the speaker but when the phrase was uttered. By relating the phrase to "when Israel went out from Egypt," the Targumist clearly sees the character in question as Israel, and the time is during the exodus. While the Scripture tells us Pharaoh and his army pursued Israel with chariots and their riders (Ex 14:7), the Targumist adds an imaginary detail that "the way was closed for them on four sides." This phrase is an adaptation or an echo of "the waters were like a wall to them on their right hand and on their left" (Ex 14:22). "On the right and left were wildernesses that were full of fiery serpents" is another adaptation or echo from Deuteronomy (Deut 8:15).

When recounting the circumstances when God dried up the sea, the Targumist continues his adaptation by saying, "He dried up the sea, but the mud he did not dry up." Then the villains, that is, the foreigners who went out from Egypt with the Israelites, challenged God's almighty power by saying, "He can dry up the waters of the Sea, but the mud he cannot dry up." Then God became furious with them, and they would have suffered the same fate as the Egyptians who were thrown into the sea had not Moses interceded on their behalf. This episode is purely constructed outside Scripture, and this reveals the Targumist's disdain for the foreigners who went out with the Israelites, as if to say they are the "bad guys" who were saved only by the prayers of Moses. In so doing, the Targumist distinguishes Israel as a special people, set apart not only from her enemy, the Egyptians, but also from the foreigners in her midst. The passage ends with the recollection that Moses and the righteous generation sang songs, corresponding to Exodus 15, where Moses and the sons of Israel sing a song to the Lord (Ex 15:1). It concludes with the comment that "the Israelites passed in the midst of the Red Sea on dry land by virtue of the merits of Abraham, Isaac, and Jacob, the beloved ones of the Lord."

By connecting the events of Exodus to Israel's patriarchs, the Targumist tied Israel's salvation history to the covenant that God made with Israel's forefathers.

Targum Song of Songs 2:9.

> The congregation of Israel said, "At the time when the glory of the Lord was revealed in Egypt on the night of the Passover, and He slew every firstborn, He rode upon the swift cloud and ran like a gazelle and like the young of the hart, and he protected the houses wherein we were. He took up a position behind our wall, looked in through the windows and peered through the lattices, and He saw the blood of the Passover sacrifice and the blood of the decree of circumcision marked on our doors. He hastened from the heavens above and saw His people eating the festival sacrifice, roasted with fire, together with chervil, endives, and unleavened bread, and He took pity on us, and did not give permission to the Destroying Angel to do us any harm."

> Hebrew text: "Like, my beloved, to a gazelle to a young stag, look! This (he) is standing behind our walls, gazing through the windows, peering through the lattices."

This verse connects the Targum to the Passover feast. In Hebrew Scripture, Song of Songs 2:9 describes the man standing behind the walls of the female protagonist and gazing through the windows. The Targum version of this verse transposes this event to the night of Passover. There God became like a gazelle, standing behind the wall of the Israelites, gazing through the window, and peering through the lattice. When he saw the blood of the Passover sacrifice on the doors of the Israelites, he hastened from heaven above and saw them eating the sacrifice of the Passover feast.

The Hebrew text does not suggest reading Song of Songs 2:9 in the context of Passover. However, the Targumist, understanding the Song as a commentary on Israel's salvation history, consequently interprets the verse in that light. Now we come to realize that the Song of Songs became associated with Passover through a metaphorical reading of the text as depicting divine love between God and Israel on the one hand, and through early rabbinic and Targumist piety perpetuating that belief through their interpretative agenda on the other.

Targum Song of Songs 4:5.

Your two deliverers, who will deliver you, the Messiah Son of David and Messiah Son of Ephraim, are like Moses and Aaron, the sons of Jochebed, who are compared to two fawns, twins of a gazelle. In virtue of their meritorious deeds, they were feeding the people of the House of Israel for forty years in the wilderness with manna, plump fowl, and water from Miriam's well.[62]

Hebrew text: "Two of your breasts, like two young stags, twins of a female gazelle, pasturing among the lilies."

Songs of Songs 4:5 appears in the second section of the Targum: the temple (Song 3:7–5:1). In the Hebrew Scripture, this section includes the wedding of Solomon (Song 3:7-11) and the praise of the woman's body (Song 4:1-7), followed by the man's praise of her beauty and inaccessibility (Song 4:8-15). It climaxes with the woman's invitation for her beloved to come to her garden and the man's response to come into the garden (Song 4:16–5:1). In the Targum, the union between the human couple in the Song transforms into the union between Israel and God in the context of temple worship.

Here in the Targum, the woman's two breasts become correlated to Israel's two redeemers: Moses and Aaron. This interpretation resembles the interpretation of Song of Songs Rabbah of the same verse. The underlying rationale of this interpretation is that both Moses and Aaron fed the people of Israel for forty years in the wilderness. While Song of Songs Rabbah identifies the two breasts as symbolizing the equality of Moses and Aaron, that one is not greater than the other, Targum Song of Songs highlights the breasts' function of nourishment in that they provided food for Israel during her wilderness wandering. Moreover, the temple theme is further reinforced by the last verse of this section, Song of Songs 5:1.

Targum Song of Songs 5:1.

The Holy One, blessed be He, said to His people, the House of Israel: "I have come into My Temple, which you have built for Me, My Sister, Assembly of Israel, who is likened to a chaste bride. I have caused My Shekhinah to reside among you. And I have received with favor the incense of your spices which you have offered for My name's sake. I have sent fire from heaven and it has

---

[62] Alexander, *Targum of Canticles*, 135.

consumed the burnt offerings and the sacrifices of holy things. The libations of red and white wine which the priests pour upon My altar have been received with favor before Me. Now come, priests, lovers of My precepts, eat what is left of the offerings, and enjoy the bounty that has been prepared for you!"[63]

Hebrew text: "I have come to my garden, my sister, (my) bride; I have plucked my myrrh with my spices; I have eaten honey comb with my honey, I have drunk my wine with my milk. Eat! O Friends, Drink! and get drunk! O Lovers."

A literal reading of the sexual union between the woman and the man in the Song becomes a metaphorical reading of the communion between the Holy One and his people Israel in the Targum. The Targum sees the context of Song of Songs 5:1 in the temple and so contextualizes it to the reign of Solomon. Compared to Song of Songs Rabbah, the same verse refers to the tabernacle during the wilderness period.[64] The various figurative descriptions of the woman's body, such as the dripping of the flowing honey, milk and honey, and fragrance all become descriptions of the temple in this Targumic version of the Song (Song 4:11). The wine, which is used to describe love and to be a comparison to love, now in the Targum becomes the wine that the priests poured out on the altar. The invitation in the Targum for the friends to eat and drink becomes the priests eating of the offerings. The temple vision epitomizes the ideal portrait of the relationship between God and Israel after the wilderness experience.

Targum Song of Songs 8:1-2.

And at that time the King Messiah will be revealed to the Assembly of Israel, the Children of Israel shall say to him, "Come, be a brother to us, and let us go up to Jerusalem and suck out with you the reasons for the Torah, just as an infant sucks at the breast of its mother. For all the time that I was wandering outside my land, when I was mindful of the Name of the Great God and gave up my life for His divinity, even the nations of the earth did not despise me. I will lead you, O King Messiah, I will bring you up into my Temple, and you will teach me to fear the Lord, and to walk in His ways.

---

[63] Alexander, *Targum of Canticles*, 146-47.

[64] Simon, *Midrash Rabbah: The Song of Songs*, 228-29. Alexander makes a helpful comparison between Song of Songs Rabbah and Targum Song of Songs on Song 5:1. His analysis shows that the Targum makes use of early exegetes' interpretative scheme but also readapts them to provide a better reasoned, more consistent reading of the biblical text. See Alexander, "Tradition and Originality," 323-24.

There we will partake of the feast of Leviathan and we will drink (from) old wine which has been preserved in its grapes from the day that the world was created, and from pomegranates and fruits which are prepared for the righteous in the Garden of Eden."[65]

Hebrew text: "Who gives you like a brother to me, who nursed at the breasts of my mother, then I will find you outside, and I will kiss also, they will not despise me. I would lead you, I would bring you to the house of my mother, she taught me. . . . I will give you drink from the spice wine, from the sweet wine of pomegranates."

These verses belong to the fifth section of the Targum of the Song of Songs: the final exile, redemption, and the temple (Song 7:10–8:14). In a literal reading, this passage belongs to a speech by the female protagonist to her beloved. In the Targum, the passage becomes a conversation from Israel to her Messiah, the brother. They are to go to Jerusalem to study the law as an infant sucks at his mother's breasts. It also acknowledges the experience of the exile and the wish to be mindful of the name of God. Song 8:2 continues the theme of worshiping at the temple by appealing to the Garden of Eden scene.

Targum Song of Songs 8:6.

The Children of Israel will say on that day to their Lord, "We beseech You, set us like the engraving of a signet ring upon Your heart, and like the engraving of a signet ring upon Your arm, so that we shall never be exiled again, for the love of your divinity is as strong as death, and the jealousy which the nations bear us is as harsh as Gehinnom and the enmity which they harbor against us is like the blazing coals of Gehinnom, which the Lord created on the second day of the creation of the world to burn therein idolaters."[66]

Hebrew text: "Put me like a seal upon your heart, like a seal upon your arm because strong like death is love, severe like Sheol is jealousy, her flames are flames of fire, a blazing flame (or a flame of Yahweh)."

While in the Hebrew Scripture the woman says to her beloved, "Put me like a seal," in the Targum it is Israel who says to God, "Set us as the seal." "For love is strong as death" in the Targum refers to "the love of your divinity" specifically. "Jealousy" becomes the jealousy that the nations harbor against

---

[65] Alexander, *Targum of Canticles*, 189-91.
[66] Alexander, *Targum of Canticles*, 196.

Israel. *Gehinnom* is a Greek equivalence for the Hebrew word *Sheol*, demonstrating the Targum's Greek influences.

In summary, the Targum of the Song of Songs presents a systematic hermeneutical strategy to read the Song as a chronicle of Israel's salvation history from the creation of Adam to the messianic age, between which lie events of Israel's wilderness wandering, the temple, the exile, and the return from exile. In retelling Israel's salvation history through the Song, frequent references are made to the book of Exodus, such as the Red Sea, the golden calf, the law, Mount Sinai, and the temple. Song of Songs 2:9 further places it in the context of Passover, where God is the gazelle standing behind the walls of the Israelites on the eve of Passover and passing through their doors when he sees the blood of the sacrifice. The identification of the Song as a parable for the exodus event and as Israel's salvation history strongly grounds it to the presence of God among his chosen people Israel. The absence of God in the Song may be a problem for contemporary readers, but not for early Jewish readers. On the contrary, they see that the presence of God permeates the Song. The annual reciting of the Song of Songs during the Passover serves to perpetuate this metaphorical reading up to this day.

Song of Songs and Passover. Why do the Jewish people sing the Song of Songs on Passover? The answer is that it developed over a long period of time with multiple layers of interpretative tradition through a metaphorical reading of the Song of Songs. The early Tannaim tradition read it as a divine love song, and this influenced subsequent interpretations. Song of Songs Rabbah and Targum Song of Songs are two crucial consequences of that tradition. The rabbis consider the Song a midrash to the Torah, one that includes several key themes such as the temple, the law, and the exodus. These motifs form the basis of Jewish belief and piety. Targum Song of Songs explicitly connects the Song to Passover, which reinforces the Song's liturgical uses to this day. Reading the Song of Songs in the plain sense does not yield an immediate association with Passover. Yet, when read with a Jewish mind, particularly with the understanding that the Song is a divine love song, its connection with the exodus event, epitomized in the feast of Passover, becomes clear.

Over the course of history, Passover has developed into more than a Jewish festival; indeed, it has also influenced Christian liturgy. Churches of various denominations around the world practice the ritual of the Lord's Supper (or Holy Communion) as a way to remember the death of Jesus. The bread and the cup become two symbols of his body dying on the sinner's behalf. In Christian appropriation, the Passover feast has been transformed into a metaphor for remembering the sacrifice of Jesus on the cross in the Lord's Supper. The blood of the lamb splattered on Israelites' doorpost has metaphorically come to represent the blood of Jesus. Jesus is that sacrificial lamb.

While in Exodus, Passover symbolizes the deliverance of the Hebrews from Egyptian slavery, in the Christian context it becomes the deliverance from a spiritual slavery—the bondage of sin. In other words, there is no trace of divine absence in Passover. On the contrary, Passover accentuates the memory of God's deliverance of his people through the exodus event. The Song of Songs, with its explicit absence of God's name, comes to be associated with this very festival that places God and his salvific act front and center. We cannot help but reflect on the nature of divine presence in our lives as we observe Passover, or eat at the table of the Passover Seder, or partake of the Lord's Supper. The absence of God's name does not prevent the celebration of God's deliverance in the past, nor does it prevent us from entreating him for his mercy in the present.

Dianne Bergant considers Passover a sacred event performed in a sacred time. In observing Passover, we reinforce our identity, both personal and communal. Just as creation is about reordering the world, the ritual of Passover is a reordering of one's life, from chaos to new creation.[67] Since *Seder* means "order," observing the Passover Seder itself symbolizes one's reordering of life. The same goes for the Lord's Supper, before which observers examine their life and reorient it toward God.

Tamara Prosic sees Passover as a rite of passage. She notes that where Passover is mentioned in Scripture, it often occurs after a major event in Israel's life and is often connected with the temple building or rebuilding.[68] As a rite of passage, Passover marks one's "passing over" from an old order to a new order of life. Reading through the lens of the early Jewish interpreters, Song of Songs, then, is not merely a love song but a divine love song that sings of God's

---

[67]Dianne Bergant, "An Anthropological Approach to Biblical Interpretation: The Passover Supper in Exodus 12:1-20 as a Case Study," *Semeia* 67 (1994): 55, 57.

[68]Tamara Prosic, "Passover in Biblical Narratives," *JSOT* 82 (1999): 48-49, 53.

love for his people, even though his name is absent in the text. The annual reenactment of the Passover feast not only forges one's identity with the salvation history of God's people but also recalls God's faithfulness in the past. The Jewish way of reading the Song of Songs offers a vision of love and hope in the midst of one's mundane or even adversarial circumstances. The presence of God is presupposed within the text when early Jewish exegetes read the Song of Songs metaphorically as depicting the love between God and Israel.

THE BOOK OF ESTHER

Unlike in the Song of Songs, where the reader has to retrieve its early Jewish interpretations in order to discover its connection with the Passover and thus the presence of God, Purim presents itself unhidden within the text of Esther. In fact, many commentators suggest that the purpose of the Esther scroll is to explain the origin of Purim. For instance, Lewis Bayles Paton states, "The purpose of the Book of Esther is to commend the observance of the feast of Purim by an account of the way in which this feast originated."[69] Berlin also asserts that the very reason for the existence of Esther is to establish Purim as a Jewish holiday for all generations.[70] Fox identifies the primary genre based on the intrinsic importance of Esther as "festival etiology" and its present function as "festival lection."[71] Frederic Bush states that the agenda for Esther and Mordecai is to institute the festival celebrating the joy of deliverance in the diaspora.[72] Given the undeniable evidence presented within the text of Esther that the story does narrate the origin of Purim and gives it meaning and purpose within the salvation history of the Jewish people, it is clear that the story of Esther and Purim are intimately linked and inseparable.

---

[69]Lewis Bayles Paton, *The Book of Esther: A Critical and Exegetical Commentary*, International Critical Commentary (Skokie, IL: Varda Books, 2016), 54. This edition is based on the original edition published by T&T Clark in Edinburgh, 1908.

[70]Adele Berlin, *Esther: The Traditional Hebrew Text with the New JPS Translation*, JPS Bible Commentary (Philadelphia: Jewish Publication Society, 2001), xv.

[71]Fox explains, "Everything in the Masoretic version of Esther leads up to the establishment of Purim as a two-day holiday." He believes that the Purim theme has been crafted on to the older salvation theme in Esther 1–8. See Michael V. Fox, *Character and Ideology in the Book of Esther* (Grand Rapids, MI: Eerdmans, 1991), 151.

[72]Frederic William Bush, *Ruth, Esther*, WBC 9 (Dallas: Word Books, 1996), 314.

While God commanded the Israelites and their subsequent generations to observe Passover as a way to commemorate God's deliverance of Israel from Egypt (Ex 12:24), the peculiarity of Purim lies in that it is unsanctioned by divine command but justified by historical experience and communal declaration.[73] It is also the only festival established outside the Torah. Therefore, questions about the nature of Purim as well as its significance abound. Below I draw attention to the origin of Purim, the timing of Purim, and the connection between Purim and Passover as a means to address the question, What do Song of Songs and Esther, texts that do not include the divine name but are associated with Passover and Purim, mean to communities of faith? I demonstrate that while both books lack explicit reference to God's name, the two feasts, in association with the books, recall and commemorate God's faithfulness and deliverance all year round. Thus, the books' connection with the two feasts testifies to faith communities' perception of divine presence in the wake of God's literary absence.

The origin of Purim. The word *Purim* comes from *pur*, meaning "lot" (as in casting lots). *Purim* is the plural form of *pur*, referring to "lots." However, its etymology has been traced to many languages, including Hebrew, Old Persian, Babylonian, and Assyrian.[74] Theologically, Karen Jobes thinks that *lot* introduces the element of destiny into the story. She cites Psalm 16:5-6, where David praises God because "The LORD is the portion of my inheritance and my cup; You support my lot. The lines have fallen to me in pleasant places; Indeed, my heritage is beautiful to me." The verses are rooted in the context of Joshua's division of the land by casting lots. Jobes also cites Proverbs 16:33, "The lot is cast into the lap, but its every decision is from the LORD." Seeing *lot* in this light, it becomes clear that the date of the lot being cast was not determined by Haman or any human agent but by God alone.[75] Daniel Polish notes how Julius Lewy traces the etymology of Purim to the Babylonian *puru*, which conveys the idea of "fate."[76]

---

[73]Fox, *Character and Ideology*, 151.

[74]Carey A. Moore, *Esther*, AB (Garden City, NY: Doubleday, 1971), xlvii.

[75]Karen H. Jobes, *The NIV Application Commentary: Esther* (Grand Rapids, MI: Zondervan, 1999), 124-25.

[76]Daniel F. Polish, "Aspects of Esther: A Phenomenological Exploration of the Megillah of Esther and the Origin of Purim," *JSOT* 85 (1999): 103.

Scholars speculate on the origin of Purim. Some think that Purim has a Babylonian origin, while others think that it has a Persian or even Jewish origin.[77] Since the names of Esther and Mordecai are associated with or even originate in the Babylonian deities Ishtar and Marduk, whereas the names of Haman and Vashti are associated with the Elamite gods Humman and Mashti, it is possible to connect Purim with the Babylonian origin or the word. Some scholars think that Purim is comparable to the Babylonian New Year festival, celebrated in the month of Nisan. People cast lots in this festival as a part of its major foci.[78] Others think that Purim is a Jewish appropriation of a non-Jewish celebration of New Year called Sacae, a festival associated with a substitute king.[79]

There are also scholars who suggest Purim originated as a political festival called the Accession Days, to affirm Mordecai's accession as a Jewish viceroy in the Persian court. It then evolved and was gradually replaced by Purim.[80] The earliest source regarding a Day of Mordecai celebrated on the fourteenth of Adar is 2 Maccabees 15:36 and may lend support to this proposal. Yet other scholars propose that Purim had a Palestinian origin since it is an adaptation of the festival held on the thirteenth of Adar to celebrate Judas Maccabeus's victory over Nicanor in 161 BCE, based on 1 Maccabees 7:26-50.[81] Nicanor Day and the Day of Mordecai were two rival festivals held on succeeding days, Nicanor Day on the thirteenth of Adar and the Day of Mordecai (Purim) on the fourteenth of the same month. Their exact relationship is the subject of speculation. The fact is that after the destruction of the second temple, Nicanor Day vanished, but Purim continues to this day.[82]

---

[77] Moore, *Esther*, xlvii–xlviii. Gerleman suggests Purim originated among the Jews. See Gillis Gerleman, *Esther*, 2nd ed., Biblischer Kommentar: Altes Testament 21 (Neukirchen-Vluyn: Neukirchener Verlag, 1982).

[78] B. C. Gregory, "Purim," *DOTWPW* 632.

[79] Polish, "Aspects of Esther," 85–106.

[80] Jona Schellekens, "Accession Days and Holidays: The Origins of the Jewish Festival of Purim," *JBL* 128, no. 1 (2009): 115–34. In the second to first century BCE, the Day of Mordecai, which was celebrated on the fourteenth of Adar, appeared in 2 Maccabees and may provide evidence for this possibility. Schellekens uses biblical type scenes, juxtaposing the story of Esther with other biblical narratives such as the stories of Moses, Joseph, and Joash to support his thesis.

[81] Roger Heist, "The Purim Connection," *Union Seminary Quarterly Review* 32 (1978): 139–45; Gregory, "Purim," 632.

[82] Hayyim Schauss, *The Jewish Festivals: History and Observance* (New York: Schocken Books, 1938), 251–52.

Outside the biblical canon, the origin of Purim is difficult to trace, and all proposals are merely conjectures. There are also scholars who believe that Purim does not originate in the book of Esther at all but existed and was practiced long before the Esther scroll. In this understanding, the book of Esther was created as an explanation for the festival.[83] That said, among the Megilloth, the association between Purim and the book of Esther is the least contested. By the first century CE, the Esther scroll was being recited during the Purim festival. By the second century CE, the observance of Purim was reinforced by several events, including the fall of the second temple in 70 CE, the failure of the Bar Kokhba revolt in 135 CE, and the confirmation of the canonical status of the Esther scroll. From the second century on, reading the Esther scroll has been a central feature in the celebration of Purim.[84]

The installation of Purim. Three accounts exist in Esther, providing the customs and practices associated with Purim. All appear in Esther 9. They are Esther 9:16-19, 20-28, 29-32. Esther 9:17-19 explain the two-day festival as follows:

> The remainder of the Jews who were in the provinces of the king were as-sembled and mustered. And have rest (deposed) from their enemies, and killed those who hate them 750,000 but the spoil, they did not send their hand.
>
> (These were done) on the thirteenth day for the month Adar. And (they) rested on the fourteenth day of it, and (they) made it a day of feasting and rejoicing.
>
> But the Jews who were in Shushan were assembled on the thirteenth in it and on the fourteenth in it, then (they) rested on the fifteenth in it and made it a day of feasting and rejoicing. (Esther 9:16-19)[85]

Three days are involved in the Purim festival. The Jews outside Shushan gathered on the thirteenth day of Adar, and then rested on the fourteenth day of Adar, with feasting and rejoicing. As for the Jews in Shushan, they gathered on the thirteen and fourteenth of Adar, then they rested on the fifteenth of Adar, with feasting and rejoicing. The feasting motif forms a reversal of the banquet motif found at the beginning of the Esther story, where the Persian banquets give way to the feasting of the Jews. The rejoicing

---

[83]E.g., Schauss, *Jewish Festivals*, 250.
[84]B. C. Gregory, "Megillot and Festivals," *DOTWPW* 463.
[85]"Mustered" literally means "stood for their soul."

motif of Purim echoes the rejoicing motif in Esther 8 when Mordecai went out from the presence of the king in royal robes with a golden crown. There was joy for the Jews. Whenever the king's decree allowing the Jews to avenge themselves arrived, there was gladness and joy (Esther 8:15-17). A transfer of power as well as a transfer of joy from Persians to the Jews was in view. Therefore, Purim was characterized by resting, feasting, and rejoicing.

Esther 9:20-28 provides a detailed account of the installation of Purim with emphasis on the manner of confirmation, the practice, and the naming of it. Mordecai records the events that happened concerning the king's decree and sends letters to all the Jews who are in the provinces of the king, confirming the decree to observe the fourteenth and the fifteenth of Adar annually (Esther 9:20-21). The practice of Purim involves not only feasting and rejoicing but also sending portions (of food) to one another as well as to the poor (Esther 9:22). Then the text recounts the naming of Purim:

> For Haman son of Hammedatha the Agagite, the adversary of all the Jews, plotted against the Jews to destroy them and he casted a *pur*, that is, a lot, in order to confuse them and to destroy them.
>
> But when she came before the king, he said with the book, "Let his evil thought which he plotted against the Jews be returned upon his head." So they hanged him and his sons, upon the tree.
>
> Therefore, they called these days "Purim," according to the name "the Pur." (Esther 9:24-26)

This passage takes the reader back to Esther 3:7, where Haman casts the lot in order to determine the date on which to annihilate the Jews. However, the meaning of Purim as derived from *pur* seems dubious to some, since casting a lot was never the focus of the Esther scroll. It is likely that *pur* and *purim* is another example of soundplay.[86] What is significant about *pur* is its meaning. The Hebrew equivalence for *pur* is "lot" (גּוֹרָל), which not only refers to a dice-like object but also to "fate" that comes from God (Ps 16:5).[87] On the surface, the casting of lots seems to resort to the realm of unknown or random chance, but it may reflect the divine will. Thus, the uncertainty of divine involvement in Esther abounds.

---

[86]Berlin, *Esther*, xlvii.
[87]Karen H. Jobes, "Esther 1, Book of," *DOTWPW* 166.

The last passage concerning Purim is recorded in Esther 9:29-32:

Then Esther the queen, the daughter of Abihail, wrote and (with) Mordecai the Jew, all the power to confirm the letter of this Purim the second time.

Then he sent the documents to all the Jews, 127 provinces of the kingdom of Ahasuerus the words of peace and truth.

To confirm these days of Purim in their appointed time just as Mordecai the Jew and Esther the Queen confirmed for them and just as they confirmed upon their soul and upon their seed the words of their fast and their cry.

And the word of Esther confirmed the words of these Purim and it was written in the book.

Over the course of the narrative, Esther ascends from inactivity to activity and then to a position of authority.[88] She writes with all the power, that is, with all her authority, to confirm the letter of the installation of Purim. Esther's purpose is to add the weight of her authority to that of Mordecai so that she can secure the official observance of the Purim festival.[89] Carol Bechtel highlights the significance of the power of the written word. She notes the presence of at least sixty-three references to writing or written texts in Esther and posits that during the times of the book, the written word and the spoken word were paired up.[90] The festival of Purim not only commemorates the victory of the Jewish people in defending their lives through annual observance, but is also remembered forever by being present in the written word. Through the written word and through celebrating Purim annually, the memories of Esther, Mordecai, and the courageous Jewish people live on.

The connections between Purim and Passover. A major component in the celebration of Purim is the reading of the Esther scroll in its entirety. During the morning service, the Torah reading that is read alongside Esther is Exodus 17:8-16, the story about the Amelekites raging war against the Israelites. God says to Moses that he will blot out the memory of Amelek from under heaven. Then Moses builds an altar to the Lord and names it, "The LORD is my banner." Moses also says, "The LORD has sworn; the LORD

---

[88]Fox, *Character and Ideology*, 196.

[89]Paton, *Book of Esther*, 300.

[90]The list includes "to write," "law/decree/edict," "letter/letter-writer," "copy," "letter/missive," "annals," "decree." See Carol M. Bechtel, *Esther*, Interpretation (Louisville, KY: Westminster John Knox, 2002), 14-15.

will have war against Amalek from generation to generation" (Ex 17:15-16). Since the ancestry of Haman is traced back to the Amalek (Esther 3:1; 1 Sam 15:8-9), the association between Exodus and Esther is evident.

Furthermore, a blessing formula always follows the reading of the Esther scroll during the Purim festival: "Blessed are you, O Lord, the King of the universe, who pleads our cause, who renders judgment on our behalf, who avenges us, who fulfills retribution on the enemies of our life, and exacts recompense for us from our foes. Blessed are you, O Lord, who exacts recompense for his people Israel from all their foes, the God who saves" (Babylonian Tamud Megillah 21b).[91] This liturgical function of Esther during the Purim festival provides yet another close association between the scroll and the salvific theme in Exodus. As Song of Songs is read during Passover, Esther is recited during Purim. As Passover originates from Exodus and Esther has affinity with Exodus on multiple levels, the correlation between Purim and Passover not only sheds light on the two scrolls' connection with Exodus, but also illuminates the other on the theme of salvation.

Timing of Purim and Passover. In the Hebrew Masoretic Text, an account for the origin of Purim is stated clearly in Esther 3 and Esther 9. In Esther 3, when Haman sees that Mordecai does not bow to or prostrate himself before him, he is filled with rage. He then seeks to exterminate all the Jews in all the kingdom of Ahasuerus, the people of Mordecai (Esther 3:5-6). Killing Mordecai alone is not enough to appease his rage; Haman intends to annihilate the whole Jewish race. Then the text says: "In the first month, that is the month of Nisan, in the twelfth year of King Ahasuerus, a Pur, that is, the lot [הִפִּיל פּוּר הוּא הַגּוֹרָל], was cast before Haman, from day to day, and month to month, twelfth month, that is, the month of Adar" (Esther 3:7). Then Haman incites the king and accuses a people group within the king's realm who do not subject themselves to the king's law but practice their own. As if this is not enough to move the king to action, Haman pledges to send ten thousand talents of silver to the treasury of the king if this people are destroyed. The king agrees immediately, without any hesitation. Then the scribes of the king are called in on the thirteenth day of the first month (Esther 3:8-12). The next verse recounts, "Written documents were sent by the hand of the runners to all the provinces of

---

[91]Gregory, "Megillot and Festivals," 463.

the king to exterminate, to kill, to destroy all the Jews, from young to old, children and women, on one day, on the thirteenth day of the twelfth month, that is, the month of Adar, to plunder them to take as spoils" (Esther 3:13).

In the mind of a Jewish reader and in the mind of those who are familiar with the Passover tradition, the timing of casting the lot cannot be mere coincidence. The date when Haman casts lots to annihilate the Jews falls on the thirteenth day of the first month, the month of Nisan, in the twelfth year of King Ahasuerus (Esther 3:7). This is precisely one day before Passover. In other words, the day Haman casts lots falls on the eve of Passover. In the Jewish liturgy, the first day of Passover begins after sunset on the fourteenth of Nisan and ends at sunset on the fifteenth day of Nisan.

Subsequently, the lot to determine the date of annihilating the Jews falls eleven months later, on the thirteenth day of the twelfth month, the month of Adar. This is exactly one month before Passover (Esther 3:13).

Below is the Babylonian calendar with Hebrew and Gregorian equivalences:

Table 5.2

Jewish Month	Hebrew Equivalent	Gregorian Equivalent	Purim	Passover
1	Nisan	March/April	Haman cast lot on 13th Nisan	14th of Nisan
2	Iyyar	April/May		
3	Sivan	May/June		
4	Tammuz	June/July		
5	Ab	July/August		
6	Elul	August/September		
7	Tishri	September/October		
8	Marheshvan	October/November		
9	Kislev	November/December		
10	Tebeth	December/January		
11	Shebat	January/February		
12	Adar	February/March	the lot fell on 13th Adar	

Passover marks the beginning of a year (Ex 12:1), and Purim marks the end of a year. Therefore, the timing of Purim and Passover is closely connected and difficult to overlook. Although Haman had an ill intent for the Jews, that the lot that he cast fell on the eve of Passover must have suggested that something supernatural was at work. What was meant to be evil to the Jews turned out to be redemption for them. The following diagram provides another illustration to the relationship between these two feasts:

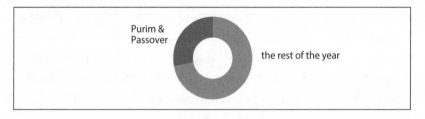

Figure 5.1

This diagram shows that Purim and Passover are back to back in the liturgical calendar. The timing of the two festivals as well as their common symbolism of salvation cannot be coincidental. Neither can the literary absence of the divine name in the book of Esther and Song of Songs be coincidental. Therefore a logical conclusion seems to be: while God is absent in Esther and Song of Songs, he is present in the rest of the Hebrew canon.[92] For God, there is a time to be absent and a time to be present.

Purim and Passover in the Syriac version of Esther. In addition to the close proximity of the timing of Purim and Passover and their back-to-back connection in the liturgical calendar, there is yet another connection between the two festivals. Michael Wechsler notes a verse in Peshitta Esther that has a strong Purim-Passover connection. *Peshitta* means "the simple (translation)." It is the standard Bible for the Syriac tradition, a dialect of Aramaic. It is

---

[92]Webb connects Passover and Purim to the call of Abraham and says that they "testify to two complementary aspects of a single reality: the election of Israel, which had its beginning historically in the call of Abraham." When God said to Abraham "whoever curses you, I will curse," it became realized in the Amalekites and their descendant Haman, who tried to destroy Israel. Barry G. Webb, *Five Festal Garments: Christian Reflections on the Song of Songs, Ruth, Lamentations, Ecclesiastes, and Esther* (Downers Grove, IL: InterVarsity Press, 2000), 128.

believed that the Old Testament of the Peshitta was translated into Syriac from Hebrew, probably in the second century CE.[93] The verse is Esther 9:26:

עַל־כֵּן קָרְאוּ לַיָּמִים הָאֵלֶּה פוּרִים עַל־שֵׁם הַפּוּר :MT

My translation: Therefore, they called those days "Purim," according to the name "the Pur."

Peshitta: Therefore, they called those days *puraye* (i.e., Purim) in accord with the name *pesha* (i.e., Passover).[94]

In the Hebrew text, *Pur* and *Purim* not only create a pun but also tie in with their respective meanings. It is odd that Peshitta renders the word *Pur* as *pesha* when it translates the same word in other places as "lot" (Peshitta Esther 3:7; 9:24). Wechsler suggests that the rendering of *pesha* in Peshitta Esther 9:26 could be a result of Jewish exegetical influence or oral tradition, specifically a tradition that links Purim-Passover with their common themes of national redemption. In Exodus, the Passover event centers on God's "passing over" to secure the release of God's people from Egypt, whereas in Esther, God works through the lot to overturn the evil intended by Haman and turn it into the assurance of deliverance for God's people.[95]

The ritual aspect of Purim and its connection with Passover. In his study of the nature of Purim from a ritual perspective, Jeffrey Rubenstein observes that the festival of Purim involves liminality and *communitas* as defined by anthropologist Victor Turner. Turner defines liminality as an in-between time, "betwixt and between," or a threshold period. Power and status come to a halt at this point of in-betweenness. Turner considers *communitas* to be a space where equality, immediacy, and the lack of social rank and roles occur. All members within the *communitas* are equal in spite of their social and hierarchical differences. The practice of Purim resembles theatrical performances or a carnival, where people wear masks, dress in the clothing of the opposite gender, and put on costumes of Esther, Mordecai, and Haman. These practices flatten the differences between rich and poor, the powerful and the oppressed, the religious and the nonreligious.

---

[93]Emanuel Tov, *Textual Criticism of the Hebrew Bible*, 2nd ed. (Minneapolis: Fortress, 2001), 152.
[94]Michael G. Wechsler, "Critical Notes: The Purim-Passover Connection: A Reflection of Jewish Exegetical Tradition in the Peshitta Book of Esther," *JBL* 117, no. 2 (1998): 321.
[95]Wechsler, "Critical Notes," 326.

After Mordecai's ascension, many people of the land profess to be Jews (Esther 8:17), which suggests a leveling of the boundaries between Gentiles and Jews.[96] Reversal is a core motif in the book of Esther. Polish observes that Esther 9:1, where the phrase "it is completely overturned" or "the opposite happened" occurs, could very well serve as the emblem of the entire book because everything in Esther exists in a dialectical relationship with its opposite.[97]

If flattening and leveling of boundaries between social, economic, and religious differences characterizes the Purim festival, then Purim represents antistructure. By contrast, Rubenstein observes that Passover symbolizes not only the beginning of the liturgical and agricultural year but also the beginning of the Jewish people and the giving of the law. Passover celebrates God's deliverance of the Israelites from slavery in Egypt. Because of this newfound identity, Israel was able to receive the divine law to be God's people. In this sense, Passover symbolizes order and structure, whereas Purim symbolizes antistructure, a state prior to the establishment of order, society, and the legal system. In the Talmud, the rabbis advise people to ask questions concerning the laws of Passover during Purim. The Purim feast goes on late into the night, and the preparation for the Passover starts in the morning. These ancient traditions acknowledge a special relationship between Purim and Passover. According to this ritual perspective, going from Purim to Passover means that people enter from a state of disorder to order.[98] The Purim-Passover connection and its multiple symbolisms cannot be easily dismissed.

Purim: Salvation with a twist. How do we understand the nature and the work of God in the two texts that are connected with Israel's feasts but do not include the name of God? In light of the Purim and Passover connections, their symbolism of salvation is evident through the respective timing of the feasts and Jewish exegetical interpretations on the subject. Some scholars and commentators see more than a dozen elements that the

[96]Jeffrey Rubenstein, "Purim, Liminality, and Communitas," *Association for Jewish Studies Review* 17, no. 2 (1992): 247-77, esp. 250-51, 260-61.
[97]Polish, "Aspects of Esther," 89.
[98]Rubenstein, "Purim, Liminality, and Communitas," 267. Rubenstein adds that the leveling of boundaries in the Purim celebration also anticipates the world to come, where there will be universal love, peace, and the absence of society and structure, the ultimate *communitas*.

stories of Passover and Purim have in common, such as the setting of both stories being at a foreign court. There is a mortal threat endangering God's people. There is deliverance, revenge, and triumph. There is the establishment of a festival to commemorate the deliverance.[99] However, Purim has a major variance that sets it apart from Passover.

In the event of the Passover, God occupies center stage. God speaks, commands, gives law and ordinances, kills the firstborn sons of the Egyptians, and enables the Israelites to leave Egypt (Ex 12:1-13). God even gives the Israelites favor in the eyes of the Egyptians so they plunder the Egyptians and receive their articles of silver, gold, and clothing upon leaving Egypt (Ex 12:35-36). When the Egyptians change their mind and start pursuing the Israelites in the Reed Sea, God appears to be ever more vindictive and powerful. He fights for the Israelites by moving the pillar of cloud from before the Israelites to behind them, preventing the Egyptians from getting too close to them. God then sweeps the sea by a strong east wind and turns the sea into dry land. As a result, the Israelites go through the midst of the sea on dry ground. As if this were not enough, God then confuses the Egyptian army and causes their chariot wheels to swerve. God then asks Moses to stretch out his hand over the sea so that the water will come back and drown the Egyptians who go after the Israelites. Therefore, God overthrows the Egyptians into the midst of the sea. Not even one of them remained alive (Ex 14:19-28).

In that Passover event, God is visible, vocal, mobile, and powerful. The symbolism of Passover as commemorating God's deliverance of the Israelites fits perfectly with the narrative unfolded in the exodus account. In response to God's deliverance, Moses praises God as "a man of war" (Ex 15:3, my translation) whose right hand is majestic in power and whose left hand shatters the enemy (Ex 15:6). God appears to be a warrior, fighting for his people and triumphing over the enemy.

By striking contrast, in Esther there is salvation of the Jews, but God's name is not mentioned. Koller states blatantly that "the book describes a 'salvation' with no God."[100] In Esther, God is invisible, silent, hidden, and

---

[99]For instance, Gerleman is a proponent of this view (*Esther*, 14).
[100]Koller, *Esther in Ancient Jewish Thought*, 92.

opaque. Some even doubt he is there at all. In Esther the salvation of the Jews seems to be accomplished by humans alone without God's direct intervention. The book and Purim revolve around human beings. God is nowhere to be seen. Unlike Exodus, where the status of the Israelites drastically transforms from slaves to free people after divine deliverance, the status of the Jews is not changed in Esther, even after the edict of genocide has been averted. There is also no geographical movement for the Jews in Persia, in contrast to the Israelites who migrate from Egypt on the way to the Promised Land.[101]

While Passover was instituted by God, Purim was established and confirmed by human beings. If this is not enough of a difference, Passover was part of the Israelite law code to be observed throughout their generations. Purim, on the other hand, is the only festival recorded in the Scripture that is outside the law and practiced outside the land of Israel. In other words, Purim serves as a symbol of salvation, but with a twist—a salvation without God's direct involvement. In this sense, Esther is responding to Exodus in terms of salvation of God's people that God's people will be delivered. However, Esther also responds to Exodus deconstructively, by suggesting that salvation can be achieved without God's overt assistance.

The rabbinic commentary, Megillat Ta'anit, juxtaposes Purim and Passover. Some rabbis even claim that the two festivals happened on the same night "so as to juxtapose redemption to redemption."[102] This forces the reader to reflect on the different types of redemption they commemorate. Passover is by God's direct intervention and Purim by divine hiddenness or, worse, by divine absence. Whether in God's overt or covert action, salvation is accomplished at the end. Even if "salvation without God" indeed happens, one can't help but wonder whether God has been involved somehow behind the scenes. This resonates with what Rabbi Hutner says about Purim and Passover: that they represent alternative modes by which Israel may recognize God, who is both the "I" in "I will hide my face on that day" and the "I" in "I am the LORD your God who brought you out of the

---

[101]Koller remarks that the book of Esther has a radical focus on the present, with no hint of a promise for the future (*Esther in Ancient Jewish Thought*, 93).

[102]Koller, *Esther in Ancient Jewish Thought*, 202-3.

land of Egypt."[103] Therefore, the two feasts, Passover and Purim, illuminate each other on the theme of salvation complementarily and present a dynamic God who acts according to his freedom in human history whether in his presence or absence.

FEAST: IN THE ABSENCE OF GOD

In the absence of God's name in the Song of Songs and Esther, their connection with the feasts of Passover and Purim demonstrates the scrolls' religious significance to Jewish communities of faith. The two feasts' concern with the exodus event points to the scrolls' particular influence in the Jewish community as well as the Jewish identity. During the postexilic time, when the temple is no longer in sight and when divine presence becomes a matter of faith rather than a visible icon, Purim recalls Passover. In times when God is absent, the two feasts form two responses to God's deliverance in Exodus and evoke his faithfulness all year round. Even if the name of God does not present itself explicitly in these two books, God is not entirely absent either. The Song of Songs is still sung annually during Passover season as a way to commemorate God's deliverance of his people in Exodus. Likewise, the book of Esther is recited annually during Purim to recall the salvation of the Jews. Through these two feasts associated with the two scrolls, God is present in his absence.

The arrangement of Song of Songs heading the Megilloth and Esther ending it suggests an intentional design of the compiler, who was familiar with Israel's exodus narrative and attempts to ground their faith in that national identity. Through Passover and Purim, the presence of God is invoked in the midst of his absence in the texts. In one sense, the feasts remember God's past salvation and offer the hope of his present and future deliverance. In another sense, although the feasts resonate in texts in which the name of God is absent, the texts nonetheless remind of God's presence and faithfulness at other times.

For postexilic Jewish communities, with the destruction of the temple, divine presence became an abstract concept. The annual observance of

---

[103] Avivah Gottlieb Zornberg, *The Murmuring Deep: Reflections on the Biblical Unconscious* (New York: Schocken Books, 2009), 131.

Passover and Purim reminds observers to look beyond their current circumstances by revisiting the past, where God delivered his people visibly and powerfully. Hence, ritual ties the past with the present.

For contemporary readers, in the absence of God, we can look back to the past, where God could be found, and then remember his faithfulness to us in life's ups and downs. Just as God has been faithful to us in the past, so too will he get us through the trials of the present. In the absence of God, we can also look forward to the future, trusting God that he will act on our behalf to ensure his presence with us. Our trust in God's future deliverance is based on his past faithfulness to us. Therefore, even in the midst of God's absence, there is still hope to be found. This hope is grounded in reading the text from a perspective of God's active presence in history and from one's persistent trust in that presence in the midst of divine absence.

6

CANON
RESONANCES *and* DISSONANCES

*All Scripture is inspired by God and profitable for teaching,
for reproof, for correction, for training in righteousness.*

2 TIMOTHY 3:16

ALTHOUGH THE BOOKS OF RUTH AND ESTHER traditionally have
been grouped together due to their similarities, in recent years scholars
have noticed that Song of Songs and Esther both echo the tripartite division
of the Hebrew Bible. For example, David Carr has used the garden metaphor to position Song of Songs within the Hebrew canon, linking the
garden in the Song to the Garden of Eden and Isaiah's vineyard images.[1]
Nathan Ward sees the interbiblical dialogue within the biblical canon as a
clue to deciphering the book of Esther. He argues that allusions from all
three sections of the Hebrew Scripture frame Esther as a canonical book.[2]
Both authors adopt the method of interbiblical or innerbiblical allusions,
connecting the contents, motifs, and images of Song of Songs or Esther to
the rest of the Hebrew Scripture.[3]

---

[1]David McLain Carr, *The Erotic Word: Sexuality, Spirituality, and the Bible* (New York: Oxford
University Press, 2005).

[2]Nathan Ward, *God Unseen: A Theological Introduction to Esther* (Chillicothe, OH: DeWard, 2016).

[3]I use the terms *innerbiblical* or *intertextual* not in their technical sense, but rather for convenience
to refer to the shared imagery, concept, or theology that emerges from texts in the Hebrew
Scripture when juxtaposed with one another. For a recent study on various definitions for

This chapter considers how the motifs and "type-scenes" of Song of Songs and Esther relate to the rest of the Hebrew Scripture.[4] The focus on the motifs of the texts is different from focusing on the linguistic or literary and rhetorical aspects of the texts. A motif is more conceptual and includes images and ideas rather than specific words or expressions. The aforementioned authors focus on the similarities between the two scrolls with the rest of the Hebrew canon, but they fail to identify their dissimilarities with the rest of the Hebrew canon. As we will observe, Song of Songs and Esther serve both as echoes and as counterechoes in relation to the rest of the Hebrew Scripture. As echoes, the motifs of both books resonate with other biblical texts; as counterechoes, they challenge, critique, and evaluate the normative motifs manifested in the rest of the canon. In so doing, these two books form a conversation with the rest of the canon, providing a fuller picture of biblical revelation as well as the multidimensionality of the divine human relationship. Reading Song of Songs and Esther in the context of the Hebrew canon shows that the lack of explicit reference to the name of God is to be understood as an integral part of the Scripture as well as an aspect of the manifestation of divine activities. While God should be present at all times ontologically, nevertheless he is sometimes perceived as absent in the human experience.

Situated within the Hebrew canon, Song of Songs and Esther present themselves as two texts in the tradition of the sacred Scriptures as well as two texts that counter that same tradition. While the books' motifs that are shared with the rest of the canon suggest that God must be present in these two books as he is in other biblical books, these motifs also display apparent variations from the norm and suggest the possibility of divine absence. It is with these resonances and dissonances of the two books in relation to the rest of the Hebrew canon that this chapter intends to grapple. What do

---

intertextuality, see Havilah Dharamraj, *Altogether Lovely: A Thematic and Intertextual Reading of the Song of Songs* (Minneapolis: Fortress, 2018), 12-16. See my earlier discussions on intertextuality in chapter four.

[4]Robert Alter, *The Art of Biblical Narrative* (New York: Basic Books, 1981), 51. Alter's "type-scenes" focus on narratives, yet in the poetic world of Song of Songs, this type-scene is applicable too. The way I use the motifs in the Song of Songs as echoes to other texts reflects Russell Meek's definition for innerbiblical exegesis, where the receptor text in some way modifies the source text. See Russell L. Meek, "Intertextuality, Inner-Biblical Exegesis, and Inner-Biblical Allusion: The Ethics of a Methodology," *Biblica* 95, no. 1 (2014): 290.

these resonances and dissonances say about the nature of God and his activities? How should we think of God when dissonances appear? What should we do when those dissonances emerge in our lived experiences?

With these questions in mind, we will first consider the various motifs in Song of Songs that bear resemblance to and share similar scenes with the rest of the Hebrew canon, such as the Eden motif, the prophet theme, and the women figures in Proverbs. At the same time, these shared motifs are not entirely similar but display apparent differences in the Song. We will then consider the motifs in Esther that share striking resemblances with the motifs elsewhere in other biblical books, including the temple theme, the Joseph narrative, the exodus story, Saul and the Amalekites, the Daniel narrative, and the story of Ruth, for these very motifs occur with disparities in Esther. Therefore, the motifs of Song of Songs and Esther, by conforming to the rest of the Hebrew canon and by diverging from or subverting them, point to the fact that these two books are indeed an integral part of the sacred Scripture but offer an alternative voice. They are, on the one hand, witnesses to the scriptural tradition, and on the other hand, challengers to that normative tradition. It is in this unique combination of resonances and dissonances that Song of Songs and Esther contribute to the canon and speak to the lived experience of believers that life does not always turn out in the way that the rest of the Scripture suggests. Primarily, they show that God is not always present and visible, as other biblical books indicate. God is full of surprises, and this means there will be surprises in the journey of life and faith.

Before we move on to Song of Songs, a word about the definition of canon needs to be said. For the purposes of this chapter, by *canon* I refer to the Masoretic Text in its final form with its three divisions: Torah, Prophets (Nevi'im), and Writings (Ketuvim).[5] Since the focus of the canonical approach centers on its final form and the meaning of the canonical books for the faith community, the dating of the books and the order of the books become relatively insignificant.[6] John Goldingay divides canonical

---

[5] This method was first proposed by Brevard Childs. See Brevard S. Childs, *Introduction to the Old Testament as Scripture* (Philadelphia: Fortress, 1979), 73.
[6] By this method, Childs intends to study the canonical books in relation to their usage among the Israelite community. James Sanders diverges from Childs and stresses that *canon* means different

interpretation into two strands: individual books and the collection as a whole.[7] For individual books, one interprets each individual book in light of the canon. For the collection as a whole, the interpreter takes different individual books in the canon and brings them into conversation with one another on various subjects such as God, the relationship between man and woman, and the problem of suffering.[8] It is this latter approach that I use to make sense of the canonical status of the two books that leave the name of God out of the text.

READING SONG OF SONGS AS HEBREW SCRIPTURE

In the entire Scripture, there is no book like the Song of Songs. After all, where else in Scripture do we find a book that from beginning to end describes erotic love between a man and a woman? Where do we find a book that lavishes uninhibited praise on the human body, both female and male? Where do we encounter the kind of heartbreak and lovesickness that characterizes the female lover? Other than Esther, where in the Bible do we find a book that makes no explicit reference to the name of God? Throughout the two thousand years of its interpretative history, Song of Songs has remained utterly fascinating to interpreters. In what follows, I position Song of Songs among the three aforementioned divisions of the Hebrew Bible and note in what ways it resonates with or is dissonant with the images of the selected books in these divisions.

Song of Songs and the Torah. *Genesis 2: Garden.* In chapter four of this book, we explored the connection between the garden imagery in the Song of Songs and in the Garden of Eden in Genesis. The garden is one of the Song's dominant settings. It is both a physical garden and a metaphorical

---

things to different faith communities, so the idea of canon and its interpretations is ongoing and adapting alongside the evolvement of the faith communities in which these canons are received. See James A. Sanders, *Canon and Community: A Guide to Canonical Criticism* (Philadelphia: Fortress, 1984), 15. House sees the canonical approach as involving the intertextual connections between the individual book and the rest of the canon, and thus illuminates the thematic wholeness of Hebrew Scripture. See Paul R. House, *Old Testament Theology* (Downers Grove, IL: InterVarsity Press, 1998), 57.

[7]John Goldingay, "Hermeneutics," *DOTWPW* 267-80.

[8]For example, Goldingay writes, "In Genesis 1–2, the relationship between a man and a woman is a practical one; in the Song of Songs, it is a romantic one. We learn from the conversation within the Writings and between the Writings and other Scriptures about these questions" ("Hermeneutics," 274).

image for the woman's body (Song 4:12, 16; 5:1). Along with this garden imagery comes the presence of fountains, streams, trees, fruits, jewelry, and animals. The composer uses poetic images from nature to conjure up a paradise as well as a garden of delight. In the Song, the garden is where love blossoms. The female and male lovers unreservedly lavish praise on each other. They are naked but not ashamed. These images bear striking similarities to the descriptions of the lovers in the Garden of Eden. In Eden, there are also two human lovers in the garden, likewise with trees, fruits, streams, jewelry, and animals. The woman is brought together to be with the man. They are naked but not ashamed. When reading the whole biblical narrative together, one can see the broad strokes of the story line in which human beings are created by God, and the woman is described as being bone of the man's bones and flesh of his flesh (Gen 2:23). But their relationship goes wrong after the fall (Gen 3:16-17). Their relationship is restored in the Song of Songs, where the human lovers once again enjoy each other's love. They are once again naked but not ashamed. At the end, Edenic love is restored. This is what chapter four delineated. Yet, as good as it sounds, this story line only presents a partial story, for the dissonances between the two gardens are just as significant as their resonances.

In the Garden of Eden, the man is the dominant figure. God creates the man first, then the woman (Gen 2:7, 22). God gives the man the responsibility to till and to keep the garden, whereas the woman is his helper (Gen 2:15, 18). Although being a helper does not suggest inferiority or lack of privilege, it is certainly not the same as being the "person in charge." It is the man who names the woman (Gen 2:23), thus projecting the image of him as the one who has authority over her. It is also the man who shall leave his father and his mother and cleave to his wife. Therefore, the man appears to be the leader of the house. In the Edenic narrative, the man speaks about the woman in a poetic utterance: she is "bone of my bones and flesh of my flesh." The woman remains silent and passive.

These dynamics of the man and the woman in the Garden of Eden are reversed in the Song of Songs. Here the woman becomes the more prominent character. It is she who opens the Song and expresses her desire for his kisses. It is also she who closes the Song with her desire for him to return to her. In the middle of the Song are two night scenes about the woman. In both of her dreamlike visions, she experiences his absence and is anxious over this liminal existence of missing her beloved. It is she who searches for him, yearns for him, and desires him. He, on the other hand, appears to be distant and emotionally removed. Although he also desires her and praises her, his physical presence is not constant. There is no doubt that the woman occupies center stage in the Song. Her inner world as well as her words and actions are depicted more transparently than those of her beloved. Whether there is one Song or an anthology of songs in the Song of Songs, the woman is the leading lady. While the couple's roles in the Genesis narrative focus on the functional level of their relationship, the roles of the couple in the Song of Songs focus on the erotic, romantic, and sensual aspects of their relationship.

Because of this striking difference from the woman in the Garden of Eden, Song of Songs has attracted particular attention from female readers and feminists alike. Some construe her as a figure who "redeemed the love that had been lost in Eden."[9] Others champion her as an embodiment of desire and passion.[10] Some see the woman in the Song as in a mutual, harmonious and equal relationship with the man, thus reversing the male-dominated picture portrayed in the Garden of Eden.[11] Others see the two gardens as inversions of each other.[12] Still others see the woman in the Song not as the man's equal but as "less" than the man since his presence is elusive. It is always he who is bouncing off the hills somewhere, while she wants him to stay indoors with her. Also, it is always she who looks for him and not the other way around.[13] Clearly, the dynamics of the human couple in the Song are not the same as of the human couple in the Garden of Eden.

In light of these different views of the Song and the Garden of Eden, questions emerge as to the exact relationship between these two texts: Is the

---

[9]For example, Phyllis Trible, *God and the Rhetoric of Sexuality* (Philadelphia: Fortress, 1978), 144-65.

[10]For example, Carey Ellen Walsh, *Exquisite Desire: Religion, the Erotic, and the Song of Songs* (Minneapolis: Fortress, 2000), 7.

[11]For example, Trible, *God and the Rhetoric*, 144-65.

[12]Francis Landy, "The Song of Songs and the Garden of Eden," *JBL* 98, no. 4 (1979): 513-28.

[13]For example, J. Cheryl Exum, "Ten Things Every Feminist Should Know About the Song of Songs," in *A Feminist Companion to the Song of Songs*, ed. Athalya Brenner and Carole R. Fontaine, FCB 2/6 (Sheffield: Sheffield Academic Press, 2000), 30.

love portrayed in the Song of Songs a restoration of Edenic love or a correction of the Edenic love? Which text is presented as the ideal portrait of love? Is the male-female dynamics in the Song an inversion of the male-female relationship in the Garden of Eden? The two versions of the garden form a tension between a harmonious portrait of the human couple and a dynamic relationship that involves the highs and lows of love. Both texts present aspects of the ideal setting for love and the portrait of an ideal couple, but they do not present the whole picture of love.

In Eden, the setting of love is uncontaminated by sin. Yet the relationship portrayed of the human couple is one in which the man is in a dominant position but nevertheless regards the woman as his flesh and bone. The male dominance thus can be perceived to reflect the harmonious order of the relationship rather than portraying a dominant party overpowering the subordinate one. This harmonious order is thwarted when they eat the fruit from the tree of the knowledge of good and evil and receive divine punishment, which results in a relationship rife with tension. Henceforth, although the woman's desire (תְּשׁוּקָה) will be for her husband, he will rule over her (Gen 3:16-17). This desire, when read together with Genesis 4:7, yields a picture of dominance and subjugation. By contrast, in the Song of Songs the love between the man and the woman involves aspects of both the ideal and reality. The woman's words to the man—"I am my beloved's and his desire [תְּשׁוּקָה] is for me" (Song 7:10)—change the desire to dominate into a desire for erotic love.[14] In this sense, the love that has been lost in Eden is found in the Song of Songs.

However, the love between the human couple in the Song is not entirely ideal. There are angry brothers who oppose their little sister's love, or at least the woman perceives this to be the case (Song 1:6); the woman has an inferiority complex (Song 1:5); her love does not seem to be acknowledged in public and has to remain secret (Song 8:1). Additionally, there are little foxes in their garden (Song 2:15). Worse is the presence of recurrent dreamlike visions in which the woman searches for her beloved but he is nowhere to be found (Song 3:1-5; 5:2-7). Worse yet, in one of these visions, guards in

---

[14]The word "desire" (תְּשׁוּקָה) only appears three times in the entire Hebrew Scripture (Gen 3:17; 4:7; Song 7:10), suggesting the connection between those instances and stories.

the city strike and beat her (Song 5:7). Love elates and intoxicates her, but love also makes her faint and sick (Song 5:8).[15] Her comparison of the force of love to death in Song of Songs 8:6 presupposes the existence of death and sin. The world of Song of Songs is mixed with both the ideal and reality, which forms a drastic difference from the scene of the Garden of Eden, a prefall state.

Therefore, the two texts with two gardens share both symmetry and asymmetry in the portrayal of love. By presenting a portrait of love that is both heart-racing and heart-rending, the poet offers an alternative reality to the love in Eden. In the Hebrew canon, Song of Songs critiques and supplements the Edenic story, but the whole story remains to be told in the eschaton. The love presented in the Song of Songs is reminiscent of "love already but not yet."[16] It is a love on earth in the here and now. It tells the love between the fall and the final vision in the eschaton, where God and humanity will be joined into one (Rev 21:1-4). The love in the Song is indeed an in-between love. Whether it is human love or divine-human relationship, we are all in this in-between state, awaiting the final consummation with God in the new heaven and new earth.

Genesis 12: Abraham. In the Hebrew Scripture, the expression "go forth" (לֶךְ־לְךָ) appears twice in Genesis, once in God's calling of Abraham (Gen 12:1), the other in God's command to Abraham to sacrifice Isaac (Gen 22:2). Throughout the entire Hebrew Scripture, this expression occurs only in these two verses. However, a similar construction with a variation of gender endings appears in Song of Songs, where the male lover invites his female lover to come away (לְכִי־לָךְ; Song 2:10, 13).[17] This constitutes the third appearance of the expression "go forth" or "come away" in the Hebrew Bible.

> My beloved spoke and he said to me, "Arise! Go! my darling, my beautiful, and come away [לְכִי־לָךְ]!
>
> For look! The winter is passed. The rain has passed through and gone.

---

[15]Richard M. Davidson, "Theology of Sexuality in the Song of Songs: Return to Eden," *Andrews University Seminary Studies* 27 (1989): 1-12, esp. 6.

[16]Longman writes, "In a word, relationships, broken by sin, may experience the healing of redemption, but it is an already-not yet phenomenon." See Tremper Longman III, *Song of Songs*, New International Commentary on the Old Testament (Grand Rapids, MI: Eerdmans, 2001), 66.

[17]Here the ending is feminine, whereas in Gen 12:1; 22:2, the endings are masculine.

The blossoms appear in the land. The time of pruning has arrived. The sound of the turtle doves is heard in our land.

The fig tree has ripened her early fig and the vines (in) blossom have given forth fragrance. Arise! Go! my darling, my beautiful, and come away [לְכִי־לָךְ]!" (Song 2:10-13)[18]

In Genesis, God's call to Abraham to go (לֶךְ־לְךָ) from his land, his kindred, and his father's house to a land he will show him involves tremendous risk. Abraham has to leave everything behind—his roots, his culture, his relatives, his community, and his gods. The author of the book of Hebrews says, "He went out, not knowing where he was going," and accredits his action to faith (Heb 11:8). Then, when God asks Abraham to sacrifice his son Isaac, Abraham encounters the second-greatest risk of his life. This time it is larger than life. Isaac is the long-awaited son, the promised son, the one to whom Abraham will give his inheritance and blessings. It is through Isaac that God's promise to Abraham to become the father of nations will be realized. In other words, Isaac is everything to Abraham, but now God tells him to go (לֶךְ־לְךָ) to the land of Moriah and sacrifice him as a burnt offering. The first call is about God's promise of the land, while the second call is about the promised seed. Abraham's obedience to the two divine imperatives to "go" sets him apart from all the spiritual giants and defines who he is as an emblem of faith, sacrifice, and devotion.[19]

A similar but different picture emerges in the Song of Songs. Here the male lover invites the woman to arise and go out with him because spring has arrived. The same construction of the Hebrew expression in Genesis 12:1; 22:2 appears precisely at a point at which the man asks the woman for a decision.[20] In this context, the woman faces the risk of going out, not

---

[18]For "Go," the Masoretic Text reads לָךְ (same with Song 2:13), but the critical apparatus indicates Cairo Geniza Kethiv, Septuagint, and Vulgate have לָךְ (to/for you), whereas Cairo Geniza Qere has לְכִי (Go!). "Pruning" could also be translated "singing." "Has ripened" could also be translated "made spicy."

[19]Although, in the binding of Isaac, philosophers and scholars question Abraham's obedience and argue that he should have protested God's command to sacrifice his own son. See Jon D. Levenson, "Abusing Abraham: Traditions, Religious Histories, and Modern Interpretations," *Judaism* 47, no. 3 (1998): 259-77; Isaac Kalimi, "'Go. I Beg You, Take Your Beloved Son and Slay Him!' The Binding of Isaac in Rabbinic Literature and Thought," *Review of Rabbinic Judaism* 13, no. 1 (2010): 1-29.

[20]An imperative "go" + preposition + pronominal suffix.

knowing what awaits her. She also needs to leave behind her safe indoor setting to venture outside to his world and to the outside world. Perhaps she needs to leave her mother and brothers, who may object to her departure. Although the context in the Song's passage diverges from those in Genesis, they do share something on the conceptual level of letting go and taking a risk. Klara Butting provides an illuminating insight into the two texts. She observes the parallel between the objects of seeing. In Genesis 12:1, God will let Abraham see the land, whereas in Song of Songs, the male lover desires to see her form (Song 2:14). Butting asks, "This land, with its blossoms and buds, has already revealed itself in the Song of Songs (Song 2:12). But can the lover, a woman who, like Sarah, is 'beautiful of appearance,' let her face be seen in this land?" Butting also connects the woman in the Song to the land of Israel. Just as the Promised Land flows with milk and honey, likewise the male lover finds for his beloved "a land flowing with milk and honey" (Song 5:1). His also lets her know that "honey and milk are under your tongue" (Song 4:11). The original promise to Abraham regarding the land is newly defined in Song of Songs.[21] Perhaps it is too much of a stretch to say that the woman in the Song is a new Abraham, but the shared semantics between the two texts do link them together as people who are called to let go of their own comfort space by going out and taking a risk.

Exodus: Chariots of Pharaoh, wilderness, and tabernacle. The male lover in the Song opens by saying to the woman, "To a mare in the chariots of Pharaoh, I compare you, my darling" (Song 1:9). The image of the chariots of Pharaoh echoes the chariots of Pharaoh in Exodus. There Pharaoh and his chariots are overthrown by God in the midst of the sea while pursuing the Israelites. The water covers the chariots, the horsemen, even the entire army of Pharaoh that had gone into the sea after the Israelites; not even one of them remains alive (Ex 14:27-28). Subsequently, Moses composes a song celebrating the event, singing "Pharaoh's chariots and his army He has cast into the sea" (Ex 15:4). The judgment motif of the chariots of Pharaoh is transformed into a language of praise for the woman in the Song of Songs.[22]

---

[21]Klara Butting, "Go Your Way: Women Rewrite the Scriptures (Song of Songs 2:8-14)," in Brenner and Fontaine, *Feminist Companion to the Song of Songs*, 145, 150.

[22]Early Jewish exegetes have noticed this intertextual connection and offered interesting

In the wedding scene of the Song, a voice speaks: "Who is this coming up from the wilderness, like columns of smoke, perfumed (with) myrrh and frankincense of all the powders of the merchant?" (Song 3:6). The image of the wilderness and columns of smoke evokes the Israelites' journey in the wilderness, where there is a column of cloud by day and a column of fire by night to guide them as they travel (Ex 13:21-22).[23] Myrrh is one of the ingredients used in the perfume mixture as a holy anointing oil to anoint the tabernacle and the ark of the testimony, the table of showbread and its utensils, the lampstand and its utensils, the altar of incense, the altar of burnt offering and all its utensils, and the laver and its stand (Ex 30:22-28). In other words, myrrh is an essential ingredient in anointing the tabernacle and its furniture in order to consecrate it. In Song of Songs, myrrh appears in the garden metaphor for the woman (Song 4:14). When the man comes into the "garden," he expresses his satisfaction that "I have come to my garden, my sister, (my) bride; I have plucked my myrrh with my spices" (Song 5:1). There is also a "mountain of myrrh," possibly describing the woman (Song 4:6).

Frankincense is used as an ingredient not only in making the holy incense in the tabernacle (Ex 30:34-37) but also in grain offerings. The priest would make the grain offering on the altar as an offering by fire of a soothing aroma to God (Lev 2:1-2). In addition, priests are instructed to put frankincense on each row of the bread inside the tabernacle as an offering by fire to God (Lev 24:7). In Song of Songs, frankincense appears in Song of Songs 3:6 describing the woman and in Song of Songs 4:6 designating a metaphorical "hill of frankincense," possibly referring to the woman.[24]

The combined imagery of the wilderness and the column of smoke, along with the myrrh and frankincense, echo the images in Exodus, thus connecting the two texts. It is highly likely that the poet of the Song was quite familiar with the exodus tradition and reused its imagery in the Song to describe the woman. No wonder Jewish commentators thought of the woman in the Song metaphorically as the embodiment of Israel.

---

interpretations. See Jonathan Kaplan, *My Perfect One: Typology and Early Rabbinic Interpretation of Song of Songs* (New York: Oxford University Press, 2015), 75-76.

[23] The column or pillar of cloud and fire are also mentioned in Numbers and Deuteronomy (Num 14:14; Deut 31:15).

[24] Frankincense also appears in 1 Chron 9:29; Neh 13:5, 9; Is 60:6; Jer 6:20; Mt 2:11; Rev 18:13.

Exodus 33: Divine presence and hiddenness. One of the dominant theological themes in the book of Exodus is the visible and powerful presence
of God. God is present in initiating salvation for his people, in making
covenant with them, in issuing laws governing the moral code of his people
as well as in instructing Moses how to build the tabernacle so that God may
dwell among his people. After the golden-calf incident, divine presence has
been affected and divine hiddenness comes to the fore. The motif of
presence and hiddenness also appears in Song of Songs.

When describing the hiddenness of his darling, the male lover utters,
"My dove, in the clefts of the rock, in the hiding places of the steep, let me
see your appearance; let me hear your voice, because your voice is sweet
and your appearance is comely" (Song 2:14).[25] This expression of hide and
seek, presence and absence, finds resonance in the scene where Moses desires to see the glory of God but God says, "You cannot see My face, for no
man can see Me and live" (Ex 33:20). God goes on to say, "Behold, there is
a place by Me, and you shall stand *there* on the rock; and it will come about,
while My glory is passing by, that I will put you in the cleft of the rock and
cover you with My hand until I have passed by. Then I will take My hand
away and you shall see My back, but My face shall not be seen" (Ex 33:21-23).

Although the exact wordings for the "clefts of rock" in these two texts are
different in Hebrew, the shared images are implied or alluded to. We can
say that the Song alludes to the image in Exodus but transcends it to fit its
own context. Walsh interprets the "cleft of rock" in Exodus as a symbol of
safety when viewed from the perspective of the one who desires to see the
other's face, whereas in the Song the "cleft of rock" becomes the hiding spot
of the shy other. She further imagines the male lover in the Song as God.
Instead of being overbearing and protecting the other human from a fatal
sighting, the male lover has become curious and inquisitive about the one
hiding in the cleft. He has taken an interest in knowing the other.[26] This
creates a reversal of the "hide and seek" portrait in Exodus. Again, the poet
of the Song adapts an earlier text in Exodus and revises it into something
new but also familiar.

---

[25]"Steep" could also be translated "cliff."

[26]Carey Ellen Walsh, *Exquisite Desire: Religion, the Erotic, and the Song of Songs* (Minneapolis:
   Fortress, 2000), 208.

As we can see, Song of Songs resonates with the Garden of Eden, the call of Abraham to go out, the wilderness motif, the tabernacle imagery, and the motif of presence and hiddenness in Exodus. Yet, Song of Songs also counters and reconfigures these resonances to form its own portrait of love, of taking risk, of the whole range of dynamic emotions in the relationship between a man and a woman. Therefore, the Song creates its own voice by forming both resonances and dissonances with the Torah.

Song of Songs and the Prophets. Use of the marriage metaphor to depict the relationship between God and Israel has been prevalent and indeed dominant in the prophetic literature, especially in the books of Hosea, Isaiah, Jeremiah, and Ezekiel. T. Drorah Setel states that while the images of female sexuality appear in texts earlier than the prophetic texts, "these books seem to be the first to use objectified female sexuality as a symbol of evil."[27] The negative portraits of love revealed in these texts form a stark contrast with the love expressed in the Song of Songs.

Hosea 1–3: Marrying an adulterer. Hosea was an eighth-century prophet ministering to the Israelites in the northern kingdom at a time when worship of Baal was prevalent in the land. The book of Hosea is one of the first prophetic books to employ the marriage metaphor, in this case to the relationship between God and Israel.[28] Gerlinde Baumann asserts that the marriage metaphor in the book of Hosea serves as the "Primal Text."[29] Numerous scholars, among them Julia O'Brien, use Hosea as a case study to explore its marriage metaphor and offer challenges to its underlying gender and theological bias.[30] *The Feminist Companion to the Latter Prophets*

---

[27]T. Drorah Setel, "Prophets and Pornography: Female Sexual Imagery in Hosea," in *The Feminist Companion to the Song of Songs*, ed. Athalya Brenner, FCB (Sheffield: Sheffield Academic Press, 1993), 143-55.

[28]For using various theories of reading Hosea, such as sign language, deconstruction, and feminist readings, see Yvonne Sherwood, *The Prostitute and the Prophet: Hosea's Marriage in Literary-Theoretical Perspective*, GCT 2, JSOTSup 212 (Sheffield: Sheffield Academic Press, 1996).

[29]Gerlinde Baumann, *Love and Violence: Marriage as Metaphor for the Relationship Between YHWH and Israel in the Prophetic Books*, trans. Linda M. Malony (Collegeville, MN: Liturgical Press, 2003), 85.

[30]Julia M. O'Brien, *Challenging Prophetic Metaphor: Theology and Ideology in the Prophets* (Louisville, KY: Westminster John Knox, 2008). These challenges include presupposing the reader as male, perpetuating patriarchal ideology, and projecting theological language as political language.

devotes eleven chapters to the book of Hosea, exploring various theological, ethical, and hermeneutical issues that the book raises.[31] For instance, Alice Keefe states, "From whatever critical perspective a feminist reader might approach Hosea, the text offers offense."[32] Here God asks Hosea to marry a prostitute as an object lesson for Israel to visualize and comprehend how God loves her even when she goes after other gods.[33] "When the LORD first spoke through Hosea, the LORD said to Hosea, 'Go, take to yourself a wife of harlotry and *have* children of harlotry; for the land commits flagrant harlotry, forsaking the LORD'" (Hos 1:2).

The root of the word "harlotry" (זְנוּנִים) appears four times in the above half-verse.[34] Sometimes it is translated as "prostitution" or "promiscuity." Metaphorically, it refers to "improper intercourse with foreign nations (religious references sometimes involved)."[35] "The land commits flagrant harlotry" refers to the people of Israel following after other gods and thus committing harlotry. Setel says this word appears eighty-four times in the entire Hebrew Bible, of which fifty-one times are in the Latter Prophets. Hosea uses its root, *zānāh*, twenty times. Its frequent occurrence in Hosea suggests its significance to the book. Behind the words of God to Hosea lies a historical reality of Canaanite religion, which often entailed ritual sexual activity in which human sexuality was perceived as a way to induce procreative power from Baal.[36] In the eyes of God, Israel is like an adulterer and a prostitute. The marriage metaphor between God and Israel cannot be more apparent here. Hosea obeys by marrying Gomer, and she bears him three children. Their names symbolically reflect the estranged marital status between God and Israel and that God will judge Israel for her adultery.[37] Then God issues a warning to Israel:

[31] Athalya Brenner and Carole R. Fontaine, *A Feminist Companion to the Latter Prophets*, FCB 8 (Sheffield: Sheffield Academic Press, 1995).

[32] Alice A. Keefe, *Woman's Body and the Social Body in Hosea*, GCT 10, JSOTSup 338 (Sheffield: Sheffield Academic Press, 2001), 146.

[33] For challenges of identifying God and Israel in this marriage metaphor, see O'Brien, *Challenging Prophetic Metaphor*, 31-35.

[34] In Hebrew, "flagrant harlotry" repeats the root word for "harlotry" twice.

[35] *BDB* 275.

[36] Setel, "Prophets and Pornography," 148, 150.

[37] The name of the first child is Jezreel, which means both "punish" and "sow." The name of the second child is Lo-ruhamah, which means "no mercy." The name of the third child is Lo-ammi, which means "not my people."

And let her put away her harlotry from her face
And her adultery from between her breasts,
Or I will strip her naked
And expose her as on the day when she was born.
I will also make her like a wilderness,
Make her like desert land
And slay her with thirst. (Hos 2:2-3)

The language of divine judgment in the act of "strip her naked" evokes the similar image in Ezekiel 16 and Song of Songs 5:7. In the prophetic books, Israel is the one who has sinned against God. God in turn becomes a wounded lover. In his love, there is justice, as expressed by his punishment of "strip her naked." By contrast, in Song of Songs, the woman becomes that wounded lover who seeks her beloved in the streets at night, then is wounded by the city guard and has her shawl taken away from her. On the other hand, the male lover also seeks out the woman to come along with him to the countryside (Song 2:10-13). He searches for her in clefts of the rock and in the secret place of the steep pathway, desiring to see her form and hear her voice (Song 2:14). Ellen Davis rightly considers the Song of Songs a healing text, one that redeems the love gone wrong in the prophetic texts.[38] Havilah Dharamraj observes that the seeking woman in the Song is a perfect equivalent to the seeking husband in Hosea, but she replaces the woman in Hosea as a better partner. In this sense, Song of Songs, when placed side by side with Hosea, presents a "human ideal of love-in-separation."[39]

In Hosea, Israel has mistaken Baal and other gods as the ones who provide her with food and clothing. Little does she know that it is Yahweh who is her real provider. This is an aspect of perceived negativity in the male-female relationship, in which the woman depends on the man for her sustenance.

[38]Ellen F. Davis, *Proverbs, Ecclesiastes, and the Song of Songs*, Westminster Bible Companion (Louisville, KY: Westminster John Knox, 2000), 231, 253.
[39]Dharamraj, *Altogether Lovely*, 77. Concerning the parallel texts of Hosea and Song of Songs 5:2–6:3, she concludes, "If not for the Song of Songs, the Hebrew Bible would lack a woman whose tenacious pursuit of her separated beloved matches that of the husband in Hosea. If not for the Song, the Old Testament's divine-human marital metaphor would locate the devotee in the company of sundry lovers, leaving deity inhabiting a state of love-in-separation" (*Altogether Lovely*, 82).

> For their mother has played the harlot;
> She who conceived them has acted shamefully.
> For she said, "I will go after my lovers,
> Who give *me* my bread and my water,
> My wool and my flax, my oil and my drink." (Hos 2:5)
> She will pursue her lovers, but she will not overtake them;
> And she will seek them, but will not find *them*.
> Then she will say, "I will go back to my first husband,
> For it was better for me then than now!"
> For she does not know that it was I who gave her the grain, the new wine and
>   the oil,
> And lavished on her silver and gold,
> *Which* they used for Baal. (Hos 2:7-8)

The image of Israel seeking but not finding her lovers evokes two similar scenes in Song of Songs where the woman seeks but cannot find her beloved (Song 3:1-2; 5:6). However, while the scenes of seeking and finding appear in both texts, there is no trace of either the female or the male providing sustenance in the Song of Songs. The images of food in the Song of Songs are only used to describe the woman's body (Song 4:14, 16; 5:1) and her desire for him (Song 2:3). In the Song of Songs, the wine (יַיִן) and oil (שֶׁמֶן) in Hosea 2:8 are transformed into the language of love and desire. She expresses to him that his love is better than wine (Song 1:2). He reciprocates by saying that her love is also better than wine (Song 4:10). To her, his name is the finest oil (Song 1:3). For him, the fragrance of her oils is better than all kinds of spices (Song 4:10).

In most prophetic texts, God's judgment against Israel closes with a message of hope and restoration. God speaks to Israel:

> I will betroth you to Me forever;
> Yes, I will betroth you to Me in righteousness and in justice,
> In lovingkindness and in compassion,
> And I will betroth you to Me in faithfulness.
> Then you will know the LORD. (Hos 2:19-20)

"Betroth" appears in the context of marriage. God will remarry Israel in spite of her unfaithfulness. Larry Lyke points out that this message of hope means to have Israel returned to the former state in which she had not committed adultery, the youthful state in which God and Israel were in their prime. This picture of a youthful love reflects the love between the human couple in Song of Songs.[40] God loves Israel. He would defy or reverse his own law in order to reaccept Israel as his beloved. The ancient Near Eastern law code always ends with statements of blessing and cursing. Blessing often involves protection of the sovereign party, and cursing often involves the language of stripping one's clothing or the wife of the offending party being raped by others.[41] In the Mosaic law, an adulterer receives capital punishment by stoning (Deut 22:22-24). However, in the book of Hosea, it is Israel (Gomer) who commits adultery. Not only is she not being punished, but God tells Hosea to marry her on more than one occasion (Hos 3:1-2). God is the lord of the law, and therefore he is not bound by it, but he re-writes law in order for Israel to return to him.

At the center of the book of Hosea and the Song of Songs is love. Hosea accentuates God's divine love for wayward Israel, whereas Song of Songs manifests the woman's erotic love for her beloved, which is as strong as death and as severe as Sheol (Song 8:6). If we identify the woman in the Song metaphorically as a symbol of Israel, then the interbiblical reading of these two texts presents a picture in which Israel, symbolized by the woman in the Song of Songs, responds to God in Hosea, saying, "I am reciprocating your love." In this way, Israel (Gomer) redeems and reinvents herself as a faithful lover in the Song of Songs.

Isaiah 5: Vineyard. Isaiah's vineyard metaphor imprints in its audience's mind a vivid but twisted picture of passion and betrayal. It is a song of love spurned and gone awry. Couched between the passages of judgment, the song of the vineyard provides an illuminating image for why God should judge Israel. Terence Fretheim sees God in this text as lover and judge. Because God loves, he judges. Even when he judges, he loves.[42] The song opens

---

[40]Larry L. Lyke, *I Will Espouse You Forever: The Song of Songs and the Theology of Love in the Hebrew Bible* (Nashville: Abingdon, 2007), 9.

[41]Baumann, *Love and Violence*, 76. Carr also interprets the language of Hosea in terms of its an-cient Near Eastern military metaphors, referring to when tyrants would threaten their subjects with rape or sexual humiliation (*Erotic Word*, 68-69).

[42]Terence E. Fretheim, "What Kind of God Is Portrayed in Isaiah 5:1-7?," in *New Studies in the Book of Isaiah: Essays in Honor of Hallvard Hagelia*, ed. Hallvard Hagelia and Markus Philipp Zehnder, Perspectives on Hebrew Scriptures and Its Contexts 21 (Piscataway, NJ: Gorgias, 2014), 53-67, esp. 57-58.

with, "Let me sing now for my beloved, a song of my beloved concerning His vineyard" (Is 5:1).

The phrase "let me sing a song" (אָשִׁירָה שִׁירַת) recalls "Song of Songs" (שִׁיר הַשִּׁירִים). The address "to my beloved" (לִידִידִי) echoes "to/belonging to my beloved" (לְדוֹדִי) in Song of Songs (Song 5:5, 6; 6:3; 7:10, 11). What is more, the vineyard in Isaiah evokes the vineyard metaphor in the Song of Songs. For those who are familiar with these Hebrew expressions, it is natural to link the two texts together. However, the gender dynamics in the two texts are reversed. While in Isaiah, God is the lover singing to his beloved, Israel, in the Song of Songs the woman is the lover singing to her male beloved. The outcomes of these two love relationships also diverge drastically from each other. The song of vineyard goes on:

> My well-beloved had a vineyard on a fertile hill.
> He dug it all around, removed its stones,
> And planted it with the choicest vine.
> And He built a tower in the middle of it
> And also hewed out a wine vat in it;
> Then He expected *it* to produce *good* grapes,
> But it produced *only* worthless ones.
> And now, O inhabitants of Jerusalem and men of Judah,
> Judge between Me and My vineyard.
> What more was there to do for My vineyard that I have not done in it?
> Why, when I expected *it* to produce *good* grapes did it produce worthless ones? (Is 5:1-4)

Here God compares himself to or transposes himself with the owner of the vineyard, who cares for it, tends it, prunes it, maintains it, and expects it to produce good grapes. The vineyard, in the context of the Hebrew Bible, refers to the wife.[43] Unfortunately, to his surprise and disbelief, the vineyard yields worthless grapes or sour grapes that are inedible. God then calls the inhabitants of Jerusalem and inquires, "Why?" but there is silence. We do not know whether the people of Jerusalem are too ashamed to respond, or

---

[43]See Dharamraj, *Altogether Lovely*, 172. The association between vineyard and wife lies in the intoxication effect and the maintenance factor. Just as a vineyard needs to be carefully tended, pruned, and watered, so too the wife in the marriage relationship requires careful attention from her husband.

are simply speechless about the charge, or whether perhaps God is so upset that he does not give them time to respond. God continues:

> So now let Me tell you what I am going to do to My vineyard:
> I will remove its hedge and it will be consumed;
> I will break down its wall and it will become trampled ground.
> I will lay it waste;
> It will not be pruned or hoed,
> But briars and thorns will come up.
> I will also charge the clouds to rain no rain on it. (Is 5:5-6)

Because of the unfavorable outcome of the sour (בְּאֻשִׁים) grapes and God's "frustrated expectations," God issues his verdict to remove, destroy, and stop caring for the vineyard.[44] The last verse of the song discloses the identities of the vineyard and its owner, which might have been a shocking revelation for Isaiah's original audience:

> For the vineyard of the LORD of hosts is the house of Israel
> And the men of Judah His delightful plant.
> Thus He looked for justice [מִשְׁפָּט], but behold, bloodshed [מִשְׂפָּח];
> For righteousness [צְדָקָה], but behold, a cry of distress [צְעָקָה]. (Is 5:7)

In a prophetic pronouncement, God identifies the guilty party as the house of Israel. The crime they have committed is bloodshed. In a series of poetic alliterations, God says that he looked for justice (מִשְׁפָּט), but saw bloodshed (מִשְׂפָּח); righteousness (צְדָקָה) but saw distress (צְעָקָה). The dire condition of Israel is symbolized both artistically and appallingly by the metaphor of the vineyard.

By contrast, the vineyard in the Song of Songs presents a picture of pleasant, luxurious, and fruitful imagery. According to Edmee Kingsmill's study, the word *vineyard* occurs nine times in the Song of Songs (Song 1:6 [2×], 14; 2:15 [2×]; 7:13; 8:11-12 [3×]). When it is read with Isaiah 5 and the

---

[44]Dharamraj's study indicates that the word "sour" (בְּאֻשִׁים) is used to describe food that goes bad with maggots (Ex 16:20), the smell given off by piles of dead frogs (Ex 8:14), mounds of human corpses (Is 34:3), wounds that fester (Ps 38:6), and ointment smelling foul because of decomposing flies (Eccles 10:1). In Is 5, the sour grapes refer to the children that Israel bore out of wedlock (see Dharamraj, *Altogether Lovely*, 181). See also Gary Roye Williams, "Frustrated Expectations in Isaiah 5:1-7: A Literary Interpretation," *VT* 35, no. 4 (1985): 459-65. For Williams, the frustrated expectations involve both God in Is 5 and the interpreters of that parable.

parables of the vineyard in the New Testament, she interprets the vineyard
in the Song as representing Israel.[45] The word *vineyard* in Song of Songs is
used both literally to refer to a physical vineyard and metaphorically to refer
to the woman's body (Song 1:6). It also symbolizes the setting where *eros*
can be threatened or can blossom (Song 2:15; 7:13).

The enigmatic verses of Solomon's vineyard and "my vineyard is mine"
in Song of Songs 8:11-12 pose quite a challenge to interpreters. Should we
interpret these vineyards literally or metaphorically? Or do they encompass
both levels of meanings and beyond? Othmar Keel thinks that in the metaphorical language of Song of Songs, vineyard always stands for the woman
as well as a related metaphor of the garden. Therefore, Keel takes it that
Solomon's vineyard refers to women in his harem.[46] Fishbane states that in
context, these verses are both symbolic and ironic. Symbolically, Solomon's
thousand talents hint at his harem. Ironically, this episode mocks those who
would use money to buy love.[47]

The vineyard imagery in Song of Songs, when juxtaposed with the
vineyard of Isaiah 5, yields two contrasting images of Israel. In Isaiah 5, it
is a love that is disdained, whereas in Song of Songs, it is a love that is desired. The initial condition of the vineyard in Isaiah 5 and the condition of
the woman as the garden in Song of Songs 4:12–5:1 share images of abundance and fertility. Both are also well tended. However, their respective
outcomes differ drastically. Another striking contrast between the two texts
is the gender reversal in Isaiah 5, where God appears to be the "conde-
scending" character, tirelessly tending his vineyard, whereas in Song of
Songs the woman in the make-believe context appears as the goddess of
love who is in a transcending position, in the cleft of the rock, but she vol-
unteers to "condescend" to meet her human lover.[48] Last but not least, if we
identify the woman in the Song metaphorically as Israel, then along with
the theological premise of Deuteronomy, the portrait of the vineyard in
Isaiah 5 is the result of a curse due to covenant disobedience on the part of

---

[45]See Edmee Kingsmill, *The Song of Songs and the Eros of God: A Study in Biblical Intertextuality* (Oxford: Oxford University Press, 2009), 110-13.

[46]Othmar Keel, *The Song of Songs*, Continental Commentary (Minneapolis: Fortress, 1994), 281.

[47]Michael Fishbane, *Song of Songs: The Traditional Hebrew Text with the New JPS Translation*, JPS Bible Commentary (Philadelphia: Jewish Publication Society, 2015), 219.

[48]Dharamraj, *Altogether Lovely*, 188-90.

Israel, while the image of the vineyard in Song of Songs is the result of blessings due to the covenant obedience of Israel. While Isaiah 5 illustrates the example of love gone wrong, Song of Songs presents a vision of what love ought to be like.

Isaiah 49; 54; 62: Wife, widow, bride, and bridegroom. One of the prominent metaphors of God in the prophetic texts is the marriage metaphor— God is the husband of Israel, and Israel is his wife. The relationship between God and Israel is based on a covenant, reminiscent of a marriage covenant between a man and a woman. When Israel goes after other gods, she becomes a whore. Consequently, Israel experiences exile as a result of her husband/God's fury, which then makes her a widow, forsaken by her husband—God. However, when this husband/God retakes her as wife through Israel's returning from the exile, she is once again a married woman who regains her honorable status. In the metaphorical language of marriage, divorce, and remarriage, the relationship between God and Israel is presented nakedly right in front of its audience's eyes.

Feminist scholars often protest the seemingly gendered language in the prophetic metaphor of marriage between God and Israel, where God is portrayed as a powerful monarch with male prestige talking down to Israel while Israel remains silent. Worse yet, her body often becomes the object of divine punishment, which is construed as rape in that cultural and moral context. For example, Renita Weems summarizes the relationship between God and Israel as one that is unequal, since the burden of the relationship falls on the subordinate partner, whose responsibility is not to offend or bring dishonor to the dominant party, and says that God, with the dominant power, directs the relationship in ways that will ensure the relationship conforms to social standards of the time.[49] Julia O'Brien also notes, "Feminist criticism marks one of the first cases in prophetic imagination in which the interpreter overtly resists at least certain aspects of the text's presentation of God."[50] In my opinion, the hermeneutical and theological challenges of the negative image of God in the marriage metaphor of the prophetic texts are countered by the inclusion of Lamentations in the

---

[49]Renita J. Weems, *Battered Love: Marriage, Sex, and Violence in the Hebrew Prophets*, Overtures to Biblical Theology (Minneapolis: Fortress, 1995), 33-34.

[50]O'Brien, *Challenging Prophetic Metaphor*, 39.

biblical canon, in which Daughter Zion "talks back" to the prophets and to God by expressing her inner thoughts and emotions as well as questioning divine cruelty toward her.[51]

In the context of the exile, Isaiah 49:14-23 uses the marriage metaphor of God as the husband of Israel (Zion) and Israel as his wife, in response to Zion's lament that "YHWH has forsaken me, and YHWH has forgotten me." God says, "Can a woman forget her nursing child and have no compassion on the son of her womb? Even these may forget, but I will not forget you" (Is 49:14-15). Here, the marriage metaphor is apparent, but a parent metaphor is also prominent. Instead of portraying God as the father of Israel, God assumes the role of a mother in this text. God is both Israel's husband and her mother, a mixing of metaphors.[52] God has his rough side, but he also shows his tender side to Israel. Both sides of God are in tension but also in a complementary relationship to each other. Therefore, to emphasize or defend one aspect of God obscures a fuller picture of who God is. The mixed metaphors of husband, father, mother, and children point to the metaphor of a family where God takes on multiple roles in his relationship with Israel.

In Isaiah 54:1-8, the marriage metaphor resurfaces again. Here in the context of the exile, Israel is metaphorically represented first as a barren woman, "Shout for joy, O barren one, you who have borne no *child*; Break forth into joyful shouting and cry aloud, you who have not travailed; for the sons of the desolate one *will be* more numerous Than the sons of the married woman" (Is 54:1). As a nation in exile, Israel becomes a barren woman without children, but God provides a vision for her future, that she will once again bear children. Then God goes on to say,

Fear not, for you will not be put to shame;
And do not feel humiliated, for you will not be disgraced;
But you will forget the shame of your youth,
And the reproach of your widowhood you will remember no more.
For your husband is your Maker,

---

[51]A very helpful book in this regard is Carleen Mandolfo, *Daughter Zion Talks Back to the Prophets: A Dialogic Theology of the Book of Lamentations*, Semeia Studies 58 (Atlanta: Society of Biblical Literature, 2007).

[52]Sarah J. Dille, *Mixing Metaphors: God as Mother and Father in Deutero-Isaiah*, GCT 13, JSOTSup 398 (London: T&T Clark, 2004).

Whose name is the LORD of hosts;
And your Redeemer is the Holy One of Israel,
Who is called the God of all the earth. (Is 54:4-5)

In the Old Testament world, a barren woman suffered shame and humiliation because she failed to provide an heir for her husband's household and
therefore failed to perpetuate the family line of her husband. Barrenness
was such a disgrace that a woman would rather die than bring dishonor to
herself and her clan (Gen 30:1). Examples of the desolation of barren
women are everywhere in the Old Testament, including Sarah, Rebekah,
Rachel, and Hannah. Barrenness and widowhood are closely connected.
Israel is barren because her husband—God—forsook her, but only for a
brief moment. God continues his promise to Israel in the following verses:

"For the LORD has called you,
  Like a wife forsaken and grieved in spirit,
  Even like a wife of *one's* youth when she is rejected,"
  Says your God.
"For a brief moment I forsook you,
  But with great compassion I will gather you.
  In an outburst of anger
  I hid My face from you for a moment,
  But with everlasting lovingkindness I will have compassion on you,"
  Says the LORD your Redeemer. (Is 54:6-8)

The husband/God of Israel forsook her for a brief moment during exile, but
he will once again be her husband and redeemer. The marriage metaphor
between God and Israel attains its fullest expression in these passages.

There is yet another passage in Isaiah about God as the bridegroom and
Israel as his bride. In the language of restoration, God says to Israel:

It will no longer be said to you, "Forsaken,"
  Nor to your land will it any longer be said, "Desolate";
  But you will be called, "My delight is in her,"
  And your land, "Married";
  For the LORD delights in you,
  And to *Him* your land will be married.
  For *as* a young man marries a virgin,

So your sons will marry you;
And *as* the bridegroom rejoices over the bride,
So your God will rejoice over you. (Is 62:4-5)

In the theological and cultural context of the Old Testament, God, Israel, and land form a triangular relationship. When Israel sinned against God, this had consequences for the land. The barren state of Israel parallels the desolate state of her land. Here in this passage, God compares himself to a bridegroom who rejoices over the bride, Israel. We see a similar metaphor of bride and bridegroom emerge in the poetic world of the Song of Songs. Song of Songs 3:6-11 depicts a scene of Solomon's wedding procession. Immediately following that wedding scene is a *wasf* in which the bridegroom lavishes praises on his bride's body (Song 4:1-7). Then, for the first time in the Song, the man addresses his lover as "my bride" in a series of yearning and admiring declarations about her (Song 4:9-12). This series of acclamations culminates in Song of Songs 5:1, when the man says: "I have come to my garden, my sister, (my) bride; I have gathered my myrrh with my spices; I have eaten honeycomb with my honey, I have drunk my wine with my milk." In the plain sense of the Song, we have a wedding scene, followed by the first night of intimate encounter, in which the bridegroom and the bride consummate their marriage.

In the metaphorical sense, the bride can be seen both as a symbolism for the land of Israel and the embodiment of Israel as a nation. Davis provides profound insight in terms of reading the woman in the Song iconographically as the land of Israel. The frequent occurrence of Lebanon calls to mind the image of the temple. Davis interprets Song of Songs 5:1 as evoking the experience of the pilgrim, since the temple was a place of feasting as well as a place of consummation between worshipers and God.[53] The place names and geographical sites mentioned in the Song of Songs, such as Gilead, the tower of David, Lebanon, and Hermon, all conjure up images of the land of Israel. Davis thus sees the Song as a healing text—healing the relationship between God and Israel in both erotic and ecological terms.[54] I find Davis's

---

[53]Davis, *Proverbs, Ecclesiastes, and the Song of Songs*, 274.

[54]Ellen F. Davis, "Reading the Song Iconographically," in *Scrolls of Love: Ruth and the Song of Songs*, ed. Peter S. Hawkins and Lesleigh Cushing Stahlberg (New York: Fordham University Press, 2006), 172-84, esp. 176, 183; Davis, "Romance of the Land in the Song of Songs," *Anglican Theological Review* 80, no. 4 (1998): 533-46.

interpretation particularly compelling because it takes account of the triangular relationship between God, Israel, and the land expressed in the metaphorical language of the Song.

The image of widowhood and barrenness as reflected in Isaiah disappears in Song of Songs. The image of the bride and the bridegroom remains in the Song in its purest form. When juxtaposed with Isaiah 54, the language of the Song can be read as a healing or a restorative text to the shame of widowhood in exile. However, when we read the Song with the Edenic text, the image of the bride and the bridegroom evokes the kind of love that God originally intended for the human couple in Eden, only that the *eros* in the Song appears to be more intense and dynamic than that of the human couple in Eden.

In light of these connections, the marriage metaphor in the Song of Songs resonates with both the prophetic texts and the Edenic text. At the same time, it departs from them and reconfigures to form its own text. The marriage metaphor in the Song presents an alternative vision of erotic love that transcends both Isaiah and Eden. It envisions a love that is intoxicating, passionate, fierce, and shameless.

Jeremiah 2–3; 31: Yearning for lost love. The marriage metaphor continues in the book of Jeremiah. In the opening prophetic oracle, God asks Jeremiah to proclaim to Jerusalem:

> I remember concerning you the devotion of your youth,
> The love of your betrothals,
> Your following after Me in the wilderness,
> Through a land not sown. (Jer 2:2)

In the current state of Israel's apostasy, God recalls the early days, when Israel's relationship with him was right. This was their first love. "The love of your betrothals" evokes the covenant between Israel and God that she would obey the divine commandments and ordinances (Ex 24:3-8). "Your following after me" expresses the ideal state of their earlier relationship, in contrast to the present estrangement. "In the wilderness" brings to mind the journey of the wilderness wandering. For Israel, the experience of the wilderness wandering was a punishment for her rebelliousness and distrust, yet God now considers those days nothing compared to the present apostasy.

By recalling the earlier days, God romanticizes the past relationship and mourns for the lost love. By contrast, in the Song of Songs, although there are episodes of "hide and seek" and "search for him but not found," the love between the human lovers is relatively equal, in that they show mutual passion and desire for each other, reminiscent of the first love between Israel and God.

In Jeremiah 3, the metaphor of marriage continues. God speaks to Israel,

> "If a husband divorces his wife
> And she goes from him
> And belongs to another man,
> Will he still return to her?
> Will not that land be completely polluted?
> But you are a harlot *with* many lovers;
> Yet you turn to Me," declares the LORD. (Jer 3:1)

The law indicates that if a man takes a wife and then divorces her, if she then becomes another man's wife and that man also divorces her, her first husband cannot take her back again, since she has been polluted, for that is an abomination to the Lord (Deut 24:1-4). By contrast, God tells Israel that even if she goes after other gods, she can still return to him. Here God applies the marriage law to his own relationship with Israel. Therefore, the metaphor of marriage for the human couple and the God-Israel relationship finds its parallel in Jeremiah and in the Song of Songs.

There is yet another passage in Jeremiah that speaks about God's yearning for Israel:

> "Is Ephraim My dear son?
> Is he a delightful child?
> Indeed, as often as I have spoken against him,
> I certainly *still* remember him;
> Therefore My heart yearns for him;
> I will surely have mercy on him," declares the LORD. (Jer 31:20)

Davis notices the connection between "my heart yearns for him" and the erotic words in Song of Songs 5:4: "My beloved extended his hand from the hole [opening], and my inward parts growled [or roared] upon it." "My heart" in Jeremiah 31:20 is literally "my inward parts" (מֵעַי). The same word appears in Song of Songs 5:4. "Yearn" (הָמָה) in Jeremiah 31:20 is the same word for "growl" in Song of Songs 5:4. It designates an animal kind of roar, murmur, or growl. Davis uses the translation of "heave or churn of one's gut" to describe the sticky and tortuous feeling toward someone. The same combination of "my inward parts" and "growl" also appears in Isaiah 63:15. Therefore, Davis understands this combination as an expression of hope, since God's guts churn for Israel. If the reader identifies the woman in Song of Songs as a symbol for Israel, then she is expressing her hope, desire, and yearning for God, rather than merely her erotic desire for her beloved. Thus, when the Song is read metaphorically, the woman in the Song is reciprocating God's visceral attachment to her, as is indicated in the prophetic texts.[55]

Reading the book of Jeremiah and the Song of Songs intertextually, we see that they form two inverted portraits of a relationship. In Jeremiah, God yearns for the lost love when Israel goes after other gods. His inward parts churn for her. In Song of Songs, the woman's inward parts churn for her beloved in his absence. When the two texts are brought together, they form a dialogue of love, loss, and longing. It is as if the woman in the Song is responding to her God/husband in Jeremiah 31:20, "Your heart churns for me. My heart churns for you too."

Ezekiel 16: Stripping her clothes. The prophet Ezekiel conducted his ministry during the darkest time in the history of Israel. This was when Israel entered into exile in Babylon. Both Ezekiel 16 and Ezekiel 23 use the marriage metaphor to depict Yahweh's relationship with Israel, but here I focus on Ezekiel 16. Ezekiel 16 provides a lengthy parable of Israel, first as an unwanted infant but then adopted by God, who raised her, nurtured her, and clothed her until her fame spread among the nations. Ezekiel uses graphic language to unfold this lengthy metaphor of a twisted love between Israel and God. Weems says that the lucid "pornographic" language of Ezekiel would make even modern audiences blush.[56] Julie Galambush highlights the distinctiveness of Ezekiel's marriage metaphor when compared with the same metaphor in earlier prophetic texts. Ezekiel's distinctiveness includes its literary style, its contents, and its placement in the book.

---

[55]Davis, *Proverbs, Ecclesiastes, and the Song of Songs*, 278.
[56]Weems, *Battered Love*, 60.

Galambush also remarks that Ezekiel 16 provides a coherent and elaborate biography for Hosea's Gomer and the adulterous Israel in Isaiah and Jeremiah.[57]

Ezekiel 16 begins with a parable of an unwanted infant:

> "When I passed by you and saw you squirming in your blood, I said to you *while you were* in your blood, 'Live!' Yes, I said to you *while you were* in your blood, 'Live!' I made you numerous like plants of the field. Then you grew up, became tall and reached the age for fine ornaments; *your* breasts were formed and your hair had grown. Yet you were naked and bare.
>
> Then I passed by you and saw you, and behold, you were at the time for love [דֹּדִים]; so I spread My skirt over you and covered your nakedness. I also swore to you and entered into a covenant with you so that you became Mine," declares the LORD God. (Ezek 16:6-8)

God found Israel when she was squirming in her blood and revived her. When she was ready for love (דֹּדִים), God betrothed her by spreading his skirt over her. The same gesture is taken by Ruth toward Boaz in the context of a marriage proposal (Ruth 3:9). Here, "skirt" (כָּנָף) is also the word for "wing" (כָּנָף), symbolically referring to the protection of marriage. Entering into covenant reflects a double entendre of human marriage as well as divine-human marriage. God married Israel. In Song of Songs, "love" (דֹּדִים or דּוֹד) occurs frequently in the mouths of the human lovers (Song 1:2, 4; 4:10; 7:13). However, when Israel became famed among the nations, she trusted in her beauty and played the harlot with the nations. She took some of her clothes and made for herself high places—places where she would be worshiped. Not only that, but she took the jewels, gold, and silver that God gave her and used them to make images of idols. She used embroidered cloth to cover the idols and offered the oil and incense that God had given her to worship them instead. Worse yet, she took her sons and daughters whom she had borne to God and sacrificed them to idols, passing them through the fire (Ezek 16:15-21). Because of these abominations that Israel committed against God, God pronounced his judgment against her:

---

[57]Julie Galambush, *Jerusalem in the Book of Ezekiel: The City as Yahweh's Wife* (Atlanta: Scholars Press, 1992), 62, 78-79.

Therefore, O harlot, hear the word of the LORD. Thus says the LORD God, "Because your lewdness was poured out and your nakedness uncovered through your harlotries with your lovers and with all your detestable idols, and because of the blood of your sons which you gave to idols, therefore, behold, I will gather all your lovers with whom you took pleasure, even all those whom you loved *and* all those whom you hated. So I will gather them against you from every direction and expose your nakedness to them that they may see all your nakedness. Thus I will judge you like women who commit adultery or shed blood are judged; and I will bring on you the blood of wrath and jealousy." (Ezek 16:35-38)

God explicitly calls Israel a harlot here. He promises to judge her as one who has committed adultery. Then God says, "I will also give you into the hands of your lovers, and they will tear down your shrines, demolish your high places, strip you of your clothing, take away your jewels, and will leave you naked and bare" (Ezek 16:39). One vivid manifestations of divine judgment on Israel is the stripping away of her clothing. This is in a metaphorical sense reminiscent of the night scene in Song 5 where the woman goes out to search for her beloved but he is nowhere to be found. She then encounters the guards, and they strike her, wound her, and take her shawl away from her: "The watchmen, the ones patrolling the city, found me, they struck me, they bruised me; they lifted up my shawl from upon me, the watchers of the walls" (Song 5:7). Although the words in both texts for "strip" or "take away" are different, the underlying images are the same. Being stripped away of one's clothing and having one's shawl taken away both convey terror, violence, and punishment.[58] Only in the latter case is the exact meaning cryptic. Keel indicates that in the Old Testament context, a woman wandering in the streets at night would have been perceived as an adulteress or prostitute (Prov 7:11-12). The guards would have treated such a woman by arresting her. They could also take her clothing and strike her fifty times with a club as a punishment.[59] It is possible that the woman in the Song, in seeking her beloved on the streets at night, is identified as a prostitute by the guards. The poem may intend to express what she has suffered for the sake of her beloved.

---

[58]Similar imagery appears in Jer 13:22, 26.
[59]Keel, *Song of Songs*, 195.

Davis offers another interpretation. She proposes that the hostile re-
action of the city guards may serve a symbolic function, since in the
Song, the city and the garden do not connote different geographical
locations but two poles of experience. The city of Jerusalem, on the one
hand, represents the positive image of the place for intimate encounter
between God and humanity, as the psalmists and prophets celebrate. On
the other hand, Jerusalem also stands for "the city of blood" (Ezek 22:2;
24:6, 9), a negative image of those who seek to destroy what is holy and
true.[60] Paul Griffiths offers yet another interpretation. He asserts that
the woman is the true city and the night encounter in the city is the false
city. Those who guard the streets, therefore, must oppose her, and they
do it by beating her and wounding her. Griffiths understands the wound
as a "love wound," since the same word appears in Song of Songs
4:9, where the male lover is "wounded" by her eyes.[61] In fact, a
history of interpretation based on Song of Songs 5:7 alone would yield
a fascinating book.

Ezekiel 16 does not end with a message of judgment but a beacon of hope
and restoration. "Nevertheless, I will remember My covenant with you in
the days of your youth, and I will establish an everlasting covenant with you"
(Ezek 16:60). "In the days of your youth" recalls "the devotion of your youth"
in Jeremiah 2:2. Israel's youth symbolizes her first love with God. It also
echoes the kind of love portrayed in the Song of Songs, where the woman's
love and devotion for her beloved is pure and without blemish. Various
images that appear in Ezekiel 16, such as the woman as a metaphor for Israel,
her pure love in her youth, and her waywardness and her punishment, as
well as God's words of restoration, find resonances in the Song of Songs. At
the same time, these images in the Song also counter Ezekiel 16 by presenting a portrait of an ideal love of a woman who suffers for the sake of her
beloved. The poet adapts the images of Israel in Ezekiel 16 to fit his own
purpose in the Song of Songs. Another aspect of the resonance and dissonance between Ezekiel 16 and Song of Songs is the female body. While
Ezekiel 16 exhibits the female body in a way that prompts its readers to

---

[60]Davis, *Proverbs, Ecclesiastes, and the Song of Songs*, 279.
[61]Paul J. Griffiths, *Song of Songs*, Brazos Theological Commentary on the Bible (Grand Rapids, MI:
  Brazos, 2011), 124-25.

recoil (Ezek 16:25, 36), Song of Songs depicts the female body as beautiful, desirable, and erotic (Song 4:1-7; 7:1-7).

In this regard, I agree with Weems and Davis's assertion that Song of Songs is a healing text, restoring what is lost in the Prophets.[62] While the prophetic texts portray a love gone wrong, the Song of Songs portrays a love restored. The love in the Song of Songs resonates with the love of God for Israel in the prophetic texts. At the same time, it counters them by presenting a relatively mutual, passionate, and youthful love between the man and the woman. This love is unlike the love between God and Israel when Israel goes after other gods, but it is likened to the love between God and Israel in their youthful stage in the wilderness. Therefore, Song of Songs both resonates and departs from the image of love in the prophetic texts and asserts the woman's own voice in the Hebrew canon. The resonances suggest that the Song of Songs is intended to be read as Scripture. The dissonances point to the Song's distinct contribution to the canon as both a healing text and a restorative text.

Song of Songs and the Writings. *Proverbs 1–9: Woman Wisdom and Lady Folly.* The similarities between Song of Songs and Proverbs 1–9 are striking. Perhaps this is because both books are associated with Solomon, the emblem of wisdom. Just as the boundary between human sexuality and divine-human relationship in Proverbs 1–9 is fuzzy, so too is it in the Song of Songs. Furthermore, the woman in the Song shares several images with the wife as well as the adulterous woman (woman folly) in Proverbs 1–9. For instance, the woman in the Song is described as

> A garden locked, my sister, (my) bride; a fountain locked, a spring sealed. (Song 4:12)

> A spring, gardens (garden spring), a well of the water of life and the ones flowing from Lebanon. (Song 4:15)

In Proverbs, similar imagery of water and fountain is employed to describe the wife of a young man:

---

[62]Weems, *Battered Love*, 12-44; Davis, "Reading the Song Iconographically," 176, 183. LaCocque deviates from Weems and Davis. He sees the Song of Songs as in a horizontal axis about human-human *eros*, whereas the prophetic texts present a vertical axis of divine-human relationship. In so doing, the Song deconstructs the prophetic metaphor and reconfigures it as "*eros* is found in agape." See Andre LaCocque, *Romance, She Wrote: A Hermeneutical Essay on Song of Songs* (Harrisburg, PA: Trinity Press International, 1998), 54-56.

Drink water from your own cistern
And fresh water from your own well.
Should your springs be dispersed abroad,
Streams of water in the streets?
Let them be yours alone
And not for strangers with you.
Let your fountain be blessed,
And rejoice in the wife of your youth. (Prov 5:15-18)

By contrast, an adulterer or Lady Folly describes herself as "the stolen water" (Prov 9:17), that is, a wife who belongs to another man. It is likely that both the authors of Song of Songs and Proverbs are drawing this image of water as wife from a common stock of poetic convention at their time. Nevertheless, the close affinity of this imagery in association with Solomon connects the two books.

Additionally, spices such as myrrh appear in both texts. Myrrh here refers literally and metaphorically to both the woman and the man. The woman compares a pouch of myrrh to her beloved: "A pouch of myrrh is my beloved to me; between my breasts, he lodged" (Song 1:13). He also compares her to a garden in which are found various precious spices, including myrrh: "Nard and saffron, reed and cinnamon, with all the trees of frankincense, myrrh and aloes, with all the top spices" (Song 4:14). When she describes her hands, she employs the imagery of myrrh as well: "I arose, I, to open to my beloved, and my hands dripped (with) myrrh, and my fingers flowing myrrh upon the palms of the bolt" (Song 5:5).[63] Myrrh is not reserved for the woman alone. When she describes her lover's cheeks, she employs the same poetic imagery: "His cheeks, like beds of spices, towers of perfume, his lips, lilies dripping flowing myrrh" (Song 5:13).

While myrrh is used to describe both genders in Song of Songs, myrrh in Proverbs is attributed only to Lady Folly: "I have sprinkled my bed with myrrh, aloes and cinnamon. Come, let us drink our fill of love until morning; Let us delight ourselves with caresses" (Prov 7:17-18). Another image shared by both Song of Songs and Proverbs 1–9 is that of a female

---

[63]For "flowing myrrh" NASB has "liquid myrrh." "Palms" could also be translated "handles."

gazelle (צְבִיָּה). In Song of Songs, a female gazelle is used to describe the woman's breasts: "Two of your breasts, like two young stags, twins of a female gazelle, pasturing among the lilies" (Song 4:5; 7:3). A gazelle is also used in the adjuration refrain in the Song that the woman utters: "I adjure you, daughters of Jerusalem, by female gazelles or by hinds of the field, do not stir up and do not arouse love until it desires" (Song 2:7; 3:5; see Song 5:8).

Likewise, in Proverbs, a doe or deer describes the wife's breasts. Although the author chooses another word for doe (אַיָּלָה), which is different from "female gazelle" in the Song of Songs, the image of a gazelle or a deer is a close analogy. Both convey a youthful, refreshing, lively, and soft image: "*As a loving hind and a graceful doe, Let her breasts satisfy you at all times; Be exhilarated always with her love*" (Prov 5:19).[64] There is yet another shared image between Song of Songs and Proverbs 1–9—lips dripping honey. Like the imagery of myrrh, dripping honey in Proverbs is used for the adulterous woman and not the wife. The man in the Song says to his bride, both before and after he enters into his "garden":

> Flowing honey dripped (from) your lips, (my) bride; honey and milk under your tongue; the fragrance of your robes like Lebanon. (Song 4:11)

> I have come to my garden, my sister, (my) bride; I have gathered my myrrh with my spices; I have eaten honeycomb with my honey, I have drunk my wine with my milk. (Song 5:1)

Inside the metaphorical garden depicting the woman's body, there are honey and milk, thus evoking the image of the land of Israel as a land flowing with milk and honey. The expression "honey dripped from lips" appears also in Proverbs, where it describes the adulterous woman:

> My son, give attention to my wisdom,
> Incline your ear to my understanding;
> That you may observe discretion
> And your lips may reserve knowledge.
> For the lips of an adulteress drip honey
> And smoother than oil is her speech. (Prov 5:1-3)

---

[64]The NASB translates "a female gazelle" as "a graceful doe" (ESV). The NIV translates it as "a graceful deer."

The meaning of "lips dripping honey" in and of itself is neutral, depending on its context. In Song of Songs, the image evokes a soft, soothing, and sweet sensation. But when it describes the adulterous woman's lips dripping honey in Proverbs, it points to her smooth but deceitful tongue and her enticement, which paints a negative portrait of a woman. There are resonances between Song of Songs and Proverbs, such as the idea of seeking and finding (Song 3:1-2; 5:6; Prov 8:17, 35) and "call her blessed" (Song 6:9; Prov 31:28-29). Through these resonances, the Song of Songs echoes and counterechoes images in Proverbs.

Reading both texts together forms an intertextual reading of two women. The woman in the Song resonates with both the image of the wife and of the adulterous woman in Proverbs. In this sense, we may interpret the woman in the Song as embracing and sharing qualities of the two contrasting women in Proverbs. How do we make sense of this fact? The so-called strange-woman tradition includes two modes of literary expression: admonition and scenario, just like the Song of Songs. In the Song, the Shulamite and the daughters of Jerusalem represent the instructor and students in the admonishment, whereas the scenes between the Shulamite and Solomon function as scenario. Therefore, Martin Hauge argues that Proverbs 2–7 frames the Song of Songs but also reinterprets the tradition in Proverbs.[65] Annette Schellenberg offers an alternative reading of Song of Songs and Proverbs 5:19. Suggesting that the wisdom tradition holds an ambivalent attitude toward female sexuality, she argues that rather than Song of Songs being adapted from Proverbs, it is Proverbs that reacts against the sexual freedom in Song of Songs through demonizing and domesticating the erotic woman in the Song.[66] The implication of this understanding, she argues, is that the author of Proverbs reads the Song literally as opposed to allegorically. Kingsmill, by contrast, considers Proverbs as predating the Song of Songs, and so the Song is "redeeming" Proverbs rather than the other way around.[67] Andruska argues for the Song's

---

[65]Martin Ravndal Hauge, *Solomon the Lover and the Shape of the Song of Songs*, HBM 77 (Sheffield: Sheffield Phoenix, 2015).

[66]Annette Schellenberg, "May Her Breasts Satisfy You at All Times (Prov 5:19)," *VT* 68 (2018): 252-73.

[67]Kingsmill, *Song of Songs*. Kingsmill identifies similarities between Prov 7:6-23 and Song 3:1-4 and suggests they should be well qualified to be Wisdom books, and also that there is an *eros*

influence on Proverbs, stating that the motifs that appear in Proverbs 7 are distinctive of the Song of Songs, such as the search for the lover on the city streets as well as the bed perfumed with myrrh and aloes. These motifs are unique in the Song and are not found elsewhere in ancient Near Eastern texts. She suggests that Proverbs 7 modifies the motifs in the Song for the purpose of aligning them with its own argument.[68]

While it may be difficult to date the two books precisely, what we can deduce is that Proverbs and Song of Songs share a common poetic world. The key difference between the woman in the Song and the adulteress in Proverbs lies in the boundary of marriage. Within the boundary of marriage, a woman can be like the adulterous woman, preparing her bed with myrrh and having lips dripping honey and speaking soft words to her husband. However, when a woman engages in such activities outside the bounds of marriage, she becomes an adulteress, like the one condemned in Proverbs. The genius of the poet of Song of Songs is exactly that while they employ the literary conventions of the time, they adapt it to fit the purposes of the Song. In so doing, the poet creates an artful portrait that both conforms to and departs from the cultural expectations for seeing women as only one of two extremes poles—wife or adulteress. Reading the two texts together in a canonical context and in their final form results in one illuminating the meaning of the other, regardless of which direction one is going.

Proverbs 30: The way of a man with a maid. Proverbs 30 records the words of Agur, the son of Jakeh. Though his identity is obscure and cannot be verified definitively, it is believed that Agur was a collector who pulled together a collection of proverbs that celebrate divine power and wisdom, the wonder of creation, and the limits of human knowledge in regard to God's creation.[69] In Proverbs 30:18-19, Agur writes: "There are three things which are too wonderful for me, Four which I do not understand: The way of an eagle in the sky, The way of a serpent on a rock, The way of a ship in the middle of the sea, And the way of a man with a maid." Here Agur

---

strand in Wisdom books. Other similarities between these books include the images of wine, milk, honey, lips, and the tongue.

[68] J. L. Andruska, *Wise and Foolish Love in the Song of Songs*, Oudestamentische Studiën 75 (Leiden: Brill, 2019), 35-41.

[69] Christine Roy Yoder, *Proverbs*, Abingdon Old Testament Commentaries (Nashville: Abingdon, 2009), 278.

ponders the "four wonders of the world," the fourth of which—"the way of
a man with a maid"—is intimately connected to the Song of Songs, which
is all about the way of a man with a maid. The word "maid" (עַלְמָה) used here
refers either to a virgin or to a woman of marriageable age (Gen 24:43; Ex
2:8; Song 1:3; 6:8; Is 7:14). The ambiguity of the word matches the ambiguity
of the sexuality of the woman in the Song where it is not clear at what point
she is married or remains a virgin. In the Christian Bible, Song of Songs
follows right after Proverbs and Ecclesiastes. It is conceivable to read the
story of "the way of a man with a maid" in the Song after reading
Proverbs 30:18-19.

Ecclesiastes 9:9: Rejoice with the wife whom you love. Although Solomonic authorship of both Ecclesiastes and Song of Songs is contested, one
cannot deny both books' association with Solomon. Song 1:1 states, "The
Song of Songs [שִׁיר הַשִּׁירִים], which is Solomon's." Ecclesiastes 1:2 employs
a similar refrain, "vanity of vanities" (הֲבֵל הֲבָלִים). Its contents suggest the
author is using a Solomonic persona to probe the meaning of life under
the sun. As we discussed in chapter one, strictly speaking Song of Songs
does not belong to the Wisdom corpus. Rather, it is a cousin of wisdom,
and as such it is affiliated with Israel's wisdom tradition on love and life.
As one reads Song of Songs and Ecclesiastes, the figure of Solomon,
whether positively or negatively portrayed, becomes seared into the mind
of the reader.

If one reads the woman in the Song as an epitome of wisdom through its
intertextual links with Proverbs 1–9, then the Song is about Solomon's
pursuit of Wisdom. This reading would affirm Gerhard von Rad's understanding of the development of the wisdom tradition in Israel, namely, that
it began as objectified wisdom and evolved into a personified sense of
Wisdom, which appears as a woman.[70] This personification of "Lady
Wisdom" becomes apparent in Proverbs 1–9. Could it be that the woman in
the Song of Songs represents the same Lady Wisdom?

As for the other wisdom book, Ecclesiastes, the central thought is death.
Because of the absolute certainty of death, life becomes ephemeral, and
because of the brevity of life, Qoheleth exhorts his readers to enjoy life

---

[70]Gerhard von Rad, *Wisdom in Israel* (Harrisburg, PA: Trinity Press International, 1972), 171-73.

while they can. Ecclesiastes 9 begins with the grave concern about death, namely, that it happens to all (Eccles 9:1-6). Death shows no partiality or preference. Then Qoheleth turns from this gloomy reality to a positive note, telling his audience to eat and drink, to take care with one's appearance, to enjoy life with the woman one loves, and to work with all diligence as ways to cope within the inescapable fate of death (Eccles 9:7-10). As early as Baba Batra, the book of Ecclesiastes is followed by Song of Songs. One reads the exhortation "to enjoy life with the woman you love" in Ecclesiastes 9:9 followed immediately by Song of Songs, whose contents reflect and expand on that very verse.

Steinberg sees Song of Songs as a realization or application of Ecclesiastes 9:9. In such a reading, Song of Songs belongs to the wisdom tradition and functions as applied wisdom, as I argued in chapter two.[71] Melton considers Song of Songs as an intertext to Ecclesiastes 9:9. She suggests that Ecclesiastes predates Song of Songs, since Qoheleth admits in Ecclesiastes 7:28 that he cannot find a worthy woman among all those he has found. Had he found the love of his life, like the woman in Song of Songs, he would not have uttered what he says in Ecclesiastes 7:28. Melton also points out the significant link between love and death. Song of Songs focuses on love, while Ecclesiastes focuses on death. Though their respective starting points differ, they both urge one to celebrate life by spending it with the one's love.[72]

Through its association with wisdom, Song of Songs resonates with Proverbs and Ecclesiastes. At the same time, it retains its distinct voice as a book that counters the adulteress in Proverbs and extends both the word of Agur in Proverbs 30:18-19 and the exhortation of Qoheleth in Ecclesiastes 9:9. What is more, since God created human sexuality in Eden, the sexuality expressed in Proverbs, Ecclesiastes, and Song of Songs links them to the creator God and to human beings' desire to find order and meaning in the area of human sexuality.

---

[71]See Julius Steinberg and Timothy J. Stone with the assistance of Rachel Marie Stone, *The Shape of the Writings*, Siphrut 16 (Winona Lake, IN: Eisenbrauns, 2015), 152, 160.

[72]Brittany N. Melton, "Solomon, Wisdom, and Love: Intertextual Resonances Between Ecclesiastes and Song of Songs," in *Reading Ecclesiastes Intertextually*, ed. Katherine Dell and Will Kynes (London: T&T Clark, 2014), 130-41, esp. 138-39.

Daniel 2: Male statue. In the Song of Songs, when the woman describes her beloved's body, she uses language reminiscent of the statue of a god in Daniel 2:31-45, where King Nebuchadnezzar dreams of a statute, which Daniel interprets as representing Nebuchadnezzar himself:

> You, O king, were looking and behold, there was a single great statue; that statue, which was large and of extraordinary splendor, was standing in front of you, and its appearance was awesome. The head of that statue *was made* of fine gold, its breast and its arms of silver, its belly and its thighs of bronze, its legs of iron, its feet partly of iron and partly of clay. (Dan 2:31-33)

> My beloved is dazzling and ruddy, more prominent than ten thousand.
>   His head, gold, refined gold, his locks of hair, black like the raven.
>   His eyes, like doves, upon the streams of water, washing in milk and sitting upon the rim.
>   His cheeks, like beds of spices, towers of perfume, his lips, lilies dripping flowing myrrh.
>   His hands, rods of gold, are being filled with yellow jasper; his belly, an ivory plate, being covered (with) sapphires.
>   His legs, (are like) pillars of alabaster, being founded upon a pedestal of refined gold,
>   His appearance is like the Lebanon, being chosen like cedars. (Song 5:10-15)[73]

Both of these descriptions go from top to bottom. Tremper Longman III regards the woman's description of her beloved as "God-like" in appearance. She is using godlike language to describe her man. From her perspective, he appears to be "larger than life," and such is her vision of love.[74] Kingsmill also notices the similar imagery of a male statue in Song of Songs 5 and their contrasts. She indicates that the contrasts are found between "the silver, brass, iron and clay of Nebuchadnezzar's image, and the beryl, ivory, sapphires and marble of the beloved." The woman ends her description of this contrast in Song 5:16 by noting that "all of him is pleasant."[75] We may well conclude that the description of the beloved's body in the Song both resonates with that of the statute in Daniel 2 and also counters it, since the

---

[73]For "yellow jasper," NASB/JPS has "set with beryl." "Alabaster" could also be translated "marble."
[74]Longman, *Song of Songs*, 171, 173.
[75]Kingsmill, *Song of Songs*, 182.

beloved's body is all pleasant, whereas Nebuchadnezzar's statue is stiff and then degenerates from head to feet.

Esther: Women, temple, feast, and wine. That Song of Songs bears striking similarities to the book of Esther has been overlooked in the past. For example, both books accentuate female characters with supportive male characters. Both female characters start out as Cinderella figures and later are transformed into royal figures. Both books find resonance with temple images as well as Israel's wisdom tradition. Both books are associated with feasts and wine and are recited annually at the feasts. Both books are a part of the Megilloth. Most significantly, both books refrain from explicit reference to the name of God. Both books center on human beings and their actions in the world. Both books demonstrate elements of applied wisdom in love and life. At the same time, each book is quite unique in its own ways. For example: Their portrayal of time is different. The focus of the Song is on Jerusalem, whereas the focus of Esther is on Shushan. In the Song, the woman marries for love, while Esther marries out of a sense of duty. One compares love to death, the other confronts evil with possible death. Therefore, Song of Songs and Esther are both echoes and counterechoes not only to each other but also to the rest of the Hebrew Scripture.

Conclusion on Song of Songs and the Hebrew Scripture. So far, we have seen glimpses of the interbiblical resonances and dissonances between Song of Songs and the rest of the Hebrew Scripture. The motifs of Song of Songs run across the entire Hebrew canon from the Torah, to the Prophets, and on to the Writings. If one judges the Song by the contents of the Song alone, one might come up with different ways of reading and interpreting it, such as that the Song is about sexual love or unrestrained free love or even soft pornography.[76] However, when one reads the Song as a book within the Hebrew canon, it is difficult to ignore or overlook its interconnectedness with the rest of the biblical books. Through its echoes, the Song becomes a sounding board to the canon, and through its counterechoes, it asserts its own voice as a unique book among Hebrew Scripture. Although explicit reference to the name of God is absent in the Song, through the Song's intertextual links

---

[76]For example, David Clines, "Why Is There a Song of Songs and What Does It Do to You if You Read It?," *Jian Dao* 1 (1994): 3-27.

with the canon, it functions as an echo chamber, reflecting the presence of God through images of nature, through garden-temple imagery, and through the erotic love expressed in the Song.[77] As it is a book infused with wisdom, the presence of God is expressed subtly and not overtly. It is to be discerned through association with creation and anthropology. This aspect of God in the Song of Songs, then, is precisely a distinctive appeal of the book, one that contributes to the understanding of God as both present and absent—absent in presence as well as present in absence.

READING ESTHER AS HEBREW SCRIPTURE

The book of Esther is particularly known for its lack of any reference to the name of God. Its first chapter reflects a secular setting of Gentile indulgence in licentious drinking parties and pleasure-seeking endeavors. Yet the feast of Purim also borders on merrymaking without any religious significance. Andre LaCocque, for example, says that Purim as carnival reflects its a-religiosity.[78] Past reception history of Esther falls into two camps at opposite ends of the spectrum. At one end of the spectrum Martin Luther, emblematic of those who strictly uphold the authority of the Scripture, wrote: "I am so great an enemy to the second book of the Maccabees, and to Esther, that I wish they had not come to us at all, for they have too many heathen unnaturalities."[79] Also, John Calvin wrote a commentary on every book of the Bible except for the Song of Songs and Esther. There is no evidence that any New Testament writers quote or allude to the book of Esther. The church fathers also rarely make reference to the book.[80] Additionally, Esther is not found among the Dead Sea Scrolls.[81] On the other end of the spectrum, many Protestant interpreters see the hidden presence or the providence of God as

[77]Ellen Davis, "Losing a Friend: The Loss of the Old Testament to the Church," *Pro Ecclesia* 9, no. 1 (2000): 83.

[78]Andre LaCocque, *Esther Regina: A Bakhtinian Reading* (Evanston, IL: Northwestern University Press, 2008), 42.

[79]Martin Luther, *Table Talk* 24, quoted in John Anthony Dunne, *Esther and Her Elusive God: How a Secular Story Functions as Scripture* (Eugene, OR: Wipf & Stock, 2014), 97.

[80]Jo Carruthers, *Esther Through the Centuries* (Malden, MA: Blackwell, 2008), 13.

[81]Carey A. Moore, *Esther*, AB (Garden City, NY: Doubleday, 1971), xxxi. Dunne suspects that the Qumran community deliberately excluded the book of Esther from its collection of texts. See Dunne, *Esther and Her Elusive God*, 99-100; Peter H. W. Lau, *Esther*, Asia Bible Commentary (Carlisle, UK: Langham Global Library, 2018), 20-21.

an inherent part of the book.[82] For example, Jobes asserts, "Christian theology is concerned with the character of the unseen God, who manifests himself in the events of human history. The Esther story is an example of how at one crucial moment in history the covenant promises God had made were fulfilled, not by his miraculous interventions, but through completely ordinary events."[83] Anthony Tomasino has highlighted Haman's demise as visible evidence of divine providence, noting that "God is most manifest in the irony of Haman, impaled on the gallows that he had prepared for another man. . . . We see that God has not died and has not been absent."[84]

Jewish traditions tend to be more sympathetic toward the book of Esther than their Christian counterparts. For the Jewish people, the book of Esther is known as the Megillah, which means "the scroll." Esther is the scroll par excellence. This revered term makes apparent the book's preeminence. The celebration of Purim further emphasizes the book's significance to the Jewish communities throughout the world. For Jewish medieval scholars, Esther is "a book which exemplifies, vividly and concisely, the eternal miracle of Jewish survival."[85] The book's relevance lasts until the present day, especially after the modern history of the Holocaust and the issue of anti-Semitism.[86]

Reading Esther apart from the rest of Scripture may yield an interpretation that emphasizes human characters achieving salvation without divine intervention or assistance in any form. Nevertheless, when we read Esther as an integral part of Hebrew Scripture, the book sets itself apart as both an echo and a counterecho to the rest of Scripture. Some scholars tend to focus on the book's echoes without drawing attention to its counterechoes.[87] Others focus on its counterechoes more than its echoes.[88] The

---

[82]For example, Barry G. Webb, "Reading Esther as Holy Scripture," *Reformed Theological Review* 52, no. 1 (1993): 23-35. See chap. 1 for more examples of these scholars.

[83]Jobes, *NIV Application Commentary: Esther*, 41.

[84]Anthony Tomasino, *Esther*, Evangelical Exegetical Commentary (Bellingham, WA: Lexham, 2016), 128.

[85]Carruthers, *Esther Through the Centuries*, 12.

[86]Richard Bauckham, *The Bible in Politics: How to Read the Bible Politically* (Louisville, KY: Westminster John Knox, 1989), 118-30. As I was writing this chapter, ten Jews were murdered at the Tree of Life synagogue in Pittsburgh, the targets of a hate crime.

[87]For example, Gillis Gerleman, *Esther*, 2nd ed., Biblischer Kommentar: Altes Testament 21 (Neukirchen-Vluyn: Neukirchener Verlag, 1982), 11-23; Ward, *God Unseen*.

[88]For example, Aaron Koller, *Esther in Ancient Jewish Thought* (Cambridge: Cambridge University Press, 2014), 90-106. Koller considers Esther as a text of "anti-Exodus."

book's unique contribution to Old Testament theology lies precisely in this resonance and dissonance with the other books in the Hebrew canon. In this sense, like the Song of Songs, Esther also makes its mark, complementing and supplementing what is lacking in the rest of the Hebrew Scripture on the nature of God and the manifestation of his activities.

Through an interbiblical reading with Esther, the book's motifs run across the three major divisions of the Hebrew Bible and therefore confirm the notion that the book of Esther is intended to be read as a part of Scripture. *How* to read this book as Scripture is a different question entirely; as Timothy Beal remarks, Esther is both strange and familiar.[89]

Esther and the Torah. *Genesis 12:3: Abrahamic covenant.* The book of Esther is known for its lack of explicit religious content, such as references to the covenant between God and Israel, to salvation history, worship, prayers, offering sacrifices, and to observing the Mosaic law. While it is true that the book does not include any overt references to God's covenant with Israel, there is, however, an element in Esther that ties it to the Abrahamic covenant in Genesis 12:1-3, namely, the curse and the demise of Haman. In Genesis 12:3, God speaks to Abram: "I will bless those who bless you, and whoever slights you I will curse" (my translation). At a time of postexilic Jewish diaspora in Persia, though the Jewish people in Shushan did not express an intent to return to Jerusalem, their status as the people of God remained. As Jews, they were the descendants of Abraham, and they knew that whoever belittled them would be cursed. The plight of Haman, from his ascent to his downfall, demonstrates precisely the outworking of the Abrahamic covenant that God will curse those who act against his chosen people.

By attempting to annihilate the entire Jewish race in Persia, Haman becomes the archenemy of God. Even his wife recognizes this reality. When Haman comes back from the palace, knowing that the king will honor Mordecai instead of him, his wife, Zeresh, says to him, "If Mordecai whom you begin to fall before him is from the Jewish seed, then you will not overcome him, indeed, you will surely fall before him " (Esther 6:13). God is on the side of his chosen people, and whoever is against them God will curse. The

---

[89]Timothy K. Beal, *Esther*, Berit Olam (Collegeville, MN: Liturgical Press, 1999), ix.

miraculous reversal of fortunes in both Mordecai and Haman's ordeals is thus a direct consequence and realization of the Abrahamic covenant. In addition, Haman is hanged on the gallows he made for Mordecai. The word "gallows" in Hebrew is literally "the tree," which recalls the Mosaic law that "whoever is hanged on a tree is cursed" (Deut 21:23). Therefore, though Esther does not directly mention or hint at the Abrahamic covenant, its story line resonates with it.[90]

Genesis 37–50: Joseph. In her influential dissertation, Sandra Berg provides detailed intertextual connections between the story of Esther and the Joseph narrative.[91] Indeed, their characters and journeys are strikingly similar. For example, both protagonists are native Hebrew/Jewish and survive and thrive at a foreign court. Both characters are beautiful in appearance and in form (Gen 39:6; Esther 2:7). Both characters find favor in the eyes of others (Gen 39:4; Esther 2:9, 17). Both characters use wisdom to negotiate or "manipulate" their surroundings to their own advantage. They both appear to be wise courtier figures. Both characters exist between two cultures, Joseph as a Hebrew-Egyptian and Esther as a Jewish-Persian. Both characters speak at least two languages. Both marry a Gentile. Both experience a time of lowly status, Joseph when sold into Egypt by his brothers, and Esther as an orphan. However, both ascend to the highest status one can possibly achieve at a foreign court. Both Joseph and Esther save their own people and more. Both Joseph and Esther also hide their true identity at first and only later reveal who they are. Joseph first hides his identity from his brothers (Gen 42:7; 43:30-31), and Esther hides her Jewish identity from those in the Persian court, as Mordecai commands her (Esther 2:10, 20).

Clothing also plays a significant role in both stories. Joseph's long coat becomes the cause of his demise (Gen 37:3, 31, 33). When Joseph meets

---

[90]For more details on the relationship between Esther and the Abrahamic covenant, see Chloe Sun, "Ruth and Esther: Negotiable Space in Christopher Wright's *The Mission of God*?," *Missiology* 46, no. 2 (2018): 150-61. Webb also sees the intertextual connection between the story of Esther and that of the Abrahamic covenant. He goes even further, linking Esther and Mordecai to Christ (Webb, "Reading Esther as Holy Scripture," 33).

[91]Sandra Beth Berg, *The Book of Esther: Motifs, Themes, and Structure*, Society of Biblical Literature Dissertation Series 44 (Missoula, MT: Scholars Press, 1979), 123-43. Berg provides linguistic evidence and the motifs and themes as well as the structure of the two texts. As regards the linguistic evidence, Berg notices the similar choice of words and sentence constructions, such as Gen 39:10 and Esther 3:4 as well as Gen 44:34 and Esther 8:6.

Pharaoh, he changes his clothes (Gen 41:14). Joseph gives Benjamin five changes of clothes, while he gives only one change of clothes to the other brothers (Gen 45:22). For each of these scenes, the narrator employs the motif of clothing to reflect Joseph's status and to drive the story line forward. In Esther, Clines notices that there are two types of clothing, the formal and what one might call the deformed, which mediate between the powerful and the powerless. Mordecai first tears his clothes when informed of the genocide, and when Esther gives him a normal change of clothes, he refuses to wear them (Esther 4:1-4). Later, Esther wears royal robes when standing before the king (Esther 5:1). In light of these examples, Clines argues that clothing serves as a "conspicuous code signaling where one stands on the power axis."[92] Banquets serve as another common motif between the two texts. It is after the banquet scene that Joseph reveals his identity to his brothers (Gen 45:3). In Esther, it is during the banquet scene that she reveals her identity to Ahasuerus and Haman (Esther 7:3-4).

The settings of the two texts are also similar. For example, both stories present a time when God's people lived in a Gentile domain. In the Joseph narrative the Israelites live in Egypt, while in Esther the Jewish people have settled in Persia. Beyond that, both stories involve a death threat. For Joseph, it is the presence of the famine. For Esther, it is the annihilation of the Jewish people. Berg notices also that both stories involve eunuchs who act against the king but also function as bridges in enabling a reversal of events (Gen 40:1-3; Esther 2:21-23).[93] In addition, both stories exemplify a diaspora setting, in which God's people are scattered far from the Promised Land.

These echoes connect the two stories. It is highly likely that the author of Esther constructed his tale based on the Joseph story or at least with the story of Joseph in mind.[94] Rachel Adelman's comparison of the two stories

---

[92]David J. A. Clines, "Reading Esther from Left to Right: Contemporary Strategies for Reading a Biblical Text," in *The Bible in Three Dimensions: Essays in Celebration of Forty Years of Biblical Studies in the University of Sheffield* (Sheffield: University of Sheffield Press, 1990), 31-52, esp. 39.

[93]Berg, *Esther*, 126.

[94]Berg, *Esther*, 142. This is supported by the linguistic similarities of the two texts. See also Klara Butting, "Esther: A New Interpretation of the Joseph Story in the Fight Against Anti-Semitism and Sexism," in *A Feminist Companion to Ruth and Esther*, ed. Athalya Brenner, FCB 2/3 (Sheffield: Sheffield Academic Press, 1999), 234-48. Butting thinks that the character of Joseph is recreated in Esther in two persons: Esther and Mordecai. In Esther, the old story is told in a new way as a story of a woman.

also describes the similarities between Joseph and Esther, particularly in their respective transformation from passive to active, from archetypally feminine to masters of their own narratives.[95] However, I disagree with her treatment of the hidden nature of God in both narratives. Regarding the presence of God in the two stories, apparent differences emerge, rather than what Adelman conceives as similarities. In the Joseph narrative, the work of God is not as overt as in the stories of the patriarchs, where God appears, speaks, walks, interacts, and makes covenant with human beings. In fact, God never speaks directly to Joseph. Rather, God speaks and reveals his will through dreams, both to Joseph and to Pharaoh. The narrator's repeated remark that "God is with Joseph" makes clear, if not overtly, that God's presence is behind the scenes (Gen 39:2-3, 21). The narrator sees the hand of God behind the story line of Joseph in both the highs and lows of his life. In such remarks, the narrator provides a theological framework for the activities of God, who works behind the scenes to ensure the survival of the people at the time of the famine through Joseph. In Esther, no such theological framework appears. There is no mention of God or the implication of any veiled reference to suggest his presence. If the author of Esther had the story of Joseph in mind during his writing process, the absence of any reference of God must have been deliberate, so as to make a drastic distinction from the activity of God in the Joseph narrative.

One can argue based on canonical similarities between the two texts that if God is with Joseph in Egypt, God is also with Esther, even though his name is not mentioned. However, one can also argue the other way— that if God is with Joseph in the course of history, why does the author of Esther omit God's name in that book? This conspicuous absence of God in Esther is precisely the book's contribution to the canon. One may construe this absence of God as a manifestation of the postexilic theology, where divine presence becomes elusive when compared with the preexilic and exilic periods. One may also consider this absence of God in Esther as a critique of the presence of God in Joseph, that God does not always work the way one would expect him to. God can choose the manner of his

---

[95]Rachel E. Adelman, *The Female Ruse: Women's Deception and Divine Sanction in the Hebrew Bible*, HBM 74 (Sheffield: Sheffield Phoenix, 2015), 198-230. The table on pages 228-30 comparing the analogies between the Joseph and Esther narratives is particularly helpful.

manifestations, whether explicit or implicit or absent entirely. The absence of God in Esther may also be due to the book's association with wisdom books, in which divine presence does not manifest the same way as in the Torah and the Prophets.

By leaving the name of God out of the text, the author of Esther creates a strong counterecho to the story of Joseph. He shows that these two stories are different theologically and in essence. Therefore, through these echoes and counterechoes, Esther retains its own distinctiveness as a unique book in the Hebrew canon. The resonance it forms with the Joseph narrative makes a canonical connection, yet its dissonance with that story also presents an alternative voice, one that in effect tells the reader that there is a time when divine presence and activity are absent or at least perceived to be so. In such a time as this, human beings need to act on their own wisdom to discern the moral order of the world and then exercise justice in the face of evil.

Exodus: Moses, law, and tabernacle. Gerleman demonstrates the resonances between the story of Esther and the Exodus narrative, including life at a foreign court, God's people who are facing death threats, experiencing deliverance, executing revenge, gaining victory, and feasting.[96] Indeed, both stories are set in a foreign nation where the people of God suffer persecution and death threats, but in the end they emerge triumphant, escaping the annihilation of their respective foreign powers. Both stories include a feast associated with the deliverance. In Exodus, it is the Passover. In Esther, it is Purim. The casting of lots to determine the date for the feast of Purim happens on the eve of the Passover, thus connecting the two feasts. The two feasts also appear back to back in the Jewish liturgical calendar, as if Passover marks the beginning of the year and Purim marks the end of the year. Adele Berlin adds that in a rabbinic text, the sleepless night of Ahasuerus occurs on "the night of watching" (Ex 12:42), which is exactly the night when the exodus occurs. Also, Haman is impaled on the sixteenth of Nisan, during Passover. Berlin also cites examples of rabbinic sources that regard the deliverance of the Jews in Esther in terms of their deliverance from Egypt in Exodus.[97]

---

[96]Gerleman, *Esther*, 11-23.
[97]Adele Berlin, *Esther: The Traditional Hebrew Text with the New JPS Translation*, JPS Bible Commentary (Philadelphia: Jewish Publication Society, 2001), xxxvii-xl.

Moses and Esther, though they differ in gender, culture, and time period, share similarities as well. For example, Moses is the adopted son of Pharaoh, and Esther is the adopted daughter of Mordecai. Moses is bicultural, familiar with both Hebrew and Egyptian customs. Esther is also bicultural, embodying both Jewish and Persian cultures. Both Moses and Esther marry persons from a different race, and both ascend to positions of considerable power in a foreign court. Both characters save their own peoples. Additionally, both Moses and Esther are associated with writing law. Moses receives the Ten Commandments and the covenant code from God (Ex 20:1-23:33). He also writes the law according to divine revelation (Deut 31:9, 24). Esther also writes law—a remarkable feat, considering she is a woman. Carol Bechtel observes the frequent appearance of vocabulary associated with the notions of "writing," "law," "copying," "letter," "annals," and "decree" in the book and consequently suggests that the book of Esther can be considered as an extended meditation on the power of the written word.[98] Some scholars even regard Esther as the "new Moses."[99]

The glaring difference between Moses and Esther lies in the portrayal of divine presence. While God calls Moses, speaks to him face to face and mouth to mouth (Ex 33:11; Num 12:8; Deut 34:10), commands him, reveals his back to him, and talks to him on top of Mount Sinai, instructing him how to construct the tabernacle, there is no such textual evidence in the Hebrew version of the book of Esther that indicates God's presence with Esther. While Moses prayed and interceded for his people on various occasions, no such acts appear in Esther. Although Esther requests her people to fast, this does not explicitly suggest she is asking them to seek God's presence. Mordecai's reference to "another place" also may not imply God's help.[100] Koller identifies the book of Esther as in many ways an "anti-Exodus" and as offering "salvation without God."[101]

Yet the two books cannot be more different in the portrayal of God and his activities in human history. The God of the exodus is visible, vocal,

---

[98]Carol Bechtel, *Esther*, Interpretation (Louisville, KY: Westminster John Knox, 2002), 14.

[99]For example, C. E. Hambrick-Stowe, "Ruth the New Abraham, Esther the New Moses," *Christian Century* (1983): 1130.

[100]See chap. 2.

[101]Koller, *Esther in Ancient Jewish Thought*, 90, 92; LaCocque, *Esther Regina*, 42.

active, present, powerful, authoritative, commanding, and glorious, whereas the God of Esther is invisible, silent, inactive, or perhaps even indifferent to human affairs. Divine intervention in Esther, as if God is working behind the scenes, only appears in the Greek versions of the book, not in the Hebrew Masoretic Text. Yet many Christians still regard the book as reflecting God's providential protection for his people. Therefore, Exodus and Esther form two ends of the continuum with respect to the presence of God. In this regard, the Hebrew Masoretic version of Esther forms a countervoice to the theme of divine deliverance in Exodus. As Barry Webb indicates, the deliverance in Esther is of a different kind—a kind that emerges in the midst of life with its apparently normal flux of events. He suggests that readers identify themselves with the Persian king and Haman, and warn of anti-Semitism, instead of seeing themselves in the characters of Esther and Mordecai, because the book is about God's deliverance of a particular kind of people—his chosen people.[102]

Reading Esther canonically, we may reach two radically opposite conclusions. On the one hand, one may consider Esther a book about God's hidden presence, when read intertextually with Exodus. Just as God is present with his people and with Moses visibly in the Exodus experience, God is also present with his people behind the scenes in the book of Esther. God's people, such as Esther and Mordecai, serve as faithful witnesses to the divine covenant with their ancestors. Such an interpretation reflects a common Christian view of the book. On the other hand, one may consider the book of Esther as one in which God is completely absent. His people are compromised through assimilating into the Persian culture and worldview. In this reading, the book is about a secularized people of God who, though they were unfaithful to God, are saved through God's grace.[103] Koller reads it as a "desacralized" story.[104] If the book of Esther is read individually in its own right without taking it as a part of the Scripture, then any hint of the presence of God and his involvement in human history remains a reading through the lens of faith. Due to Esther's echoes and counterechoes with the book of Exodus, it retains its own voice as a part of the

---

[102]Webb, "Reading Esther as Holy Scripture," 30.
[103]This latter position is articulated in Dunne, *Esther and Her Elusive God*, 4-5.
[104]Koller, *Esther in Ancient Jewish Thought*, 96.

Scripture that critiques and reassesses divine presence in other books such as Exodus. It says to God's people that there are times when God is present, but there are also times when God is absent or seems absent. In the latter times, God's people need to act on their own initiative to discern the order of things and to exercise justice in an unjust world.

Last but not least, the descriptions of the Persian palace are remarkably similar to the descriptions of the tabernacle in Exodus. For a Jewish reader familiar with the Hebrew language, various descriptions—such as the pillars of the Persian palace, the colors of the palace and the royal robe of Mordecai—evoke the image of the tabernacle. The details of their similarities are stated in chapter four of this book. Through these similar descriptions, Esther forms another echo to Exodus. However, one cannot help but observe the counterechoes. While the tabernacle is the temporary dwelling of God, the Persian palace reflects the dwelling of an earthly Gentile monarch—a spineless, comical one. The royal robe of Mordecai echoes the Levitical priestly garment in Exodus 28, yet it is worn by a Jew in a foreign court. Does Mordecai's clothing suggest divine presence or absence? Such is the ambiguity that is left for the reader to confront.

Whatever the case, through a series of echoes and counterechoes, Esther continues to fascinate readers with its meaning and place in the Hebrew canon. Through its intertextual connections with Exodus, the book is linked to the rest of the biblical canon, and through its counterechoes, it asserts its own voice, which challenges the normative notions of divine presence and activity in the canon and reminds us that there are times when God is present and times when he is not, at least not in the way we humans expect. The fact remains in Esther that even when God is absent or hidden, history moves according to the direction God intends, God's people will survive, and the enemy of God's people will be defeated. When reading Esther retrospectively, the understanding of the providence of God (rather than the absence of God) that governs and protects his people is a possible hermeneutical trajectory.

Deuteronomy: I will hide my face. The connection between Deuteronomy 31:18 and Esther lies in the meaning of the name Esther. In Talmud Megillah 13a, Rabbi Judah says that although the actual name of Esther was Hadassah,

she was called Esther "because she hid facts about herself." Rabbi Judah is
referring to Esther hiding her Jewish identity in Esther 2:10, 20.[105] The consonants of the name Esther in Hebrew (אסתר) are exactly the same as in the
word "I will hide" (אסתר) in Deuteronomy 31:18. Judging from the context
of Deuteronomy 31, God foresaw the future apostasy of Israel and warned
Moses that the Israelites would play the harlot with the strange gods of the
land into which they were going and would forsake God's covenant. Then
God says,

> My anger will be kindled against them in that day, and I will forsake them
> and hide [הסתרתי] My face from them, and they will be consumed, and many
> evils and troubles will come upon them; so that they will say in that day, "Is
> it not because our God is not among us that these evils have come upon us?'
> But I will surely hide [אסתר] My face in that day because of all the evil which
> they will do, for they will turn to other gods. (Deut 31:17-18)

If the name of Esther conveys the meaning of divine hiddenness, the
logical implication is that the book is indeed a book about God's hiding.
Based on the intertextual reading with Deuteronomy 31, the reason for
God's hiding in Esther is the sin of his people, the breaking of the covenant. Thus, God's hiding becomes a form of punishment. If this is indeed
the appropriate reading of the two texts, then this reading brings no
comfort to the people of God and reinforces the notion of divine absence,
as Beal indicates.[106] Another possible understanding of the two texts is
that God is hiding in Esther, but for a different reason—God wants to stay
back and see what human beings will do in the face of evil without his
direct intervention into the matter. In this sense, God's hiding is not for
the purpose of punishment but to give human beings an opportunity to
achieve their own salvation. In other words, God's hiding can be understood in terms of a test from God—a test to see what human beings will
do. Still another likely reading is that God hides in plain sight, but he
continues to work providentially to protect his people. Therefore, Deuteronomy 31:18 provides both resonance and dissonance with Esther, both
ambiguity and clarity.

---

[105]Beal, *Esther*, xx.
[106]Beal, *Esther*, xxi.

Esther and the Prophets. 1 *Samuel 15: Kish, Benjaminite, and Agag.* The closest connection between Esther and the Former Prophets lies in the connection between the story of Saul and Mordecai. In Esther 2:5-6, the connection between these two figures is difficult to overlook: "A Jewish man was in Shushan the citadel, and his name was Mordecai, the son of Jair, the son of Shimei, the son of Kish, a Benjaminite, who had been exiled from Jerusalem with the exile whom was exiled with Jeconiah, king of Judah whom Nebuchadnezzar, king of Babylon, exiled." The ancestry of Mordecai, as the son of Shimei, son of Kish, and a Benjaminite, recalls the ancestry of Saul. In 1 Samuel 9:1-2, the narrator introduces the father of Saul as a Benjaminite whose name is Kish. This similarity cannot be a mere coincidence. It suggests that Mordecai is linked to Saul in ancestry, although Mordecai is from a different time period from that of Saul's father. He could well be a distant relative to Saul. The name Shimei also recalls another Shimei in David's time, who was a relative of Saul and who cursed David when David fled from Absalom (2 Sam 16:6-7, 13). This Shimei also appears on the death list of David (1 Kings 2:8-9).

In addition, the story of Saul involves killing the Amalekites. In 1 Samuel 15:2-3, God commands Saul to destroy the Amalekites without pity: "Thus says the LORD of hosts, 'I will punish Amalek *for* what he did to Israel, how he set himself against him on the way while he was coming up from Egypt. Now go and strike Amalek and utterly destroy all that he has, and do not spare him; but put to death both man and woman, child and infant, ox and sheep, camel and donkey.'" Saul obeys the divine command by attacking the Amalekites and defeating them. Conversely, against God's direct will, Saul spares Agag, king of the Amalekites, together with the best of the sheep, the oxen, the fattened calves, and the lambs (1 Sam 15:7-9), thus preserving Agag and his descendants.

This preservation of Agag's life finds its dire consequence in Esther. The author of Esther introduces Haman as the Agagite (Esther 3:1), which evokes the image of Agag, king of the Amalekites in 1 Samuel 15. In this way, readers realize that the hostility between Mordecai and Haman goes way back to their respective ancestors. History seems to have a way of coming full circle despite the distance in time. What Saul sows in 1 Samuel

15, his descendant Mordecai reaps in Esther 3. Based on the backdrop of Saul in relation to Agag, the hostility between Mordecai and Haman becomes intelligible. The hanging of Haman in Esther also is a form of poetic justice for what Saul failed to do in 1 Samuel 15, as LaCocque remarks: "The story of Esther is the redemptive sequence of the unfinished business reported in 1 Samuel."[107]

Yitzhak Berger argues that it is Esther who is linked to the ancestry of Saul rather than Mordecai. By overcoming Haman's plot to annihilate the Jewish race, Esther redeems what Saul failed to do. Furthermore, the heroism of Esther also counteracts the theme of Davidic moral superiority in the realm of justice and retribution as depicted in 1 Samuel.[108]

With heroes modeled on Saul rather than David, with no loyalty to the city of Jerusalem, with no intention to return to Judah, the story of Esther proves to be a challenge to those who believe that Jewish destiny is dependent on physical and hereditary links.[109] The echoes and counterechoes between Esther and 1 Samuel coexist on multiple levels.

Joel 2 and Jonah 3: Who knows? Mordecai's famous words to Esther in 4:14, "Who knows whether for such a time like this you have reached royalty?!" have become a sounding board, reverberating through earlier appearances of the phrase in Joel 2:14 and Jonah 3:9. Scholars have understood this rhetorical question in two divergent ways. One is to see it as an indication of faith and the possibility of hope for deliverance. The other is to take it as meaning "no one knows." While in the contexts of Joel and Jonah the same question seems to reflect the possibility of hope, when it appears in Proverbs 24:22 and Ecclesiastes 2:19; 3:21; 6:12, it suggests something else.[110] Jobes, for instance, reads the question "who knows" in Esther 4:14 as depending on Joel 2:14 and involving the act of repentance. Dunne, however, objects to this interpretation by asserting there is a lack of repentance in the context of Esther.[111] Therefore, is "who knows" in Esther an indication of hope or simply a desperate declaration that no one knows?

---

[107]LaCocque, *Esther Regina*.
[108]Yitzhak Berger, "Esther and Benjaminite Royalty: A Study in Inner-biblical Allusion," *JBL* 129, no. 4 (2010): 625-44.
[109]Koller, *Esther in Ancient Jewish Thought*, 53.
[110]See chap. 2.
[111]Jobes, *Esther*, 135; Dunne, *Esther and Her Elusive God*, 51-53.

The answer to that seems to be as cryptic as the absence of God in Esther. The echo to other biblical references of "who knows" is evident, but whether there are true counterechoes remains unclear.

Together, these echoes and counterechoes point to the fact that Esther is to be read as a part of the Hebrew canon. Yet the counterelements suggest that the divergent voice in Esther is also an integral part of Scripture. The tension between the echoes and the counterechoes is not to be lessened or resolved but held in balance.

Esther and the Writings. *Song of Songs: Women, feasts, absence.* As a part of the Megilloth, Esther and Song of Songs share multiple similarities, as described elsewhere in this book. The prominence of women, the Cinderella motif, the ascent of the female character to a royal status, the temple-palace connection, the feasts of Passover and Purim, the motif of absence, and the affiliation with wisdom all bind the two books together. Nonetheless, the two books differ tremendously including in primary genre, historical context, characterization, literary devices, theological and ethical messages. Both books connect canonically to other books in the Hebrew Scripture and form countervoices to those books. As I have argued elsewhere in this book, the motif of absence in these two scrolls offers an alternative perspective to the theology of presence in the rest of the Hebrew Scripture. As regards Old Testament theology, Song of Songs and Esther contribute to a richer profile of God and his involvement in the world where humans live.

Ruth: Esther's counterpart. Scholars have long noticed the similarities between Esther and Ruth. These two books are the only books in the entire Scripture that use women's names as the book titles. Some consider them as bookends to the Megilloth, while others read them as book pairs or parallel texts.[112] Lengthy monographs devoted to the study of the two scrolls are abundant, which demonstrates the scholarly consensus in terms of reading them as a pair or counterparts.[113] Indeed, numerous echoes can be

---

[112]Davis, e.g., considers them bookends to the Megilloth; see Andrew R. Davis, "Ruth and Esther as the Thematic Frame of the Megilloth," in *Megilloth Studies: The Shape of Contemporary Scholarship*, ed. Brad Embry (Sheffield: Sheffield Phoenix, 2016), 17. Goldingay, e.g., reads them as book pairs or parallel texts; see "Hermeneutics," 275-76.

[113]For example, Frederic William Bush, *Ruth, Esther*, WBC 9 (Dallas: Word Books, 1996); Athalya Brenner, ed., *A Feminist Companion to Reading the Bible: Approaches, Methods and Strategies*

found between these two books. Both books center on female protagonists. Both Ruth and Esther ascend from a lowly status to enjoy royal status. Ruth as a Moabite woman carries the stigma of being a "foreign seductress," as described in Numbers 25:1-3 and Proverbs 1–9. She then becomes the wife of Boaz, a Judahite, and the great-grandmother of David. Ruth eventually makes it into the genealogy of Jesus in Matthew 1:5. Esther first appears as an orphan, then ascends to become the queen of Persia. Both characters are first Cinderella figures. Both Ruth and Esther are also bicultural, married to a person of prominence and of a different race. Both characters have their respective older mentors who guide them in their paths. For Ruth it is Naomi, and for Esther it is Mordecai. Both characters also display elements of wisdom. Both Ruth and Esther appear to be wise in their own dealings with their circumstances. Boaz regards Ruth as a "woman of excellence" (Ruth 3:11), reminiscent of the Proverbs 31 woman.[114] As Ruth finds favor (חֵן) in the eyes of Boaz (Ruth 2:13), so does Esther find favor (חֵן) in the eyes of all who see her (Esther 2:15), and in the eyes of the king (Esther 2:17).

Both story lines involve a death threat. In Ruth, a famine occurs in the land, while in Esther there is a genocidal attempt to wipe out the Jewish race. The idea of salvation also emerges from both books. In Ruth, God visits his people and gives them food (Ruth 1:6). By providing Ruth a child, God helps in preserving the family line of Elimelech (Ruth 4:13). In Esther, the courageous actions of Esther ensure the survival of her people. Both the scrolls of Ruth and Esther are a part of the Megilloth and are recited during two Jewish festivals, the feast of Pentecost and the feast of Purim. The similarities between the two books are too many to recount here; I have mentioned only a few of them. Through these similarities, Esther forms recurring echoes to the book of Ruth.

However, Ruth and Esther also exhibit considerable differences. Ruth is a Moabite woman, a Gentile, married to an Israelite. She crosses the border from Moab to Bethlehem. She observes the Mosaic law by proposing to

---

(Sheffield: Sheffield Academic Press, 1997); Brenner, *Feminist Companion to Ruth and Esther*; Anne-Mareike Wetter, *"On Her Account": Reconfiguring Israel in Ruth, Esther, and Judith*, LHBOTS 623 (London: T&T Clark, 2015); Orit Avery, *Liminal Women: Belonging and Otherness in the Books of Ruth and Esther* (Jerusalem: Hartman Institute, 2015).

[114] In the Masoretic Text, the book of Ruth is placed right after Proverbs, suggesting that the compiler considers Ruth to be the woman of excellence referred to in Prov 31.

Boaz as a way to extend Elimelech's family line.[115] Esther is a Jew, married
to a Gentile. She never crosses a geographical border. There is no indication
that she observes the Jewish dietary laws in the Persian palace. Yet the most
obvious difference is the presence and the activity of God. God's activity in
Ruth appears to be behind the scenes, as God provides food for his people
and allows Ruth to become pregnant. His name is mentioned frequently in
the mouths of Ruth, Naomi, and Boaz as well as in the narrator's comments
in Ruth 1:6; 4:13. God's hidden presence is overt in Ruth rather than covert.
By contrast, the name of God or explicit reference to divine activity is completely absent in Esther. God does not appear in the mouths of the characters, even when Mordecai has the chance to use it, for example when he
says obliquely that "deliverance will arise from another quarter" (Esther
4:14). The complete absence of any reference to God in Esther forms the
loudest counterecho to the book of Ruth.

Melton identifies the waiting motif in both books to suggest divine providence. At the same time, she astutely observes that the degree of divine
involvement varies between the books. The means of divine intervention as
well as the time when it occurs are different. She concludes with three statements: "(1) Permanent versus temporary gapping yields less certainty about
divine involvement in Esther, (2) God seems to work through characters in
Ruth versus situations in Esther, and (3) intermittent divine intervention is
possible in Esther as opposed to God's continuous involvement which can
be inferred in Ruth."[116] While her reading accentuates the ambiguity of
divine action in both books, the problem of divine activity in Esther receives more theological discussion than that in Ruth.

Reading Ruth and Esther intertextually, one may take the position of
seeing the hidden hand of God behind the coincidences and the dramatic
reversals in the book of Esther, just like how God works in the story of Ruth.
However, one may also interpret the literary absence of God in Esther as a
critique of the book of Ruth and understand that sometimes God works
behind the scenes to ensure the survival of his chosen people. Other times

---

[115]Although what appears in Ruth is not strictly a Levirate marriage, it is a form of application of
   that law in a local context (see Bush, *Ruth, Esther*, 166-69).
[116]Brittany N. Melton, *Where Is God in the Megilloth? A Dialogue on the Ambiguity of Divine Presence
   and Absence* (Leiden: Brill, 2018), 158-62.

God may leave the fate of his people entirely to the hands of human beings, who will have to act with their best wisdom to do justice and to ensure the salvation of God's people. Both readings are plausible. Again, the tension between two possible but contrasting readings is not to be minimized but honored.

Daniel: Esther's other counterpart. Like the story of Joseph and Esther, the story of Daniel bears striking resemblances to Esther. Both Daniel and Esther are young and beautiful in appearance (Dan 1:4; Esther 2:7). Both of them grow up in the foreign court and eventually rise to prominence, influencing the decisions of kings. Both characters employ wisdom in confronting the kings to do their own bidding (Dan 2:16; Esther 7:3-4). Both Daniel and Esther also risk their lives when disobeying the king's order (Dan 6:10; Esther 4:16). Daniel risks his life by praying to his God, while Esther risks her life by appearing unsummoned before the king.

Both story lines are set in a foreign court, in the context of the exile (Dan 1:2; Esther 2:6). Both kings show favor (חֵן), respectively, to Daniel and Esther, and grant their wishes (Dan 2:46-48; Esther 2:17; 5:3; 7:2). The kings are surrounded by courtiers and advisers. Banquet scenes and drinking parties also appear in both stories (Dan 5:1-12; Esther 1:2-9). When Daniel and Mordecai rise to power, they are endowed with royal clothing of purple (Dan 5:29; Esther 8:15). Villains oppose them and threaten their lives, but both Daniel and Esther emerge as heroes in their stories (Dan 6:4; Esther 3:1-15). Both stories involve establishing laws and decrees (Dan 6:9; Esther 1:19; 2:12; 8:9-10; 9:29). Berlin says the shared motifs and linguistic evidence in these two stories probably suggest they originated in the same period.[117]

At the same time, Daniel and Esther form a contrasting pair. During the exile, Daniel refrains from contaminating himself with the king's food, while Esther assimilates into Persian culture quite successfully. While Daniel gets down on his knees and prayed to God three times a day (Dan 6:10), there is no such religious devotion recorded in Esther, except for her asking the Jews in Shushan to fast for her for three days after she becomes aware of Haman's plot (Esther 4:16). Daniel and his friends are open about who they are and whom they serve (Dan 2:28; 3:16-18), whereas Esther

---

[117]Berlin, *Esther*, xl.

conceals her Jewish identity, as Mordecai commands her to do (Esther 2:10, 20). Koller sums it up well: he says that the Jewish identity in Daniel is overt, whereas the Jewish identity in Esther is covert.[118] Dunne observes, "What becomes apparent is that [we have here a] juxtaposition between two very different responses to life in the pagan palace, and ultimately, to exile."[119] Daniel's piety and resistance to assimilate in the midst of the exilic experience contrast sharply with Esther's lack of religious sensibilities and assimilation into the Persian culture in relatively the same period of time.

Last but not least, God is present with Daniel through his adventures in the palace. Even the Gentile king acknowledges this reality when he issues a decree that all people should tremble and fear before the God of Daniel (Dan 6:20, 26-27). By contrast, the name of God is absent in Esther. Therefore, Esther forms counterechoes to Daniel precisely in the area of personal piety, resistance, and assimilation as well as the presence of God.

Seeing the two stories from an intertextual perspective, the books of Daniel and Esther reflect two quite different responses to divine presence. There was a time in the darkest period of Israel's history in exile when God was present with his people, as demonstrated by Daniel's story. But there was also a time when God was absent, as illustrated by the story of Esther. God's presence and absence are solely dependent on his freedom. This counterecho of Esther marks the book as an invaluable source of divine mystery. The tension between divine presence and absence in exile lingers.

Ezra and Nehemiah: Esther as a postexilic anomaly. Ezra, Nehemiah, and Esther occur in the postexilic context, where the temple in Jerusalem has been destroyed and God's people have been carried into exile in Babylon and then Persia against their will. All three books are considered to belong to the historical corpus of Hebrew Scripture. The close canonical distance of Esther to Ezra-Nehemiah reflects this understanding. In both Jewish and Christian traditions, Ezra and Nehemiah are considered as one composite book. This is shown by the Tanakh's arrangement of the material as one book, namely, Ezra-Nehemiah. In the Christian canon, the two books, though separated into two documents, are back to back in the

---

[118]Koller, *Esther in Ancient Jewish Thought*, 65.
[119]Dunne, *Esther and Her Elusive God*, 124.

chronological order. Many commentaries and monographs also place the two books together as one entity.[120] Sternberg's structural-canonical understanding places the book of Esther in the "national-historical" realm, along with Lamentations, Daniel, Ezra-Nehemiah, and Chronicles, pointing to the way the nation moves back to God, from sorrow to joy.[121] This theme of restoration, however, does not occur in Esther.

The internal evidence reveals the close affinity and similarities between Ezra and Nehemiah. For example, both books reflect a time of restoration in which the Jewish people desire to return to Judah in order to rebuild the temple and their country. Both books center on a male character, Ezra and Nehemiah, and the books are named after them. While Ezra attempts to rebuild the people of God by rebuilding the temple and by stressing the significance of the Torah to the identity of God's people, Nehemiah strives to rebuild the wall of Jerusalem as a way to ensure the well-being of his people. Both books end in Judah with a strong message about preserving the holiness of God's people by condemning interracial marriage, which was prevalent during this time. In addition, resistance to assimilation forms a major thrust of both books. In both books, God's people encounter opposition from non-Jewish groups. Both books include first-person memoirs (Ezra 7:27-28; 8:1-34; 9:1-15; Neh 1:1-7:5; 12-13) and various name lists (Ezra 2; Neh 7:5-73; 11:1-26).

In Ezra-Nehemiah, God is present. Though he does not speak directly to his servants or perform miraculous actions, his name appears constantly in the mouths of Ezra and Nehemiah. Mark McEntire researches the presence of God in Ezra-Nehemiah and asserts that divine behavior in these two books is subtle and indirect. God is the subject of about 103 verbal statements in Ezra-Nehemiah, 38 of which describe God's actions or potential actions. These verbs include "God delivers" (Ezra 8:31), "God gives" (Ezra 1:2; 9:8), "God stirred up" (Ezra 1:1), "God charged" (Ezra 1:2), "Our God will fight for us" (Neh 4:20), and "God put into my heart" (Neh 2:12; 7:5).

---

[120]To name a few: Joseph Blenkinsopp, *Ezra-Nehemiah: A Commentary*, OTL (Philadelphia: Westminster, 1988); Mark A. Throntveit, *Ezra-Nehemiah*, Interpretation (Louisville, KY: John Knox, 1989); Matthew Levering, *Ezra-Nehemiah* (Grand Rapids, MI: Brazos, 2007); James M. Hamilton Jr., *Exalting Jesus in Ezra-Nehemiah*, Christ-Centered Exposition (Nashville: B&H, 2014); Donna Laird, *Negotiating Power in Ezra-Nehemiah* (Atlanta: SBL Press, 2016).

[121]Steinberg and Stone, *Shape of the Writings*, 153.

Furthermore, in Ezra-Nehemiah, God's actions in Israel's history are repeatedly mentioned both in and beyond Nehemiah 9:6-37. By evoking these divine actions through Israel's history, McEntire suggests that Nehemiah seems to compare and question the lack of involvement of God in the present moment. He then asks: "Has God disappeared, diminished or matured?"[122] Compared to the early history of God in Exodus, God's presence and actions in Ezra and Nehemiah seem to retreat to the background and become visible only in the faith statements and prayers of Ezra and Nehemiah. Yet when juxtaposed with Esther, this indirect presence of God renders Esther even more of an anomaly.

Contrary to Ezra-Nehemiah, the book of Esther is set in the Persian court rather than Judah. Esther is the only book in the Bible whose context is the Jewish diaspora in Persia. There is no evidence in Esther to suggest that the Judahites desire to return to Judah, to rebuild the temple, to observe the Mosaic law, or to reconnect with their God in worship. The concept of the covenant, the significance of Israel's history and creedal statements, resistance to assimilation into the Gentile world, the religious act of praying, and opposition against interracial marriage all vanish in the pages of Esther. Both Mordecai and Esther seem well adjusted to life at the court. Mordecai even commands Esther to hide her Jewish identity (Esther 2:10, 20). Esther herself marries a Gentile king. There is no hint of evidence to suggest they retain Jewish dietary laws or show any intention of returning to Jerusalem. No wonder some consider Esther and Mordecai to be "compromisers."[123] The secularity of the book is "as good as it can get." Moreover, Mordecai is a Benjaminite who claims to be a Jew rather than from the tribe of Judah, a perceived "legitimate Jew."[124] The central locale of the story is Shushan, as opposed to Jerusalem. Also, the Gentile palace replaces the temple as the focus of the story. Most baffling of all is of course the lack of any explicit reference to God or his name.

---

[122]Mark McEntire, *Portraits of a Mature God: Choices in Old Testament Theology* (Minneapolis: Fortress, 2013), 180-81, 184-87.

[123]These compromises include interracial marriage, hiding one's Jewish identity, and not expecting help from God (Dunne, *Esther and Her Elusive God*, 15-67). See also Ronald W. Pierce, "The Politics of Esther and Mordecai: Courage or Compromise?," *Bulletin for Biblical Research* 2 (1992): 75-89.

[124]Koller points out that to introduce Mordecai as a Jew (Jehudi) is to assert that those in Jerusalem do not have a monopoly on the term. See Koller, *Esther in Ancient Jewish Thought*, 49.

Timothy Laniak casts the centrality of the book of Esther as "volkcentrism." He argues that the book reframes postexilic Judaism by reminding
the Jewish people that Israel is a people first, and then the place; by creating
new Torah through the annual reenactment of Purim; by reconfiguring
Natocentric Judaism by positioning Esther as both a countercharacter as
well as one who follows the rules of patriarchy; and by reframing Yahweh-
centric Judaism by excluding the name of God in the text. At the end,
Laniak raises a pertinent question that expresses both theological ambiguity
and theological possibility: "Is it possible that this 'secular' book, by
deliberate indirection, understatement, 'implicity' and intertextuality,
provides an unanticipated perspective on God that ultimately supports
traditional theology?"[125]

Although closely associated with Ezra-Nehemiah, the book of Esther is
an anomaly and thus serves as a counterecho to Ezra-Nehemiah in terms
of postexilic themes in general and divine presence in particular. Esther's
shared similarities with Ezra-Nehemiah fade in comparison with its distinctiveness in both contents and theology to Ezra-Nehemiah.

Conclusion on Esther and the Hebrew Scripture. Esther forms numerous
echoes and counterechoes with the three divisions of the Hebrew Scripture.
By functioning as an echo chamber, reminiscent of the Song of Songs,
Esther is intended to be read as Scripture. Yet canonically speaking, although Esther resonates with other books in the Writings, such as Song of
Songs, Ruth, Daniel, and Ezra-Nehemiah, its dissonances regarding the
absence of God are simply too strong to be overlooked.[126] By differentiating
itself, especially in the motif of the absence of God, Esther offers a critique,
a challenge, and a countervoice to the motifs in other books of the sacred
Scripture. In this way, it asserts a voice of its own, shouting out loud to the

---

[125]Timothy S. Laniak, "Esther's *Volkcentrism* and the Reframing of Post-exilic Judaism," in *The Book of Esther in Modern Research*, ed. Sidnie White Crawford and Leonard J. Greenspoon, JSOTSup 380 (New York: T&T Clark, 2003), 77-90.

[126]Goswell argues that the absence of God's name in Esther is the author's deliberate effort to present a theology that highlights human responsibility in a non-Christian environment. See Gregory R. Goswell, "Keeping God out of the Book of Esther," *Evangelical Quarterly* 82, no. 2 (2010): 99-110. Beal considers Esther as a fracture in the biblical canon. It interrogates biblical authority from within, and it crosses boundaries on multiple levels. See Timothy K. Beal, *The Book of Hiding: Gender, Ethnicity, Annihilation, and Esther* (London: Routledge, 1997), 118-19, 123.

audience that yes, God is present in history, but there are also times when God is absent, times when God's people need to take matters into their own hands and act on their own wisdom to do justice and ensure the survival of God's people.

CANON: IN THE ABSENCE OF GOD

Both Song of Songs and Esther function as sounding boards, echoing various motifs that occur across the three divisions of the Hebrew Scripture. At the same time, their respective tunes vary from the expected norm as reflected in other books of the canon. On the one hand, these echoes connect the two books with the rest of the Scripture and thus position the two books as canonical, intending the audience to read them as such. On the other hand, the counterechoes provide an alternative voice, creating a disharmonic symphony. These dissonances in the scriptural symphony create tension with the resonances and thus force the audience to rethink Scripture and the God it reveals.

The literary absence of God in Song of Songs and Esther suggests that God does not always conform to the expectations of the normal pattern of Scripture, such as the books of Exodus and Daniel. God does not always speak to his people or disclose his plans to human beings, as when God sings the vineyard song to Israel or when God commands Saul to destroy the Amalekites. Sometimes, God is visible, vocal, and performs miracles. At other times, he lays low and prefers to work through human beings, as in the book of Ruth. At still other times, God remains incomprehensible and distant, as in Ecclesiastes. At yet other times, he appears to be silent, invisible, and beyond the grasp of human intellect. In terms of presence and absence, God reserves his sovereign freedom. While the visible presence of God makes him "real" from the perspective of the reader, his invisible presence creates doubt, unease, and puzzlement in the human experience of the divine. Therefore, by including Song of Songs and Esther in the Hebrew Scripture, the real, lived experience of readers, which encompasses both divine presence and absence, finds its reality in Scripture and affirms that there are times when human beings may experience divine absence. It is times like these that compel us to rethink God, ourselves, our world, and our relationship with God. It is also times like these that open us up to honest conversations with an incomprehensible God.

Hence, the absence of God creates an opportunity for reflection, contemplation, and dialogue with God. This is a time of journey upward toward God, to inquire of him: "Where are you, God?" "What are you doing in this particular situation?" "How do you want me to respond?" "What should I do?" At the same time, this is also a time of journey inward, to inquire of ourselves: "Who am I in relation to God?" "Can I still trust this God when I do not even perceive or sense his presence?" "How may I discern God's presence through my circumstances and current events?"

Reading Song of Songs and Esther canonically enables us to regard divine absence as a reality in the human realm. This reality also appears in the psalmist's experience: "My God, my God, why have You forsaken me?" (Ps 22:1), as well as in the mouth of Jesus on the cross (Mt 27:46; Mk 15:34).[127] What is remarkable about this divine forsakenness is that even in these darkest moments of divine absence, God's will is fulfilled. As Henri Nouwen observes: "Where God's absence was most loudly expressed, God's presence was most profoundly revealed. The mystery of God's presence therefore can be touched only by a deep awareness of God's absence."[128]

In this regard, God's absence is not the end. Rather, his presence is. Through his absence, we may sense his presence—the accomplishment of his divine will.

In times when God is absent, we may also find his presence in unexpected places as well as in astonishing and subtle ways. For instance, God's presence permeates creation. It can be found in the garden, in his cosmic temple, in trees, plants, flowers, and animals. God's presence can be sensed through the love between a man and a woman, which is as strong as death. God's presence can also be found in human wisdom, courage, goodness, and justice as well as in one's sacrifice for the benefit of another. God's presence also occurs in various chance events and in the realm of mystery.

---

[127]Zornberg notes the midrash evidence about Esther's prayer. In the midst of divine abandonment, Esther prays, "My God, my God! Why have you abandoned me?" Avivah Gottlieb Zornberg, *The Murmuring Deep: Reflections on the Biblical Unconscious* (New York: Schocken Books, 2009), 125.

[128]Henri J. M. Nouwen with Michael J. Christensen and Rebecca J. Laird, *Spiritual Direction: Wisdom for the Long Walk of Faith*, repr. (New York: HarperOne, 2015), 80.

Thus, divine presence and absence are not mutually exclusive but are often held in creative tension.

Last but not least, reading Song of Songs and Esther canonically points to the fact that even though God is not overtly present in these two books, he is present everywhere in the rest of the Scripture. The literary absence of God in these two books reminds us that although there are times when we may not sense his presence, through his presence in other books and other times we may find hope for his past and future presence. Divine absence does not have the final word in the Scripture. Divine presence does.

CONCLUSION

AS A PART OF THE COLLECTION OF THE MEGILLOTH, Song of Songs and Esther are commonly associated with the five scrolls and the annual Jewish feasts. However, these two books also stand out as the only two books in the biblical canon that never refer explicitly to God. In this monograph, I have investigated, reflected on, and juxtaposed the theology of absence in these two books in order to search for its theological significance, particularly its place in Old Testament theology, the books' interconnectedness, and the implications of divine absence in believers' lives.

As we have seen, the absence of any explicit reference to God's name does not preclude one from doing theological discourse or inquiring into theological matters. On the contrary, its absence compels the reader to rethink the nature of God and his activities in the world. The normative mode of divine presence and activity in the early books of the Hebrew Scripture is countered by the absence and inactivity of God in Song of Songs and Esther. Both modes are an integral part of Scripture, and both reflect the nature of God and the dynamics of divine-human relationship. There are times when God is actively present. There are other times when God is covertly present. There are still other times when God seems completely absent or is present only in silence. Placing Song of Songs and Esther front and center in Old Testament theology yields a portrait of a God who neither works according to human beings' expectations nor conforms to his own pattern of presence in the past. In terms of presence and absence, God has absolute freedom.

As these books are a part of the Megilloth and the Writings, the way in which God works in these two books differs from that of the Torah and the Prophets. God's presence is not confined to the dominant model, as in

Exodus. Rather, God works mysteriously. Sometimes he works behind the scenes, and other times he refrains from being visible to the human eye. At still other times, he is simply absent. Therefore, these two scrolls complement and supplement what the rest of the biblical canon lacks. An Old Testament theology without Song of Songs and Esther would obscure a fuller picture of who God is and how human beings relate to him.

The question of the absence of God involves time, space, and relationship. Divine presence is experienced in the human consciousness of time. Outside the realm of time, divine presence becomes unintelligible and only appears in philosophical abstraction. Divine presence is also a matter of space. When God is said to be present, he has to be sensed and perceived at a particular time and space. When the male lover is absent in Song of Songs 5, the female protagonist, in dire agony, attempts to search for him. His absence is perceived in the context of time and space of the human realm. In Esther, the absence of the name of God parallels the male lover's absence in the Song. In these scenarios, on the one hand, the absence of the other creates a relational crisis. On the other hand, the desire to seek the one who is absent intensifies. In times of divine absence, God is present in the minds of those who desire his presence. Therefore, a theology of presence in absence emerges in Song of Songs and Esther, albeit in different ways and varied degrees.

The Edenic temple setting in Song of Songs evokes the presence of God in the garden. The erotic love between the two lovers in the garden, which is as strong as death, presents an alternative way to comprehend the love of God. The intertextual allusions between the Persian palace and the tabernacle contribute another aspect of the theology of absence. While the decorations and the descriptions of the Persian palace bear striking resemblances to the descriptions of the tabernacle, the conspicuous absence of the temple causes dissonance in readers' mind. If the temple symbolizes divine presence, the absence of it suggests divine absence. Theologically, this absence can be traced back to the sin of the preexilic Israelite community, to whom God said he would hide his face (Deut 31:17). However, this position oversimplifies the matter. Does the diasporic Jewish community deserve to be wiped out if they assimilate to the dominant Gentile culture without adhering to Mosaic law? The answer is no. The close resemblance of Mordecai's clothing to the Israelite priestly garment points to a theological possibility that God's presence is with his people. At the same time, it also suggests theological ambiguity: Is Mordecai's ascension aided by the hidden hand of God, or can it all be credited to human endeavor? Through this theological ambiguity, the story of Esther forms a conversation with the rest of the canon and directs readers' attention to divine incomprehensibility.

The liturgical arrangement of Song of Songs and Esther makes the two scrolls bookends of the Megilloth, with Passover launching the year and Purim ending it. These two festivals are celebrated back to back, pointing to the deliverance of God's people. While God is absent in these two books, by associating the books with the two Jewish feasts, the Jewish faith community receives these two books as a part of their religious tradition. In the absence of God, the faith community can look back for the presence of God in history and look forward to his presence in the future. The cycle of the liturgical calendar, which includes both the presence and the absence of God, testifies to the reality of the lived experience of believers, for whom oftentimes God's presence and absence alternate, but overall his presence prevails over his absence.

Canonically, Song of Songs and Esther resonate with the tripartite division of the Hebrew Scripture, and thus they are intended to be read as Scripture. At the same time, they critique and counter the motifs in the rest of the canon through their dissonances. This countering voice situates the two scrolls as indispensable in articulating a canonical reading of divine presence and absence. Reading Song of Songs and Esther canonically points to the fact that even though God is not present in these two books, he is present elsewhere in the rest of the Scripture. The absence of God in these two books reminds us that although there are times when we may not sense his presence, through his presence in other books and times we may find hope for his past and future presence. Reading resonance and dissonance together enriches our understanding of God and his involvement in human experience, especially when we live in between his presence and absence.

HOW DO WE THINK OF GOD WHEN HE IS
ABSENT OR PERCEIVED TO BE ABSENT?

This book has shown that the theology of the absence of God is an integral part of Scripture and ought not to be relegated to obscurity or ignored in Old Testament theology. Understanding the absence of God paints a fuller picture of who God is, which challenges the reductionist notion of divine presence. The realization and the acknowledgment of divine absence in human history (such as in the Holocaust, the Nanking massacre, the Rohingya genocide, numerous mass shootings in recent US history, and natural disasters) and in the lived experience of human beings (death of loved ones, depression, poverty, divorce, oppression, unemployment, all forms of abuse and injustice, as well as COVID-19) helps believers align Scripture with reality. Therefore, divine absence is a theological necessity. The experience of the absence of God creates doubt and despair, but it also elicits faith and prayer. The absence of God forces us to redefine his presence. God's presence may not be manifested in his action, words, or the narrator's evaluation. Rather, through Song of Songs and Esther, God's presence may be found through his creation, through nature, garden, animals, plants, streams, fountains, and love that is as strong as death. In Esther, God's presence can be found in the miraculous merging of times, in the victory of God's people over their enemies. Even if we take God as completely absent in Esther, we may find his presence elsewhere in Scripture through a canonical reading of the text. As Song of Songs and Esther are associated with wisdom, the search for order in the world is manifested in the search for the beloved (or the Other) in his elusive presence and the search for justice in an unjust world.

WHAT DO WE DO WHEN GOD IS SILENT OR HIDDEN?

For believers, experiencing an intimate relationship with God is an innate desire, so the experience of the absence of God or a silent God is excruciating. Based on a metaphorical reading of the Song of Songs and a literal reading of Esther, we realize that experiencing divine absence is a part of the faith journey. There are times now and there will be times in the future when we do not sense the presence of God. We do not or will not know for certain whether God is involved in the world and in our lives. We may be skeptical and wondering whether God is still in control of human history, especially when disaster strikes or when evil emerges or in the midst of the COVID-19 pandemic. Such times should draw us to prayer, as the psalmists do. This is a time to ask God honest questions: "How long will you forget me?" "Where are you?" "Are you there?" "Do you see what is going on with my life?" "Why do you allow this to happen?" Times of divine absence are also opportunities to express to God our feelings of frustration or pain: "God, I cannot bear it anymore." "God, do you see me?" "God, I am suffering." Christian faith is a dialogic faith. Through prayer and interaction with God, we may find the dynamics of a Christian journey that involves doubt, protest, lament, faith, and hope. In other words, when we sense God's silence, we do not keep silent. We voice our thoughts to him and we take action using the best of our knowledge to enact change and to maintain order as much as we are able.

Second, when we experience divine absence, it is time to go out and see God's creation. God's presence is inherently bound up with his creation. "The heavens are telling of the glory of God; And their expanse is declaring the work of His hands" (Ps 19:1). The setting for love in the Song of Songs is within the garden. The garden is where love blossoms. Along with garden imagery, there is also a stream, fountain, water, and the natural world of flora and fauna. When we see the majestic mountains, the clear river streams, the bubbling fountains, the enchanting flowers, trees and plants, and various kinds of animals, they evoke their maker—the creator God. Connecting with nature enables one to sense God's infusing presence in the world.

Third, in the absence of God, his presence can be sensed through love, both the erotic love between human beings, as in the Song of Songs, and the loyal love (חֶסֶד) between humans that Esther models to her Jewish people. As God is love, whenever there is love, there is God's presence (1 Jn 4:16). In the human world, love is God incarnate. In times of divine absence, it is important to be connected with a loving human being or a loving human community. It is in the context of love that the presence of God resides.

By including the Song of Songs and Esther in the biblical canon, Scripture bears witness to the multifaceted as well as the mysterious nature of God. God is both present and absent, active and passive, vocal and silent, accessible and unreachable. The reality of divine absence opens up opportunities for honest dialogue with God and with oneself. Recall the psalmist who in his most desperate and agonizing moment utters, "My God, my God, why have You forsaken me?" (Ps 22:1). Reflecting on this prayer, Henri Nouwen suggests,

> In prayer and meditation, God's presence is never separated from God's absence, and God's absence is never separated from God's presence in the heart. The presence of God is so much beyond the human experience of being near to another that it quite easily is misperceived as absence. The absence of God, on the one hand, is often so deeply felt that it leads to a new sense of God's presence.[1]

God's presence and absence are integrally connected and sometimes, more often than not, coexist harmoniously. Although this book ends here, its implications and ramifications for the theological quest for divine presence will continue, as will the human response to divine absence. In this sense, reading Song of Songs and Esther in light of divine absence is not just an intellectual pursuit but also an integral part of spiritual journey, until the day we behold the beauty of the Lord and inquire in his temple about all the grandeurs and mysteries of the divine (Ps 27:4). For those who seek to find God in their own lives, the path to comprehend the intricacies of the dynamic between God's presence and absence will go on.

---

[1]Henri Nouwen with Michael J. Christensen and Rebecca J. Laird, *Spiritual Direction: Wisdom for the Long Walk of Faith* (New York: Harper One, 2006), 79.

BIBLIOGRAPHY

Abrams, M. H. *A Glossary of Literary Terms*. 4th ed. New York: Holt, Rinehart and Winston, 1981.

Ackroyd, P. R. "Two Hebrew Notes." *Annual of the Swedish Theological Institute* 5 (1966–1967): 82-86.

Adelman, Rachel E. *The Female Ruse: Women's Deception and Divine Sanction in the Hebrew Bible*. HBM 74. Sheffield: Sheffield Phoenix, 2015.

Al-Fayyumi, Saadiah Ben Joseph. *The Book of Theodicy: Translation and Commentary on the Book of Job*. Translated by L. E. Goodman. New Haven, CT: Yale University Press, 1988.

Alexander, Philip S. "Jewish Aramaic Translations of Hebrew Scriptures." Pages 217-53 in *Mikra: Text, Translation, Reading and Interpretation of the Hebrew Bible in Ancient Judaism and Early Christianity*. Peabody, MA: Hendrickson, 2004.

———. *The Targum of Canticles: Translated with a Critical Introduction, Apparatus, and Notes*. Aramaic Bible 17A. Collegeville, MN: Liturgical Press, 2003.

———. "Tradition and Originality in the Targum of the Song of Songs." Pages 318-39 in *The Aramaic Bible: Targums in Their Historical Context*. JSOTSup 166. Sheffield: Sheffield Academic Press, 1994.

———. "'Translation and Midrash Completely Fused Together?' The Form of the Targums to Canticles, Lamentations and Qohelet." *Aramaic Studies* 9, no. 1 (2011): 83-99.

Alter, Robert. *The Art of Biblical Poetry*. New York: Basic Books, 1985.

Anderson, Bernhard W. *Contours of Old Testament Theology*. Minneapolis: Fortress, 1999.

Andruska, J. L. *Wise and Foolish Love in the Song of Songs*. Oudestamentische Studiën 75. Leiden: Brill, 2019.

Ansberry, Christopher B. "Wisdom and Biblical Theology." Pages 174-93 in *Interpreting Old Testament Wisdom Literature*, edited by David G. Firth and Lindsay Wilson. Downers Grove, IL: IVP Academic, 2017.

Arbel, Daphna V. "'My Vineyard, My Very Own, Is for Myself.'" Pages 90-101 in *The Feminist Companion to the Song of Songs*, edited by Athalya Brenner and Carole R. Fontaine. FCB. Sheffield: Sheffield Academic Press, 2000.

Archer, Gleason. *Introduction to the Old Testament*. Chicago: Moody, 1964.

Assis, Eliyahu. *Flashes of Fire: A Literary Analysis of the Song of Songs*. LHBOTS 503. New York: T&T Clark, 2009.

Avery, Orit. *Liminal Women: Belonging and Otherness in the Books of Ruth and Esther*. Jerusalem: Hartman Institute, 2015.

Avery-Peck, Alan J. "Midrash and Exegesis: Insights from Genesis Rabbah on the Binding of Isaac." Pages 441-57 in *Method Matters: Essays on the Interpretation of the Hebrew Bible in Honor of David L. Petersen*, edited by Joel M. LeMon and Kent Harold Richards. Atlanta: Society of Biblical Literature, 2009.

Balentine, Samuel E. *The Hidden God: The Hiding of the Face of God in the Old Testament*. Oxford Theological Monographs. Oxford: Oxford University Press, 1983.

Bar-Efrat, Shimon. *Narrative Art in the Bible*. London: T&T Clark, 1989.

Bauckham, Richard. *The Bible in Politics: How to Read the Bible Politically*. Louisville, KY: Westminster John Knox, 1989.

Baumann, Gerlinde. *Love and Violence: Marriage as Metaphor for the Relationship Between YHWH and Israel in the Prophetic Books*. Translated by Linda M. Malony. Collegeville, MN: Liturgical Press, 2003.

Beal, Timothy K. *The Book of Hiding: Gender, Ethnicity, Annihilation, and Esther*. London: Routledge, 1991.

———. *Esther*. Berit Olam. Collegeville, MN: Liturgical Press, 1999.

Beale, G. K. *The Temple and the Church's Mission: A Biblical Theology of the Dwelling Place of God*. Downers Grove, IL: InterVarsity Press, 2004.

Beaton, R. "Song of Songs 3: History of Interpretation." *DOTWPW* 760-69.

Bechtel, Carol M. *Esther*. Interpretation. Louisville, KY: Westminster John Knox, 2002.

Belcher, Richard P., Jr. *Finding Favor in the Sight of God: A Theology of Wisdom Literature*. NSBT 46. Downers Grove, IL: IVP Academic, 2018.

Beller, David. "A Theology of the Book of Esther." *ResQ* (1997): 1-15.

Berg, Sandra Beth. *The Book of Esther: Motifs, Themes, and Structure*. Society of Biblical Literature Dissertation Series 44. Missoula, MT: Scholars Press, 1979.

Bergant, Dianne. "An Anthropological Approach to Biblical Interpretation: The Passover Supper in Exodus 12:1-20 as a Case Study." *Semeia* 67 (1994): 43-62.

Berger, Yitzhak. "Esther and Benjaminite Royalty: A Study in Inner-biblical Allusion." *JBL* 129, no. 4 (2010): 625-44.

Berlin, Adele. *Esther: The Traditional Hebrew Text with the New JPS Translation*. JPS Bible Commentary. Philadelphia: Jewish Publication Society, 2001.

————. *Poetics and Interpretation of Biblical Narrative*. Winona Lake, IN: Eisenbrauns, 1994.

Black, Fiona C. "Nocturnal Egression: Exploring Some Margins of the Song of Songs." Pages 93-104 in *Postmodern Interpretation of the Bible: A Reader*, edited by A. K. M. Adam. St. Louis: Chalice, 2001.

Bland, David. "God's Activity as Reflected in the Books of Ruth and Esther." *ResQ* 24 (1981): 129-41.

Blenkinsopp, Joseph. *Ezra-Nehemiah: A Commentary*. OTL. Philadelphia: Westminster, 1988.

Bloch, Ariel, and Chana Bloch. *The Song of Songs*. New York: Random House, 1995.

Block, Daniel I. "Divine Abandonment: Ezekiel's Adaptation of an Ancient Near Eastern Motif." Pages 15-42 in *The Book of Ezekiel: Theological and Anthropological Perspectives*, edited by Margaret S. Odell and John T. Strong. Atlanta: Society of Biblical Literature, 2000.

Blumenthal, David R. "Where God Is Not: The Book of Esther and the Song of Songs." *Judaism* 44, no. 1 (1995): 81-92.

Boyarin, Daniel. *Intertextuality and the Reading of Midrash*. Bloomington: Indiana University Press, 1990.

Brady, Christian M. M. "The Use of the Eschatological Lists Within the Targumim of the Megilloth." *JSJ* 40 (2009): 493-509.

Brenner, Athalya, ed. *A Feminist Companion to Reading the Bible: Approaches, Methods and Strategies*. FCB. Sheffield: Sheffield Academic Press, 1997.

————, ed. *A Feminist Companion to Ruth and Esther*. FCB. Sheffield: Sheffield Academic Press, 1999.

————, ed. *A Feminist Companion to the Song of Songs*. FCB. Sheffield: Sheffield Academic Press, 1993.

Brenner, Athalya, and Carole R. Fontaine, eds. *A Feminist Companion to the Latter Prophets*. FCB 8. Sheffield: Sheffield Academic Press, 1995.

————, eds. *Feminist Companion to the Song of Songs*. FCB 2/6. Sheffield: Sheffield Academic Press, 2000.

Brown, William P. *The Seven Pillars of Creation: The Bible, Science, and the Ecology of Wonder*. Oxford: Oxford University Press, 2010.

————. "Theological Interpretation: A Proposal." Pages 387-405 in *Method Matters: Essays on the Interpretation of the Hebrew Bible in Honor of David L. Petersen*, edited by Joel M. LeMon and Kent Harold Richards. Atlanta: Society of Biblical Literature, 2009.

————. *Wisdom's Wonder: Character, Creation, and Crisis in the Bible's Wisdom Literature*. Grand Rapids, MI: Eerdmans, 2014.

Brueggemann, Walter. "The Costly Loss of Lament." *JSOT* 36 (1986): 57-71.

———. *Old Testament Theology: Essays on Structure, Theme, and Text.* Edited by Patrick D. Miller. Minneapolis: Fortress, 1992.

———. *Old Testament Theology: An Introduction.* Nashville: Abingdon, 2008.

———. "Texts That Linger, Not Yet Overcome." Pages 21-41 in *Shall Not the Judge of All the Earth Do What Is Right? Studies on the Nature of God in Tribute to James L. Crenshaw*, edited by David Penchansky and Paul L. Redditt. Winona Lake, IN: Eisenbrauns, 2000.

———. *Theology of the Old Testament: Testimony, Dispute, Advocacy.* Minneapolis: Fortress, 1997.

———. *An Unsettling God: The Heart of the Hebrew Bible.* Minneapolis: Fortress, 2009.

Bundvad, Mette. *Time in the Book of Ecclesiastes.* Oxford: Oxford University Press, 2015.

Burnett, Joel S. "The Question of Divine Absence in Israelite and West Semitic Religion." *CBQ* 67 (2005): 215-35.

———. *Where Is God? Divine Absence in the Hebrew Bible.* Minneapolis: Fortress, 2010.

Busatta, S. "The Perception of Color." *Antrocom Online Journal of Anthropology* 10, no. 2 (2014): 317-19.

Bush, Frederic William. *Ruth, Esther.* WBC 9. Dallas: Word Books, 1996.

Butting, Klara. "Esther: A New Interpretation of the Joseph Story in the Fight Against Anti-Semitism and Sexism." Pages 239-48 in *A Feminist Companion to Ruth and Esther*, edited by Athalya Brenner, FCB 2/3. Sheffield: Sheffield Academic Press, 1999.

———. "Go Your Way: Women Rewrite the Scriptures (Song of Songs 2:8-14)." Pages 142-51 in *The Feminist Companion to the Song of Songs*, edited by Athalya Brenner and Carole R. Fontaine, FCB 2/6. Sheffield: Sheffield Academic Press, 2000.

Carr, David McLain. *The Erotic Word: Sexuality, Spirituality, and the Bible.* New York: Oxford University Press, 2005.

Carr, G. Lloyd. *The Song of Solomon.* Tyndale Old Testament Commentaries 19. Downers Grove, IL: InterVarsity Press, 1984.

Carruthers, Jo. *Esther Through the Centuries.* Malden, MA: Blackwell, 2008.

Childs, Brevard S. *Introduction to the Old Testament as Scripture.* Philadelphia: Fortress, 1979.

Chisholm, Robert, Jr. *From Exegesis to Exposition: A Practical Guide to Using Biblical Hebrew.* Grand Rapids, MI: Baker Books, 1998.

Clarke, Rosalind. "Seeking Wisdom in the Song of Songs." Pages 100-112 in *Interpreting Old Testament Wisdom Literature*, edited by David G. Firth and Lindsay Wilson. Downers Grove, IL: IVP Academic, 2017.

Clifford, Richard J. *The Wisdom Literature*. Interpreting Biblical Texts. Nashville: Abingdon, 1998.

Clines, D. J. A. *The Esther Scroll: The Story of the Story*. JSOTSup 30. Sheffield: University of Sheffield Press, 1984.

———. *Ezra, Nehemiah, Esther*. New Century Bible Commentary. Grand Rapids, MI: Eerdmans, 1984.

———. "Quarter Days Gone: Job 24 and the Absence of God." Pages 242-58 in *God in the Fray: A Tribute to Walter Brueggemann*, edited by Tod Linafelt and Timothy K. Beal. Minneapolis: Fortress, 1998.

———. "Reading Esther from Left to Right: Contemporary Strategies for Reading a Biblical Text." Pages 31-52 in *The Bible in Three Dimensions: Essays in Celebration of Forty Years of Biblical Studies in the University of Sheffield*. Sheffield: University of Sheffield Press, 1990.

———. "Why Is There a Song of Songs and What Does It Do to You if You Read It?" *Jian Dao* 1 (1994): 3-27.

Cohen, Gerson D. "The Song of Songs and the Jewish Religious Mentality." Pages 1-17 in *Studies in the Variety of Rabbinic Cultures*, edited by Gerson D. Cohen. Philadelphia: Jewish Publication Society, 1991.

Craig, Kenneth. *Reading Esther: A Case for the Literary Carnivalesque*. Louisville, KY: Westminster John Knox, 1995.

Crawford, Sidnie White. "Esther: A Feminine Model for Jewish Diaspora." Pages 161-77 in *Gender and Difference in Ancient Israel*, edited by Peggy Lynne Day. Minneapolis: Fortress, 1989.

Crenshaw, James L. "The Expression MÎ YÔDĒAʿ In the Hebrew Bible." *VT* 26 (1986): 279-85.

———. "In Search of Divine Presence: Some Remarks Preliminary to a Theology of Wisdom." *Review and Expositor* 74, no. 3 (1977): 353-69.

———. "Method in Determining Wisdom Influence upon Historical Literature." *JBL* 88, no. 2 (1969): 129-42.

———. *Old Testament Wisdom: An Introduction*. 3rd ed. Louisville, KY: Westminster John Knox, 2010.

———. *Reading Job: A Literary and Theological Commentary*. Macon, GA: Smyth & Helwys, 2011.

———. *Sipping from the Cup of Wisdom*. Vol 1. Macon, GA: Smyth & Helwys, 2017.

Currie, Mark. *About Time: Narrative, Fiction, and the Philosophy of Time*. Edinburgh: University of Edinburgh Press, 2007.

Dalferth, Ingolf U. "God, Time, and Orientation: 'Presence' and 'Absence' in Religious and Everyday Discourse." Pages 1-20 in *The Presence and Absence of God:*

Claremont Studies in the Philosophy of Religion, Conference 2008, edited by Ingolf U. Dalferth, RPT 42. Tübingen: Mohr Siebeck, 2009.

Davidson, Richard M. "Theology of Sexuality in the Song of Songs: Return to Eden." *Andrews University Seminary Studies* 27 (1989): 1-12.

Davis, Andrew R. "Ruth and Esther as the Thematic Frame of the Megilloth." Pages 7-19 in *Megilloth Studies: The Shape of Contemporary Scholarship*, edited by Brad Embry. Sheffield: Sheffield Phoenix, 2016.

Davis, Ellen F. "Losing a Friend: The Loss of the Old Testament to the Church." *Pro Ecclesia* 9, no. 1 (2000): 73-84.

———. *Proverbs, Ecclesiastes, and the Song of Songs*. WBC. Louisville, KY: Westminster John Knox, 2000.

———. "Reading the Song Iconographically." Pages 172-84 in *Scrolls of Love: Ruth and the Song of Songs*, edited by Peter S. Hawkins and Lesleigh Cushing Stahlberg. New York: Fordham University Press, 2006.

———. "Romance of the Land in the Song of Songs." *Anglican Theological Review* 80, no. 4 (1998): 533-46.

———. *Swallowing the Scroll: Textuality and the Dynamics of Discourse in Ezekiel's Prophecy*. JSOTSup 78. Sheffield: Sheffield Academic Press, 1989.

Davis, Stephen T. "God as Present and God as Absent." Pages 147-60 in *The Presence and Absence of God: Claremont Studies in the Philosophy of Religion, Conference 2008*, edited by Ingolf U. Dalferth, RPT 42. Tubingen: Mohr Siebeck, 2009.

Day, Linda. *Esther*. Abingdon Old Testament Commentaries. Nashville: Abingdon, 2005.

De Moor, J. C. "The Love of God in the Targum to the Prophets." *JSJ* 24, no. 2 (1993): 257-65.

De Troyer, Kristin, and Leah Rediger Schulte. "Is God Absent or Present in the Book of Esther? An Old Problem Revisited." Pages 35-40 in *The Presence and Absence of God: Claremont Studies in the Philosophy of Religion, Conference 2008*, edited by Ingolf U. Dalferth, RPT 42. Tübingen: Mohr Siebeck, 2009.

Delitzsch, Franz. *Commentary on the Song of Songs and Ecclesiastes*. Translated by M. G. Easton. Edinburgh: T&T Clark, 1891.

Dell, Katherine J. "Deciding the Boundaries of Wisdom: Applying the Concept of Family Resemblances." Pages 145-60 in *Was There a Wisdom Tradition? New Prospects in Israelite Wisdom Studies*, edited by Mark R. Sneed. Atlanta: SBL Press, 2015.

———. "Does the Song of Songs Have Any Connections to Wisdom?" Pages 8-25 in *Perspectives on the Song of Songs*, edited by Anselm C. Hagedorn, Beihefte zur Zeitschrift für die Alttestamentliche Wissenschaft 346. Berlin: de Gruyter, 2005.

Deventer, Hans van. "Daniel, Prophet of Divine Presence and Absence." Pages 221-34 in *The Lion Had Roared: Theological Themes in the Prophetic Literature of the Old Testament*, edited by H. G. L. Peels and S. D. Snyman. Eugene, OR: Pickwick, 2012.

Dharamraj, Havilah. *Altogether Lovely: A Thematic and Intertextual Reading of the Song of Songs*. Minneapolis: Fortress, 2018.

Dille, Sarah J. *Mixing Metaphors: God as Mother and Father in Deutero-Isaiah*. GCT 13. JSOTSup 398. London: T&T Clark, 2004.

Dobbs-Allsopp, F. W. *On Biblical Poetry*. Oxford: Oxford University Press, 2015.

Doyle, Brian. "Where Is God When You Need Him Most?" Pages 339-90 in *The Composition of the Book of Psalms*, edited by Erich Zenger. Leuven: Peeters, 2010.

Duguid, Iain M. "But Did They Live Happily Ever After?: The Eschatology of the Book of Esther." *Westminster Theological Journal* 68, no. 1 (2006): 85-98.

———. *Esther and Ruth*. Reformed Expository Commentary. Phillipsburg, NJ: P&R, 2005.

Dunn, Steven. *The Sanctuary in the Psalms: Exploring the Paradox of God's Transcendence and Immanence*. Lanham, MD: Lexington Books, 2016.

Dunne, John Anthony. *Esther and Her Elusive God: How a Secular Story Functions as Scripture*. Eugene, OR: Wipf & Stock, 2014.

Duvall, J. Scott, and J. Daniel Hays. *God's Relational Presence: The Cohesive Center of Biblical Theology*. Grand Rapids, MI: Baker Academic, 2019.

Eichrodt, Walter. *Theology of the Old Testament*. 2 vols. Translated by J. A. Baker. Philadelphia: Westminster, 1961, 1967.

Embry, Brad. *Megilloth Studies: The Shape of Contemporary Scholarship*. Sheffield: Sheffield Phoenix, 2016.

Erickson, Amy, and Andrew R. Davis. "Recent Research on the Megilloth (Song of Songs, Ruth, Lamentations, Ecclesiastes, Esther)." *Currents in Biblical Research* 14, no. 3 (2016): 298-318.

Exum, J. Chery. *Song of Songs: A Commentary*. OTL. Louisville, KY: Westminster John Knox, 2005.

———. "Ten Things Every Feminist Should Know About the Song of Songs." Pages 24-35 in *A Feminist Companion to the Song of Songs*, edited by Athalya Brenner and Carole R. Fontaine, FCB 2/6. Sheffield: Sheffield Academic Press, 2000.

Falk, Marcia. *Love Lyrics from the Bible: The Song of Songs*. New York: HarperSanFrancisco, 1990.

Firth, David G. *The Message of Esther*. Downers Grove, IL: InterVarsity Press, 2010.

Fisch, Harold. *Poetry with a Purpose: Biblical Poetics and Interpretation*. Bloomington: Indiana University Press, 1988.

Fishbane, Michael A. *The Kiss of God: Spiritual and Mystical Death in Judaism.* Seattle: University of Washington Press, 1994.

——. *Song of Songs: The Traditional Hebrew Text with the New JPS Translation.* JPS Bible Commentary. Philadelphia: Jewish Publication Society, 2015.

Fox, Michael V. *Character and Ideology in the Book of Esther.* 2nd ed. Grand Rapids, MI: Eerdmans, 2001.

——. *Ecclesiastes.* JPS Bible Commentary. Philadelphia: Jewish Publication Society, 2004.

Freedman, Amelia Devin. *God as an Absent Character in Biblical Hebrew Narrative: A Literary-Theoretical Study.* New York: Peter Lang, 2005.

Freehof, Solomon B. "The Song of Songs: A General Suggestion." *Jewish Quarterly Review* (1948): 397-402.

Fretheim, Terrence E. *God and World in the Old Testament: A Relational Theology of Creation.* Nashville: Abingdon, 2005.

——. *The Suffering of God: An Old Testament Perspective.* Overtures to Biblical Theology 14. Philadelphia: Fortress, 1984.

——. "What Kind of God Is Portrayed in Isaiah 5:1-7?" Pages 53-67 in *New Studies in the Book of Isaiah: Essays in Honor of Hallvard Hagelia,* edited by Hallvard Hagelia and Markus Philipp Zehnder, Perspectives on Hebrew Scriptures and Its Contexts 21. Piscataway, NJ: Gorgias, 2014.

Freud, Sigmund. *Interpretation of Dreams.* Sioux Falls, SD: NuVision, 2007.

Fried, Lisbeth S. *The Priest and the Great King: The Temple-Palace Relations in Persian Empire.* Winona Lake, IN: Eisenbrauns, 2004.

Friedman, Richard Elliot. *The Disappearance of God: A Divine Mystery.* Boston: Little, Brown, 1995. Rev ed., *The Hidden Face of God.* New York: HarperSanFrancisco, 1997.

Galambush, Julie. "Jerusalem in the Book of Ezekiel: The City as Yahweh's Wife." Atlanta: Scholars Press, 1992.

Galvin, Garrett. "Horizontal Theology in the Megilloth." Pages 125-40 in *Megilloth Studies: The Shape of Contemporary Scholarship,* edited by Brad Embry. Sheffield: Sheffield Phoenix, 2016.

Garrett, Duane. *Song of Songs.* WBC 23B. Nashville: Thomas Nelson, 2004.

Gault, Brian P. "A 'Do Not Disturb' Sign? Reexamining the Adjuration Refrain in Song of Songs." *JSOT* 36, no. 1 (2011): 93-104.

Gerleman, Gillis. *Esther.* 2nd ed. Biblischer Kommentar: Altes Testament 21. Neukirchen-Vluyn: Neukirchener Verlag, 1982.

Gharipour, Mohammad. *Persian Gardens and Pavilions: Reflections in History, Poetry and the Arts.* London: I. B. Tauris, 2013.

Gledhill, Tom. *The Message of the Song of Songs*. Downers Grove, IL: InterVarsity Press, 1994.

Godzieba, Anthony J. *A Theology of the Presence and Absence of God*. Collegeville, MN: Liturgical Press, 2018.

Goldingay, John. "Hermeneutics." *DOTWPW* 267-80.

——. *Old Testament Theology*. Vol. 2, *Israel's Faith*. Downers Grove, IL: IVP Academic, 2006.

——. *Old Testament Theology*. Vol. 3, *Israel's Life*. Downers Grove, IL: IVP Academic, 2009.

Goodman, William. *Yearning for You: Psalms and the Song of Songs in Conversation with Rock and Worship Songs*. Bible in the Modern World 46. Sheffield: Sheffield Phoenix, 2012.

Goswell, Gregory R. "Keeping God Out of the Book of Esther." *Evangelical Quarterly* 82, no. 2 (2010): 99-110.

——. "The Temple Theme in the Book of Daniel." *Journal of the Evangelical Theological Society* 55, no. 3 (2012): 509-20.

Goulder, Michael D. *The Song of Fourteen Songs*. JSOTSup 36. Sheffield: University of Sheffield Press, 1986.

Grasham, William W. "The Theology of the Book of Esther." *ResQ* 16, no. 2 (1973): 99-111.

Gregory, B. C. "Megillot and Festivals." *DOTWPW* 457-64.

——. "Purim." *DOTWPW* 631-34.

Griffiths, Paul J. *Song of Songs*. Brazos Theological Commentary on the Bible. Grand Rapids, MI: Brazos, 2011.

Grossman, Jonathan. *Esther: The Outer Narrative and the Hidden Reading*. Siphrut 6. Winona Lake, IN: Eisenbrauns, 2011.

Hallo, William W., ed. *The Context of Scripture: Monumental Inscriptions from the Biblical World*. 2 vols. Leiden: Brill, 2003.

Hambrick-Stowe, C. E. "Ruth the New Abraham, Esther the New Moses." *Christian Century* (1983): 1130-34.

Hamilton, James M., Jr. *Exalting Jesus in Ezra-Nehemiah*. Christ-Centered Exposition. Nashville: B&H, 2014.

Hancock, Rebecca S. *Esther and the Politics of Negotiation: Public and Private Spaces and the Figure of the Female Royal Counselor*. Emerging Scholars. Minneapolis: Fortress, 2013.

Harding, Kathryn. "'I Sought Him but I Did Not Find Him': The Elusive Lover in the Song of Songs." *Biblical Interpretation* 16, no. 1 (2008): 43-59.

Hauge, Martin Ravndal. *Solomon the Lover and the Shape of the Song of Songs*. HBM 77. Sheffield: Sheffield Phoenix, 2015.

Hausmann, J. "*Mōr.*" Pages 559-60 in vol. 8 of *Theological Dictionary of the Old Testament*, edited by G. Johannes Botterweck and Helmer Ringgren, translated by John T. Willis et al. Grand Rapids, MI: Eerdmans, 1974–2006.

Hawkins, Peter S., and Lesleigh Cushing Stahlberg. *Scrolls of Love: Ruth and the Song of Songs*. New York: Fordham University Press, 2006.

Hays, Christopher B. *Hidden Riches: A Sourcebook for the Comparative Study of the Hebrew Bible and Ancient Near East*. Louisville, KY: Westminster John Knox, 2014.

Heist, Roger. "The Purim Connection." *Union Seminary Quarterly Review* 32 (1978): 139-45.

Hertig, Young Lee. "The Subversive Banquets of Esther and Vashti." Pages 15-29 in *Mirrored Reflections: Reframing Biblical Characters*, edited by Young Lee Hertig and Chloe Sun. Eugene, OR: Wipf & Stock, 2010.

House, Paul R. *Old Testament Theology*. Downers Grove, IL: InterVarsity Press, 1998.

Humphrey, W. Lee. "A Life-Style for Diaspora: A Study of the Tales of Esther and Daniel." *JBL* 92 (1977): 211-23.

Imes, Carmen Joy. "Between Two Worlds: The Functional and Symbolic Significance of the High Priestly Regalia." Pages 29-62 in *Dress and Clothing in the Hebrew Bible: "For All Her Households Are Clothed in Crimson,"* edited by Finitsis Antonios. LHBOTS 679. London: T&T Clark, 2019.

James, Elaine T. *Landscapes of the Song of Songs: Poetry and Place*. New York: Oxford University Press, 2017.

Jobes, Karen H. "Esther 1, Book of." *DOTWPW* 160-70.

——— . *The NIV Application Commentary: Esther*. Grand Rapids, MI: Zondervan, 1999.

John of the Cross. *Dark Knight of the Soul*. Translated by E. Allison Peers. New York: Doubleday, 1959.

Jung, Carl G. *Answer to Job*. Translated by R. F. C. Hull. Princeton, NJ: Princeton University Press, 1969.

Kaiser, Walter C. Jr. *Toward an Old Testament Theology*. Grand Rapids, MI: Zondervan, 1978.

Kalimi, Isaac. "'Go. I Beg You, Take Your Beloved Son and Slay Him!' The Binding of Isaac in Rabbinic Literature and Thought." *Review of Rabbinic Judaism* 13, no. 1 (2010): 1-29.

Kaplan, Jonathan. *My Perfect One: Typology and Early Rabbinic Interpretation of Song of Songs*. New York: Oxford University Press, 2015.

Kates, Judith A. "Entering the Holy of Holies: Rabbinic Midrash and the Language of Intimacy." Pages 201-13 in *Scrolls of Love: Ruth and the Song of Songs*, edited by

Peter S. Hawkins and Lesleigh Cushing Stahlberg. New York: Fordham University Press, 2006.

Keefe, Alice A. *Woman's Body and the Social Body in Hosea*. GCT 10. JSOTSup 338. Sheffield: Sheffield Academic Press, 2001.

Keel, Othmar. *The Song of Songs*. Continental Commentary. Minneapolis: Fortress, 1994.

Kessler, John. *Old Testament Theology: Divine Call and Human Response*. Waco, TX: Baylor University Press, 2013.

Kingsmill, Edmee. "The Song of Songs: A Wisdom Book." Pages 310-35 in *Perspectives on Israelite Wisdom: Proceedings of the Oxford Old Testament Seminar*, edited by Oxford Old Testament Seminar and John Jarick, LHBOTS 618. London: Bloomsbury T&T Clark, 2016.

———. *The Song of Songs and the Eros of God: A Study in Biblical Intertextuality*. Oxford: Oxford University Press, 2009.

Koller, Aaron. *Esther in Ancient Jewish Thought*. Cambridge: Cambridge University Press, 2014.

Kristeva, Julia. "Word, Dialogue and Novel." Pages 34-61 in *The Kristeva Reader*, edited by Toril Moi. New York: Columbia University Press, 1986.

Kuan, Jeffrey Kah-Jin. "Daisporic Reading of a Diasporic Text: Identity Politics and Race Relations and the Book of Esther." Pages 161-73 in *Interpreting Beyond Borders*, edited by Fernando F. Segovia. Sheffield: Sheffield Academic Press, 2000.

Kutsko, John F. *Between Heaven and Earth: Divine Presence and Absence in the Book of Ezekiel*. Winona Lake, IN: Eisenbrauns, 2000.

Kynes, Will. *An Obituary for "Wisdom Literature": The Birth, Death, and Intertextual Reintegration of a Biblical Corpus*. Oxford: Oxford University Press, 2019.

LaCocque, Andre. *Esther Regina: A Bakhtinian Reading*. Evanston, IL: Northwestern University Press, 2008.

———. *Romance, She Wrote: A Hermeneutical Essay on Song of Songs*. Harrisburg, PA: Trinity Press International, 1998.

Laird, Donna. *Negotiating Power in Ezra-Nehemiah*. Atlanta: SBL Press, 2016.

Landy, Francis. "Beauty and the Enigma: An Inquiry into Some Interrelated Episode in the Song of Songs." *JSOT* 17 (1980): 55-106.

———. *Paradoxes of Paradise: Identity and Difference in the Song of Songs*. 2nd ed. Sheffield: Sheffield Phoenix, 2011.

———. "The Song of Songs and the Garden of Eden." *JBL* 98, no. 4 (1979): 513-28.

Laniak, Timothy S. "Esther's *Volkcentrism* and the Reframing of Post-exilic Judaism." Pages 77-90 in *The Book of Esther in Modern Research*, ed. Sidnie White Crawford and Leonard J. Greenspoon. JSOTSup 380. New York: T&T Clark, 2003.

Lau, Peter H. W. *Esther: A Pastoral and Contextual Commentary*. Asia Bible Commentary Series. Carlisle, UK: Langham Global Library, 2018.

Leonard, Jeffrey M. "Identifying Inner-biblical Allusions: Psalm 78 as a Test Case." *JBL* 127, no. 2 (2008): 241-65.

Levenson, Jon D. "Abusing Abraham: Traditions, Religious Histories, and Modern Interpretations." *Judaism* 47, no. 3 (1998) 259-77.

―――. *Esther: A Commentary*. OTL. Louisville, KY: Westminster John Knox, 1997.

Levering, Matthew. *Ezra-Nehemiah*. Grand Rapids, MI: Brazos, 2007.

Lewis, Theodore J., trans. "El's Divine Feast." Pages 193-96 in *Ugaritic Narrative Poetry*, edited by Simon B. Parker, Writings from the Ancient World. Atlanta: Scholars Press, 1997.

Lim, Timothy H. "The Defilement of the Hands as a Principle Determining the Holiness of Scriptures." *Journal of Theological Studies* 61, no. 2 (2010): 501-15.

Linafelt, Tod. "The Arithmetic of Eros." *Interpretation* (2005): 244-58.

―――. "Lyrical Theology: The Song of Songs and the Advantage of Poetry." Pages 291-305 in *Toward a Theology of Eros: Transfiguring Passion at the Limits of Discipline*, edited by Catherine Keller and Virginia Burrus. New York: Fordham University Press, 2006.

―――. *Ruth and Esther*. Collegeville, MN: Liturgical Press, 1999.

Longman, Tremper, III. *The Fear of the Lord Is Wisdom: A Theological Introduction to Wisdom in Israel*. Grand Rapids, MI: Baker Academic, 2017.

―――. "Refrain." *DOTWPW* 641-43.

―――. *Song of Songs*. New International Commentary on the Old Testament. Grand Rapids, MI: Eerdmans, 2001.

Lyke, Larry L. *I Will Espouse You Forever: The Song of Songs and the Theology of Love in the Hebrew Bible*. Nashville: Abingdon, 2007.

Lyons, Michael A. "Marking Inner-biblical Allusion in the Book of Ezekiel." *Biblica* 88 (2007): 245-50.

Mandolfo, Carleen. *Daughter Zion Talks Back to the Prophets: A Dialogic Theology of the Book of Lamentations*. Semeia Studies 58. Atlanta: Society of Biblical Literature, 2007.

Manguno, John M., Jr. "Accident or Acronomy: The Tetragrammaton in the Masoretic Text of Esther." *Bibliotheca Sacra* 171 (October–December 2014): 440-51.

McDonald, Nathan, and Izaak J. De Hulster, eds. *Divine Presence and Absence in Exilic and Post-exilic Judaism*. Tübingen: Mohr Siebeck, 2013.

McEntire, Mark. *Portraits of a Mature God: Choices in Old Testament Theology*. Minneapolis: Fortress, 2013.

McGeough, Kevin M. "Esther the Hero: Going Beyond 'Wisdom' in Heroic Narratives." *CBQ* 70, no. 1 (2008): 44-65.

Meek, Russell L. "Intertextuality, Inner-biblical Exegesis, and Inner-biblical Allusion: The Ethics of a Methodology." *Biblica* 95, no. 1 (2014): 280-91.

Meinhold, Arndt. "Zu Aufbau und Mitte des Estherbuches." *VT* 33 (1983): 435-45.

Melton, Brittany N. "Miqreh in Retrospect: An Illumination of Miqreh." Pages 30-42 in *Megilloth Studies: The Shape of Contemporary Scholarship*, edited by Brad Embry. Sheffield: Sheffield Phoenix, 2016.

———. "'Oh, That I Knew Where I Might Find Him': Aspects of Divine Absence in Proverbs, Job and Ecclesiastes." Pages 205-26 in *Interpreting Old Testament Wisdom Literature*, edited by David G. Firth and Lindsay Wilson. Downers Grove, IL: IVP Academic, 2017.

———. "Solomon, Wisdom, and Love: Intertextual Resonances Between Ecclesiastes and Song of Songs." Pages 130-41 in *Reading Ecclesiastes Intertextually*, edited by Katherine Dell and Will Kynes. London: T&T Clark, 2014.

———. *Where Is God in the Megilloth?: A Dialogue on the Ambiguity of Divine Presence and Absence*. Leiden: Brill, 2018.

Menn, Esther M. "Thwarted Metaphors: Complicating the Language of Desire in the Targum of the Song of Songs." *JSJ* 34, no. 3 (2003): 237-73.

Meredith, Christopher. *Journeys in the Songscape: Space and the Song of Songs*. HBM 53. Sheffield: Sheffield Phoenix, 2013.

Middlemas, Jill. "Divine Presence in Absence: Aniconism and Multiple Imaging in the Prophets." Pages 183-211 in *Divine Presence and Absence in Exilic and Postexilic Judaism*, edited by Nathan McDonald and Izaak J. De Hulster. Tübingen: Mohr Siebeck, 2013.

———. *The Templeless Age: An Introduction to the History, Literature, and Theology of the "Exile."* Louisville, KY: Westminster John Knox, 2007.

Miles, Jack. *God: A Biography*. New York: Vintage Books, 1995.

Miller, Geoffrey D. "Intertextuality in Old Testament Research." *Currents in Biblical Research* 9, no. 3 (2010): 283-309.

Miller, Patrick D. "Prayer and Divine Action." Pages 211-32 in *God in the Fray: A Tribute to Walter Brueggemann*, edited by Tod Linafelt and Timothy K. Beal. Minneapolis: Fortress, 1998.

Miller, Tricia. *Three Versions of Esther: Their Relationship to Anti-Semitic and Feminist Critique of the Story*. Contributions to Biblical Exegesis & Theology 74. Leuven: Peeters, 2014.

Moberly, R. W. L. *Old Testament Theology: Reading the Hebrew Bible as Christian Scripture*. Grand Rapids, MI: Baker Academic, 2013.

Moore, Carey A. *Esther*. AB. Garden City, NY: Doubleday, 1971.

Morales, L. Michael. *The Tabernacle Pre-figured: Cosmic Mountain Ideology in Genesis and Exodus*. Biblical Tools and Studies 15. Leuven: Peeters, 2012.

Munro, Jill M. *Spikenard and Saffron: A Study in the Poetic Language of the Song of Songs*. JSOTSup 203. Sheffield: Sheffield Academic Press, 1995.

Murphy, Roland E. *The Tree of Life: An Exploration of Biblical Wisdom Literature*. Anchor Bible Reference Library. New York: Doubleday, 1992.

———. "The Unity of the Song of Songs." Pages 148-55 in *Poetry in the Hebrew Bible: Selected Studies from Vetus Testamentum*. Leiden: Brill, 2000.

Myers, Carol. "Gender Imagery in the Song of Songs." Pages 197-213 in *A Feminist Companion to the Song of Songs*, edited by Athalya Brenner, FCB 2/6. Sheffield: Sheffield Academic Press, 2001.

Neusner, Jacob. *Israel's Love Affair with God: Song of Songs*. Valley Forge, PA: Trinity Press International, 1993.

———. *The Midrash: An Introduction*. London: Jason Aronson, 1990.

———. *Song of Songs Rabbah: An Analytical Translation*. 2 vols. Brown Judaic Studies 197. Atlanta: Scholars Press, 1989.

———. *The Talmud of Babylon: An American Translation*. Vol. 23C, *Tractate Sanhedrin, Chapters 9–11*. Chico, CA: Scholars Press, 1985.

Niditch, Susan. "Esther: Folklore, Wisdom, Feminism and Authority." Pages 26-46 in *A Feminist Companion to Esther, Judith and Susanna*, edited by Athalya Brenner. FCB. Sheffield: Sheffield Academic Press, 1995.

Noble, Paul R. "Esau, Tamar, and Joseph: Criteria for Identifying Inner-biblical Allusions." *VT* 52 (2002): 219-52.

Nouwen, Henri, with Michael J. Christensen and Rebecca J. Laird. *Spiritual Direction: Wisdom for the Long Walk of Faith*. New York: HarperOne, 2006.

O'Brien, Julia M. *Challenging Prophetic Metaphor: Theology and Ideology in the Prophets*. Louisville, KY: Westminster John Knox, 2008.

O'Donnell, Douglas Sean. *The Song of Solomon: An Invitation to Intimacy*. Wheaton, IL: Crossway, 2012.

Oosthuizen, Marlene. "Reading Song of Songs as Wisdom Literature: An Interpretive Approach Integrating Sexuality and Spirituality." PhD diss., University of the Free State, 2014.

Ostriker, Alicia. "A Holy of Holies: The Song of Songs as Countertext." Pages 36-54 in *A Feminist Companion to the Song of Songs*, ed. Athalya Brenner and Carole R. Fontaine, FCB 2/6. Sheffield: Sheffield Academic Press, 2000.

Pardes, Ilana. *The Song of Songs: A Biography*. Lives of Great Religious Books. Princeton, NJ: Princeton University Press, 2019.

Parker, Simon B. ed., *Ugaritic Narrative Poetry*. Writings from the Ancient World. Atlanta: Scholars Press, 1997.

Paton, Lewis Bayles. *The Book of Esther: A Critical and Exegetical Commentary*. International Critical Commentary. Skokie, IL: Varda Books, 2016.

Patrick, Dale. *The Rendering of God in the Old Testament*. Philadelphia: Fortress, 1981.

Paz, Octavio. *The Double Flame: Love and Eroticism*. San Diego: A Harvest Book, 1993.

Pennington, M. Basil. *Song of Songs: A Spiritual Commentary*. Woodstock, VT: Skylight Paths, 2004.

Perdue, Leo G. *Reconstructing Old Testament Theology: After the Collapse of History*. Minneapolis: Fortress, 2005.

———. *Wisdom and Creation: The Theology of Wisdom Literature*. Nashville: Abingdon, 1994.

———. *Wisdom Literature: A Theological History*. Louisville, KY: Westminster John Knox, 2007.

Pierce, Ronald W. "The Politics of Esther and Mordecai: Courage or Compromise?" *Bulletin for Biblical Research* 2 (1992): 75-89.

Pitkanen, Pekka. "Temple Building and Exodus 25-40." Pages 225-80 in *From the Foundations to the Crenellations: Essays on Temple Building in the Ancient Near East and Hebrew Bible*, edited by Mark J. Boda and Jamie Novotny. Münster: Ugarit-Verlag, 2010.

Pleins, J. David. "Why Do You Hide Your Face? Divine Silence and Speech in the Book of Job." *Interpretation* (July 1994): 229-38.

Polish, Daniel F. "Aspects of Esther: A Phenomenological Exploration of the Megillah of Esther and the Origin of Purim." *JSOT* 85 (1999): 85-106.

Pope, Marvin H. *Song of Songs*. AB 7C. Garden City, NY: Doubleday, 1977.

Prosic, Tamara. *The Development and Symbolism of Passover Until 70 CE*. London: T&T Clark, 2004.

———. "Passover in Biblical Narratives." *JSOT* 82 (1999): 45-55.

Queen-Sutherland, Kandy. "Ruth, Qoheleth, and Esther: Counter Voices from the Megilloth." *Perspectives in Religious Studies* 43, no. 2 (2016): 227-42.

Rad, Gerhard von. *Old Testament Theology*. 2 vols. Translated by D. M. G. Stalker. Edinburgh: Oliver & Boyd, 1962, 1965.

———. *Wisdom in Israel*. Harrisburg, PA: Trinity Press International, 1972.

Reid, Debra. *Esther*. Tyndale Old Testament Commentaries 13. Downers Grove, IL: IVP Academic, 2008.

Ricoeur, Paul. *Time and Narrative*. Vol. 3. Translated by Kathleen Blamey and David Pellauer. Chicago: University of Chicago Press, 1985.

Roaf, Michael. "Palaces and Temples in Ancient Mesopotamia." Pages in 423-41 in vol. 1 of *Civilizations of the Ancient Near East*, edited by Jack M. Sasson. Peabody, MA: Hendrickson, 1995.

Root, Margaret Cool. "Palace to Temple—King to Cosmos: Achaemenid Foundation Texts in Iran." Pages 165-210 in *From the Foundations to the Crenellations: Essays on Temple Building in the Ancient Near East and Hebrew Bible*, ed. Mark J. Boda and Jamie Novotny. Münster: Ugarit-Verlag, 2010.

Rubenstein, Jeffrey. "Purim, Liminality, and Communitas." *Association for Jewish Studies Review* 17, no. 2 (1992): 247-77.

Ruiz-Ortiz, Francisco-Javier. *The Dynamics of Violence and Revenge in the Hebrew Book of Esther*. Supplements to Vetus Testamentum 175. Leiden: Brill, 2017.

Ryken, Leland. *How to Read the Bible as Literature*. Grand Rapids, MI: Zondervan, 1984.

Sanders, James A. *Canon and Community: A Guide to Canonical Criticism*. Philadelphia: Fortress, 1984.

Schachter, Lifsa. "The Garden of Eden as God's First Sanctuary." *Jewish Bible Quarterly* (2013): 73-77.

Schauss, Hayyim. *The Jewish Festivals: History and Observance*. New York: Schocken Books, 1938.

Schellekens, Jona. "Accession Days and Holidays: The Origins of the Jewish Festival of Purim." *JBL* 128, no. 1 (2009): 115-34.

Schellenberg, Annettte. "May Her Breasts Satisfy You at All Times (Prov 5:19)." *VT* 68 (2018): 252-73.

Schellenberg, Annette, and Ludger Schwienhorst-Schönberger, eds. *Interpreting the Song of Songs: Literal or Allegorical?* Biblical Tools and Studies 26. Leuven: Peeters, 2016.

Scolnic, Benjamin Edidin. "Why Do We Sing the Song of Songs on Passover?" *Conservative Judaism* 48, no. 4 (1996): 53-72.

Seow, Choon Leong. *Ecclesiastes: A New Translation with Introduction and Commentary*. Anchor Yale Bible. New Haven, CT: Yale University Press, 1997.

———. "Qoheleth's Eschatological Poem." *JBL* 118 (Summer 1999): 209-34.

Setel, Drorah. "Prophets and Pornography: Female Sexual Imagery in Hosea." Pages 143-55 in *A Feminist Companion to the Song of Songs*, edited by Athalya Brenner, FCB. Sheffield: Sheffield Academic Press, 1993.

Sherwood, Yvonne. *The Prostitute and the Prophet: Hosea's Marriage in Literary-Theoretical Perspective*. GCT 2. JSOTSup 212. Sheffield: Sheffield Academic Press, 1996.

Simon, Maurice, trans. *Midrash Rabbah: Esther*. London: Soncino, 1939.

————. *Midrash Rabbah: The Song of Songs*. London: Soncino, 1939.

Smith, Mark S. "Like Deities, Like Temples (Like People)." Pages 3-27 in *Temple and Worship in Biblical Israel*, edited by John Day, LHBOTS 422. London: T&T Clark, 2005.

Snaith, John G. *Song of Songs*. New Century Bible Commentary. Grand Rapids, MI: Eerdmans, 1993.

Sneed, Mark S. "'Grasping After the Wind': The Elusive Attempt to Define and Delimit Wisdom." Pages 39-67 in *Was There a Wisdom Tradition? New Prospects in Israelite Wisdom Studies*, edited by Mark R. Sneed. Atlanta: SBL Press, 2015.

Sparks, Kent. "The Song of Songs: Wisdom for Young Jewish Women." *CBQ* 70, no. 2 (2008): 277-99.

Steinberg, Julius. "The Place of Wisdom Literature in an Old Testament Theology: A Thematic and Structural-Canonical Approach." Pages 147-73 in *The Shape of the Writings*, edited by Julius Steinberg and Timothy J. Stone with the assistance of Rachel Marie Stone, Siphrut 16. Winona Lake, IN: Eisenbrauns, 2015.

Steinberg, Julius, and Timothy J. Stone with the assistance of Rachel Marie Stone. *The Shape of the Writings*. Siphrut 16. Winona Lake, IN: Eisenbrauns, 2015.

Stern, Elsie R. "Esther and the Politics of Diaspora." *Jewish Quarterly Review* 100, no. 1 (Winter 2010): 25-53.

Sternberg, Meir. "Time and Space in Biblical (Hi)story Telling: The Grand Chronology." Pages 81-145 in *The Book and the Text: The Bible and Literary Theory*, ed. Regina M. Schwartz. Oxford: Basil Blackwell, 1990.

Stone, Timothy J. *The Compilational History of the Megilloth*. Tübingen: Mohr Siebeck, 2013.

Stordalen, Terje. *Echoes of Eden: Genesis 2–3 and Symbolism of the Eden Garden in Biblical Hebrew Literature*. Contributions to Biblical Exegesis and Theology 25. Leuven: Peeters, 2000.

Strollo, Megan Fullerton. "Initiative and Agency: Towards a Theology of the Megilloth." Pages 150-60 in *Megilloth Studies: The Shape of Contemporary Scholarship*, edited by Brad Embry. Sheffield: Sheffield Phoenix, 2016.

Strong, John T. "God's *Kābôd*: The Presence of Yahweh in the Book of Ezekiel." Pages 69-95 in *The Book of Ezekiel: Theological and Anthropological Perspectives*, edited by Margaret S. Odell and John T. Strong. Atlanta: Society of Biblical Literature, 2000.

Sun, Chloe. "As Strong as Death: The Immortality of Allegory in the Chinese Reception of the Song of Songs." Pages 217-46 in *Honoring the Past, Looking to the Future: Essays from the 2014 International Congress of Ethnic Chinese Biblical*

Scholars, edited by Gale A. Yee and John Y. H. Yieh. Hong Kong: Divinity School of Chung Chi College, 2016.

———. "Ecclesiastes Among the Megilloth: Death as an Interthematic Link." *Bulletin for Biblical Research* 27, no. 2 (2017): 185-206.

———. *Oxford Bibliographies: Song of Songs.* Oxford: Oxford University Press, 2016. www.oxfordbibliographies.com/view/document/obo-9780195393361/obo-9780195393361-0215.xml?rskey=XjUbjK&result=1&q=Song+of+Songs#first Match.

———. "Ruth and Esther: Negotiable Space in Christopher Wright's *The Mission of God?*" *Missiology* 46, no. 2 (2018): 150-61.

Sweeney, Marvin A. "Absence of G-d and Human Responsibility in the Book of Esther." Pages 264-75 in *Reading the Hebrew Bible for a New Millennium: Form, Concept, and Theological Perspective*, edited by Wonil Kim, Deborah Ellens, Michael Floyd, and Marvin A. Sweeney. Harrisburg, PA: Trinity Press International, 2000.

———. "Foundations for a Jewish Theology of the Hebrew Bible: Prophets in Dialogue." Pages 161-86 in *Jewish Bible Theology: Perspectives and Case Studies*, ed. Isaac Kalimi. Winona Lake, IN: Eisenbrauns, 2012.

———. *Reading the Hebrew Bible After the Shoah: Engaging Holocaust Theology.* Minneapolis: Fortress, 2008.

———. "What Is Biblical Theology? With an Example on Divine Absence and the Song of Songs." Pages 31-55 in *Theology of the Hebrew Bible*, vol 1, *Methodological Studies*, edited by Marvin A. Sweeney. Atlanta: SBL Press, 2019.

Talmon, Shemaryahu. "'Wisdom' in the Book of Esther." *VT* 13, no. 4 (1963): 419-55.

Terrien, Samuel. *The Elusive Presence: The Heart of Biblical Theology.* Cambridge: Harper & Row, 1978.

Thöne, Yvonne Sophie. *Liebe zwischen Stadt und Feld: Raum und Geschlecht im Hohelied.* Berlin: LIT Verlag, 2012.

Throntveit, Mark A. *Ezra-Nehemiah.* Interpretation. Louisville, KY: John Knox, 1989.

Tomasino, Anthony. *Esther.* Evangelical Exegetical Commentary. Bellingham, WA: Lexham, 2016.

Tooman, William A. "Covenant and Presence in the Composition and Theology of Ezekiel." Pages 151-82 in *Divine Presence and Absence in Exilic and Post-exilic Judaism*, edited by Nathan McDonald and Izaak J. De Hulster. Tübingen: Mohr Siebeck, 2013.

Tournay, Raymond Jacques. *Word of God, Song of Love: A Commentary on the Song of Songs.* Translated by J. Edward Crowley. New York: Paulist, 1988.

Tov, Emanuel. *Textual Criticism of the Hebrew Bible*. 2nd ed. Minneapolis: Fortress, 2001.

Treat, Jay C. "The Aramaic Targum to Song of Songs." August 12, 2004. http://ccat.sas.upenn.edu/~jtreat/song/targum/.

Trible, Phyllis. *God and the Rhetoric of Sexuality*. Philadelphia: Fortress, 1978.

Tuell, Steven S. "Divine Presence and Absence in Ezekiel's Prophecy." Pages 97-116 in *The Book of Ezekiel: Theological and Anthropological Perspectives*, edited by Margaret S. Odell and John T. Strong. Atlanta: Society of Biblical Literature, 2000.

Vanhoozer, Kevin J., ed. *Theological Interpretation of the Old Testament: A Book-by-Book Survey*. Grand Rapids, MI: Baker Academic, 2008.

Vaux, Roland de. "The Presence and Absence of God in History According to the Old Testament." Pages 7-20 in *The Presence of God*, edited by Pierre Benoit, Roland Murphy, and Bastiaan van Iersel. New York: Paulist, 1969.

Wahl von Harald, Martin. "Das Motiv des 'Aufstiegs' in der Hofgeschichte: Am Beispiel von Joseph, Esther und Daniel." *Zeitschrift für die alttestamentliche Wissenschaft* 112 (2000): 59-74.

Walsh, Carey Ellen. *Exquisite Desire: Religion, the Erotic, and the Song of Songs*. Minneapolis: Fortress, 2000.

Waltke, Bruce K. *An Old Testament Theology: An Exegetical, Canonical, and Thematic Approach*. Grand Rapids, MI: Zondervan, 2007.

Waltke, Bruce K., and M. O'Connor. *An Introduction to Biblical Hebrew Syntax*. Winona Lake, IN: Eisenbrauns, 1990.

Walton, John H. "Eden, Garden of." Pages 202-7 in *Dictionary of the Old Testament: Pentateuch*, edited by T. Desmond Alexander and David W. Baker. Downers Grove, IL: InterVarsity Press, 2002.

———. *The Lost World of Genesis One: Ancient Cosmology and the Origins Debate*. Downers Grove, IL: InterVarsity Press, 2009.

Ward, Nathan. *God Unseen: A Theological Introduction to Esther*. Chillicothe, OH: DeWard, 2016.

Webb, Barry G. *Five Festal Garments: Christian Reflections on the Song of Songs, Ruth, Lamentations, Ecclesiastes, and Esther*. Downers Grove, IL: InterVarsity Press, 2000.

———. "Reading Esther as Holy Scripture." *Reformed Theological Review* 52, no. 1 (1993): 23-35.

Wechsler, Michael G. "Critical Notes: The Purim-Passover Connection: A Reflection of Jewish Exegetical Tradition in the Peshitta Book of Esther." *JBL* 117, no. 1 (1998): 321-35.

Weeks, Stuart. "The Place and Limits of Wisdom Revisited." Pages 3-23 in *Perspectives on Israelite Wisdom: Proceedings of the Oxford Old Testament Seminar*, edited by John Jarick. London: Bloomsbury T&T Clark, 2016.

Weems, Renita J. *Battered Love: Marriage, Sex, and Violence in the Hebrew Prophets.* Overtures to Biblical Theology. Minneapolis: Fortress, 1995.

Weiland, Forrest S. "Literary Clues to God's Providence in the Book of Esther." *Bibliotheca Sacra* 160 (2003): 34-47.

Westermann, Claus. "The Complaint Against God." Translated by Armin Siedlecki. Pages 233-41 in *God in the Fray: A Tribute to Walter Brueggemann*, edited by Tod Linafelt and Timothy K. Beal. Minneapolis: Fortress, 1998.

Wetter, Anne-Mareike. *"On Her Account": Reconfiguring Israel in Ruth, Esther, and Judith.* LHBOTS 623. London: T&T Clark, 2015.

Wiebe, John M. "Esther 4:14: 'Will Relief and Deliverance Arise for the Jews from Another Place?'" *CBQ* 53 (1991): 409-15.

Williams, Gary Roye. "Frustrated Expectations in Isaiah 5:1-7: A Literary Interpretation." *VT* 35, no. 4 (1985): 459-65.

Wills, Lawrence M. *The Jew in the Court of the Foreign King: Ancient Jewish Court Legends.* Harvard Dissertations in Religion 26. Minneapolis: Fortress, 1990.

Wilson-Wright, Aren. "Love Conquers All: Song of Songs 8:6b-7a as a Reflex of the Northwest Semitic Combat Myth." *JBL* 134, no. 2 (2015): 333-45.

Yoder, Christine Roy. *Proverbs.* Abingdon Old Testament Commentaries. Nashville: Abingdon, 2009.

Zhang, Sarah. *I, You, and the Word God: Finding Meaning in the Song of Songs.* Siphrut 20. Winona Lake, IN: Eisenbrauns, 2016.

Zimmerli, Walther. *Old Testament Theology in Outline.* Translated by David E. Green. Edinburgh: T&T Clark, 1978.

———. "The Place and Limit of Wisdom in the Framework of Old Testament Theology." *SJT* 17 (1964): 146-58.

Zornberg, Avivah Gottlieb. *The Murmuring Deep: Reflections on the Biblical Unconscious.* New York: Schocken Books, 2009.

AUTHOR INDEX

SUBJECT INDEX

SCRIPTURE INDEX

SONG OF SONGS
RABBAH INDEX

TARGUM INDEX